FOURTH EDITION

UNDERSTANDING READING

A Psycholinguistic Analysis of Reading and Learning to Read

FRANK SMITH

LAWRENCE ERLBAUM ASSOCIATES, PUBLISHERS
1988 Hillsdale, New Jersey   Hove and London

Lawrence Erlbaum Associates, Inc., Publishers
365 Broadway
Hillsdale, New Jersey 07642

Library of Congress Cataloging-in-Publication Data
Smith, Frank, 1928-
  Understanding reading.
  Bibliography: p.
  Includes index.
  1. Reading. 2. Learning, Psychology of.
3. Written communication. I. Title.
LB1050.S574 1988 428.4 87-33045
ISBN 0-89859-855-9
ISBN 0-89859-879-6 (pbk.)

Printed in the United States of America
10 9 8 7 6 5 4 3 2

CONTENTS

PREFACE TO THE FOURTH EDITION

If a single factor had to be identified as the predominating influence in reading research and theorizing during the 1980s, for good or for ill, it would have to be the computer. Computers have been employed in scattered areas of psychology and education for several decades, but in recent years the technology has determined the way many people think about literacy and literacy instruction. Often this influence is unsuspected—the implicit basis of new ways of conceptualizing reading and teaching—with consequences that may sometimes be inappropriate and even misleading.

The influence of computer technology can be discerned in three areas of concern in this book. The first area is instruction. All the major publishers of instructional materials in reading, and many others as well, have now produced computer-based programs, usually emphasizing repetitive exercises, frequent tests, and elaborate record-keeping and other "classroom management" facilities. Many educational administrators and instructional developers appear to believe that anything done by computer must be more effective than traditional teaching methods. The main issues are considered toward the end of the present book.

The second area in which computers have become prominent is laboratory research into reading, primarily in a revival of detailed analyses of eye movements and visual perception, but also in studies of comprehension and memory. It remains to be seen what such research can add to a general understanding of reading, apart from specialized questions related to what the eyes might be doing while the brain is making sense of print. But a tendency to restrict thinking about reading, memory, and comprehension to experimental procedures that can be conducted by computer warrants caution. Recent findings have contributed new references to several chapters in the present volume.

The most pervasive influence of computers has come about indirectly and almost imperceptibly through a new academic discipline called *cognitive science*, embracing much of the more established academic areas of psycholinguistics and cognitive psychology and including specialists in computer systems design and artificial intelligence. Many of the most active theorists and experimenters in reading today are "cognitive scientists." The new discipline is primarily concerned with highly abstract questions of how complex organizations of knowledge can most efficiently be constructed, stored, and utilized, especially through the medium of language. Psychologists are naturally interested in such questions because of the insights they might gain about how human beings acquire and employ knowledge. The computer experts are vitally concerned with such questions in the pursuit of "fifth-generation" computers able to understand and produce human language. To do this, computers must understand what humans talk about, which means they must share knowledge with humans. How "knowledge" can best be represented in computers, and how they can acquire it, is not clearly understood, so the computer programmers have been interested in what psychology can tell them about knowing and learning, especially through language.

The result—almost imperceptibly and insidiously—has been that human brains and electronic computers have come to be regarded as similar systems. The computer has been changing the way many people think about reading, readers, and learning to read. There has been a significant interchange of metaphors. The computer is seen as a "thinking" system, which has a "memory", "reads" instructions, and has other human characteristics. On the other hand, the human brain has come to be regarded as an information-processing device which receives, stores, and operates upon data according to formalized "programs" and procedures. The word "process" has become ubiquitous in the psychological and educational research literature, with reading, writing, comprehension, and thinking almost invariably being referred to as *processes* which can be broken down into linear sequences of automatized operations. Mental states and acts are seen in the same terms as the representation and manipulation of data on computers.

Computer models and metaphors can distort perceptions of the nature of reading and other aspects of mental life. Fortunately, an alternative, contrasting point of view has also become prominent during the decade, attracting the attention of investigators from such diverse fields as psychology, linguistics, sociology, and anthropology, but not from computer science. This alternative perspective concerns the way people learn to read, or become literate generally. The learning is seen, not as a consequence of specific instruction, but of demonstrations and collaboration by other people, a sociocultural phenomenon. From this point of view, much of the work in cognitive science—and in neurophysiology—becomes a side issue, interesting sometimes, but occasionally irrelevant and even misleading. The focus in studies of learning has turned to what people surrounding the learner are doing. Learning, it has become recognized, is a social phenomenon.

Cognitive science has not led me to make radical changes in matters concerning theories of reading in the present edition of *Understanding Reading*, although it has caused me to be more cautious in my own use of words like "information." But sociocultural considerations about how literacy develops have encouraged me to expand considerably my discussions of learning generally and of learning to read in particular. Because of these recent trends, and to emphasize what I consider to be the most important aspects of reading, I have opened this new edition with the topic of comprehension. Further details of fourth edition changes are given at the beginning of the Notes at the end of the book.

AIMS

My aim in this fourth edition of *Understanding Reading* continues to be what it was when the first edition was published in 1971, to attempt to shed light on fundamental aspects of the complex human act of reading—linguistic, physiological, psychological, and social—and on what is involved in learning to read. One topic, inseparable from reading, that has not perhaps been covered to the extent that it warrants, is writing. The neglect is primarily because I have discussed the subject at length in a companion volume *Writing and the Writer* (Smith, 1982).

There is no comparison of instructional methods, nor any effort to promote one instructional program at the expense of another. My early researches persuaded me that learning to read resulted from practical and meaningful interactions between teachers and students, rather than from exercises and drills. Consequent experience with many hundreds of teachers and classrooms, and the research of a growing band of "naturalistic" researchers, has confirmed that the essential element in literacy instruction is the teacher. Literacy is not accomplished through the external controls of prescribed programs and formalized tests, but through sensitive teachers who understand what they teach and who also understand the students for whose learning they are responsible.

Reading cannot be understood without consideration of perceptual, cognitive, linguistic, and social factors, not just in reading but in thinking and learning in general. Reading defies a simplistic analysis, just as teaching reading confounds simplistic solutions. Reading is complex, but so also are walking, talking, and making sense of the world in general—and children are capable of achieving all of these provided the environmental circumstances are appropriate. What is difficult to describe is not necessarily difficult to learn. One consideration that this book emphasizes is that children are not as helpless in the face of learning to read as often is thought.

Because an understanding of reading requires acquaintance with research in a variety of disciplines, more than half of the book is devoted to such general topics as language, memory, learning, the development of spoken language ability, and the physiology of the eye and brain. The aim is to make these topics comprehensible, with the assumption that many readers will have neither the time nor the experience to undertake deep or specialized study in these areas. At the risk of offending specialists, diverse subject areas have been covered only to the extent that they are relevant to reading. For those who wish to pursue any topic further, some introductory sources are listed in the Notes. In general, this book is designed to serve as a handbook for language arts teachers, a college text for a basic course on the psychology of reading, a guide to relevant research literature on reading, and an introduction to reading as an aspect of thinking and learning.

I have tried to provide an integrated discussion of reading, a coherent theoretical position, rather than a compendium of research. I have not attempted to cover all contemporary research and theorizing into literacy, but I have tried to indicate at least one specific source of evidence for every assertion I make, and occasionally an alternative point of view. In general, I have tried to postpone multiple citations and detailed discussions until the extensive Notes section at the end of the book, where general references for further reading on major topics are also found.

The manner in which I have interpreted the evidence and tried to construct a coherent picture reflects basically my own thinking. My guide in all my excursions into the vast and shadowy forests of research into language, thought, and learning has always been the insights I have gained from the explorers to whom this book is dedicated—the teachers and learners of literacy.

Frank Smith

INTRODUCTION

There is nothing special about reading, apart from everything that reading enables us to do. The power that reading provides is enormous, not only in giving access to people far distant and possibly long dead, but also in allowing entry into worlds which might otherwise not be experienced, which might otherwise not exist. Reading enables us to manipulate time itself, to involve ourselves in ideas or events at a rate and in a sequence of our own choosing, quite independently of the manner in which the text was produced or printed. We do not have such power when we listen to speech or watch a movie.

But there is nothing special about reading in terms of what a reader has to do. Reading does not make any exclusive or esoteric demands on the brain. There are no unique kinds of movements that the eyes must make in reading that they do not make when we examine a picture or glance around a room. No particular kind or degree of visual ability is required to discriminate among printed letters or words. And there is nothing exceptional about the language that we read either. Written language is not the same as speech; each has its own characteristics and conventions. But there is nothing the brain must do to make sense of language that is written that it doesn't do to comprehend speech. There is nothing distinctive about learning to read. Reading requires no special talent or unique brain development. Any child who can see well enough to distinguish one face from another in a photograph and who can understand the familiar language of family and friends has the ability to learn to read.

The difficulty some children experience in learning to read often is attributed to some kind of minimal and undetectable brain damage, but there is no convincing evidence that a particular part of the brain is uniquely responsible for reading. It is, of course, possible—though by no means as common as some reading authorities would suggest—for an occasional child to have a brain injury that would affect language ability, but such an injury would not interfere with reading yet leave the comprehension of speech untouched. Children can obviously have visual defects that will interfere with reading, but these are problems that would show up in other visual activities as well. None of this is to say that it is impossible for a child to fail to learn to read despite perfectly adequate vision and spoken language ability; there are enough counterexamples in our schools. But there are many other possible reasons for reading difficulty apart from hypothetical brain disorders. Personal, social, or cultural conflicts can interfere critically with a child's motivation or ability to learn to read, and it is also possible for something to go wrong during instruction. Children can develop reading habits that make comprehension impossible.

All of the assertions made so far are reflections of the theoretical perspective of this book. There are other points of view. There is, for example, a traditional belief that reading is simply a matter of "decoding" the letters of written words into the sounds of speech, that it is basically a mechanical process, and that teaching children to read must involve drilling them in the recognition and blending of the sounds of letters. But analysis of the relationships between print and speech shows that the "rules" relating spelling to the sounds of speech in English are inordinately complicated and unreliable, and also that they are largely irrelevant to reading in any language. Reading is less a matter of extracting sound from print than of bringing meaning to print. The sounds that are supposed to reveal the meaning of sequences of letters cannot in fact be produced unless a probable meaning can be determined in advance. It is a universal fact of reading rather than a defect of English spelling that the effort to read through decoding is largely futile and unnecessary.

The point of view of this book is that reading and learning to read are essentially meaningful activities; that they are not passive and mechanical but purposeful and rational, dependent on the prior knowledge and expectations of the reader (or learner). Reading is a matter of making sense of written language rather than of decoding print to sound.

PERSPECTIVE

It is a question of who is in charge. From the decoding point of view, the reader is under the control of the text and must mechanically identify every letter and word in front of the eyes. But the meaningful perspective holds that what goes on behind the eyes is the critical factor. Reading is seen as a creative and constructive activity having four distinctive and fundamental characteristics—it is *purposeful, selective, anticipatory,* and based on *comprehension,* all matters where the reader must clearly exercise control.

The purposeful nature of reading is central, not simply because one normally reads for a reason, whether to find a telephone number or to enjoy a novel, but because the understanding which a reader must bring to reading can only be manifested through the reader's own intentions. A person who has no purpose in reading can bring nothing to the reading, and the activity is bound to be meaningless. Reading is selective because we normally only attend to what is relevant to our purposes. To read any kind of text without discrimination, whether a novel or a set of instructions, is as pointless as reading every number in the telephone directory when we are looking for only one. Reading is anticipatory because we are rarely surprised by what we read—our purposes define our expectations. And reading is based on comprehension because despite an ever-present possibility of ambiguity, the act (if not the content) rarely leaves us confused. Understanding is the basis not the consequence of reading. All these are matters that are of general concern throughout this book.

These matters also serve to underline that there is far more to reading than meets the eyes. In fact, because of certain fundamental characteristics of the human visual system and of language, fluent reading depends on the ability to use the eyes as little as possible. Such an ability is not taught. It is acquired by children as they employ perceptual and cognitive skills common to many everyday aspects of making sense of the visual world.

PREVIEW

Because reading should not be regarded as a special kind of activity but rather one that involves far broader aspects of human thought and behavior, an understanding of reading cannot be achieved without consideration of the nature of language and of various operating characteristics of the human brain. Consequently, the first half of this book is devoted to such topics as comprehension, knowledge, language, vision, and memory. These opening chapters are by no means intended to be comprehensive or even balanced disquisitions on the subjects covered; this is not a book about physiology, linguistics, or cognitive psychology. Instead, the chapters offer the minimum of background fact and theory that is necessary and relevant for an analysis of reading. A few suggestions are made in the Notes at the end of the book to set interested readers on the trail of more detailed sources.

Such a broadly based approach to reading has some incidental advantages. The more that is said about general topics at the beginning, the less that remains to be added when a detailed analysis of reading begins in the second half of this book, at which point much of the basic ground will have been covered. Questions related to learning and to how reading should be taught are left to the final chapters, partly because the pedagogical emphasis of this book is on enabling teachers to make informed decisions rather than on telling them what to do; partly because inferences about how reading should be taught become clearer as reading itself becomes more fully understood. The main instructional implication of the analysis of this book is that children learn to read by reading and by being read to. Drills, exercises, and rote learning play little part in learning to read and in fact may interfere with comprehension, giving a distorted idea of the nature of reading. The function of teachers is not so much to *teach* reading as to help children read. How this can be done—and the resolution of the paradox that children must read to learn to read—must of course eventually be faced. But for the moment it is more appropriate to postpone the ultimate issues and to look at the route by which the concluding portions of the book are reached.

Chapter 1, "Knowledge and Comprehension," examines the nature and organization of the knowledge we all carry around in our heads, and discusses the manner in which it is used to comprehend the world, whether through language or more directly.

Chapter 2, "Language: Spoken and Written," considers the special demands that language in all its aspects makes on listeners and readers, and also the rather subtle differences that exist between speech and print.

Chapter 3, "Information and Experience," shows how information aspects of reading (and other forms of language) can be conceptualized technically and even measured. But there is much more to reading than the acquisition of information, which plays only a small and even incidental role in many kinds of reading, for "pleasure" or for experience.

Chapter 4, "Between Eye and Brain" goes behind the eyes to discuss the major contribution that "prior knowledge" already possessed by the reader must make to reading. There are also limitations on how the brain can cope with what is going on in the world beyond the eyes, with the result that reading must be fast, selective, and anticipatory.

Chapter 5, "Memory and its Bottlenecks" is concerned with another major source of the brain's strengths but also of its limitations, again emphasizing the critical importance in reading of what the reader knows in advance about the text being read.

Chapter 6, "Letter Identification" is the first of four chapters that make a detailed theoretical analysis of reading, based on the preceding discussions. For ease of exposition, the topics of these four chapters start with letters and end with meaning, which is the reverse of the order in which reading is normally accomplished or learned. Readers usually focus their attention on meaning, and become concerned with individual words, and occasionally letters, only when understanding fails. But an analysis of letter identification demonstrates the possible mechanism by which words and even complex meanings can be ascertained.

Chapter 7, "Word Identification" shows how words can be identified "as wholes," without the prior identification of individual letters. The chapter also demonstrates how it is more economical, and generally essential, to recognize entire words "immediately" as perceptual units rather than to construct them out of individual letters.

Chapter 8, "Phonics and Mediated Word Identification" is concerned with the alternatives that are available when words cannot be recognized as wholes. "Phonics"—a system supposed to construct the identification of words from the sounds of individual letters—is shown to be cumbersome and unreliable. There are more productive alternatives available to readers when words cannot be identified immediately.

Chapter 9, "The Identification of Meaning" is directed to the ultimate purpose of reading—the understanding of the text in ways relevant to the reader's purposes in reading in the first place. It shows how "meanings" can be identified without the prior identification of individual words, just as words can be identified without the identification of component letters.

Chapter 10, "Reading, Writing, and Thinking" brings together the entire picture, summarizing and elaborating upon the act of reading, and also discussing the relationships between reading and writing. Reading and writing are both "thinking activities," and thinking is a complex topic in its own right. The chapter concludes with a brief attempt to relate reading and writing to more general aspects of thinking.

Chapter 11, "Learning about the World and about Language" outlines some basic principles of learning, because children do not need—nor can they lack—unique abilities for learning how to read. Rather they must use quite fundamental approaches to learning to solve the particular problems that literacy presents. The chapter emphasizes the social nature of learning.

Chapter 12, "Learning to Read and to Write" reviews the conditions under which children learn to become literate (once again, reading and writing cannot be separated), and includes a brief discussion of the relevance of different kinds of instruction, by teachers and by computers.

Notes to the Preface and Introduction begin on page 217, covering

Psycholinguistics
Research
On Not Being Eclectic
Changes in the Fourth Edition
Acknowledgements

Chapter 1
KNOWLEDGE AND COMPREHENSION

Understanding, or *comprehension*, is the basis of reading and of learning to read. What is the point of any activity if there is no understanding? Comprehension may be regarded as relating relevant aspects of the world around us—written language in the case of reading—to the intentions, knowledge, and expectations we already have in our heads. And learning can be considered as the modification of what we already know as a consequence of our interactions with the world around us. We learn to read, and we learn through reading, by adding to what we know already. Thus, comprehension and learning are fundamentally the same, relating the new to the already known. To understand all this, we must begin by considering what it is that "we already have in our heads" that enables us to make sense of the world. We must begin by comprehending comprehension.

COGNITIVE STRUCTURE

There are several terms that can be used to refer to the knowledge we carry around in our heads all the time. I shall speak of the *prior knowledge* or *nonvisual information* stored in the brain that enables us to make sense of the *visual information* that comes through the eyes when we read. I shall examine *long-term memory*, our permanent source of understanding of the world. But the different terms do not refer to distinct areas or aspects of the brain; they are synonymous. The knowledge that we must already possess in order to understand written language (like the knowledge we need for the understanding of speech) must reside in long-term memory. And remembrance of the sense we have made of past experience is the foundation of all new understanding of language and the world. In more general contexts, this basis of understanding is also referred to by psychologists as *cognitive structure*. The term is apt because "cognitive" means "knowledge" and "structure" implies organization, and that indeed is what we have in our heads—an organization of knowledge.

Certainly, it would be simplistic to suggest that what we carry around in our heads is just "memories." The brain is not a souvenir album filled with an assortment of snapshots and tape recordings of bits of the past. At the very least we would have to say that the brain contains memories-with-a-meaning; our memories are related to everything else that we know. Cognitive structure is much more like a summary of our past experience. I do not want to remember that on 16 July I sat on a chair, and that on 17 July I sat on a chair, and on 18 July I sat on a chair. I want to remember that chairs are for sitting on, a summary of my experience. We remember specific events only when they are exceptions to our summary rules or when they have some particularly dramatic or powerful or emotional significance. And even then our memories, when we "recall" them, turn out to be highly colored by our present intentions and perspectives about the world (Bartlett, 1932). Specific memories that cannot be related to our summary, to our present general understanding, will make little sense, which may be the reason we can recall so little of our childhood.

But it would also be an oversimplification to suggest that our heads are filled with an accumulation of facts and rules. The brain is not like a library where useful facts and procedures are filed away under appropriate headings for possible future reference. And certainly the human brain is not like a bank in which we save nuggets of information deposited by teachers and textbooks. Instead, the system of knowledge in our heads is organized into an intricate and internally consistent working model of the world, built up through our interactions with the world and integrated into a coherent whole. We know far more than we were ever taught.

THE THEORY OF THE WORLD
IN OUR HEADS

What we have in our heads is a *theory* of what the world is like, a theory that is the basis of all our perceptions and understanding of the world, the root of all learning, the source of hopes and fears, motives and expectancies, reasoning and creativity. And this theory is all we have. If we can make sense of the world at all, it is by interpreting our interactions with the world in the light of our theory. The theory is our shield against bewilderment.

As I look around my world, I distinguish a multiplicity of meaningful objects that have all kinds of complicated relations to each other and to me. But neither these objects nor their interrelations are self-evident. A chair does not announce itself to me as a chair; I have to recognize it as such. Chairs are a part of my theory. I recognize a chair when my brain decides that a chair is what I am looking at. A chair does not tell me that I can sit on it, or put my coat or books or feet on it, or stand on it to reach a high shelf, or wedge it against a door that I do not wish to be opened. All this is also part of my theory. I can only make sense of the world in terms of what I know already. All of the order and complexity that I perceive in the world around me must reflect an order and complexity in my own mind. Anything I cannot relate to the theory of the world in my head will not make sense to me. I shall be bewildered.

The fact that bewilderment is an unusual state for most of us despite the complexity of our lives is a clear indication that our theory of the world in the head is very efficient. The reason we are usually not aware of the theory is that it works so well. Just as a fish takes water for granted until deprived of it, so we become aware of our dependence on the theory in our head only when it proves inadequate, and the world fails to make sense. That we can occasionally be bewildered only serves to demonstrate how efficiently our theory usually functions. When were you last bewildered by something that you heard or read? Our theory of the world seems ready even to make sense of almost everything we are likely to experience in spoken and written language—a powerful theory indeed.

And yet, when was the last time you saw a bewildered baby? Infants have theories of the world too, not as complex as those of adults, but then children have not had as much time to make their theories complex. But children's theories seem to work very well for their needs. Even the smallest children seem able most of the time to make sense of their world in their own terms; they rarely appear confused or uncertain. The first time many children run into a situation that they cannot possibly relate to anything they know already is when they arrive at school, a time when they may be consistently bewildered if they are confronted by circumstances that make no sense to them. Children are often denied credit for knowing very much. But, in fact, most of our knowledge of the world—of the kind of objects it contains and the way they can be related—and most of our knowledge of language, is in our heads before we arrive at school. At age five or six the framework is there, and the rest is mainly a matter of filling in the details.

For the remainder of this chapter I talk a little more about how this theory in the head is organized, and then discuss how it is used so that we can comprehend the world.

Comprehension is more than understanding the circumstances we are in; it is the way in which we learn. This is the reason I have put the topic of comprehension first in this book and left learning until the end. This may be the reverse of the situation that often exists in school, where children often are expected to learn in order to understand. But learning is more a result of comprehension than its cause. Learning to read is literally a matter of "understanding reading."

THE STRUCTURE OF KNOWLEDGE

The system of knowledge that is the theory of the world in our heads has a structure just like any other theory or system of organizing information, such as a library. Information systems have three basic components—a set of categories, some rules for specifying membership of the categories, and a network of interrelations among the categories—and I shall briefly examine each component in turn.

Categories

To categorize means to treat some objects or events as the same, yet as different from other objects or events. All human beings categorize, instinctively, starting at birth. There is nothing remarkable about this innate propensity to categorize, because living organisms could not survive if they did not in fact treat some objects or events as the same, yet as different from other objects and events.

No living organism could survive if it treated everything in its experience as the same; there would be no basis for differentiation and therefore no basis for learning. There would be no possibility of being systematic. Just as a librarian cannot treat all books as the same when putting them on the shelves, so all human beings must differentiate throughout their lives. In our culture at least, everyone is expected to be able to distinguish dogs from cats, tables from chairs, and the letter *A* from the letter *B*.

But similarly, no living organism could survive if it treated everything in its experience as different. If there is no basis for similarity there is still no basis for learning. Thus the librarian must treat some books as the same in some senses—so that all chemistry books are stacked in the same area—even though these books may differ in size, color, and author's name. In the same way everyone, in our culture at least, is expected to ignore many differences in order to treat all dogs as the same, all cats as the same, and many different shapes like A, *Я, Ә,* a, *ɑ* , as the letter "a."

In other words, the basis of survival and of learning is the ability to ignore many potential differences so that certain objects[1] will be treated as the same, yet as different from other objects. All objects that belong to one category are treated as the same, yet as different from objects belonging to other categories.

The categories that we all observe, which are part of our theories of the world, are visually quite arbitrary; they are not generally imposed on us by the world itself. The world does not force us to categorize animals into dogs and cats and so forth—we could divide them up in other ways, for example treating all green-eyed animals as the same, in contrast to those with other eye colors, or differentiating those over 15 inches in height from those under 15 inches. The librarian could very neatly organize books on the basis of the color of their covers, or their size, or the number of pages. But we cannot usually invent categories for ourselves—hence the qualification "in our culture at least" in previous paragraphs. The reason we divide animals on a cat and dog basis and not on the basis of size or eye color is that the categories we have are part of our culture. Categories are *conventions*. In part, to share a culture means to share the same categorical basis for organizing experience. Language reflects the way a culture organizes experience, which is why many of the words in our language are a clue to the categories in our shared theories of the world. We have the words "dog" and "cat" but not a word for animals with green eyes or less than 15 inches in height. When we have to learn new categories, the existence of a name in the language tends often to be the first clue that a category exists.

Not that words are essential prerequisites for the establishment of categories. Quite the reverse—categories can exist for which we have no names. I can easily distinguish certain mottled brown and gray birds that come to my garden every morning, but I do not know a name for them. To know a name without an understanding of the category that it labels is meaningless. In fact, the existence of a category is a prerequisite for learning how to use words, since words label categories rather than specific objects. What we call a dog is any individual animal that we put in the category with the name "dog."

The category system that is part of our theory of the world in our heads is essential for making sense of the world. Anything we do that we cannot relate to a category will not make sense; we shall be bewildered. Our categories, in other words, are the basis of our perception of the world. Perception must be regarded as decision-making. We "see" what the brain decides we are looking at, which means the category to which visual information is allocated. If I see a chair in front of me, then I must have a category for chairs in my theory of the world, and I must have decided that what I am looking at belongs to that

---

[1] From this point on, I refrain from the cumbersome practice of talking all the time about "objects or events." But every reference to "objects" applies in general to "events" as well.

category. If I can see the word "cat" when I read, then I must have a category for that word quite independent of my knowledge of its name or possible meanings, just as I must have categories for the letters *c*, *a*, and *t*, if I can distinguish those in the word. Interestingly, we cannot see things in more than one category at a time; it is not possible to see the letters "c," "a," and "t" and the word "cat" simultaneously in the visual configuration *cat*, which is why children may find learning to read more difficult if they are required to concentrate on the individual letters in words. Usually you only see what you are looking for, and remain quite unaware of other possibilities. If I ask you to read the address 4IO LION STREET you will probably not notice that the numerals IO in 4IO are the same characters as the letters IO in LION. When you look for the category of numerals you see numerals and when you look for the category of letters you see letters. Even now that you are aware of what I am doing, you cannot look at IO and see both letters and numerals simultaneously, any more than you can see the faces and the vase simultaneously in the ambiguous illustration of Figure 1.1. The brain can make decisions about only one category at a time in relation to a single visual configuration (although we could see the face and vase in Figure 1.1 simultaneously if they did not share a common contour). And if there is no category to which we can relate an object or event to which we are exposed, the brain can make no decision at all; the world will not make sense to us. The brain, like every other executive, needs categories in order to make decisions, categories that embrace not only sights and sounds, but tastes, odors, feelings, and sensations, as well as many kinds of events, patterns, and relationships.

Rules for Category Membership

Categories in themselves are not enough. The category "chemistry books" is useless if a librarian has no way of recognizing a chemistry book when confronted by one, just as a child can make no use of the information that there are cats and dogs in the world without some notion of how to distinguish one

FIGURE 1.1.   Ambiguous visual information.

from the other. A child who can recite the alphabet has established a set of 26 categories but may not be able to recognize a single letter. For every category that we employ there must be at least one way of recognizing members of that category. Every category must have at least one set of rules, a specification, that determines whether an object (or an event) belongs in that category. Sometimes a single category may have more than one set of rules—we can distinguish an object as an onion by its appearance, feel, smell and taste. We can recognize the letter "a" in a number of different guises. But just as we must have a category for every object we can distinguish in the world, so we must have at least one set of rules—a list of significant attributes or *distinctive features*—for allocating that object to a particular category. These are not usually rules that we can put into words, any more than we can open a window into our brains and inspect the categories we have there. Knowledge of this kind is *implicit*—we can only infer that we have the categories or rules by the fact that we can make use of them.

The question of what constitutes the rules that differentiate the various categories that we employ in reading and language generally demands a good deal of attention in later chapters—especially when we see that "teaching" is often little more than telling children that a category exists, leaving them to discover for themselves what the rules are.

Category Interrelations

Rules permit the categories in a system to be used, but they do not ensure that the system makes sense. A library does not make sense simply because all the chemistry books are stacked together in one place and all the poetry books in another. What makes a library a system is the way in which the various categories are related to each other, and this is the way the system in our brains makes sense as well.

It is not possible to list all the different interrelations among the categories in the theory of the world in our heads. To do so would be to document the complexity of the world as we perceive it. Everything that we know is directly or indirectly related to everything else, and any attempt to illustrate these relationships risks becoming interminable.

For example, consider an onion. We know what that particular object is called—in more than one language perhaps—and also the names of several kinds of onion. All these are relations of the particular object to language. We also know what an onion looks, feels, smells, and tastes like, again perhaps in more than one way. We know where an onion comes from—how it is grown—and we probably have a good idea about how it gets to the place where we can buy one. We know roughly what we have to pay to buy one. We know how an onion can be used in cooking, and probably some other uses as well. We may know half a dozen different ways of cooking onions (with different names), and we certainly know a number of things that can be eaten with onions. We know a number of instruments for dealing with onions—knives, graters, and blenders, for example. We not only know what we can do with onions, we also know what onions can do to us, both raw and cooked. We know people who love onions and people who hate them; people who can cook them and people who cannot. We may even know something about the role of onions in history. One enormous ramification of our knowledge of onions is related to the fact that we can call them by more than one name. An onion can also be called a vegetable, which means that everything we know about vegetables in general applies to onions in particular. Indeed, every time we relate an onion to something else—to a knife, a frying pan, or a particular person—then we discover that what we know about onions is part of what we know about knives, frying pans, and people. There is no end.

Many cognitive interrelations pertain to the system of language that is such an important part of everyone's theory of the world. One complex set of interrelations is called *syntax*, the rules of which determine how elements of language must be related to each other in speech or writing. Syntactic rules enable us to put words together in ways sometimes called "grammatical," although people whose speech is often characterized as "ungrammatical" do not normally lack syntax; they follow other rules. Another set of interrelations is called *semantics*, concerned with the way language is related to the world at large (or rather, to perception of the world). The semantic richness of words determines to some extent the complexity we perceive in the world. Cultures with many words for different kinds of snow see snow differently from individuals who know only the one word (Whorf, 1956). Knowledge of language must also include extensive understanding of the conventional ways in which language and other systems of communication are used on particular occasions, sometimes referred to as *pragmatics* or as *semiotics*. And a good deal of our knowledge of the world is actually held in the form of language, in verbal *descriptions* of things that we know. Our heads can also contain a host of *propositions*, ranging from simple facts (Paris is the capital of France, two times two is four), through proverbs and other compact bundles of ideas or common sense, to complex verbal formulas and even entire segments of prose or poetry. All of this verbal prior knowledge can become available to us at relevant times to help us to comprehend and even to bring about particular sets of circumstances.

Scenes, Scenarios, and Stories

Many important sets of cognitive relations are mental representations of places and scenes with which we are familiar. We carry around in our heads detailed specifications of the spatial organization of familiar landscapes and locations—

the beach where we played as children, the family living room, or our first classroom. We are quickly aware if something in a familiar setting has changed (even if we cannot immediately determine what exactly is different). In addition to these "photographic" images, our theory also contains many more symbolic representations, such as maps (which is the primary way most of us understand the geography of the world, and of familiar countries and cities), and diagrams, some of which we may have constructed in our own minds without ever seeing or putting them on paper.

But our heads also contain extensive representations of more general patterns or regularities that occur in our experience. These representations are called *schemes* (or occasionally schemas or schemata). Most of us have a complex "generic" scheme for what classrooms are like, for example. We can recognize and make sense of classrooms we have never been in before, just because they contain familiar arrangements of familiar elements. Our cognitive structures similarly include schemes of department stores and restaurants, for example, which enable us to make sense of new experiences and to behave appropriately. Many experiments have demonstrated that our ability to recognize scenes and to remember them depends on the extent to which they conform to our expectations of what such scenes should be like, to the schemes that we already have in our heads.

Readers develop and require a large number of spatially organized schemes related to the way in which books and other kinds of written texts are organized. Among such schemes are those of specific *genres*—newspapers are not set out in the way that magazines, novels, or textbooks are. All of these schemes, or specifications for various kinds of texts, are conventional. The appearance and organization of a book or a newspaper can vary considerably from one community or culture to another, and their schemes have to be known to us if we are to make sense of them. Other conventional rules of written *discourse structure* include organization into paragraphs, chapters, or sections, with titles and other kinds of heading, which readers as well as writers have to observe and expect.

The examples of schemes I have so far given have all been spatial, the way things are laid out, primarily for comprehension visually. Our brains also contain innumerable schemes for other sense modalities—for arrangements of sounds, tastes, and smells and a variety of tactile sensations, many of them closely related to each other and to patterns of events in the visual world.

But many of our most important schemes are also laid out in time, they have a serial or temporal organization. Time and change are essential aspects of the way we perceive the world—how otherwise could we understand language, music, or even a football match? Schemes that have a temporal as well as a spatial basis are often referred to as *scenarios* or *scripts*. A department store script sets out expected and conventional patterns of behavior for ourselves and for others when we go out to shop, even when we are purchasing unfamiliar items in stores we have never been to before. An absence or mismatch of scripts can result in confusion, embarrassment, and misunderstanding. Collectively, scripts, scenarios, and schemes are sometimes referred to as *event knowledge* (Nelson, 1986).

Knowledge of relevant schemes is obviously essential if we are to read any kind of text with comprehension. A child who does not have a scenario about farming is unlikely to understand a story about farming, or a reference to farming in a textbook. But there are special kinds of language schemes that readers particularly require. If we are readers, or if we hope to become readers, our theories of the world in our heads must contain *story schemes,* specifications of how stories are organized, and how they unfold. We must know that stories comprise particular kinds of plots, characters, and episodes. How well a story is understood and remembered depends on how well it conforms to conventional schemes for stories—and on how well the reader is familiar with those schemes.

Time and change are also an essential part of the way individuals operate upon the world. One thing has to follow another in a particular way, in an invariant sequence, often at a specific moment or rate. Complex serial and temporal schemes include the multiplicity of *skills* that all human beings acquire, depending on their physical capabilities, experience, and interests— feeding and dressing ourselves, tying shoelaces, riding bicycles, playing chess, programming computers—and of course reading and writing.

The complexity of cognitive structure in the human brain is indeed astounding. Our prior knowledge resists all efforts to catalog it, or to reduce it to a few simple categories. Attempts to "simplify" the organization or operation of the brain can only mislead, especially if they are made the basis of instructional or diagnostic practices in education. The enormous power of every brain is frequently overlooked if there is an emphasis on "weaknesses" or "disabilities." Think for a moment of the complexity of the world in which we all live, of the multitude of individuals with different personalities, roles, and patterns of behavior; of the multitude of animate and inanimate objects in the world, and of all the multifarious ways in which these people and objects can be related to each other. Any circumstance or situation to which we cannot bring a relevant cognitive structure—including categories, sets of distinctive features, and a multiplicity of spatial, temporal, and other cognitive relations—will confuse or bewilder us. Our ability to make sense of the world, like our ability to remember events, to act appropriately, and to predict the future, is determined by the complexity of the knowledge we already possess.

My emphasis in this book is on the many kinds of things everyone's brain does well. One of these superb but commonplace mental abilities is the storing of vast amounts of useful knowledge, of potential understanding, as a result both of experience and creative imagination. Another powerful yet everyday constant achievement of the brain is to make use of all this prior knowledge, the topic to which I now turn.

THE DYNAMICS OF COGNITIVE STRUCTURE

Cognitive structure, the theory of the world in our heads, may so far have seemed rather a crowded and static place, not very different in essence from a collection of facts and procedures. But the theory of the world in our heads is *dynamic*, and not just in the sense that it is constantly being added to and changed, particularly during that lively period of intense exploration and learning we call childhood. We can do much more with the theory of the world in our heads than make sense of the world and interact with it. We can live in the theory itself, in worlds that exist only in the imagination. Within this theory we can imagine and create, testing provisional solutions to problems and examining the consequences of possible behaviors. We can explore new worlds of our own, and can be led into other worlds by writers and artists.

But the aspect of imagination with which we will be most concerned is more mundane, although at first encounter it may sound quite exotic. We can use the theory of the world in our heads to predict the future. This ability to predict is both pervasive and profound, because it is the basis of our comprehension of the world, including our understanding of spoken and written language. Reading depends on prediction.

The Pervasiveness of Prediction

Everyone predicts—including children—all the time. Our lives would be impossible, we would be reluctant even to leave our beds in the morning, if we had no expectation about what the day will bring. We would never go through a door if we had no idea of what might be on the other side. And all our expectations, our predictions, can be derived from only one source, the theory of the world in our heads.

We are generally unaware of our constant state of anticipation for the simple reason once again that our theory of the world works so well. Our theory is so efficient that when our predictions fail, we are surprised. We do not go through life predicting that anything might happen—indeed, that would be contrary to prediction, and in that case nothing could surprise us. The fact that something always could rhinoceros take us by surprise—like the word *rhinoceros* a few words ago—is evidence that indeed we always predict but that our predictions are usually accurate. It is always possible that we could be surprised, yet our predictions are usually so appropriate that surprise is a very rare occurrence. When was the last time you were surprised?

We drive through a town we have never visited before, and nothing we see surprises us. There is nothing surprising about the buses and cars and pedestrians in the main street; they are predictable. But we do not predict that we might see anything—we would be surprised to see camels or submarines in the main street. Not that there is anything very surprising or unpredictable about camels or submarines in themselves—we would not be surprised to see camels if we were visiting a zoo or to see submarines at a naval base. In other words, our predictions are very specific to situations. We do not predict that anything will happen, nor do we predict that something is *bound* to happen if it is only *likely* to happen (we are no more surprised by the absence of a bus than we are by the presence of one), and we predict that many things are unlikely to happen. Our predictions are remarkably accurate—and so are those of children. It is rare to see a child who is surprised.

The Need for Prediction

Why should we predict? Why not expect that anything could happen all the time, and thus free ourselves from any possibility of surprise? I can think of three reasons. The first reason is that our position in the world in which we live changes constantly, and we are usually far more concerned with what is likely to happen in the near and distant future than we are with what is actually happening right now. An important difference between a skilled driver and a learner is that the skilled driver is able to project the car into the future while the learner's mind is more closely anchored to where the car is now—when it is usually too late to avoid accidents. The same difference tends to distinguish skilled readers from beginners, or from anyone having difficulty with a particular piece of reading. In fluent reading the eye is always ahead of the brain's decisions, checking for possible obstacles to a particular understanding. Readers concerned with the word directly in front of their nose will have trouble predicting—and they will have trouble comprehending.

The second reason for prediction is that there is too much ambiguity in the world, too many ways of interpreting just about anything that confronts us. Unless we exclude some alternatives in advance, we are likely to be overwhelmed with possibilities. Of the many things I know about onions, I do not want to be concerned with the fact that they are dug from the ground, or that they bring my cousin George out in spots, if all I want is garnish for a hamburger. What I see is related to what I am looking for, not to all possible interpretations. Words have many meanings—*table* can be several kinds of verb as well as several kinds of noun—but there is only one meaning that I am concerned with, that I predict, if someone tells me to put my books on the table. All the everyday words of our language have many meanings and often several grammatical functions—*table, chair, house, shoe, time, walk, open, narrow*—but by predicting the range of possibilities that a word is likely to be, we are just not aware of the potential ambiguities.

The final reason for prediction is that there would otherwise be far too many alternatives from which to choose. The brain requires time to make its decisions about what the eyes are looking at, and the time that it requires depends on the number of alternatives. We take longer to decide that we are looking at the letter *A* when it could be any one of the 26 letters of the alphabet than when we know that it is a vowel or that it is either *A* or *B*. It takes much longer to identify a word in isolation compared with a word in a meaningful sentence. The fewer the alternatives, the quicker the recognition. If there are too many alternatives confronting the eyes, then it is much harder to see or to comprehend.

Prediction is the core of reading. All of the schemes, scripts, and scenarios we have in our heads—our prior knowledge of places and situations, of written discourse, genres, and stories—enable us to predict when we read, and thus to comprehend, experience, and enjoy what we read. Prediction brings potential meaning to texts, reducing ambiguity and eliminating in advance irrelevant alternatives. Thus, we are able to generate comprehensible experience from inert pages of print.

Prediction is not reckless guessing, nor does it involve taking chances by betting everything on the most likely outcome. We do not go through life saying "Round the next corner I shall see a bus," or "The next word I read will be *rhinoceros.*" We predict by opening our minds to the probable and by disregarding the unlikely. Here is a formal definition: *Prediction is the prior elimination of unlikely alternatives.* It is the projection of possibilities. We predict to reduce our uncertainty and therefore to reduce the amount of external information that we require. Our theory of the world tells us the most probable occurrences, leaving the brain to decide among those remaining alternatives until uncertainty is reduced to zero. And we are so good at predicting only the most likely alternatives that we are rarely surprised.

Put more informally, prediction is a matter of asking specific questions. We do not ask "What is that object over there?" but "Can we put our books on it?" or whatever we want to do. We do not look at a page of print with no expectation about what we shall read next, instead we ask "What is the hero going to do?" "Where is the villain going to hide?" And "Will there be an explosion when liquid A is mixed with powder B?" And provided the answer lies within the expected range of alternatives—which it usually does if we are reading with comprehension—then we are not aware of any doubt or ambiguity. We are neither bewildered nor surprised.

Prediction and Comprehension Related

Now at last prediction and comprehension can be tied together. Prediction means asking questions, and comprehension means being able to get some of the questions answered. As we read, as we listen to someone talking, as we go through life, we are constantly asking questions, and if we are able to find answers to those questions, then we comprehend. The person who does not comprehend how to repair a radio is the one who cannot ask and find answers to such questions as "Which of these wires goes where?" at appropriate times. And the person who does not comprehend a book or newspaper article is the one who cannot find relevant questions and answers concerning the next part of the text. There is a *flow* to comprehension, with new questions constantly being generated from the answers that are sought.

Such a view of comprehension differs from the way the word is often used in school. So-called comprehension tests in school are usually given after a book has been read, and, as a consequence, are more like tests of long-term memory. (And because the effort to memorize can drastically interfere with comprehension, the test may finish up by destroying what it sets out to measure.) If I say that I comprehended a certain book, it does not make sense to give me a test and argue that I did not understand it. And a score on a test certainly would not convince me that I had really understood a book or a speaker if my feeling is that I did not.

The very notion that comprehension is relative, that it depends on the questions that an individual happens to ask, is not one that all educators find easy to accept. Some want to argue that you may not have understood a book even if you have no unanswered questions at the end. They will ask, "But did you understand that the spy's failure to steal the secret plans was really a symbol of humanity's ineluctable helplessness in the face of manifest destiny?" And if you say, "No, I just thought it was a jolly good story," they will tell you that you did not *really* comprehend what the story was about. But basically what they are saying is that you were not asking the kind of questions they think you should have asked.

THINKING AND "META-THINKING"

A comprehensive analysis of thinking would require a separate book and the critical discussion of a mountain of recent research, uncovering, perhaps, more mysteries and controversies than it could unravel. On the other hand, the topic cannot be completely ignored because thinking has become a focus of attention for many educators recently.

In part, this concentration of interest has been generated by cognitive scientists trying to develop models of thought that might serve in the development of "thinking computers," and also by cognitive psychologists involved with human thinking who nevertheless want to simulate or test their theories on computers. As a result, thinking has tended to be fragmented into distinct clusters of "information-processing" procedures, more appropriate to the programmed sequential operations of electronic technology than to humans whose thought and actions are based primarily on their intentions, interests, and values.

It could also be argued that another reason for the sudden concern about thinking is that educational research has tended to fragment reading and reading instruction into packages of decontextualized "basic skills," none of which particularly engage thinking.

Yet, reading cannot be separated from thinking. Reading is a thought-full activity. There is no difference between reading and any other kind of thought, except that with reading, thought focuses on a written text. *Reading* might be defined as thought that is stimulated and directed by written language. This entire book could be considered to be a disquisition on thinking, from a reading point of view.

Particular characteristics of the thinking ideally engaged in by readers must be separated into two categories, not always clearly recognized. The first is the thinking involved in the *act* of reading—such as drawing appropriate inferences in order to comprehend—and the other is thinking which is a *consequence* of reading, that might transpire in subsequent reflection. Reading involves no special kind of thought that is not already displayed by readers in other aspects of mental life.

Thinking should not be regarded as a set of specialized processes that are superimposed upon the organization of knowledge, the theory of the world in the head, discussed in the present chapter. Thinking is not a distinct faculty or set of skills, different from comprehension, prediction, or imagination. The theory of the world is dynamic, constantly modifying itself in relation to our current concerns and state of affairs. Thinking is the normal operation of the theory of the world, as the brain goes about its business of creating and selectively testing possible worlds, even when established patterns of behavior become hardened into "habits," which might be considered schemes for activity. The flow of thought is powered by our intentions and expectations, guided by the consequent experience. It is creative and constructive, not passive and reactive.

All of the various aspects of thought that language distinguishes can be seen as the manipulation of cognitive relationships. *Reasoning* usually refers to relationships within a series of statements or states of affairs; the way one thing follows another. *Inference* involves relationships between particular statements or states of affairs and some more general circumstances, and *problem solving* relates existing states of affairs to desired states. *Classification, categorization, concept formation,* and other manifestations of what are sometimes called *higher order* or *abstract* thinking all impose and examine relationships among statements or states of affairs. The terms I have italicized are just *words,* not different kinds of brain function. .The brain is not doing different things when we reason, draw inferences, or solve problems; they only appear different because of the context in which they are done or the consequences of doing them. They are not measurable.

The brain constantly engages in relational activities, in its everyday transactions of comprehending and learning about the world around us. What differs among individuals is not so much the general ability to think as the possibility of demonstrating aspects of thought on particular occasions. Three constraints bear on how well individuals can appear to think on particular occasions, none of them dependent on the acquisition of specialized or exotic skills. All of us on occasion find ourselves in situations in which we are unable to think—especially in "educational" contexts—but this need not be because no one has taught us specific "thinking skills."

Constraints on Thinking

The first constraint on thinking is *prior knowledge*. Like language, thought always has a subject. And just as we cannot talk or write competently if we do not know what we are talking about, so it is not possible to demonstrate thought in any way if we do not understand what we are expected or trying to think about. If I have difficulty understanding an article on nuclear physics, it is not because I am unable to draw conclusions, make inferences, follow arguments, or solve problems, but because I do not know enough about nuclear physics. And good nuclear physicists are not necessarily good writers, chess players, or automobile mechanics.

The second constraint on thinking is *disposition*. Philosopher John McPeck (1981), for example, has asserted that the "judicious suspension of belief," which is his definition of critical thinking, is a disposition rather than a skill. Whether or not we take something for granted, whether we will challenge other people's assertions or question our own opinions in the light of new evidence, depends on individual propensities to behave in those ways, not on the acquisition of abilities that can be developed through instruction or even practice. Dispositions can be innate, aspects of personality we were born with, or they can be the result of experience—"once bitten, twice shy."

And finally, whether or not anyone will exercise thought, particularly of the critical variety, depends on whether they have the *authority* to do so. Challenging conventional thought or other people's opinions, or even drawing one's own conclusions, is not something everyone is in a position to do, certainly not in every situation. In many institutions, and in many patterns of personal relations, the authority for engaging in thought of a significant nature (as opposed to accepting or providing "right answers") is not distributed equally. Thinking can upset applecarts.

Metacognition

One other topic related to thinking that is receiving considerable attention from educational researchers is *metacognition*—literally "cognition about cognition," or thought about our own thought. *Metacognitive processes* are presumed to take place when we think about our own thinking, for example when we reflect upon whether we know something, whether we are learning, or whether we have made a mistake.

Researchers with a "skills" orientation are again inclined to regard metacognitive processes as yet another special set of skills which have to be learned. On the other hand, children learn many things, including talking and much of literacy, without awareness of learning. And we are usually aware when we do not understand something (in the sense of being confused), or when we do not know something at a time when some knowledge is personally relevant and important to us.

SUMMARY

(Terms printed in **bold type** in the Summaries are key terms that can be found in the Glossary at the back of the book.)

Nonvisual information, long-term memory, and **prior knowledge** are alternative terms for describing **cognitive structure,** the theory of the world in the head. The theory includes **schemes,** or generalized representations of familiar settings and situations, essential in all understanding and remembering. The theory of the world is the source of **comprehension,** as the brain continually generates and examines possibilities about situations in real and imaginary worlds. The basis of comprehension is **prediction,** the prior elimination of unlikely alternatives. Predictions are questions that we ask the world, and comprehension is receiving relevant answers to those questions. If we cannot predict, we are confused. If our predictions fail, we are surprised. And if we have nothing to predict because we have no interest or uncertainty, we are bored. **Thinking**—including **metacognition,** or "thinking about thinking"—is not a special set of skills but the constant activity of the brain, subject only to constraints of individual prior knowledge, disposition, and authority.

Notes to Chapter 1 begin on page 222 covering

Theories of comprehension
Prediction
Categories
Schemes
The narrative brain
Thinking

Chapter 2
LANGUAGE:
SPOKEN AND WRITTEN

Language constitutes a substantial part of any human being's theory of the world and obviously plays a central role in reading. The present chapter is concerned with language from a number of perspectives, including the relationships between the sounds (and printed marks) of language and their meaning, between productive aspects of language (talking and writing) and receptive aspects (listening and reading), and between spoken and written language. The chapter also refers briefly to grammar, and to many other conventions of language.

All of these aspects of language are relevant to an understanding of reading; yet all are complex areas of study in their own right. Obviously it will not be possible to study any topic to the same theoretical depth as the professional linguist or psychologist—but fortunately such detail is also not necessary. The handful of basic insights that a student of reading must grasp are relatively easy to explain and to demonstrate. These insights, however, are not always part of the general awareness of educators in the field of reading; they are widely disregarded in many instructional programs and materials and in a good deal of reading research, so that they may appear to be new and even unfamiliar ideas. For example, one basic but neglected insight is that actual instances of language—the statements that people utter or write—do not convey meaning in any simple fashion. Meaning is not contained within the sounds of speech or the printed marks of writing, conveniently waiting to be discovered or decoded, but rather must be provided by the listener or reader. As a consequence, an understanding of reading requires a more complex theory of comprehension than one that simplistically assumes that meaning will take care of itself provided a reader can identify individual words correctly. Most of this chapter is concerned with the fundamental issue of how language is comprehended.

TWO ASPECTS OF LANGUAGE

Surface Structure and Deep Structure

There are two quite different ways of talking about language, whether spoken or written. On the one hand, you can talk about its physical aspect, about characteristics that can be measured, such as the loudness or duration or pitch of the sounds of speech, or the number, size, or contrast of the printed marks of writing. All of these observable characteristics of language that exist in the world around us may be called *surface structure*. They are the part of language accessible to the brain through the ears and eyes. Surface structure is a useful term because it is not restricted to a particular form of language, either spoken or written. Surface structure is the "visual information" of written language— the source of information that is lost to the reader when the lights go out—but it is also a part of spoken language—the part that is lost when a telephone connection is broken.

On the other hand, there is a part of language that can neither be directly observed nor measured, and that is meaning. In contrast to surface structure, the meaning of language, whether spoken or written, can be referred to as *deep structure*. The term is apt. Meanings do not lie at the surface of language but far more profoundly in the minds of the users of language: in the mind of the speaker or writer and in the mind of the listener or reader.

These two different aspects of language, the physical surface structure and the meaningful deep structure, can in fact be completely separated in the sense that it is quite possible to talk about one without reference to the other. We can say that someone is talking loudly or softly, or fast or slowly, without reference to what is being said. We can say that a line of print is five inches wide, or has eight characters to the inch, without fear that someone will contradict us by saying that we have not understood the meaning of the text. But conversely, meaning is not directly affected by the form of the surface structure. If we are told that Paris will host the next Olympic Games, we cannot reply that it depends on whether the speaker's source of information was spoken or written. Though it may be occasionally overlooked, the truth of an utterance is not related to its loudness or the number of repetitions.

All of this may seem very obvious, trite even, but the distinction between the surface and the deep structure of language is crucial for an understanding of reading for one simple reason: The two aspects of language are separated by a chasm. Surface and deep structures are not opposite sides of the same coin; they are not mirror reflections of each other. They are not directly and unambiguously related. Put into technical terms, *there is no one-to-one correspondence between the surface structure of language and meaning.* Meaning lies beyond the mere sounds or printed marks of language, and cannot be derived from surface structure by any simple or mechanistic process.

One way of exemplifying this absence of a one-to-one relationship between the two aspects of language is by showing that differences can occur in surface structure that make no difference to meaning, and that there can be differences in meaning that are not represented in surface structure (Miller, 1965). For example, here are some radically different surface structures that do not correspond to radical differences in meaning: (a) *the cat is chasing a bird;* (b) *a bird is chased by the cat;* (c) *a warm-blooded feathered vertebrate is pursued by the domesticated feline quadruped;* (d) *le chat chasse un oiseau.* Four quite different sequences of marks on paper; but all represent (in general terms at least) the same meaning. When we try to say what words mean, all we can do is offer other words (a synonym or a paraphrase) that reflect the same meaning. The actual meaning always lies beyond words. It makes sense to say that *bachelor* means (or more accurately, conveys the same meaning as) *unmarried man,* but it does not make sense to ask what the meaning is that *bachelor* and *unmarried man* have in common. Alternative verbal definitions or descriptions simply compound the problem. They are additional surface structures.

On the other hand, it is not difficult to find individual surface structures which have at least two possible meanings or interpretations. For example: *flying planes can be dangerous; visiting professors may be tedious; the shooting of the principals was terrible; the chickens were too hot to eat; she runs through the spray and waves; he enjoys talking with old men and women (all women?); Cleopatra was rarely prone to talk (and Mark Anthony was not inclined to argue).*

The examples just quoted represent a particular kind of ambiguity, namely puns. But often puns are difficult to comprehend at once—you may not have seen the alternative meanings in all of the above examples immediately—and there lies an important theoretical issue: Why are we so rarely aware of the potential ambiguity of language? It is not just puns but every possible sequence of words in our language, and just about every individual word for that matter, that is a source of potential misinterpretation. To understand why we are so rarely aware of the multiple meanings that might be attributed to surface structure of our language, we must look at a more basic question. If there is this chasm between surface structure and deep structure, how then is language comprehended in the first place? The question is of considerable relevance to reading, because if meaning is not immediately and unambiguously given by the surface structure of speech, then there is no point in expecting a reader to "decode" written language to speech in order for comprehension to occur. Speech itself needs to be comprehended, and print cannot be read aloud in a comprehensible way unless it is comprehended in the first place. Written language does not require decoding to sound in order to be comprehended; the manner in which we bring meaning to print is just as direct as the manner in which we understand speech. Language comprehension is the same for all surface structures.

Spoken language is not comprehended by "decoding" sounds, but by bringing meaning to them. Reading aloud is not a matter of decoding from the surface structure of print to the surface structure of speech, but must also be mediated through meaning. And for silent reading, attempts to understand through subvocal speech may be unnecessary as well as disabling, because meaning can be brought to print directly. Oral reading is more complex and difficult than silent reading.

The Trouble with Words

How then is language understood, whether spoken or written? The answer is not that we put together the meaning of individual words and thereby understand entire sentences. For a start, it seems very doubtful whether words can be said to exist in spoken language at all. Certainly scientific instruments cannot isolate the beginning and ending of many sounds—or even words—that we hear as quite separate. The actual flow of speech is relatively continuous and smoothly changing, and the segmentation into distinct sounds and words is largely something that listeners contribute. You can get some indication of this by uttering the two words "west end" and repeating them while listening very carefully to what you are saying. You will probably find that if you introduce any pause at all in the utterance, it will be between the /s/ and the /t/—that actually you are saying "wes tend" rather than "west end." Of course, English speakers would never think that you really said "wes tend." But only because they speak the language and are able to work out—and hear—the sounds you *thought* you were producing. The fact that you need to *know* a language in order to be able to *hear* it properly becomes apparent when you listen to a foreign language. Not only can you not distinguish what the distinctive sounds of the language are, you cannot even distinguish the number of words in an utterance. Speakers of other languages—and children—have exactly the same trouble with English. They hear *bank rate* as *bang crate* and *law and order* as *Laura Norder*.

The very existence of words may be an artifact of the writing system. At least in writing we can provide a definition of a word—as something with a white space on either side. Children learning to talk either produce groups of words that they use as one long word—"allgone," "drinkamilk," "gowalk"—or else single words that they use as entire sentences—"drink," "tired," "no."

Beginning readers often cannot say how many words are in a sentence, either spoken or written. They need to be readers to understand the question.

Words and Meanings

Another reason why it is difficult to argue that the meanings of sentences are made up of the meanings of words is that it would appear that words often get meaning as a virtue of occurring in sentences. In fact, it is very difficult to see what meaning a word in isolation can have. Even nouns, which might seem the easiest class of words to account for, present difficulties. It is certainly far from true that every object has one name and every word one meaning. Every object has more than one name. The family pet, for example, can be called a canine, a dog, a boxer, "Rover," an animal, and a variety of other titles including, of course, "family pet" and "that slavering brute." What is the "real name" of the animal? There is not one. The appropriate name for the speaker to use depends on the listener and the extent of the listener's uncertainty. In talking to a member of the family, the name "Rover" is adequate, or simply "the dog"; on other occasions no single word would be adequate and the name would have to be qualified as "that brown dog over there" or "the large boxer." Everything depends on the knowledge of the listener or reader and the alternatives from among which Rover has to be distinguished. The same animal will be described in different ways to the same person depending on the characteristics of other dogs that are around. What then does a word like "dog" mean? The dictionary tells us that it is "any of a large and varied group of domesticated animals related to the fox, wolf, and jackal." But that surely is not the meaning of "dog" in the sentence "Beware of the dog," let alone such expressions as hot dog, top dog, putting on the dog, dirty dog, dog tired, or going to the dogs.

All the common words of our language have a multiplicity of meanings, with the most common words being the most ambiguous. To test this assertion, just look up a few words in the dictionary. Words that come most immediately to mind—the everyday words like *table, chair, shoe, sock, horse, dog, field, file, take, look, go, run, raise, narrow*—require many inches and even columns of "definition." Less familiar words like *osmosis, gossamer,* or *tergiversation* are disposed of in a crisp line or two. Prepositions, which are among the commonest words of our language, have so many different senses that they are sometimes maligned as having "function" rather than "content." But it makes a difference whether something is in the box rather than on the box; prepositions have meanings—in great number. The linguist Fries (1952), for example, discovered in the Oxford Dictionary no fewer than 39 separate senses for *at* and *by,* 40 each for *in* and *with,* and 63 for *of.* You would surely have no difficulty in understanding the statement *I found the book by Charles*

Dickens by the tree by chance; I shall return it by mail by Friday—but it would be very difficult for you to tell me the meaning (or meanings) of the word "by" on all or any of its five occurrences. Prepositions in context seem full of meaning, but in isolation it is impossible to say what the meaning might be. That is why it is so difficult to translate prepositions from one language to another.

It is not necessary to pursue the argument about the nature of words, or their meaning, because it is quite clear that sentences are not understood by trying to put together meanings of individual words. *The man ate the fish* and *The fish ate the man* contain exactly the same words, yet they have quite different meanings. A *Maltese cross* is not the same as a *cross Maltese*, any more than a *Venetian blind* is a *blind Venetian*. A house that is *pretty ugly* is not exactly ugly, but is certainly not pretty. Obviously, the words in all these examples do not combine in any simple fashion to form the meaning of the whole sentence; in fact, the meaning of many of the individual words in the sentence would appear to be quite different from the meaning we might say they have in isolation.

Perhaps then the word order is the key—the word *cross* has one meaning before *Maltese* and another meaning after. But words in the same position can represent different meanings—compare the first words of *Man the boats* and *Man the hunter*—while words in different positions in a sentence may reflect the same meaning. Words that often seem to have a similar meaning, such as *look, view,* and *see* may suddenly acquire quite different meanings without any variation in position, as in *overlook, overview,* and *oversee,* while words that may seem opposite in meaning, such as *up* and *down,* may occasionally lose their distinctiveness, as in *slow up* and *slow down.*

A common explanation is that grammar makes the difference; indeed the entire theory of Chomsky (1957, 1975), is that syntax (word order) is the bridge between the surface structure of language and its deep structure. But the problem with this point of view is that often it is impossible to say what a word's grammatical function is before the sentence in which it occurs is understood. Grammar, in other words, does not reveal meaning; meaning must precede grammatical analysis. Consider again the familiar words that I have been citing like *man, table, chair, shoe, sock, file, dog, field, take, go,* and so forth; these are all words that not only have a multiplicity of meanings but also a variety of grammatical functions. To ask anyone to identify such words when they are written in isolation is rather pointless because they can commonly be both noun and adjective, or noun and verb, or adjective and verb, or perhaps all three. How do we understand a simple statement like *open the empty bottle?* Not by taking into account the fact that *open* is a verb and *empty* an adjective; because in the equally comprehensible sentence *empty the open bottle,* the two words switch grammatical roles without any difference in surface structure. This complicated ambiguity of language is the reason that computers cannot intelligently translate language or make abstracts, even when programmed with a "dictionary" and a "grammar." Computers lack the knowledge of the world that is required to make sense of language. Thus a computer is befuddled by over a dozen different possible meanings of a simple expression like *time flies.* Is *time* a noun, or a verb (as in *time the racehorses*), or an adjective (like the word *fruit* in *fruit flies*)? Is *flies* a noun or a verb? A computer is said to have interpreted *out of sight, out of mind* as *invisible and insane.*

Not only is it impossible to state the grammatical function of individual words outside of a meaningful context, it can also be impossible to state the grammatical structure of entire sentences without prior understanding of their meaning. Most English teachers would parse *the onions are planted by the farmer* as a passive sentence, since it contains the three grammatical markers of the passive form—the auxiliary *are,* the participle ending *-ed* and the preposition *by.* By certain transformational rules the sentence can be converted into the active form: *the farmer plants the onions.* But the sentence *the onions are planted by the tree* is not a passive sentence, although its surface would appear to contain the appropriate three grammatical markers. The second sentence cannot be transformed into *the tree plants the onions*—but not for any grammatical reason. Meaning determines the grammatical structure of these sentences, not the surface structure markers. In fact, *the onions are planted by the farmer* need not be a passive sentence, because it is just as ambiguous grammatically as *she was seated by the minister;* the grammar depends on the meaning.

In other words—and this must be the answer to the question at the beginning of this section—there is only one way in which language can be understood, that print can be comprehended, and that is by having meaning brought to it.

Comprehension Through Prediction

The assertion that language is understood by having meaning brought to it obviously cannot be taken to imply that any particular utterances or sentences can mean anything. Usually, there would be some broad general agreement about the main implications of statements, at least when they are made in real world situations. If someone in an elevator remarks "It is raining outside," not many people would want to claim that it could mean that the streets are dry. And by the same argument, the meanings that listeners and readers bring to language cannot be wild guesses; the usual broad general agreement about implications makes the reckless attribution of meaning unlikely as well. If most people seem to be in agreement about the kind of meaning that can be attributed to a particular sequence of words, then some explanation must be found as to why such agreement exists.

The explanation that can be offered should not be unfamiliar. Language tends to be understood in the same way on similar occasions because listeners or readers must have a pretty good idea about the meaning that was intended in the first place. To be more precise, meaning is brought to language through prediction, which you will remember from the previous chapter means the prior elimination of unlikely alternatives. Prediction does not mean staking everything on one wild guess (which would indeed run the risk of frequent error), nor does it mean that the precise meaning is known in advance (which would of course make attention to language unnecessary in the first place). Prediction simply means that the uncertainty of the listener or reader is limited to a few probable alternatives, and provided that information can be found in the surface structure of the utterance to dispose of the remaining uncertainty—to indicate which predicted alternative is appropriate—then comprehension takes place.

Prediction is the reason that the brain is not normally overwhelmed by the possible number of alternatives in language; there are actually only very few alternatives in our minds at any time that we are comprehending what is being said. And prediction is the reason we are so rarely aware of ambiguity: We expect what the writer or speaker is likely to say and just do not contemplate alternative interpretations. We interpret *The thieves decided to head for the bank* in one way if we know they were sitting in a car and in another way if they were swimming in a river. When language is comprehended, in other words, the receiver is usually no more aware of possible ambiguity than the producer. Speakers and writers are presumed to have at least a general idea of what they intend to say and are thus unlikely to consider alternative interpretations of the language they produce. The same applies to listeners or readers. The first interpretation that comes to us is the one that makes the most sense to us at the particular time, and alternative and less likely interpretations will not be considered unless subsequent interpretations fail to be consistent or to make sense, in which case we realize our probable error and try to recapitulate. One interpretation usually satisfies us, provided it makes sense, so we do not waste time looking for a second; this is the reason that puns are so very hard to see, and also why puns are mildly irritating. We do not expect to find more than one meaning for the same sequence of words.

As indicated in the previous chapter, there is nothing very remarkable or particularly clever about this process of prediction; it goes on all the time. Prediction enables us to make sense of all the events in our daily lives. And we are no more aware of our predictions when we read than we are at any other time for the simple reason that our predictions are usually so good. We are rarely surprised because our predictions rarely let us down, even when we read a book for the first time.

What exactly do we predict when we read? The fundamental answer is meaning, although of course we look at words or letters (or more precisely the *distinctive features* of words or letters) that will confirm or disconfirm particular meanings. But a number of more detailed and specific predictions may be made and tested simultaneously—and constantly modified—as we make our way through the actual text. Every specific prediction, however, no matter how detailed and transient, will be derived from our more general expectations about where the text as a whole might be leading.

Some Practical Implications

The preceding discussion should make it clear that it is misleading if not inaccurate to regard reading as a matter of "following the text" or to say that a listener "follows" the meaning of a speaker. Language is understood by keeping ahead of the incoming detail that the brain is striving to handle. By having some expectation of what the speaker or writer is likely to say, by making use of what we already know, we protect ourselves against being overwhelmed by information overload. We avoid the confusion of ambiguity and succeed in bridging the gap between the surface structure of the text and the writer's intention.

It is easy to demonstrate how the brain keeps ahead of the words that we identify as we read. Ask a friend to turn out the light while you read aloud, so that you are suddenly deprived of visual information, and you will find that your voice is able to continue "reading" another four or five words. Your eyes were a second or more—perhaps three or four fixations—ahead of the point your voice had reached when the lights went out. This phenomenon is known as the *eye-voice span*, a term that is rather misleading because it might suggest that the brain needs more than a second to organize in speech the sounds of the particular word it is looking at. But this is incorrect. The brain does not need a second to identify a word; the difference in time is not so much a reflection of how far the brain is behind the eye as of how far the brain is ahead of the voice. The brain uses the eyes to scout ahead so that it can make decisions about meaning, and thus about individual words, in advance. Indeed, the eye-voice span exists only when we can make sense of what we read. If we read nonsense—*dog lazy the over jumps fox quick the* rather than *The quick brown fox jumps over the lazy dog*—then brain, eye, and voice tend to converge on the same point and the eye-voice span disappears. The span, in fact, reflects rather precisely the sense that we make of text, since it tends to extend to the end of a meaningful phrase. The four or five word span is merely an average. If the lights go out just as we are about to read . . . *and drove off into the night* we are likely to continue aloud as far as *off* or as far as *night*, but not stop at *into* or *the*.

It is because the reader must keep ahead of the text that it is so hard for children to learn to read from material that does not make sense to them, or which is so disconnected and fragmentary that prediction is impossible. Reading is similarly much more difficult for children who have been taught that they should get the words right rather than try to make sense of what is being read. Not only is "getting the words right" very much harder and slower unless meaning is brought to the text in the first place, but identifying each successive word on the line one after the other will not, in itself, give meaning. Reading is not a matter of decoding to the surface structure of speech; the sounds will not make sense of their own accord.

The difficulty of many high school "problem readers" is not that they have failed over the years to learn how to sound out words correctly, nor that they are careless about getting every word right, but rather that they read one word at a time as if meaning should be the last concern. They expect that meaning will take care of itself, although this is the reverse of the way in which sense is made of reading.

Three Grammars of Language

Little has been said so far on the topic of grammar, apart from the assertion that it cannot be the bridge between the surface and deep structures of language. I was referring then to the formal grammar of the classroom, the grammar of the "English" textbook, with its concern for parts of speech, number and agreement, and parsing. This traditional grammar is a grammar of the surface structure; it is concerned with words (or parts of words) and their interrelationships. Formal grammar is a *descriptive grammar*. It never helped anyone to say anything or to understand what anyone else was saying.

Formal grammar is not the only kind of grammar that linguists study, however, and it is by far the least interesting from the point of view of understanding reading. There are two other kinds of grammar that are of more concern, a *semantic* grammar, which is concerned with deep structure, with meaning, and a *transformational grammar* which indeed serves as the link between meaning and surface structure. Both of these grammars are considered briefly in the next few paragraphs, and a more detailed discussion is provided in the Notes.

It may sound odd to say that meanings have a grammar, that there is a grammar of the deep structures of the mind, but meanings have component elements just like surface structure, and like the elements of surface structure the elements of meaning have relationships with each other. There would be no sense in deep structure if indeed it did not contain elements, parts of our theory of the world, related to each other in specific ways which are also parts of our theory of the world.

There are however three critical differences between the grammars of surface and deep structure. The elements of surface structure are words or parts of words, recognizable patterns of sounds in speech or of letters in writing. But the elements of deep structure are far more elusive, they are elements of thought, what are loosely called (because it is very difficult to be precise about them) concepts or ideas. The relationships among the elements are also different. In the surface structure of the sentence "A vicious cat just bit my dog in the street," the word "vicious" has an adjectival relationship to the word "cat," the word "bit" has a verbal relationship, and so forth. But in the deep structure the words (or underlying ideas) are all part of an event—the biting is what happened, the cat is what did it, the dog is what it was done to, and the street is where it was done. The relationships are meaningful, they express propositions. One interesting characteristic of the deep structure relationships of language is that they contain—or the listener or reader must bring to them—information not present in the surface structure. If I say to you "I heard a guitar playing yesterday morning" you will take it for granted that I heard it being played in a particular place and not everywhere in town, that someone was playing the guitar and that a particular melody was being played on it. I do not need to tell you anything that I can assume you know already, but this must all be part of your deep structure, part of your understanding of what I say. This is why children are likely to put back into stories expected or familiar elements which a story teller might leave out.

But the most significant difference between the grammars of surface structure and deep structure is that the former has a particulate and sequential component which is entirely missing from deep structure. Just because of the way the world is, the surface structure of sentences must be produced one word at a time, whether in spoken or written language. Try writing the words *cat, bit,* and *dog* in the same place and see how illegible it is—ᗞᴁᵹ. But this separation of the cat, the biting, and the dog does not occur in the deep structure; you cannot deal with the various elements of meaning one at a time. The whole point of the event was that the cat, the dog, and the biting existed simultaneously. Deep structure, in other words, is holistic, it is global, it does not break events or their descriptions down into elements which are fragmented, linear, and sequential. This, to my mind, is the fundamental issue and mystery in the production and understanding of language—how the global, concurrent, holistic structures of meaning are related to the fragmented, sequential, and episodic surface structures of speech and text. What is the relationship between the two quite different grammars? The solution lies in a third grammar, a *productive* grammar, which actually permits surface structure to be produced and understood. This is the grammar sometimes known as *transformational.*

No one is ever explicitly taught transformational grammar, in fact linguists have the greatest difficulty agreeing or even imagining what such a grammar must be like. But it is the grammar which all users of language must have as part of their implicit theory of the world. Without it there could be no language production or understanding. Infants start to create such a grammar the moment they begin to talk and to comprehend speech, and they rapidly extend and modify this grammar until their speech and understanding is compatible with those of the people around them, of the language community to which they belong. They may not learn to speak with the grammar of their teachers, but that is because children do not usually see themselves as members of the community of teachers. Children learn to talk *exactly* like their friends.

It is not possible to give a precise account of transformational grammar because half of it is shrouded in mystery. The surface structure (for written language) can be inspected on the page, but the deep structure can only be hypothesized and conceptualized in terms of metaphor. We must describe a bridge when we can see only one end of it, when all we know about the terrain at the other end is that it must be totally different and even unimaginable. The *actual* nature of theories of transformational grammar is not so important for teachers to understand and certainly not for them to teach; the theories are complex, contentious, and in any case largely metaphorical. But it is important to understand the role of transformational grammar and how it is learned—that it is the basis by which all language is produced and understood, that its rules are implicit, and that it is never taught explicitly. In fact it is difficult to see how anyone's transformational grammar could be taught explicitly, or why. Obviously everyone who has learned a first language has done so without explicit knowledge of the processes of transformational grammar, and we have all learned to read without the advantage of such specific knowledge. It is important to realize that the working grammar that the brain uses to produce and understand language is not the same as the formal grammar of the classroom, and that instruction in formal grammar cannot take its place but may very well interfere with its development and use.

WRITTEN LANGUAGE
AND SPOKEN LANGUAGE

Obviously spoken language and written language are not the same. It is not difficult to detect when a speaker reads from a text prepared for publication or when a passage that we read is the unedited transcription of a spontaneous talk. Speech and print are not different *languages*—they share a common vocabulary and the same grammatical forms—but they have different conventions for using vocabulary and grammar. It should not be considered surprising or anomalous that differences exist between spoken and written language; they are generally used for quite different purposes and addressed to quite different audiences. The grammar and vocabulary of spoken language itself are likely to vary depending on the purpose for which speech is used and the relationships between the people using it.

It is curious that the differences between written language and speech are often taken to reflect a defect in writing. Most people seem to assume—and probably rightly so—that spoken English is a reasonably efficient system. They may complain about the way various individuals *use* the language, but the language itself seems above criticism. We rarely hear suggestions that English would be a better spoken language if it had a few sounds more or less in it, or if one or two grammatical structures were added or eliminated. Indeed, signs that the language is changing may be the signal for considerable outrage in the newspapers.

Written language, on the other hand, is frequently the subject of calls for improvement, ranging from spelling reform to its total abolition in beginning reading texts in favor of written-down speech. I want to suggest, however, that written language is different from spoken language for the good reason that spoken language has adapted itself to being heard while written language is more appropriately read. Written language is not made more comprehensible by being translated into "speech," even into the supposed speech of the reader.

The Specialization of Language

To understand why such a specialized adaptation of spoken and written language might have come about, it is necessary to examine the different demands the two language forms make upon their recipients. There is, for example, the obvious fact that the spoken word dies the moment it is uttered and can only be recaptured if held in the listener's fallible memory or as the result of a good deal of mutual inconvenience as the listener asks the speaker to recapitulate. Even tape recording does little to mitigate the essential transience of speech in contrast to the facile way in which the eye can move backward and forward through written text. The reader has command over time, can attend to several words at once, select what those words will be, the order in which they will be dealt with, and the amount of time that will be spent on them. In other words, spoken language may make considerable demands on short-term memory which written language does not.

On the other hand, written language might seem to place a far greater burden on long-term memory—on what we already know about language and the world—than does our everyday speech. To bring meaning to spoken language, very often all we need do is consider the circumstances in which an utterance is made. Much of our everyday spoken language is directly related to the immediate situation in which it is uttered. We may pay very little attention to the actual words the speaker is using. The relevance of the utterance is as ephemeral as the words themselves—"Pass the salt, please"—and requires putting information into long-term memory as little as it requires drawing information out from long-term memory. Written language, by contrast, generally depends on nothing but what we can and do remember. Rarely can we look around the room to make sense of what we have just read in a book.

This matter of clues to meaning must be elaborated on to consider a different kind of demand that written language places on the reader, related this time not to memory but to the far more fundamental question of how we make sense of language in the first place.

The question is how the meaning of language is verified; how can we confirm that the information we are receiving is likely to be the truth, that it makes sense, or that indeed we are understanding it correctly? What is the source of the predictions that can cut through all the ambiguity inherent in language so that we make the most reasonable and reliable interpretation? For the kind of everyday spoken language I have been talking about, the answer is simple: Look around. Even if the topic of concern is not completely clarified by what our senses can tell us of present circumstances, any uncertainty we have can probably be removed by what we know already of the speaker's nature, interests, and likely intentions. But the language of texts offers no such shortcuts. There is only one final recourse if we are not sure of what we have read, and that is to return to the text itself. For verification, for disambiguation, and to avoid error, a difficult and possibly unique kind of skill is required. That is the skill of pursuing a line of thought, looking for internal consistencies, of evaluating arguments. Both the source and the test of many of the changing predictions that are necessary for the comprehension of written language must lie in the text itself, informed by the more general expectations that readers bring from their prior knowledge. The text determines what the actual alternatives might be and whether they have been successfully predicted. For that reason alone, spoken language and written language can rarely be the same.

A Different Difference in Language

The previous section began by considering some fairly obvious differences between spoken and written language, differences which should be familiar to anyone who hopes to learn to read. But it quickly became necessary to acknowledge that the general distinctions being made were between a particular kind of speech, the "everyday spoken language directly related to the situation in which it is uttered," and a particular kind of written language, namely that of "continuous texts." To present the complete picture it must now be explained that there is another distinction between forms of language that cuts right across the spoken-written dimension and that is of more importance in any analysis of reading and writing. This distinction differentiates a form of spoken and written language that functions quite differently from another form of spoken and written language.

The issue basically concerns how the words we speak or write are selected and organized in the first place. Obviously words are rarely produced at random. There is usually a necessity or reason for every word that we use, related in part to the intention we want to fulfill and to the language with which we propose to fulfill it. Both of these considerations, the reason for saying something and the linguistic vehicle we select for saying it, place considerable constraints on what we say and write. But there is a third important constraint, the one with which I am at present most concerned, and that is the environment in which the language is produced. To use language rather arbitrarily myself for the moment, I shall use the term *situation* to refer to the physical environment in which words are produced—the position in which you are standing when you say something or the location in which written words happen to be written or printed—and I use the word *context* to refer to the language environment in which spoken or written words occur. The context for the word *context* in the previous sentence, for example, is all the other words in that sentence and in the chapter as a whole. However, a distinction must be made between *situation-dependent* and *context-dependent* language.

Situation-dependent speech is the spoken language with which infants first become familiar and it is the basis upon which they begin all their learning about language. By situation-dependent I mean that the speech is directly related to the situation in which it is uttered. If someone says "Pass the salt, please" then there is likely to be some salt around, a person who would like some salt, and another person in a position to pass it. If someone says "I think it is raining again" then the streets are likely to be wet or there will be some other indication that rain has started. Given the physical situation and the speaker's intentions, it would not be possible to say anything very much different, like "I think it is raining again" if the speaker really wanted the salt passed, or vice versa.

The fact that such speech and the situation in which it is uttered (including the speaker's intentions) are closely related may seem trivial but it is in fact crucial, because it is the basis of children's language learning. It is the way in which language is first comprehended and verified. Normally we think that such language describes the situation in which it occurs. Hear someone say "Pass the salt, please" and we can construct the probable cast of characters and the major props, even if we cannot see what is going on. But the clues also work in the other direction; the situation can make sense of the language. A child who does not yet understand what "Pass the salt, please" means can work it out from the situation in which the language is uttered. Indeed, if someone actually said "I think it is raining again" and another person passed the speaker the salt, then the child might assume that "I think it is raining again" meant "Pass the salt." This strategy of using the situation to provide clues to how unfamiliar language works is not uncommon. We all tend to use it when confronted by someone speaking a foreign language or in any other situation when we do not understand what is being said. If the waiter says something incomprehensible, we look to see if we are being offered the menu, the wine, or the bill.

Because such language is closely tied to the situation in which it occurs, it cannot be arbitrarily transferred to different situations. If "Pass the salt, please" fails to get the response we want in the restaurant, it will not do us much good to repeat it out in the street. Also, because most of the meaning and the verification of such language rests in the particular situation in which it is uttered, it tends to be elliptical and brief—"Coffee?" "Thanks." Indeed, it is a characteristic of such language that it does not have much grammar of a surface structure kind (though of course the listener constructs a complex deep structure).

Just as there is a good deal of situation-dependent spoken language in the environment of most children, who use it to make their first sense of speech, so there is a good deal of situation-dependent *written* language in most contemporary environments which children can again employ to make sense of reading. I am referring now to the written language of signs and labels, the ubiquitous language that we find on every product that we buy, festooned around every store, on every wrapper, on every street sign, and as part of every television commercial. We do not have a convenient word in our language for such situation-dependent writing, so I refer to it as *print*. It functions in exactly the same way as situation-dependent speech, because it is also closely tied to the situation in which it occurs: The situation provides learners with a clue to its meaning, and it cannot be arbitrarily changed or moved without losing its sense. The word "toothpaste" tells the reader what is in the tube and the contents of the tube tell the learner what the printed word is likely to be. Indeed, some children think the printed word "Crest" says toothpaste just as they may think that the sign "McDonald's" says hamburgers. (And the advertisers of Crest and McDonald's will tell you that these are indeed what their brand names are supposed to say.) Certainly a child who finds he is brushing his teeth with shampoo or that she has poured herself a bowl of detergent does not need an adult to point out the reading error. If you do not understand what the sign or label means, look at the situation in which it occurs. Like the situation-dependent speech, such print cannot be moved to the middle of the wall because we are tired of seeing it over the door. Like situation-dependent speech, such print tends to be elliptical and independent of grammar. The situation takes the place of complexity of language.

Quite different from the situation-dependent written language of signs and labels, however, is the continuous written language of texts. This language is more complex and has to be. It does not derive or convey its meaning from the situation in which it occurs; there are no clues to its sense in its location. If you do not understand something in a newspaper or novel, it will not help you to look at where the text is located in the room or into the face of the person who gave it to you. The appropriate meaning of the text remains constant, whether you look at it now in the room or an hour later in the street. It cannot be elliptical. It requires a surface structure grammar.

Despite this independence from the specific location in which it is produced and read, however, there is just as much necessity about the written language of texts as there is about situation-dependent writing and speech. The writer is still not free to produce words arbitrarily or at random. A writer cannot decide to make the next word "rhinoceros" or "platitudinous" just because it is a long time since these words were last used. Now, however, the constraints upon the words are determined by just two things, the subject matter that the writer is talking about (what the writer wants to say) and the language the writer is employing (how the writer wants to say it). In other words, all of the constraints on what is written lie within the context of the language itself. Thus I shall call such language *context-dependent*. Not only does the intricate texture of a written context give every component word its meaning, but because of the redundancy in text it is usually possible to replace a word that has been left out or to work out the meaning of an unfamiliar word.

For children learning to read in a first language and for anyone attempting to read in a second, the ability to make use of contextual clues to meaning is crucial. But the clues embedded in the immediate language environment of context-dependent writing are not the same as those in situation-dependent writing (which is one reason that children who have essential insights into reading from print may still have difficulty with continuous text). Nor are the clues of context-dependent writing those of situation-dependent speech (which is one reason why being read to is such an enormous advantage in learning to read).

The particular requirements of context-dependent writing have so impressed some theorists (Havelock, 1976; Goody & Watt, 1972; Olson, 1977) that they have argued that written language has introduced a whole new mode of thought to our basic human repertoire of intellectual skills. But context-dependent written language is not unique. Not all our spoken language is of the "everyday," situationally verifiable kind that has been discussed. Some of our spoken language can be as abstract, argumentative, and unrelated to the circumstances in which it is comprehended as an article in a scientific journal. There is also context-dependent speech. Olson (1977) claims that our ability to produce and understand such spoken language is in fact a by-product of our being literate. It is only because of our experience in reading that we can make sense of this kind of spoken language, which, in its form, is more like writing than everyday speech. But the contrary also applies; by hearing such speech a child becomes better equipped to read.

If prediction is the basis for the comprehension of written language, then obviously an important part of the nonvisual information of readers must be familiarity with the unique characteristics of the different forms that context-dependent language takes. The more one knows about such language, the easier it will be to read continuous text, and thus to learn to read. All this is part of the reason that it must be emphasized that not only is reading learned through reading but also that learning to read begins with being read to.

THE ORGANIZATION OF TEXTS
AND COMPREHENSION

Psychologists and linguists who study how readers make sense of written language have been making some interesting explorations recently. They have observed that texts are not simply collections of facts, and other kinds of content, presented in English or whatever other language is appropriate, at least not texts that are well-written and comprehensible. Instead, the content of different kinds of text is organized and presented in distinctive and characteristic ways. Each kind of text has its own *genre schemes*—conventions of layout, typography, and style—which distinguish it from other genres or kinds of text. Novels do not have the same genre schemes as textbooks, poems, newspapers, letters, or telephone directories. Furthermore, the various kinds of text may have quite different genre schemes in different cultures. Newspapers or novels produced in France for French readers are not written and presented in the same way as those for readers elsewhere, even if they speak the same language. Often we can *see* that texts *look* different from culture to culture, even though we cannot read the language. There is nothing particularly logical or necessary about specific genre schemes—they could be different, as they usually are from one culture to another—but they have become conventional where they are employed and they serve their purposes because they are conventional.

Genre schemes help both readers and writers. Their characteristic forms help readers by giving them a basis for predicting what a text will be like, that a novel will be divided into chapters in a particular way, that a scientific article will follow a certain format, that a letter will observe typical conventions. Readers become so accustomed to the genre schemes of the texts with which they are familiar that they assume they are natural, rational, and universal. A text that is produced differently in a different culture may be regarded as an aberration. Indeed, we all tend to be chauvinistic about the language with which we are most intimately connected. Our own language is "natural" and the rest are "foreign." Genre schemes also help writers (if they know them), because they provide a framework for organizing what writers want to say and more importantly for anticipating and respecting what readers are likely to expect. Genre schemes facilitate communication.

Similarly, every kind of text, and every form of spoken language interaction too, has characteristic internal relationships, called *discourse structures*, which are again largely arbitrary and accidental but which serve their purposes because they are conventional. Discourse structures in conversation tell us when we may interrupt (at the end of a sentence) and when we may not; they protect speakers from interruptions while allowing others the opportunity to take a turn. In written language, readers can expect writers to observe conventional discourse structures and writers can expect readers to understand them. The structures form the basis of prediction. The manner in which chapters and paragraphs are organized and displayed in books is a matter of discourse structure, and so are the customary salutations at the beginning and ends of letters.

Even stories have their conventions, whether they are spoken or written. These conventional ways of telling a story, of relating sequences of events, are known as *story grammars*. They are the framework upon which various characters, plots, motives, and resolutions are linked together in related episodes and represented in ways that will be intelligible. If a story makes sense to us, if it *sounds* like a story, this is not just because the story is appropriately told but also because we know the appropriate way in which stories are told, at least in our culture. Stories must reflect the story schemes that readers have in their heads, if writers and readers are to connect.

The important function served for readers by all these conventional and characteristic structures of texts is underlined by the growing evidence that the structures are the basis for our *comprehension* of texts. If we do not know the relevant structures then we will not understand the text, or our reading of it will be distorted. Experimental psychologists have noted that readers' comprehension of texts is very similar to the structures in the text itself. Ask people to recapitulate what they read in a story and they will tend to do so with the same structural form as the story, rather than with the same words or even "their own" words. Readers not particularly familiar with the genre scheme and discourse structure of a text, with the grammar of the story, will not only fail to comprehend aspects of the text but will recapitulate what they did understand in forms closer to their own structures. Beginning readers have even been shown to insert into their retelling of stories conventional aspects which have been omitted in the telling but which are part of their own story grammars. They put more into the story than was in it originally, because this is their way of making sense of stories.

It is also the structures in the head rather than those in the text that determine our *memory* for texts; they are the forms in which texts are remembered. Discourse structures and story grammars are part of our own cognitive structure, part of the way we organize our knowledge of the world (and therefore a reason that reading is important—it provides us with new frameworks for perceiving the world and organizing experience). The more we can anticipate and employ the formal structures that an author uses, the more we can understand and remember what we read, because the structures also form the basis of our understanding and remembering. And the more an author knows and respects the forms that the reader will predict, so the text will be more readable and memorable.

In a sense, none of this is new or surprising. The British psychologist Bartlett (1932) demonstrated experimentally 50 years ago that the way stories are interpreted and remembered varies with the cultural backgrounds and expectations of their readers and listeners. Who would expect otherwise? But the recent experiments and theoretical work into these matters, among the most active areas in contemporary reading research, demonstrate convincingly what in the past has perhaps been only intuitively obvious (or should have been intuitively obvious)—that meaningfulness requires a close match between the way a text is constructed and the organization of the reader's mind.

Two brief qualifications must be added. First, the structures of texts should be seen as the basis for comprehension but not for comprehension itself. Some researchers seem to assume that the comprehension *is* the structure of the text, that if we have understood a story then our brain contains what the story contained. But comprehension is less a matter of being able to reproduce the facts in a text than of what one does or is able to do as a consequence of interacting with the structure of the text. You do not prove that you have understood anything by repeating it. And second, these structures which can be observed and analyzed in the organization of texts are *implicit* in the human brain. Their effects and existence can be demonstrated but they cannot be directly observed. The people who have them cannot usually say they have got them and they certainly cannot look into their own minds and say what they are. The knowledge that enables us to make sense of the world and of language is not knowledge of which we are aware, even if we are psychologists or linguists. There is no evidence that making these implicit structures explicit improves comprehension, or that by teaching them to children we help them understand. In fact without the prior understanding such "explanations" are themselves meaningless. Children learn the structures by being helped to understand the texts in which the structures are employed, which is not the same thing as being taught the structures. Children, like all of us, are capable of comprehending without being able to say how they do it.

THE CONVENTIONS OF LANGUAGE

There is one final characteristic of language, both spoken and written, situation-dependent and context-dependent, that I must emphasize. It is that all language is conventional. *Semiotics*—an area of study that is interesting a number of reading researchers—is specifically concerned with the nature of all different kinds of communicative conventions, their use, and how they develop. This is an enormous topic, with multiple ramifications, but I must try to deal with it briefly, first by explaining what it means to say that all language is conventional, then why the statement is critical.

All language is conventional in the sense that every aspect of language is a matter of chance and of mutual agreement. All the various forms of language must work, they must fulfill a function, but the nature of the forms themselves is always arbitrary, a matter of historical accident; they could always be different. In fact across the 3,000 or more different languages that exist in the world, every language form is different. There is no particular logic or necessity about the forms of any particular language. That is what the word "conventional" means, arbitrary forms which could be different, functioning in the way they do because their form is mutually agreed on.

Thus the use of red to mean stop in traffic signs is a matter of convention. The convention works because it is mutually accepted that red should mean stop (in those cultures where red means stop). But the fact that red rather than green means stop is a matter of chance. Things could have worked out differently. Green could mean stop tomorrow provided everyone agreed on the change; there is nothing particularly compelling (or arresting) about using red. In some cultures, in certain circumstances, it is a mark of respect to remove your hat. In other cultures the mark of respect is to keep it on. What makes removing your hat (or putting it on) a mark of respect has nothing to do with the act itself but with the mutual understanding that this is what it means.

Every aspect of language is conventional, starting from the very sounds and meanings of words we use. In English, "yes" means yes, but this is only a convention. "No" could mean yes. In other languages other words mean yes. The same applies to all the words in every language. No one has a free choice with words. No one can call anything something different from everyone else in their language community, not if they want to be understood.

Words are conventional, and so is grammar. Different languages have different grammatical forms, and there is nothing more logical or rational or efficient about one grammar than another. All languages solve the same kind of problems, but I have already noted that story grammars, discourse structures, and genre schemes are conventions. They could be different, they are different in different languages and cultures, and they function despite their arbitrary nature because they are all matters of mutual agreement among the people who employ them.

There is an enormous range of conventions in language, many of which have not yet been mentioned. For example, there are the conventions of idiom. Language is far more than grammar and vocabulary (even though a good deal of instruction in reading, in "English" and in second languages, seems to assume that this is what language consists of). Knowledge of grammar and vocabulary gives no one a mastery of language, either in producing or in understanding it. By far the greatest part of any language, the "working" part of it, is *idiom*, the way people actually speak, and by definition idiom cannot be accounted for by vocabulary and grammar. Idiom is the way words in the vocabulary and forms in the grammar are actually used in a particular language community, and this usage is a complex and constantly changing system of conventions. Idioms cannot be translated word for word from one language to another.

There are conventions of *cohesion*. Speech does not consist of one statement after another, and paragraphs are more than a simple succession of sentences. Statements and sentences are interlocked, they cohere. I can say "I looked for John. But he had gone" but not "But he had gone. I looked for John." I would have to change the sentences to something like "John had gone. I looked for him." The pronoun and the "but" are two of a number of cohesive devices which lock sentences together in English, but they are conventions because different languages cohere in different ways. You cannot change the order of sentences without having to change the sentences themselves, at least not in meaningful text. (This is a useful way of finding out whether material prepared for beginning readers is meaningful. If the order of sentences can be arbitrarily changed without anyone noticing the difference then they do not make sense, they are not normally functioning language.)

There are tremendously subtle and intricate conventions of language, both spoken and written, concerned with *register*. This term refers to the fact that you must choose and put your words together differently depending on the subject you are talking about (you do not discuss a death the way you would a picnic), the person you are talking to, and the circumstances in which you are talking. You cannot speak the language unless you employ the forms of vocabulary, grammar, idiom, and cohesion appropriate to the relevant register, which every child knows who speaks in one way to younger children, another way to age-mates, another way to teachers, and another way to other adults. All of the differences of register are conventional; there is no intrinsic logic about the particular form that comes to be appropriate at a particular time. Everyone who has traveled knows that you cannot carry your own conventions of language with you, not if you want to understand and be understood. Not even the nonverbal conventions of language, like how close you should stand to another person in conversation, are consistent from one culture to another.

Written language has its own substantial set of conventions. There are conventions of spelling, of punctuation, of the formation of letters, of the size of hand-writing or type, of capitalization, of paragraphing, of page layout, of book binding. All of these could be different, and all of them are, in other languages, other cultures. Every aspect of language, in astronomical numbers of ways, is conventional.

Why should I bother to point all this out? Because it is important for readers (and writers) to know what the conventions of written language are, and it is important for teachers and researchers to understand the conventional nature of language.

Knowledge of written language conventions is essential for readers and writers because conventions are the basis of understanding and communication. Conventions make prediction possible. The forms of conventions cannot be predicted, they vary by chance or historical accident from one language community to another and they also change with time. But knowledge of the forms makes the conventions that will be used on particular occasions predictable. To be able to read a text, we must be able to anticipate the conventions that its writer will employ. This understanding of the appropriate conventions, together with prior knowledge related to the subject matter, is the essential nonvisual information that readers must contribute to the act of reading. But the understanding must be shared. To be comprehensible, the writer must anticipate and respect the conventions that the reader will predict. Conventions are the common currency of every language transaction.

An understanding of the conventional nature of language is essential for teachers and researchers because it makes, or should make, a fundamental difference in the way language learning and language instruction are perceived. There is a tendency to think of language as "logical," as "rational," even as if it could be in our genes. But I am trying to emphasize that language is enormously complex and that all of its complexity is arbitrary and accidental. It could all be different. The implication of this is that no one ever learns language by sitting down and thinking about it, by anticipating what it will be like, or even by learning a few rules. Learning a language or learning to read involves learning a tremendous number of conventions. And these cannot be learned by rule or by rote. They must be learned, one at a time, in a sequence and context that is most meaningful for every learner.

There is one other implication of the conventional nature of language that assumes great importance when learning is considered. The conventionality of language means that language is *social*, in all its aspects. Language does things for *people*, and its particular conventions—the way it does things—are matters of social contract and social identification. We talk the way people around us talk—provided we see ourselves as that kind of person. We use language in the ways that it is used by the people around us, again provided we do not see ourselves as different from them. Above and beyond all the technical aspects of reading discussed in this book, and in many other books on the same topic, reading is a *social* activity, learned (or not learned) in a social rather than an intellectual context.

Language About Language

An interesting question about all the complexities of language that I have discussed in this chapter is how much they need to be consciously known by a learner. Is it necessary for beginning readers to be *instructed* in the difference between surface structure and deep structure, in the fine points of grammar, or in all the other essential conventions of language, both spoken and written? Should they be able to talk about language, as well as be able to use it?

There is even a special word for language about language—the word is *metalanguage*. In a general sense, this entire chapter has been written in metalanguage, because it has been on the topic of language. More specifically, there are a number of metalinguistic terms that are frequently central to any discussion involving language—terms like *noun* and *verb*, *word* and *syllable*, *phrase* and *sentence*.

The word *metalanguage* may remind you of the word *metacognition* which was introduced in Chapter 1. Metacognition is thinking (or language) about thinking, just as metalanguage is language (or thinking) about language. And there is a controversy in psychology and educational research about how important ability in both metacognition and metalanguage are for learning to read and to write.

Some researchers argue that children must be aware of their own learning processes, and able to talk about specific aspects of spoken and written language, if they are to learn to read. Downing (1979), for example, asserts that children who do not have metalinguistic competence are in a state of "cognitive confusion" when someone tries to teach them about reading. Other theorists claim that children are obviously capable of learning without being able to talk about learning—how else would babies learn to talk in the first place? We have all learned many things in our lives without being able to talk about what we were learning, or indeed, being aware at the time that we were learning. Many people can read and write phrases and paragraphs without being able to provide a linguistic definition for them, or to parse a sentence.

As for being able to understand the language of language, it is also evident that many people learn to read without understanding the meaning of many metalinguistic terms. Indeed, it could be argued that terms like *word*, *sentence*, *comma*, and *period* have no meaning until we can read. They are not parts of spoken language, certainly not in any direct or conspicuous way. Like Moliere's bourgeois gentilhomme, we all speak prose without knowing we are doing so until someone points it out to us (and explains the meaning of the word).

Why then should knowledge of metalinguistic terminology be thought to be so critical in reading instruction? The explanation seems to be that children need to understand what teachers are talking about, and if teachers find it necessary to use metalinguistic or metacognitive language, then children are in difficulties if they do not understand such language themselves. "Cognitive confusion" is caused by instruction that is not comprehensible. Whether it is in fact essential for classroom teachers to employ the abstract technical language of linguistics and other specialized disciplines in teaching reading is another topic.

SUMMARY

The sounds of language and the visual information of print are **surface structures** of language which do not represent meaning directly. Meaning resides in the **deep structure** of language, related to surface structures through a **transformational grammar** which must be part of the implicit knowledge of every language user (but not through traditional **formal gram-**

mar). Written language and spoken language are not the same, and language also differs to the extent that it is **situation dependent** or **context dependent.** The basis of comprehension is **prediction,** made possible by the complex **conventional** nature of language.

Notes to Chapter 2 begin on page 228, covering

Surface structure and deep structure
Semiotics
Discourse analysis
Text organization and comprehension
Some technical terms
More about words

Chapter 3
INFORMATION
AND EXPERIENCE

Louise Rosenblatt (1978) says there are two ways to read—for information or for experience. It is easy to tell the difference between the two. When information is what we want, we are perfectly content to get it in any way we can. No one ever says "Don't tell me that telephone number, I want the pleasure of looking it up for myself." But when we read for experience, we are reluctant to be deprived of even a moment. We do not encourage anyone else to say "Don't bother to read the last chapter—the butler did it." Often we slow down as we near the end of a novel, as we might at the end of a good meal, to protract the experience.

The distinction between information and experience is important because the two are frequently confounded in education. Books or other texts which should be read for experience are treated only as sources of information. Rosenblatt said this is because it is easier to grade readers on the information they might be expected to acquire than on the experience they might enjoy. She satirized such an approach in the title of an article called "What Facts Does This Poem Teach You?" (Rosenblatt, 1980).

It is often said that we live in an "information age"—but the word *information* is used very loosely. Usually it is taken to mean something like "facts" or "data." Despite its vagueness and ambiguity, the word has become ubiquitous in education, not only with reference to literacy but to learning and teaching as well. Reading and learning are both referred to as "the acquisition of information" and writing (and teaching) as its "transmission." But there is much more to education and to life than facts or data. The word *information* can be misused and misunderstood.

Information has in fact been given a precise technical definition—which most people in education are not aware of, although it has enabled some aspects of reading to be accurately measured. I shall use the word in this strict technical sense when I examine how the visual system solves complex problems of identifying letters and words in print. On the other hand, the widespread use of the word in a more general sense in educational and psychological research—for example in the characterization of the brain as an "information-processing device"—may distort rather than facilitate efforts to understand literacy and learning. And information, when the word is used in a more general sense, cannot be measured.

First, I will examine the technical definition of information and its relationship to another general term which can also be used technically in a very precise sense—*uncertainty*. I will also look at how information can be related to comprehension and to another important concept in reading, redundancy. I will then refer to some limitations on the way in which individuals can make use of information, and also on the way in which the word itself can be used—the contrast with "experience."

INFORMATION AND UNCERTAINTY

We should not expect to be able to identify and measure information by looking for something with unique and manifest characteristics in the world around us. Information can be found in a multitude of guises—in marks on paper, in facial expressions and other bodily gestures, in the configuration of clouds, trees (and sometimes tea leaves), and in the sounds of speech. Obviously sources of information have little in common, and neither do the channels through which information passes.

Consider the mutations of information when we listen to a broadcast recording of someone talking. What we hear begins as an intention in the speaker's mind, represented in some complex and deeply mysterious way in the flux of chemical and bioelectrical activities in the structures of the brain. This intention is then translated into bursts of neural energy, dispatched from the brain at different times, rates, and directions to the musculature of the jaw, mouth, lips, tongue, vocal cords, and chest, orchestrating the expulsion of breath in such a manner that distinctive pressure waves of contrasting intensity and frequency radiate through the surrounding atmosphere. These fleeting disturbances in the molecules of the air cause the tiny diaphragm of a microphone to resonate in sympathy, triggering a flow of electrical energy along a wire quite unlike the corresponding patterns of neural energy in the nervous systems of the speaker or listener. Amplified and modulated, the electrical impulses from the microphone impress subtle combinations of magnetic forces onto a plastic tape or etch wavy lines into a plastic disk. Through further mechanical and electronic incarnations, the information may then be diffused by radio transmission (perhaps diverting through the transistors of an earth-orbiting satellite) before being reconstituted by a receiver and loud-speaker into airborne pressure waves that lap against the listener's ear. And still the transformations are not done. The oscillation of the eardrum is conveyed to another resonating membrane of the inner ear across a tiny bridge of three articulating bones—the hammer, the anvil, and the stirrup. And then, perhaps most bizarrely, a pressure wave pulses back and forth through liquid in the coiling canals of the inner ear, a labyrinth carved into the skull itself, where microscopic hair cells wave like reeds with the movement of the fluid in which they are contained. The roots of these fronds are the tiny beginnings of the mighty auditory nerve, and they generate the final relays of neural impulses that travel its hundreds of thousands of separate nerve fibers, through half a dozen booster and transformer stations in various recesses of the brain, to be transformed at last into subjective experiences of meaningfulness and sound. And this meaningfulness of acoustic events can be congruent with a subjective meaningfulness and visual experience from perhaps the same words written down and reaching the brain by a completely different route through the eyes. How can all or even part of this complexity be identified and evaluated as "information"?

On Making Decisions

The answer is by looking at what it enables the "receiver"—the listener or the reader—to do. Information enables a person to make decisions, to choose among alternative possibilities or competing courses of action. Information can be discriminated and assessed, not from its source or from the various forms that it can take during transmission, but from what it enables the recipient to do. Reading involves decisions, whether by a child striving to identify a single letter of the alphabet or by a scholar struggling to decipher an obscure medieval text. And anything that helps a reader to make a decision is information.

Put into other words again, *information reduces uncertainty*. The change of focus from the facilitation of decisions to the reduction of uncertainty may not seem to be much of a conceptual gain, but in fact it permits information to be measured, or at least estimated comparatively. Information cannot be quantified directly—it is not possible to assess the dimensions of a piece of information, or to weigh it. In the same way the size or weight of a decision cannot be calculated directly. But it is possible to put a number to uncertainty, and thus indirectly to the amount of information that eliminates or reduces that uncertainty. The trick is accomplished by defining uncertainty in terms of the number of alternatives confronting the decision-maker. If you are confronted by a lot of alternatives you have a great deal of uncertainty; there are many different decisions you could make. If you have fewer alternatives, it may be just as hard for you to make up your mind but theoretically your uncertainty is less; there are fewer alternative decisions you might make. The argument has nothing to do with the importance of the decision to you, only with the number of alternatives. Theoretically, your uncertainty is the same whether you must decide for or against major surgery or for having your morning eggs scrambled or fried. The number of alternatives is the same in each case, and so therefore is your uncertainty.

And now information can be defined more fully: *Information reduces uncertainty by the elimination of alternatives.* Information, very reasonably, is anything that moves you closer to a decision. It is beside the point whether the decision concerns the identification of particular objects or events or the selection among various choices of action. Uncertainty and information are defined in terms of the *number* of alternative decisions that could be made no matter *what* the alternatives are. However, it is easier to reach an understanding of these concepts if particular situations are taken as examples.

Suppose that the information is available in a single letter of the alphabet. Or to put the matter into plain English, suppose a child is given the task of identifying a letter written on the chalkboard. There are 26 letters of the alphabet, and the reader's uncertainty requires a decision or choice among these 26 alternatives. If the situation involves bidding in a bridge game, then the uncertainty may perhaps concern a player's strongest suit, and the number of alternatives will be four. For the simple toss of a coin, the number of alternatives is two; for the roll of a die, it is six. Sometimes the exact number of alternatives is not immediately apparent—for example, if a word rather than a letter is being read. But it may still be possible to determine when this indefinite amount of uncertainty has been reduced—for example, if the reader learns that the word begins with a particular letter or is of a particular length. Either of these pieces of information will reduce the number of alternative possibilities of what the word might be.

We can now return to the definition of information as the reduction of uncertainty. Just as the measure of uncertainty is concerned with the number of alternatives among which the decision-maker has to choose, so information is concerned with the number of alternatives that are eliminated. If the decision-maker is able to eliminate all alternatives except one, and thus can make a complete decision, then the amount of information is equal to the amount of uncertainty that existed. A bridge player who receives the information that the partner's strongest suit is red has had uncertainty reduced by one-half; if the information is that the strongest suit is hearts, uncertainty is reduced completely. Similarly, a child who knows the letters well enough to decide that the letter on the board is a vowel has acquired information reducing uncertainty from 26 alternatives to five. If the letter is correctly identified, then the information gained from the letter must have been equal to the original uncertainty.

Some aspects of reading involve the acquisition of information in order to make decisions, to reduce uncertainty. For the visual identification of letters and words and possibly some aspects of "reading for meaning," uncertainty can be calculated, and therefore also the amount of information required to make a decision. The exact number of alternatives can be specified for letters, an approximate figure can be put to the number of words, but the number of alternatives for a meaning, if it can be estimated at all, must obviously be closely related both to the text being read and to the particular individual who is doing the reading.

COMPREHENSION AND INFORMATION

Comprehension cannot be measured in the same way that some aspects of information can. Comprehension cannot be measured at all, despite constant educational efforts to do so, because it is not a quantity of anything. Comprehension does not have dimension or weight, it is not incremental. Comprehension is not the opposite of uncertainty or even of ignorance, and therefore is not quantifiable as the accumulation of a number of facts or items of information. Rather, comprehension is more appropriately regarded as a *state*, the opposite of confusion. As I proposed in Chapter 1, comprehension is the possibility of relating whatever we are attending to in the world around us to the knowledge, intentions, and expectations we already have in our heads.

We comprehend the situation that we are in if we are not confused by it, whether we are reading a book, repairing an appliance, or trying to find our way through the traffic of an unfamiliar city. Absence of comprehension means not knowing what to do next or which way to turn—*not knowing the relevant questions to ask or not knowing how to find relevant answers*. When we cannot comprehend we cannot predict, we cannot ask questions. Absence of comprehension makes itself immediately evident to the person involved and to anyone looking on, even if it cannot be measured. I do not need a test to detect confusion in myself or in others; bewilderment does not conceal itself. If I see your brows furrow and your eyes glaze, then I know that all is not well with your comprehension. Without comprehension, there can be no reduction of uncertainty. The rote memorization of "facts" without comprehension is not uncertainty reduction. What we learn—with difficulty—under such conditions becomes informative to us only in the future, if by chance we should suddenly discover the sense it is supposed to make. Conversely, when uncertainty reduction is taking place, there must be some comprehension.

Comprehension does not entail that all uncertainty is eliminated. As readers, we comprehend when we can relate potential answers to actual questions that we are asking of the text. We usually have unanswered questions when we read a newspaper—there would not be much point in reading it if we knew everything in advance. And we do not need to have all our uncertainty reduced in order to comprehend. In fact, as we acquire information that reduces uncertainty in some ways, we usually expand our uncertainty in other ways. We find new questions to ask.

Absence of uncertainty is not a condition that we tolerate for very long; we find it boring. There is no "experience" to it. We seek uncertainty, provided we can keep it under control and clear of confusion. We comprehend when we can "make sense" of experience. Indeed, throughout the remainder of this book, I usually refer to comprehension in reading as "making sense of text," relating written language to what we know already and to what we want to know or experience.

Errors and Noise

Of course we may think we comprehend, and look as if we comprehend, but nevertheless make a mistake. Comprehension does not come with an unconditional guarantee. The way we understand something now may prove to be inappropriate later. To have a wrong idea about something is a constant possibility, but again not something that can be measured. And no one else can decide for us whether we are in a state of comprehension or confusion, though they can dispute whether we are in such a state for good reason, and even help us to move from one state to the other. Comprehension and confusion are the consequences of how well we cope with the particular situation that we happen to be in, with whether or not we feel we know what to do next. What may be comprehensible to you may not be comprehensible to me.

Similarly, what is information for you may not be information for me, if it does not contribute to my comprehension. And such negative information can have more than just a neutral, inconsequential effect. It can be positively disruptive.

A technical term for a signal or message that does not convey information is *noise*. The term is not restricted to acoustic events, but can be applied to anything that makes communication less clear or effective, such as a difficult-to-read typeface for printed material, or poor illumination, or distraction of the reader's attention. The *static* that sometimes interferes with television reception is visual noise. Any part of a text that a reader lacks the skill or knowledge to comprehend obviously becomes noise. The present chapter offers information to readers who understand its language and general theme, but it is literally only noise for anyone else. And noise cannot be easily ignored; it is not an absence of information but rather a distraction that can increase uncertainty.

Because anything becomes noise if one lacks the familiarity or knowledge to understand it, reading is intrinsically more difficult for the novice than for the experienced reader. For the beginner, everything is likely to be much noisier. On the other hand, reading can be made so difficult for experienced readers that they behave no differently from beginners.

The Relativity of Information and Comprehension

What is commonly called *information* cannot always be measured. *Facts* are often called information, but the informativeness of facts depends on the prior knowledge of the person receiving them. "Paris is the capital of France" is a fact, but it is not informative to Tom who knows it already, nor to Dick who does not understand what the word "capital" means. And although the statement is informative to Harry, who was not aware of the fact before, it is not possible to say how informative it is because Harry's uncertainty cannot be calculated. We do not know how many alternative cities Harry thought might be the capital of France, or how many countries he thought Paris might be the capital of. We do not even know if he cares. Quite possibly, "Paris is the capital of France" is a fact with no information value to Harry when he learns the fact, although it may be useful to him on a number of occasions later in his life. On the other hand, "information" that serves only to clutter the mind is really noise.

Information exists only when it reduces uncertainty, which is relative to the knowledge and purposes of the individual receiving it. And comprehension also depends on what an individual already knows and needs or wants to know. Comprehension does not entail assimilating or even examining all of the information in a text, but rather being able to make some sense of the text in terms of the reader's expectations and intentions. Even fluent readers must read some texts more than once in order to comprehend them, or to remember a lot of detail. Reading always involves asking questions of a text (the purposeful, selective aspects of reading to which I have referred) and comprehension ensues to the extent that such questions are answered. I may not comprehend a particular text in the same way as you, but then I may not be asking the same questions. Arguments about how a novel, poem, or any other text is most appropriately or "correctly" comprehended are usually arguments about the most relevant kind of questions to ask. A child who claims to have understood a story may not have understood it in the same way as the teacher, but the child was probably not asking the same questions as the teacher. The teacher's questions may be noise to the child. A large part of comprehending literature in any conventional manner is knowing the conventional questions to ask and how to find their answers.

All the preceding discussion of information and comprehension underlines the importance in reading of what goes on behind the eyes, where prior knowledge, purposes, uncertainty, and questions reside. So also do the next two major topics that are discussed, the matter of information that is available from more than one source and the importance of having more than one source of information available.

Redundancy

Redundancy exists whenever the same information is available from more than one source, when the same alternatives can be eliminated in more than one way. And one of the basic skills of reading is the selective elimination of alternatives through the use of redundancy.

An obvious type of redundancy is repetition, when for example the alternative sources of information are two identical successive sentences. A different means of having the same information twice would be its concurrent presentation to the eye and to the ear—an audiovisual or "multimedia" situation. Repetition is an eminently popular technique in advertising, especially in television commercials, exemplifying one of the practical advantages of redundancy—that it reduces the likelihood that receivers will unwittingly make a mistake, or overlook anything, in their comprehension of the message. There are other aspects of redundancy, however, that are not always as obvious but that play a more important role in reading.

Very often the fact that the same alternatives are eliminated by two sources of information is not apparent. Consider the following pair of sentences:

1. The letter of the alphabet that I am thinking of is a vowel.
2. The letter I am thinking of is from the first half of the alphabet.

At first glance the two statements might appear to provide complementary pieces of information telling us that the letter is a vowel in the first half of the alphabet. However, if we look at the alternatives eliminated by each of the two statements, we can see that they actually contain a good deal of overlapping information. Statement 1 tells us that the letter is not b, c, d, f, g, h, j, k, l, m, n, p, q, r, s, t, v, w, x, y, z, and statement 2 tells us that it is not n, o, p, q, r, s, t, u, v, w, x, y, z. Both statements tell us that the letter is not n, p, q, r, s, t, v, w, x, y, z, and it is to this extent (the extent to which the excluded sets of alternatives intersect) that the statements are redundant. In fact, the only new information provided by statement 2 is that the letter is not o or u; all the other information is already provided in statement 1.

There are frequent examples of redundancy in reading. As an illustration, consider the unfinished sentence (which could perhaps be the bottom line of a right-hand page of a book):

The captain ordered the mate to drop the an-

There are four ways of reducing uncertainty about the remainder of that sentence, four alternative and therefore redundant sources of information. First, we could turn the page and see how the last word finished—this would be visual information. But we could also make some reasonable predictions about how the sentence will continue without turning the page. For example, we could say that the next letter is unlikely to be *b, f, h, j, m, p, q, r, w,* or *z* because these letters just do not occur after *an* in common words of the English language; we can therefore attribute the elimination of these alternatives to *orthographic* (or spelling) information. There are also some things that can be said about the entire word before turning the page. We know that it is most likely to be an adjective or a noun because other types of words such as articles, conjunctions, verbs, and prepositions, for example, are most unlikely to follow the word *the;* the elimination of all these additional alternatives can be attributed to *syntactic* (or grammatical) information. Finally, we can continue to eliminate alternatives even if we consider as candidates for the last word only nouns or adjectives that begin with *an* plus one of the letters not eliminated by the orthographic information already discussed. We can eliminate words like *answer* and *anagram* and *antibody* even though they are not excluded by our other criteria because our knowledge of the world tells us these are not the kinds of things that captains normally order mates to drop. The elimination of these alternatives can be attributed to *semantic* information.

Obviously, the four alternative sources of information about the incomplete word in the above example, *visual, orthographic, syntactic,* and *semantic,* to some extent provide overlapping information. We do not need as much visual information about the next word as we would if it occurred in isolation because the other sources of information eliminate many alternatives. The four sources of information, therefore, are all to some extent redundant. And the skilled reader who can make use of the three other sources needs much less visual information than the less fluent reader. The more redundancy there is, the less visual information the skilled reader requires. In passages of continuous text, provided that the language is familiar and the content not too difficult, every other letter can be eliminated from most words, or about one word in five omitted altogether, without making the passage too difficult for a reader to comprehend.

One last point. I have talked of redundancy in reading as if it exists in the written words themselves, which of course in a sense it does. But in a more important sense, redundancy is information that is available from more than one source only when one of the alternative sources is in the reader's own head. Put another way, there is no utility in redundancy in the text if it does not reflect something the reader knows already, whether it involves the visual, orthographic, syntactic, or semantic structure of written language. The reader must know that *b* is unlikely to follow *an-* and that *anchors* are ordered dropped by captains. Redundancy, in other words, can be equated with prior knowledge. In making use of redundancy, the reader makes use of nonvisual information, using something that is already known to eliminate some alternatives and thus reduce the amount of visual information that is required. Redundancy represents information you do not need because you have it already.

LIMITS TO THE UTILITY OF INFORMATION

The reason for the importance of redundancy, and of prior knowledge in general, is that there are severe limits to the amount of new information the brain can cope with at any one time, whether through the eyes or any other sense modality. We may have questions that we want answered and potential answers to those questions may be in front of our eyes, but if our uncertainty is extensive or if we are trying to make sense of too much information, then we may not be able to handle all the information we need to reduce our uncertainty. We may fail to comprehend.

In plain language, we can try so hard to make sense and to remember more of what we read that we succeed only in confusing ourselves and learning less. Limitations of the brain and of memory are discussed in the following chapters. But there is another factor to be taken into account that may sound rather paradoxical—the more we strive to avoid error, the less likely we are to be right. We always have a choice about how wrong we will be.

Hits, Misses, and Criteria

Readers do not require a fixed amount of information in order to identify a letter or a word, but can make such decisions on more or less information, depending on a number of factors. Exactly how much information a reader will seek before making a "decision" about a particular letter, word, or meaning depends on the difficulty of the task (which must always be defined with respect to a particular reader), on the reader's skill, and on the "cost" of making a decision.

A useful term for the amount of information that individuals require before coming to a decision is their *criterion*. If the amount of information about a particular letter, word, or meaning meets a reader's criterion for making a decision, then a choice will be made at that point, whether or not the reader has enough information to make a decision correctly. We see a letter or word when we are ready and willing to decide what it is.

An important consideration is how a person decides at what level to establish a criterion—ranging from a supercautious attitude requiring almost an absolute certainty to willingness to take a chance on minimal information, even at the risk of making a mistake. But in order to understand why a particular criterion level is established, it is necessary to understand what the effect of setting a high or low criterion might be.

The concept of criterion levels for perception developed in an area of study called *signal detection theory* which upset quite a number of venerable ideas about human perception. It is traditional to think, for example, that one either sees something or one does not, and that there is no area of freedom between, within which the perceiver can choose whether something is seen or not. Signal detection theory, however, shows that in many circumstances the question of whether an object is perceived depends less on the intensity of the object—on its "clarity," if you like—than on the attitude of the observer. It is also traditional to think that there is an inverse relationship between correct responses and errors, that the more correct responses on any particular task— for example, the greater the proportion of letters or words correctly identified—the lower the number of errors must be. Signal detection theory, however, shows that the relationship is quite the reverse, and that the proportion of correct responses for a given amount of information can within limits be selected by the perceiver, but that the cost of increasing the proportion of correct responses is an increase in the number of errors. In other words, the more often you want to be right, the more often you must tolerate being wrong. The paradox can be explained by discussing in a little more detail how the theory originated.

Signal detection theory was originally concerned literally with the detection of signals—with the ability of radar operators to distinguish between the "signals" and "noise" on their radar screens with the objective of identifying aircraft presumed to be hostile. As far as the actual situation is concerned, there are only two possibilities: a particular blip on the screen is either a signal or noise; an aircraft is present, or it is not. As far as the operator is concerned, there are also only two possibilities: a decision that the blip on the screen is an aircraft, or a decision that it is not. In an ideal world, the combination of the actual situation and the operator's decision would still permit only two possibilities: either the blip is a signal, in which case the operator decides that there is an aircraft, or the blip is merely noise, in which case the decision is that there is no aircraft involved. We may call each of these two alternatives *hits* in the sense that they are both correct identifications. However, there are two other possibilities, of quite different kinds, that can be considered errors. The first type of error occurs when no aircraft is present but the operator decides that there is—this situation may be called a *false alarm*. And the other type of error occurs when there is an aircraft present but the operator decides that there is not, that the signal is actually noise—a situation that can be termed a *miss*.

The problem for the operator is that the numbers of hits, false alarms, and misses are not independent; the number of one cannot be changed without a change in the number of another. If the operator is anxious to avoid false alarms, and wants to get maximum information before deciding to report an aircraft, then there will be more misses. If, on the other hand, the operator wants to maximize the number of hits, reducing the possibility of a miss by deciding in favor of an aircraft on less information, then there will also be more false alarms.

Of course, with increased skills of discrimination radar operators can improve their level of efficiency and increase the ratio of hits to false alarms, just as increased clarity of the situation will make the task easier. But in any given situation the choice is always the same between maximizing hits and minimizing false alarms. Always the perceiver has to make the choice, to decide where to set the criterion for distinguishing signal from noise, friend from foe, *a* from *b*. The higher the criterion, the fewer will be the false alarms but the fewer also will be the hits. There will be more hits if the criterion is set lower, if decisions are made on less information, but there will also be more false alarms.

Now we can approach the question of the basis upon which the criterion is established: What makes the perceiver decide to set a criterion high or low? The answer lies in the relative costs and rewards of hits, misses, and false alarms. A radar operator who is heavily penalized for false alarms will set the criterion high, risking an occasional missed identification. One who is highly rewarded for the identification of a possible enemy, and excused for the occasional mistake, will set the criterion low.

Readers cannot afford to set a criterion level that is too high before making decisions. A reader who demands too much visual information will often be unable to get it fast enough to read for sense. Readiness to take chances is critical for beginning readers who may be forced to pay too high a price for making "errors." The child who stays silent (who "misses") rather than risk a "false alarm" may please the teacher but develop a habit of setting a criterion too high for efficient reading. Poor readers often are afraid to take a chance; they may be so concerned about not getting words wrong that they miss meaning altogether.

INFORMATION AND EXPERIENCE

I have gone to some length to present a technical consideration of the nature of information and its relevance in the study of reading. But my qualifications must be emphasized. *The information-processing point of view is appropriate and useful for thinking about decision-making aspects of reading, but not about reading as a whole.* Readers need to make sense of the visual information in a text in order to be able to read that text, but reading is much more than the identification of visual information. In a sense, reading is what you do with visual information; the visual information is just the beginning.

I am arguing against the view, currently widespread in education, that reading is the "acquisition of information" from text, or even more specifically that reading is a matter of receiving particular messages or facts put into a text by the writer. This is the common "communication model" (which I myself employed in earlier editions of this book), seeing text as some kind of channel along which information passes from writers to readers. Sometimes the communication metaphor becomes even more specific, with writers "encoding" messages in texts which readers in their turn must then "decode."

However, many kinds of texts and considerations of reading are distorted if not fundamentally misperceived if the communication and information-processing metaphors are applied too generally. As Rosenblatt pointed out, there is reading done for the sake of experience, which is usually the case with novels and poetry, and also for the stimulation and exploration of ideas. In both these cases what the reader brings to the text, looks for in the text, and does as a consequence of this interaction with the text are far more important and relevant than being able to "identify" and recall the actual content of the text. Indeed, I suspect that very little reading is done for purely factual purposes, where information provided by the text is of primary importance. Such reading (outside of formal school tasks) is rarely "cover-to-cover" but rather is extremely selective and localized, limited by the specific intentions of the reader. I am referring to the occasions upon which we consult encyclopedias, dictionaries, catalogs, television guides, and telephone directories. At other times—even with newspapers and magazines—we read more for the experience generated by the reading, for the very pleasure of the act, than for the specific information that the reading provides.

The information-transmission metaphor is currently widespread in education, where all aspects of literacy are likely to be categorized and perceived as "communication skills." The metaphor comes, of course, from the ubiquitous electronic technology in our environment, from the radio, television, telephone, and computers. But even in these contexts the information and communication perspective is limited and narrowing. For example, television is often seen as a source of either "information" or "entertainment," belittling the alternative if one does not watch programs in order to acquire facts. But not only is there another alternative, most of the so-called informational and entertainment programs in fact also present the possibility of *experience,* far more relative to each individual's knowledge and purposes than either of the other two supposed categories, and probably far more important as well. Indeed, the view that education is a matter of "acquiring information" leads not only to misconceptions about reading (and television watching), but also about learning itself, culminating in the dubious belief that children will soon be able to do all their learning (acquire all the necessary facts) at the consoles of computers. This exclusive emphasis on information-acquisition overlooks the critical importance in education, and in life in general, of experience and self-directed exploration.

The decision-making part of reading is usually only a minor part of the act as a whole, involving the identification of occasional letters, individual words, and possibly from time to time one of a limited range of meanings. Research has tended to concentrate on these restricted aspects of reading. But the information that enables you to make such identifications is not the same as the "message" that you interpret from the text, or the understanding that you bring to it, and certainly not the same as the experience that it might generate for you.

It might be best to regard the information offered by texts in a more general sense as *evidence* rather than a message, the basis for a response or understanding rather than the content of comprehension. Information may be what the brain looks for in reading, through the eyes, but it is not the end of reading. It is the basis upon which a meaning is interpreted, an experience constructed, or the exploration of an idea launched.

It is perhaps paradoxical that the concept of information is not widely understood and employed in those contexts in which it makes the most sense, namely where the reading act is limited to rather narrow identification tasks, but that it is overused and distorted as a metaphor for all of reading.

In this book, I do not use the term *information* in its broad and imprecise sense at all. Even with the general terms *visual information* and *nonvisual information* to which I have already alluded, the reference is to how uncertainty is reduced in reading, not to the experience and learning that reading provides. The term *information* is used fairly extensively in the next few chapters, but only in the strict technical sense, in discussions of how the brain resolves uncertainty related to visual "input" from the eyes. Despite the time I have spent discussing information, I do not regard it as the greatest or most important aspect of reading, especially for teachers to take into account.

What is experience? It cannot be measured and is not easily defined. Perhaps it does not need definition. Experience is synonymous with being alive, creating and exploring, interacting with worlds—real, possible, and invented. There is no need to "explain" the continual tension between the pursuit of possibilities and the reduction of uncertainty. It is an essential condition for being human and being alive.

Reading is experience. Reading about a storm is not the same thing as being in a storm, but both are experiences. We respond emotionally to both, and can learn from both. But the learning in each case is a by-product of the experience. We do not live to acquire information, but information, like knowledge, wisdom, abilities, attitudes, and satisfactions, comes with the experience of living.

SUMMARY

There are two fundamental reasons for reading—for **information** or for experience. Although it has a clearly defined meaning in a narrow sense, the word information is widely overused and misused. Information may be regarded as the reduction of uncertainty concerning the alternatives among which a reader must decide. How much visual information a reader will require is affected by the reader's willingness to risk an erroneous decision. Readers who set too high a **criterion level** for information before making decisions will find **comprehension** more difficult. Because there are limits to how much information the brain can cope with in making sense of texts, readers must make use of all forms of **redundancy** in written language—**orthographic, syntactic,** and **semantic.** Because reading is more than a matter of making decisions, the relevance of the information-processing perspective is limited.

Notes to Chapter 3 begin on page 241, covering

Measuring information and uncertainty
Measuring redundancy
Information theory and reading
Signal detection theory
Further reading
Limitations of information theory, and of "information"
Cognitive science
Computers

Chapter 4
BETWEEN EYE
AND BRAIN

The eyes are given altogether too much credit for seeing. Their role in reading is frequently overemphasized. The eyes do not see at all, in a strictly literal sense. The eyes *look,* they are devices for collecting information for the brain, largely under the direction of the brain, and it is the brain that determines what we see and how we see it. The brain's perceptual decisions are based only partly on information from the eyes, greatly augmented by knowledge that the brain already possesses.

The present chapter is not intended to be a comprehensive physiology of the visual system, but it does outline a few characteristics of eye-brain function that make critical differences to reading. To be specific, three particular features of the visual system are considered:

1. The brain does not see everything that is in front of the eyes.
2. The brain does not see anything that is in front of the eyes immediately.
3. The brain does not receive information from the eyes continuously.

Together these three considerations lead to three important implications for reading, and thus also for learning to read:

1. Reading must be fast.
2. Reading must be selective.
3. Reading depends on what the reader already knows.

The remainder of this chapter considers the preceding six points in order, after elaborating on the importance of what goes on behind the eyes in reading.

TWO SIDES OF READING

Obviously, reading is not an activity that can be conducted in the dark. To read you need illumination, some print in front of you, your eyes open, and possibly your spectacles on. In other words, reading depends on some information getting through the eyes to the brain. Let us call this information that the brain receives from print *visual information*. It is easy to characterize the general nature of visual information—it is what goes away when the lights go out.

Access to visual information is a necessary part of reading but it is not sufficient. You could have a wealth of visual information in a text before your open eyes and still not be able to read. For example, the text might be written in a language you do not understand. Knowledge of the relevant language is essential for reading, but you cannot expect to find it on the printed page. Rather it is information that you must have already, behind the eyeballs. It can be distinguished from the visual information that comes through the eyes by being called *nonvisual information*, or "prior knowledge."

There are other kinds of nonvisual information apart from knowledge of language. Knowledge of subject matter is similarly important. Give many people an article on subatomic physics, the differential calculus, or the maintenance of jet engines, and they will not be able to read—not because of some inadequacy of the text, which specialists can read perfectly well, nor because there is anything wrong with their eyes, but because they lack appropriate nonvisual information. Knowledge of how to read is another kind of nonvisual information, and of evident importance in making reading possible, although it has nothing to do with the lighting, the print, or the state of one's eyes. Nonvisual information is easily distinguished from visual information—it is carried around by the reader all the time; it does not go away when the lights go out.

The Trade-off Between Visual and Nonvisual Information

The distinction between visual and nonvisual information may seem obvious; nevertheless, it is so critical in reading and learning to read that I put it into diagram form (Figure 4.1).

The reason that the distinction between visual and nonvisual information is so important is simply stated—there is a reciprocal relationship between the two. Within certain limits, one can be traded off for the other. The more non-

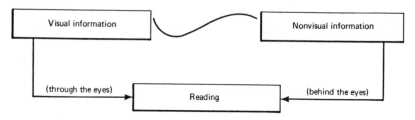

FIGURE 4.1.   Two sources of information in reading.

visual information a reader has, the less visual information the reader needs. The less nonvisual information that is available from behind the eyes, the more visual information is required. This reciprocal relationship is represented by the curved line between the two kinds of information in Figure 4.1.

Reading always involves a combination of visual and nonvisual information. It is an interaction between a reader and a text.

Informal demonstrations of the trade-off between the two sources of information in reading are not difficult to give. They are provided by the common phenomenon that popular novels and newspaper articles tend to be easy to read—they can be read relatively quickly, in poor light, despite small type and poor quality printing. They are easy to read because of what we know already; we have a minimal need for visual information. On the other hand, technical materials or difficult novels—or even the same popular novels and newspaper articles when read by someone not so familiar with the language or the conventions of writing—require more time and more effort, larger type, clearer print, and superior physical conditions. The names of familiar towns on traffic signs can be read from further away than the same size place names of unfamiliar localities. It is easier to read letters on a wall when they are arranged into meaningful words and phrases than the same size letters in the random order of an optometrist's test chart. In each case the difference has nothing to do with the quality of the visual information available in the print, but with the amount of nonvisual information that the reader can bring to bear. The less nonvisual information the reader can employ, the harder it is to read.

Making Reading Difficult

Now we can see one reason why reading can be so very much harder for children, quite independently of their actual reading ability. They may have little relevant nonvisual information. Some beginning reading materials seem to be expressly designed to prevent the use of prior knowledge. At other times adults may unwittingly or even deliberately discourage its use, by prohibiting "guessing." For whatever cause, insufficiency of nonvisual information will make reading more difficult.

Insufficiency of nonvisual information can even make reading impossible, for the simple but inescapable reason that there is a limit to how much visual information the brain can handle at any one time. There is a bottleneck in the visual system between the eye and brain, as indicated in Figure 4.2. Because of this bottleneck a reader can temporarily become functionally blind. It is possible to look but not be able to see, no matter how good the physical conditions. A line of print which is transparently obvious to a teacher (who knows what it says in the first place) may be almost completely illegible to a child whose dependence on visual information can limit perception to just two or three letters in the middle of the line.

Being unable to discern the words for the print is not a handicap that is restricted to children. Fluent readers may find themselves in exactly the same situation for essentially the same reasons—by being given difficult material to read, by being required to pay a lot of attention to every word, or by being put into a condition of anxiety, all of which increase the demand for visual information and have the paradoxical consequence of making it harder to see the text.

Later in this chapter I show how the relative proportions of visual and nonvisual information required in reading can be estimated, and also indicate how narrow the bottleneck is, so narrow that at least three-quarters of the visual information available in text must usually be ignored. As psychologist Paul Kolers (1969) wrote, "Reading is only incidentally visual." Because nonvisual information lies at the core of reading, a large part of this book is concerned with its nature, development, and use.

LIMITATIONS OF VISION

The Brain Does Not See Everything

The fact that the eyes are open is not an indication that visual information from the world around is being received and interpreted by the brain. The

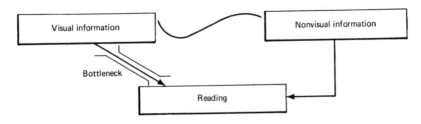

FIGURE 4.2.   The bottleneck in reading.

brain does not *see* the world as its image falls upon the eye. How could it, when that image must often be a kaleidoscopic blur as the eyes flick from place to place in their fitful investigations of the world? But the argument is more complex than the relatively simple fact that the world we see is stable although the eyes are frequently in movement. The scene perceived by the brain has very little in common with the information that the eyes receive from the surrounding world.

What goes into the open eyes is a diffuse and continual bombardment of electromagnetic radiation, minute waves of light energy that vary only in frequency, amplitude, and spatial and temporal patterning. The rays of light that impinge on the eye do not in themselves carry the color and form and texture and movement that we see; all of these familiar and meaningful aspects of perception are created by the brain itself. The image that presents itself to the eyes is actually lost the moment it gets there. The light-sensitive area of the eyeball, the *retina*, consists of millions of cells that transform light energy into neural impulses by a marvelously intricate process involving the bleaching and regeneration of pigment in the retinal cells. As a result of this chemical transformation, bursts of neural energy begin a complicated and relatively long and slow journey along the optic nerve—actually a bundle of many individual nerve fibers—from the back of the eyeballs to the visual areas of the brain, some 6 inches away at the back of the head. The messages[1] that pass from the eyes to the brain undergo a number of analyses and transformations on the way. The patterned array of light that falls on the eye and the structured percept that is produced by the brain are linked by a train of nervous impulses that itself has no simple correspondence with the occurrences at either extreme of the visual system.

Not one nerve fiber runs directly from the eye to the brain; instead there are at least six interchanges where impulses along one nerve may start—or inhibit—propogation of a further pattern of impulses along the next section of the pathway. At each of these neural relay stations there are large numbers of interconnections, some of which determine that a single impulse arriving along

---

[1] It is difficult to avoid referring to these bursts of neural energy as "messages" or "information" that the eyes send to the brain about the world. But both terms are inappropriate, with their implication that some kind of meaningful content has been put into the messages in the first place, as if the eyes know something that they are trying to communicate to the brain. It might be more apt to refer to the neural impulses that travel between eye and brain as *clues* to a world forever concealed from direct inspection. No scientist or philosopher can say what the world is "really like," because everyone's perception of the world—even when mediated by microscopes or telescopes, by photographs or x-rays—still depends on the sense the brain can make of neural impulses that have come through the dark tunnel between eye and brain. We can no more see the image of the world that falls on the retina than we can see the nerve impulses that the retina sends to the brain. The only part of vision of which we can ever be aware is the final sensation of seeing, constructed by the brain by its own private and enigmatic processes.

one section may set off a complex pattern of impulses in the next, while others may relay the message only if a particular combination of signals arrives. Each interconnection point is, in fact, a place where a complex analysis and transformation of signals takes place.

Three layers of interconnections are located in the retina of the eyes, which is, in terms of both function and embryonic development, an extension of the brain. A tremendous compression of information takes place within the retina itself. When the nerve fibers eventually leave the eye on their journey to the brain (the pencil-thick bundle of nerve fibers is collectively called the *optic nerve*) the information from about 120 million light-sensitive cells in the retina where the neural messages originate has been reduced over a hundredfold; the optic nerve consists of barely a million neural pathways.

An interesting facet of this part of the visual system is that the retina of the eye would appear to have been constructed "the wrong way round"—probably a consequence of constructing the retina from an extension of the similarly multilayered brain surface during prenatal development, beginning as early as three weeks after conception. All of the eye's three layers of nerve cells and their interconnections, together with the vessels that provide the retina with its rich blood supply, lie *between* the light-sensitive surface of the eye and the lens. The light-sensitive cells face the world through their own cell bodies, through two other layers of nerve cells, millions upon millions of interconnecting neural networks, and the curtain of their own neural processes as they converge upon the one spot (the "blind spot") to pierce the shell of the eye at the beginning of the optic nerve.

The actual nature of the message that passes along this complex cable of nerves is also very different from our perception or belief of what the visual stimulus is really like. Every nerve in our body is limited to conveying only one type of signal—either it fires, or it does not. The speed of the impulse may vary from nerve to nerve, but for any one nerve it is fixed; the response is "all or none." The nerve impulse is relatively slow: The fastest rate, for some of the long thick nerve fibers that travel several feet along the body, is perhaps 300 feet a second (about 200 miles an hour), but the smaller nerves, such as those in the visual system and brain, transmit at only a tenth of that speed (about 20 miles an hour, compared with the 186,000 miles a second at which light travels to the eye).

Many examples of the way in which the brain imposes stability upon the ever-changing perspective of the eyes are provided by what psychologists call the visual constancies. For example, we always see a known object as a constant size; we do not think that a person or automobile moving away from us gets smaller as the distance increases, although the actual size of the image on the retina is halved as the distance doubles. We do not think the world changes color just because the sun goes in, nor do we see a lawn as two shades of green because part of it is in the shade. The constancy of the visual impression belies variations in the optical information received by the eye. We "see" plates and coins as circular, although from the angle at which such objects are usually viewed the image hitting the eye is almost invariably one form of oval or another. A cat that hides behind a chair is recognized as the same cat when it comes out again, although that information is certainly not present in the input to the eye. In fact, the distinctive forms of cats, chairs, and all other objects do not organize themselves neatly for the eye—we can distinguish them because we already know the forms we want to separate. Why else should we perceive Th as T and h and not as Π and ⌐ or any other arrangement of parts?

One might think that at least the perception of movement is determined by whether or not the image that falls on the retina is moving, but that is not the case. If our eyes are stationary and a moving image falls across them, we do indeed normally see movement. But if a similar movement across the eyes occurs because we move our eyes voluntarily—when we look around a room, for example—we do not see the world moving. Our perception of whether or not something is moving depends as much on the knowledge we have about what our eye muscles are doing as on the visual information being received by the eye. We can easily fool our own brain by sending it false information. If we "voluntarily" move an eye up or down by the use of our eye muscles, we do not see the book or wall in our field of vision as in motion, but if we move the eye in the same way by poking it with a finger—moving the eye without moving the eye muscles—then we do see the book or wall in movement. The brain "thinks" that if the eye muscles have not been actively involved, then the changing image on the eye must mean external movement, and constructs our perception accordingly.

Tachistoscopes and Tunnel Vision

The preceeding discussion was not intended merely to acquaint you with some of the intricacies of the visual system. The aim was to illustrate that what we think we see at any one time may be very different from what we are actually detecting visually from the world around us. It is important to know that seeing is not a simple matter of an inner eye in the brain examining snapshots or television pictures of complete scenes from the outside world. The brain may generate a feeling that we are able to see most of what is in front of our eyes most of the time, but that is what it is—a feeling, generated by the brain. Upon analysis we may find that in fact we see very little. The eyes are not windows, and the brain does not look through them. Not only what we see, but our conviction of seeing, is a fabrication of the brain.

For a particular example, take the case of reading. When we look at a page of print we probably feel that we see entire lines at a time. In practice, we probably see very much less. And in extreme circumstances we may be almost blind. Paradoxically, the harder we try to look, the less we may actually see. To understand the research that underlies these assertions, it is necessary to acquire some familiarity with a venerable piece of psychological instrumentation and with a rather precise way of talking about very small units of time. The small unit of time is the *millisecond,* usually abbreviated to *msec.* One millisecond is a thousandth part of a second; 10 milliseconds is a hundredth of a second; 100 msec is a tenth; 250 msec, a quarter; 500 msec, a half a second; and so forth. Ten milliseconds is about the amount of time the shutter of a camera requires to be open in normal conditions to get a reasonable image on a film. It can also be sufficient time for information to be available to the eye for a single perceptual experience to result. Much more time is required for a message to get from the eye to the brain, or for the brain to make a perceptual decision.

The venerable piece of psychological equipment is the *tachistoscope,* a device that presents information to the eyes for very brief periods of time. In other words, a tachistoscope is a device for studying how much we can see at any one time. It does not allow the reader a second look.

In its simplest form, a tachistoscope is a slide projector that throws a picture upon a screen for a limited amount of time, usually only a fraction of a second. In experimental laboratories today, brief presentations are usually controlled with great precision by computers. One of the first discoveries made through the use of tachistoscopic devices during the 1890s was that the eye had to be exposed to visual information for very much less time than generally thought. If there is sufficient intensity, an exposure of 50 msec is more than adequate for all the information the brain can manage on any one occasion. This does not mean that 50 msec is adequate for identifying everything in a single glance; obviously it is not. You cannot inspect a page of a book for less than a second and expect to have seen every word. But 50 msec is a sufficient exposure for all the visual information that can be gained in a single fixation. It will make no difference if the source of the visual information is removed after 50 msec or left for 250 msec; nothing more will be seen. Eyes pick up usable information for only a fraction of the time that they are open.

The second significant finding from the tachistoscopic and other studies was that what could be perceived in a single brief presentation, in one glance, depended on what was presented and on the viewer's prior knowledge. If random letters of the alphabet were presented—a sequence like *KYBVOD*—then only four or five letters might be reported. But if words were presented for the same amount of time, two or three might be reported, comprising a total of perhaps 12 letters. And if the words happened to be organized into a short sentence, then four or five words, a total of perhaps 25 letters, might be perceived from the same exposure duration.

The preceding paragraph reports a most important finding and one that is central to an understanding of reading. To underline its importance, the main points are reiterated in the form of a diagram (Figure 4.3).

In the Notes section at the end of this book, it is shown that the eye and brain are *doing* the same amount of work in each of the three situations depicted in Figure 4.1. The eyes are sending the same amount of visual information to the brain and the brain is making sense of the same proportion of it. But the more sense the letters make—which means the more the brain is able to use nonvisual information—the more can be seen. The difference lies in the number of alternatives confronting the brain in making its perceptual decisions. If the letters are random—or as good as random to the person trying to read them—they are basically unpredictable and demand a good deal of visual information for each identification decision. The reader consequently sees very little and is in a condition known as "tunnel vision" (Mackworth, 1965), very similar to trying to examine the world through a narrow paper tube. Everyone can have tunnel vision sometimes; it has nothing to do with the health or efficiency of the eyes. Tunnel vision is a result of trying to process too much visual information. Airline pilots can suffer from tunnel vision, especially when they have so much to attend to in trying to land a big jet. That is why it takes more than one pilot to fly such planes. All readers can be afflicted with tunnel vision when the material they are trying to read is unfamiliar, opaque, or otherwise difficult—or when through the particular demands of the task or sheer anxiety they try to handle too much visual information. Beginning readers are prime candidates for having tunnel vision much of the time, especially if the books they are supposed to read from make little sense to them. Tunnel vision, in other words, is caused by information overload.

On the other hand, if the text is easily comprehended, entire lines can be seen at a time. So for a teacher who points to some words in a book and says to a child, "There, you can see that clearly enough, can't you?" the answer is

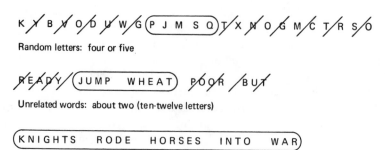

FIGURE 4.3.   What can be seen in one glance.

probably "No." The teacher who can see the entire line probably knows what the words are in the first place. The fact that the teacher is pointing can make the situation ever worse and ensure that the child sees nothing very much beyond the tip of a finger.

You cannot read if you see only a few letters at a time. Tunnel vision makes reading impossible. And the situation cannot be retrieved by trying to look at the words more often. Seeing takes time, and there is a limit to the rate at which the brain can makes its visual decisions.

Seeing Takes Time

We usually feel that we see what we are looking at immediately. But this is another illusion generated by the brain. It takes time to see anything because the brain requires time to make its perceptual decisions. And the time that is required is again directly related to the number of alternatives confronting the brain. The more alternatives the brain has to consider and discard, the longer it takes the brain to make up its mind, so to speak, and for seeing to occur.

The situation is analogous to how quickly you can identify your own car in a parking lot. No matter how well you know your vehicle, and no matter how close you are standing to it, the time it will take you to realize "That's mine" will vary with the number of other cars in the park. Only two cars in the park, and you will spot yours in a fraction of a second. Ten cars, and it will take considerably longer. A hundred cars, and you can be quite delayed.

For an experimental demonstration that the number of alternatives determines the speed of perception, the tachistoscope can again be used. If a single letter of the alphabet is briefly but clearly displayed, say A, the delay before the viewer succeeds in saying "A" will depend on the number of letters that could have occurred instead of A. Give the viewer no clue, so that the letter might be any one of 26 alternatives, and the delay—the "reaction time"—can be as long as 500 msec, half a second. Say in advance that the letter occurs in the first part of the alphabet, or that it is a vowel, and the reaction time will be much briefer. Tell the viewer that the letter is either A or B, and reaction time may drop to as little at 200 msec. With fewer alternatives the brain of the viewer has much less work to do, and the decision comes very much faster.

In reading, it is imperative that the brain should make use of anything relevant that it already knows—of nonvisual information—in order to reduce the number of alternatives. The rather slow rate at which the brain can make decisions can be extremely disruptive. If the brain has to spend too long deciding among the alternatives, the visual information that the eye makes available to the brain will be gone. That is the explanation of tunnel vision— the brain loses access to visual information before it has had time to make many decisions about it.

Visual information does not stay available to the brain for very long after being picked up by the eye. Obviously, visual information remains somewhere in the head for a short period of time, while the brain works on the information collected by the eye in the first few milliseconds of each look. Psychologists have even coined a name for the place where this information is supposed to reside between the time it has been sent back from the eye and the time the brain has made its decisions. This place is known as the *sensory store*, although it so far has remained a purely theoretical construct without any actual known location in the brain. But wherever and whatever the sensory store might be, it does not last very long. Estimates of its persistence vary from half a second to—under optimum conditions—two seconds. But it is just as well that sensory store does persist briefly because a full second is required for the brain to decide even about the limited amount that it is usually able to perceive in a single glance. The visual information that can be utilized in a single glance or tachistoscopic exposure—resulting in the identification of four or five random letters, a couple of unrelated words, or a meaningful sequence of four or five words—in fact requires a full second. The caption to Figure 4.3 could be amended to read not just "What can be seen in one glance" but also "What can be seen in one second." The basic physiological limitation on the rate at which the brain can decide among alternatives seems to put the limit on the speed at which most people can read meaningful text aloud, which is usually not much more than 250 words a minute (about 4 words a second). People who read very much faster than that rate are generally not reading aloud and not delaying to identify every word.

Information is not usually allowed to stay in sensory store for its full term of a second or so. Every time the eyes send another portion of visual information to the brain—which means every time we shift our gaze to a new focal point, or at least blink to take a second look at the same place—then the arrival of new visual information erases the previous contents of sensory store. This phenomenon is referred to as *masking*. It is by the controlled use of masking in tachistoscopic experiments that psychologists have determined that the brain does indeed require a substantial amount of time to make perceptual decisions. The experiments used to illustrate how much can be seen in a single glance only work if a second exposure to visual information does not follow the first before the brain has had time to make sense of it. If a second exposure is presented less than half a second after the first, the viewer is unlikely to report the full four or five random letters or words that would otherwise be perceived. If the two events occur too close together—say within 50 msec of each other—then the second can completely obliterate the first. Because masking occurs before the brain has time even to decide that something has taken place, the viewer will be completely unaware of a visual event that would otherwise be seen quite clearly. Seeing is a relatively slow process.

On the other hand, because information in sensory store will not persist more than about a second under most conditions, we cannot see more simply by looking longer at one spot. The eyes must be constantly active to replenish the fading stock of visual information in sensory store. A person who stares is not seeing more, but rather is having difficulty deciding what was looked at in the first place. Because the contents of sensory store decay rapidly and cannot be replenished from an eye that remains fixed in the same position, the eyes of anyone alert to the visual environment tend to be constantly on the move, even though the brain attends to only the first few moments of every new look. What the brain actually sees of the world around it is constantly subject to interruption.

Seeing Is Episodic

Our eyes are continually in movement—with our knowledge and without it. If we pause to think about it, we know that our eyes are scanning a page of text, or glancing around a room, or following a moving object. These are the movements we can see if we watch another person's face. These movements are rarely random—we would be quickly alarmed if our own eyes or someone else's began rolling around uncontrollably—but instead the eyes move systematically to where there is the most information that we are likely to need. The movements of the eye are controlled by the brain, and by examining what the brain tells the eye to do, we can get a basis for understanding what kind of information the brain is looking for.

But first, we shall consider quite a different kind of eye movement, one not apparently under the direct control of the brain, nor one that is noticeable either in ourselves or others, but that nonetheless can help to underline a point about the constructive nature of vision. Regardless of whether we are glancing around the environment, following a moving object, or maintaining a single fixation, the eyeball is in a constant state of very fast movement. This movement, or *tremor*, occurs at the rate of 50 oscillations a second. We do not notice the tremor in other people, partly because it is so fast, but also because the movement covers only a very short distance; it is more a vibration about a central position than a movement from one place to another. But although the movement is normally unnoticeable, it does have a significant role in the visual process; the tremor ensures that more than one group of retinal cells is involved in even a single glance. The tremor provides another illustration of the now familiar point that if the perceptual experience were a simple reproduction of whatever fell upon the retina, then all we should ever see would be a giddy blur.

The constant tremor of the eye is essential for vision—cancel it and our perception of the world disappears almost immediately. The cancellation is accomplished by a neat experimental procedure called "stabilizing the image" on the retina (Heckenmueller, 1965; Pritchard, 1961). To stabilize the image, the information coming to the eye is made to oscillate at the same rate and over the same distance as the movement of the eye itself. The scene can be reflected through a small mirror mounted directly on the eyeball so that the image always falls on the same position on the retina, no matter what the eye is doing. The consequence of stabilizing the image on the retina is not that the viewer suddenly perceives a super-sharp picture of the world; on the contrary, perception disappears.

The image does not seem to disappear instantaneously, nor does it fade slowly like a movie scene. Instead, entire parts drop away in a very systematic fashion. If the outline of a face has been presented, meaningful parts will vanish, one by one, first perhaps the hair, then an ear, then perhaps the eyes, the nose, until the only thing remaining may be, like the Cheshire cat, the smile. Geometrical figures break up in a similarly orderly way, losing extremities first, or one side after another. The word *BEAT* might disintegrate by the loss of its initial letter, leaving *EAT*, and then by dissolution to *AT* and *A*. By itself, the letter *B* might lose one loop to become *P* and then another to leave *I*. The phenomenon should not be interpreted to mean that the cells of the retina themselves respond to—and then lose—whole words and letters or forms; rather, it shows that the brain holds on to a disappearing image in the most meaningful way possible. Presumably the overworked retinal cells, deprived of the momentary respite the tremor can give them, become fatigued and send less and less information back to the brain, while the brain continues to construct as much of a percept as it can from the diminishing material that it receives.

Other kinds of eye movement need not detain us. There is a kind of slow drift, a tendency of the eye to wander from the point of focus, which is probably not very important because the eye has picked up all the useful information it is going to get during the first few milliseconds. There are "pursuit" movements that the eye makes when it follows a moving object. The only time that the eye can move smoothly and continuously from one position to another is in the course of a pursuit movement. Looking a person up and down with a single sweep of the eyes occurs only in fiction.

The eye movement that is really of concern in reading is, in fact, a rapid, irregular, spasmodic, but surprisingly accurate jump from one position to another. It is perhaps a little inappropriate to call such an important movement a jump, so it is dignified by the far more elegant-sounding French word *saccade* (which literally translated into English, however, means "jerk").

Fixations and Regressions

A saccade is by no means a special characteristic of reading, but rather the way we normally sample our visual environment for information about the world. We are very skilled in making saccadic movements of the eye. Guided by information received in its periphery, the eye can move very rapidly and accurately from one side of the visual field to the other, from left to right, up and down, even though we may be unaware of the point or object upon which we will focus before the movement begins. Every time the eye pauses in this erratic progression, a *fixation* is said to occur.

For reading English text, fixations are generally regarded as proceeding from left to right across the page, although, of course, our eye movements must also take us from the top of the page toward the bottom and from right to left as we proceed from one line to the next. Really skilled readers often do not read "from left to right" at all—they may not make more than one fixation a line and may skip lines in reading down the page. We shall consider in a later chapter how such a method of reading can be possible. All readers, good and poor, make another kind of movement that is just another saccade but that has got itself something of a bad name—a *regression*. A regression is simply a saccade that goes in the opposite direction from the line of type—from right to left along a line, or from one line to an earlier one. All readers produce regressions—and for skilled readers a regression may be just as productive an eye movement as a saccade in a forward, or progressive, direction.

During the saccade, while the eye is moving from one position to another, very little is seen at all. The leaping eye is functionally blind. Information is picked up between saccades when the eye is relatively still—during fixations. The qualification "relatively" still has to be made because the eye is never absolutely stationary—there are always tremors and drifts. But neither of these types of movement seems to interrupt the important business of picking up information. The sole purpose of a saccade, in whatever direction, is to move the eye from one position to another to pick up more information. It seems possible to pick up information only once during a fixation—for the few hundredths of a second at the beginning, when information is being loaded into the sensory store. After that time, the backroom parts of the visual system are busy, perhaps for the next quarter of a second, trying to make sense of the information.

Saccades are fast as well as precise. The larger saccades are faster than the small ones, but it still takes more time to move the eye a long distance than a short one. The movement of the eyes through 100 degrees, say from the extreme left to the extreme right of the visual field, takes about 100 msec—a 10th of a second. A movement of only a 20th of that distance—about two or three words at a normal reading distance—might take 50 msec.[2] But the fact

---

[2] There are some interesting analogies to be drawn between eye movements and hand movements. The top speed of movement for eye and hand are roughly similar, and like the eye, the hand moves faster when it moves over a greater distance. The hand performs the same kind of activity as the eye. It moves precisely and selectively to the most useful position, and it starts "picking up" only when it has arrived. But although the hands and eyes of children may move almost as fast and accurately as those of adults, they cannot always be used so efficiently. Children lack the experience of the adult and may not know so precisely what they are reaching for.

that a saccade can be made in 50 msec does not mean that we can take in new information by moving the eye 20 times a second. The limit on the rate at which we can usefully move from one fixation to another is set by the time required by the brain to make sense of every new input. That is why there can be little "improvement" in the rate at which fixations are made during reading. You cannot accelerate reading by hurrying the eyes along faster.

The number of fixations varies both with the skill of the reader and the difficulty of the passage being read, but not to any remarkable extent. In fact, fixation rate settles down by about Grade 4. There is a slight tendency for skilled readers to change fixations faster than unskilled readers, but the difference is only about one extra fixation a second; adults may average four while the child just starting to read changes fixation three times a second. For any reader, skilled or unskilled, reading a difficult passage may cut about one fixation a second off the fastest reading rate.

There is also not a dramatic difference between children and adults in the matter of regressions. Children do tend to make more regressions than fluent readers, but not so many more, perhaps one for every four progressive fixations compared with one in six for the adult. Once again, the rate of occurrence is determined as much by the difficulty of the passage as by the skill of the reader. Faced with a moderately difficult passage, skilled readers will produce as many regressions as beginning readers with a passage that they find relatively easy. Readers who do not make any regressions may be reading too slowly, too cautiously. When children make a lot of regressions, it is a signal that they are having difficulty, not a cause of difficulty. The number of regressions that readers make is an indication of the complexity to them of the passage they are trying to read.

In short, the duration of fixations and the number of regressions are not reliable guides for distinguishing between good and poor readers. What does distinguish the fluent from the less-skilled reader is the number of letters or words—or the amount of meaning—that can be identified in a single fixation. As a result, a more meaningful way to evaluate the eye movements of a poor reader and a skilled one is to count the number of fixations required to read a hundred words. Skilled readers need far fewer than the beginners because they are able to pick up more information on every fixation. A skilled reader at the "college graduate" level might pick up enough information to identify words at an average rate of over one a fixation (including regressions) or about 90 fixations per 100 words. The beginner might have to look twice for every word, or 200 fixations per 100 words. The beginner tends to have tunnel vision.

IMPLICATIONS FOR READING

I said at the beginning of this chapter that discussion of the visual system would lead to three important implications for reading and for learning to read—that reading must be fast, that it must be selective, and that it depends upon nonvisual information. By now the basic arguments underlying these implications may be becoming self-evident, but for emphasis they should be elaborated upon briefly.

Reading Must Be Fast

What is meant, of course, is that the brain must always move ahead quickly, to avoid becoming bogged down in the visual detail of the text to the extent that tunnel vision might result. This is not to suggest that the eyes should be speeded up. As I said earlier, reading cannot be improved by accelerating the eyeballs. There is a limit to the rate at which the brain can make sense of visual information from the eyes, and simply increasing the rate at which fixations are made would have the consequence of further overwhelming the brain rather than facilitating its decisions.

In fact, the customary reading rate of three or four fixations a second would appear to be an optimum. At a slower rate the contents of sensory store may begin to fade and the reader might be in the position of staring at nothing. At a faster rate than four fixations a second, masking can intrude so that the reader loses information before it is properly analyzed.

The "slow reading" that must be avoided is the overattention to detail that keeps the reader on the brink of tunnel vision. Trying to read text a few letters or even a whole word at a time keeps a reader functioning at the level of nonsense and precludes any hope of comprehension. The aim should be to read as much text as possible with every fixation to maintain meaningfulness. Classroom advice to slow down in case of difficulty, to be careful and examine every word closely, can easily lead to complete bewilderment.

There is no one best reading rate; that depends on the difficulty of the passage and the purposes of the reader—on whether the reader is trying to identify every word, for example, in order to read aloud, or whether the reading is "for meaning" only. The rate must be different if extensive memorization is being attempted, because rote learning cannot be accomplished quickly. Word-perfect reading aloud and extensive deliberate memorization often require that a passage should be read more than once. A reader is unlikely to comprehend while reading *slower* than 200 words a minute, because a lesser rate would imply that words were being read as isolated units rather than as meaningful sentences. As we shall see in the next chapter, limitations of memory prevent sense being built up from isolated words.

Thus, while comprehension demands relatively fast reading, memorization slows the reader down. As a consequence, comprehension may be impaired and memorization becomes pointless in any case. If the brain already has a good idea of what is on the page, then slower reading is more tolerable and more time can be spared for memorization. But heavy memory burdens should be avoided when one is learning to read or unfamiliar with the language or subject matter.

Reading Must Be Selective

The brain just does not have the time to attend to all the information in the print and can be easily inundated by visual information. Nor is memory able to cope with all the information that might be available from the page. The secret of reading efficiently is not to read indiscriminately but to *sample* the text. The brain must be parsimonious, making maximum use of what it knows already and analyzing the minimum of visual information required to verify or modify what it can already predict about the text. All this may sound very complicated, but in fact it is something that every experienced reader can do automatically, and almost certainly what you are doing now if you can make sense of what you read. It is no different from what you do when you look around a room, or at a picture.

But like many other aspects of fluent reading, selectivity in picking up and analyzing samples of the available visual information in text comes with experience in reading. Once again the initiative for how the eyes function rests with the brain. The brain tells the eyes when it has got all the visual information it requires from a fixation and directs the eyes very precisely where to move next. The saccade will be either a progressive or regressive movement, depending on whether the next information that the brain requires is further ahead or further back in the page. The brain is able to direct the eyes appropriately, in reading as in other aspects of vision, provided it understands what it needs to find out. The brain must always be in charge. Trying to control eye movements in reading can be like trying to steer a horse by the tail. If the eyes do not go to an appropriate place in reading, it is probably because the brain does not know where to put them, not because the reader has insufficient visual ability to switch gaze to the right place at the right time.

Reading Depends on Nonvisual Information

Everything I have said so far should underline this final point. The brain—with its purposes, expectations, and prior knowledge—has to be in control of the eyes in reading. To assert that reading should be fast does not mean recklessly so. A reader must be able to use nonvisual information to avoid being swamped by visual information from the eyes. To say that a reader should only sample the visual information does not imply that the eyes could go randomly from one part of the page to another. Rather, the reader should attend to just those parts of the text that contain the most important information. And this again is a matter of making maximum use of what is already known.

To recapitulate, nonvisual information is knowledge we already have in our brain that is relevant to the language and to the subject matter of what we happen to be reading, together with some additional knowledge of specific aspects of written language such as the way spelling patterns are formed. Nonvisual information is anything that can reduce the number of alternatives the brain must consider as we read. If we know that one noun cannot immediately follow another without at least a punctuation mark, then our alternatives are reduced. If we know that only a restricted range of technical terms are likely to crop up in a particular context, then again our uncertainty is reduced. Even the knowledge that certain sequences of letters are unlikely to occur in English words—for example that initial *H* will not be followed by another consonant— will enable a reader to eliminate many alternatives and see much more at any one time. But meaning is the most important nonvisual information of all.

The skilled reader employs no more *visual information* to comprehend four words in a single glance than the beginning reader who requires two fixations to identify a single word. All the additional information that skilled readers require is contributed by what they know already. When fluent readers encounter a passage that is difficult to read—because it is poorly written or crammed with new information—the number of fixations (including regressions) that they make increases, and reading speed goes down. Because of the additional uncertainty in the situation, they are forced to use more visual information to try to comprehend what they read.

The relative ability to use prior knowledge has consequences in all aspects of vision. Experts—whether in reading, art, chess, or engineering—may be able to comprehend an entire situation at a single glance while the greater uncertainty of novices handicaps them with tunnel vision. When readers in a tachistoscopic experiment are presented with words in a language they do not comprehend, they are able to identify only a few letters. The fact that the words make sense to someone who knows the language is completely irrelevant; to the uninformed reader the letters are essentially random, and inability to see very much will result.[3] The implication for anyone involved in teaching reading should be obvious. Whenever readers cannot make sense of what they are expected to read—because the material bears no relevance to any prior knowledge they might have—then reading will become more difficult and learning to read impossible.

ON SEEING BACKWARDS

One thing the eyes and the brain cannot do is see backwards. I mention this fact, which perhaps ought to be self-evident, because a belief does exist

---

[3] There are similar limitations on the amount of incoming information that can be handled by all sensory systems. For example, it is possible to have a distinct hearing loss when trying to understand speech for which there is a lack of "nonacoustic information"—which to all intents and purposes is the same as nonvisual information in reading. Thus we raise our voices when attempting to converse in an unfamiliar language—and children may often be deaf in the classroom although they appear to have no hearing problems outside.

that a visual abnormality of this kind causes some children problems in learning to read. The basis of the myth is the indisputable evidence that many children at some point in their reading careers confuse reversible letters like *b* and *d*, *p* and *q*, and even words like *was* and *saw* or *much* and *chum*. But seeing backwards is both a physical and a logical impossibility, and a much simpler explanation is available.

It is physically impossible to see *part* of the visual field in a different orientation from the rest—to see two dogs facing one way and one the other when they are all in fact looking in the same direction. And it is logically impossible to see *everything* reversed because everything would still be seen in the same relationship to everything else and therefore nothing would be different; everything would still be seen the right way round. Of course, it is possible to make a mistake, to think a dog is facing east when in fact it is facing west, especially if we are not familiar with the kind of dog, but that must be attributed to lack of adequate information or knowledge, not to a visual defect.

And indeed, the simple explanation of why so many children confuse *b* and *d* is lack of appropriate experience. The discrimination is not an easy one and can confuse adults whose information is limited, just as fluent readers of English become confused with the identification of similar letters in unfamiliar alphabets. The difference between *b* and *d* is minimal—a matter of whether the upright stroke is on the left or the right of the circle—and is not a difference that is significant or even relevant in most aspects of children's experience. A dog is a dog whichever way it faces. Those more general discriminations that do require distinctions of actual or relative direction, such as "left" and "right" or telling the time from the hands of a clock, are notoriously difficult for most children.

Fluent readers do not usually mistake *b* and *d* when they read, but that is primarily because they have so many other clues and need not be concerned with individual letters. But to distinguish *b* from *d* when they occur in isolation, one at a time, is much harder, and the fact that we can normally do so with facility must be attributed to the years of experience we have had and the amount of time we are given, relatively speaking, to inspect the evidence. Being able to distinguish *b* from *d* does not make a reader, but being a reader makes the discrimination easier.

Because the difference between *b* and *d* is both unusual and difficult to perceive, it is relatively difficult for children to learn, especially if they do not understand the significance of the difference in the first place. That is why the appropriate experience for such children is not more drills on isolated letters, which are meaningless, but more meaningful reading. Children who have the difficulty, perhaps confusing words like *big* and *dig*, must be reading words or sentences which are essentially meaningless (or as if they are meaningless). No one who is reading for sense could confuse words like *big* and *dig*, or *was* and *saw*, in a meaningful context. Unfortunately children with a "reversals problem" are often given concentrated exercises on distinguishing word pairs like *big* and *dig* in isolation, increasing their apprehension and bewilderment. And if they show no progress with words in isolation they may be restricted to drills with *b* and *d* alone. But letters in isolation are considerably more difficult than letters in words because an important relational clue has been removed. The difference between *b* and *d* at the beginning of a word is that the upright stroke is on the outside for *b* (as in *big*) but on the inside for *d* (as in *dig*). But "outside" and "inside" are meaningless for letters in isolation. There is only one possible way of making learning to distinguish *b* from *d* even more difficult, and that is to show them one at a time. This removes every relational clue, and puts the learner in the situation most likely to confound even experienced readers.

It is sometimes argued that children see letters backwards because they *write* them that way. But writing requires quite different kinds of skill. We all recognize faces and figures that we could not possibly draw. If my drawing of a face looks like a potato, that does not mean that I see a face as a potato, it means that I am a poor artist. A child may draw a human figure as a circular head with matchstick arms and legs, but show them their own distorted efforts and an artist's representation, and they will readily show you which looks most like what they see. Children do not and cannot draw what they see, and the fact that they might write a few or many letters backwards says nothing about their vision, simply that they have not yet learned the difficult task of writing letters conventionally.

A LITTLE MORE PHYSIOLOGY

Anatomically, the brain is not all of a piece. In particular it is deeply split along a center line from the back of the head to behind the nose into two roughly symmetrical hemispheres, the left and the right. These two hemispheres are relatively tenuously connected to each other, at least near the surface areas of the brain, the areas which seem to be particularly involved with the organization of cognitive and motor functions most open to conscious control. An old psychological and physiological puzzle, still not resolved, is how we piece together a coherent visual image of the scene in front of our eyes when the left half of the visual field (from both eyes) goes to one hemisphere and the right half goes to the other and there are no direct hemispheric connections between the two. Physiologically the picture is split down the middle, but subjectively the seams do not show.

It has long been known that the left hemisphere of the brain is usually largely responsible for motor and sensory control of the right side of the body and the right hemisphere for the left. Because of this general *cross-laterality*, people who suffer strokes or other forms of injury to the left side of their brain tend to lose motor control and possibly sensation in areas on the right side of their body, while damage to the right side of the brain affects the left side of the body. And it has also been known for over a century that for the majority of people, especially the right handed, areas of the left side of the brain tend to be particularly involved with language. For such people, strokes or other injuries to the right side of the brain may leave language abilities largely unimpaired, whereas accidents to the left side of the brain are more likely to be associated with language loss. However, this hemispheric specialization is by no means universal or necessary. About 10% of the population has the right hemisphere primarily involved with language functions, and children who are born with or who early in life suffer damage to the left side of the brain can develop language relatively fluently with the right, although it becomes much harder to transfer language or to relearn it with the opposite hemisphere as they get older.

More recently, many ingenious studies have been made of the general modes of functioning of the two sides of the brain, particularly with the living brains of people unfortunate enough to have had the surface connections between their two hemispheres severed by accident or unavoidable surgery. Such studies have shown that the two sides of the brain have quite different styles of operation. The left hemisphere (in most people) seems to be particularly involved in activities which are analytic and sequential (like language), for intellectual calculations and planning. In such people, the right hemisphere's characteristic responsibilities and mode of operation are more holistic and spatial; it is concerned with global, subjective, and emotional matters. The left side may be busier when we write a letter or plan an excursion, the right side when we listen to music or imagine a scene.

All this is fascinating and indeed an important step forward toward understanding the mechanisms of the brain. However, it can also be misleading and conducive to spurious and even damaging conclusions if interpreted prematurely and too literally. For the great majority of people—for at least everyone who is not institutionalized or hospitalized—the brain functions as a whole. We draw upon the resources of both hemispheres to produce and understand language, just as we use all of our brain in the rest of our experience. It is a mistake to regard the two hemispheres as separate entities which function independently and even in opposition. Unfortunately, some educators and psychologists who know little about physiology (and some physiologists and neuroanatomists who know little about language and learning) talk as if we have two brains rather than two sides of a single brain. The hemispheres are sometimes referred to as the left and right brains, although this is literally (and only approximately) true for just a handful of people whose brains have been surgically or accidentally sectioned.

One danger of such reasoning is that it confuses a structural arrangement relevant only to the internal working of the brain with the way in which a person functions as a whole. There are not people who think only with the left or the right side of their brains, even if their personalities and behavior reflect proclivities for more analytic or reflective approaches to life and learning. It is appropriate to say that a particular kind of activity or preference is dominant in a person but not that the hemisphere is dominant. It makes sense to say a person has a good spatial orientation and tends to the contemplative; this gives a way of understanding the person and perhaps adapting to idiosyncratic learning preferences. It adds nothing to say that the person is right-brain dominated, and may indeed reduce understanding by switching attention from perceptible characteristics to an assumed and probably mythical cause.

Anyone capable of learning to produce and understand the language of his or her familiar environment has the ability to use both sides of the brain and to do all those things the two hemispheres are supposed to specialize in. No child comes to school with only half a brain, and hemispheric specialization or "asymmetry" should not be proposed as an explanation of difficulty in learning to read, especially when there are, as we shall see, so many alternative possibilities. In particular it is wrong to work backward and to assume that because a child is slow or reluctant in learning to read there must be an imbalance or inadequacy of hemispheric function. There is no reading center in the brain. Many areas of the brain are active when we read, but none is involved in reading to the exclusion of anything else. Illness, injury, or very occasionally an inherent defect may affect the working of the brain so that ability to read is disturbed, but always some more general activity involving either language or vision will also be impaired. There is nothing physiologically or intellectually unique about reading. Reading does not make language demands on the brain that are not involved in the understanding of speech nor does reading make visual demands that the brain does not meet when we look around a room to locate an object or to distinguish faces. Advances in mapping the architecture of the brain help us mostly to understand the brain (or to further respect its mysteries), not to understand language or learning.

It is important to know the possibilities and limitations of the brain, which is the reason we have already been so concerned with the mechanisms of perception and memory, but the actual manner in which the brain internally organizes its own affairs does not yet have a great relevance to education. At least, that is my view. I do not believe it would or should make the slightest difference to how reading is taught if it were discovered tomorrow that we all have a critical neural center for reading in the foot (the left foot, for most people). Instruction should always be adapted to the circumstances in which an individual learns and understands best, but this is not promoted by unfounded speculation about the brain structures of the learner.

All this is stressed because there continues to be in education what I and some other researchers believe is a readiness little short of tragic to attribute learning and teaching failures to pseudomedical or scientific causes. Failures are blamed on perceptual or cognitive handicaps with evidence no more specific than the fact that the failure occurs and a convenient medical or scientific theory happens to be around. If a plausible explanation cannot be found in terms of visual, acoustic, memory, or intellectual inadequacy, then an even vaguer "minimal learning disability" may be blamed. And the current excuse, the most popular explanation, always seems to follow the area of scientific advance which is generating the most interest and receiving the most popular attention. Failure to learn is explained in terms of fad rather than fact. The specialized insights of students of the brain are important in many respects, but they do not yet explain reading or reading problems. The relating of subtle differences in learning, behavior, attitude, and personality to presumed differences in the architecture of the brain should not become a new phrenology, as unscientific as making judgments about people's character from the bumps on their skulls.

SUMMARY

Reading is not just a visual activity. Both **visual information** and **non-visual information** are essential for reading, and there can be a trade-off between the two. Reading is not instantaneous, the brain cannot immediately make sense of the visual information in a page of print. The eyes move in **saccades,** pausing at **fixations** to select visual information, usually progressing in a forward direction but, when needed, in **regressions.** Slow reading interferes with comprehension. Reading is accelerated not by increasing the fixation rate but by reducing dependency on visual information, mainly through making use of meaning.

Notes to Chapter 4 begin on page 251, covering

Vision and information
Information theory and reading
The rate of visual decision-making
On seeing backwards
Hemispheric specialization

Chapter 5
BOTTLENECKS
OF MEMORY

In Chapter 1, I talked about the diverse and massive amounts of knowledge that together comprise the theory of the world contained within the head. But I did not discuss how we managed to deposit all of this knowledge in the vaults of memory, nor how we draw on it when we need to.

Two entire chapters at the end of this book are concerned with the general topic of *learning*—with the *circumstances* in which our theory of the world develops and grows. But there are some specific issues related to *how much* can get into memory at any one time that are more appropriately considered at this point. These issues are related to the bottlenecks in *perception* which I discussed in the previous chapter—for example the fact that beginning readers (or any reader confronted by an unfamiliar text) can see only a small amount at any one time, even as little as four or five letters. Now I must turn to some additional constraints that confront all readers, but especially those in difficulty. These are constraints on how quickly specific things can be taken into or out of memory.

Why should tunnel vision, the temporary inability to see what is contained in more than a small area in front of the eyes, be such a crippling handicap for readers, whatever their experience and ability? If a beginning reader can see only a few letters at a time—say the first half of a word such as *ELEP* . . .— why cannot these letters be remembered for the fraction of a second that the child requires to make a new fixation and see the rest of the word . . . *HANT?* But unfortunately, memory has its own limitations and cannot be called upon to exceed its own capacity when the visual system is overworked. Fluent reading demands not only parsimony in the use of visual information but also restraint in the burdens placed upon memory. In both cases there are limits on how much the brain can handle. Overloading memory does not make reading easier and can contribute to making reading impossible.

There are a number of paradoxes about the role of memory in reading. The more we try to memorize, the less we are likely to recall. The more we try to memorize, the less we are even likely to comprehend, which not only makes recall more difficult—it makes recall pointless. Who wants to remember nonsense? On the other hand, the more we comprehend, the more memory will take care of itself.

An implication of these paradoxes is that the prior knowledge already in memory is far more important in reading than efforts to memorize everything in a text. To repeat a theme which by now should be familiar, the use of nonvisual information is critical (although the importance and functions of nonvisual information are rarely explained to readers, or even acknowledged).

THREE ASPECTS OF MEMORY

To begin, terms need to be clarified a little. We can use the word *memory* in a variety of ways, sometimes to refer to how well we can put something new into our minds, sometimes to how long we can retain it there, and sometimes to how well we can get it out again. In this chapter we consider four specific aspects or *operating characteristics* of memory: *input* (or how material goes in), *capacity* (how much can be held), *persistence* (how long it can be held), and *retrieval* (getting it out again). We also consider what would appear to be several kinds of memory, because memory does not always look like the same process when examined in different ways. Psychologists in fact often distinguish three kinds or aspects of memory, depending on the time that elapses between the original presentation of something to be remembered and the test to see what can be retrieved. The first aspect, termed *sensory store*, is related to information from its arrival at a receptor organ, such as the eye, until the brain has made its perceptual decision, for example, the identification of several letters or words. The second aspect, usually called *short-term memory*, involves the brief time we can maintain attention to something immediately after its identification, for example, remembering an unfamiliar telephone number as we dial it. Finally, there is *long-term memory*, which is everything we know about the world, our total amount of nonvisual information.

These three aspects of memory are often depicted in textbook "flow diagrams" as if they are separate parts of the brain or successive stages in the

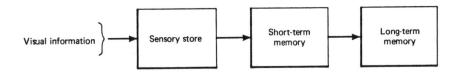

FIGURE 5.1.   A typical flow diagram for memory.

process of memorization, as indicated in Figure 5.1. But such a diagram should not be taken too literally. I am not sure that it is most appropriate to refer to different "kinds" of memory, so I use the more neutral term *aspects*. There is no evidence that different memories exist in different places in the brain, nor that one memory starts functioning when the other leaves off, as the diagram might suggest. It is definitely misleading to imply that there is movement in just one direction from short-term to long-term memory, and to ignore the fact that there is always *selectivity* about how much is remembered and the manner in which remembering takes place.

However, a discussion must begin somewhere and proceed in some kind of sequence, so for convenience the three aspects of memory are dealt with in the left-to-right order. Later in the chapter an alternative representation of memory is offered.

Sensory Store

The first aspect of memory can be quickly disposed of, because it has already been encountered in the discussion of the visual system in the preceeding chapter. Sensory store is a theoretical necessity rather than a known part of the brain. Some function or process has to be conceptualized to account for the persistence of visual information after it is received and transmitted by the eye, at the beginning of each fixation, while the brain is working on it. The operating characteristics of sensory store are quickly stated—input is very fast (the first few milliseconds of a fixation), capacity is at least large enough to hold visual information equivalent to 25 letters (although the brain may not be fast enough to identify anywhere near that number), persistence is very brief (about a second under optimal conditions, but normally erased before that time by another fixation), and retrieval depends on how fast the brain can make sense of the information.

Sensory store is of theoretical interest but has little significance for reading instruction because there is nothing that can or need be done about it. Sensory store cannot be overloaded nor can its capacity be increased by exercise. There is no evidence that children's sensory stores are less adequate than adults'. What needs to be remembered is that the brain must make sense of the contents of sensory store, but that the contents do not persist very long. As a result, there is little point in speeding up fixations (which will simply erase sensory store faster) nor in slowing them down (which will result in blank stares). What makes the difference in reading is the effectiveness of the brain in using what it already knows (nonvisual information) to make sense of the incoming information (visual information) briefly held in sensory store.

Short-Term Memory

Can you repeat the sentence you are reading at this moment, without taking a second look at it? Whatever you can do to repeat what you have just read is a demonstration of the function of short-term memory. Short-term memory is "working memory," a "buffer memory," where you retain in the forefront of your mind whatever you are attending to at a particular moment. As far as language is concerned, the contents of short-term memory are usually the last few words you have read or listened to, or whatever thoughts you had in your mind instead. Sometimes short-term memory is occupied by what you are about to say or write, by an address you are looking for or a telephone number you want to call. Short-term memory is whatever is holding your attention. And short-term memory is of central importance in reading. It is where you lodge the traces of what you have just read while you go on to make sense of the next few words. It is where you try to retain facts that you want to commit to rote memorization.

Short-term memory would appear to have both strengths and weaknesses in everyone, just by virtue of the way it functions. On the credit side, there does not appear to be any undue delay in getting something into short-term memory. In fact if someone asks you to call a certain telephone number, your best strategy is to get on your way to dial the number, not to stand around trying to commit the number to memory. Similarly, there does not appear to be any particular problem about retrieving items from short-term memory. If something is in short-term memory you can get it out again at once. Indeed, if you cannot immediately retrieve what you want, say the telephone number, then you might just as well go back and ask for it again. Either you have retained the number in short-term memory, in which case it is accessible without delay, or it is gone for good. Short-term memory is what we happen to be attending to at the moment, and if our attention is diverted to something else, the original content is lost.

But if short-term memory seems a reasonably efficient device as far as input and output operations are concerned, in other respects it has its limitations. Short-term memory cannot contain very much information at any one time—little more than half a dozen items, in fact. A sequence of seven unrelated digits is about as much as anyone can retain. It is as if a benevolent providence had provided humanity with just sufficient short-term memory capacity to make telephone calls and then had failed to prophesy area codes. For if we try to hold more than six or seven items in short-term memory, then something will be lost. If someone distracts us when we are on our way to make that telephone call, perhaps by asking us the time of day or the location of a room, then some or all of the telephone number will be forgotten and there will be absolutely no point in standing around cudgelling our brains for the number to come back. We shall just have to return and ascertain the number once again. For as much as we try to overload short-term memory, that much of its contents will be lost.

All this is the reason why short-term memory cannot be used to overcome the condition of tunnel vision. The child who has seen only *ELEP* . . . just cannot hold those letters in short-term memory, read another four or five letters, and get them all organized in a way that makes sense. As the fragments of one fixation go into short-term memory, the fragments from the previous fixation will be pushed out. This is not the same as the "masking" or erasure of sensory store—it is possible to hold a few items in short-term memory over a number of fixations. But holding such items in the forefront of our attention simply prevents very much more going in and has the obvious result of making reading much more difficult. Not much reading can be done if half your attention is preoccupied with earlier bits of letters and words that you are still trying to make sense of.

The second limitation of short-term memory involves its persistence. Nothing stays around very long in short-term memory. It is impossible to state an exact amount of time for the persistence of something in short-term memory, for the simple reason that its longevity depends on what you do with it. Ignore something in short-term memory for less than a second, and it will be gone. To retain it, you must keep giving it your attention. *Rehearsal* is the technical term often employed. To keep that telephone number in your head, you keep repeating it; it cannot be allowed to elude your attention. Theoretically, material can be kept in short-term memory indefinitely, but only if constantly rehearsed, a procedure that is generally impractical because it prevents you from thinking about anything else. Because we can rarely devote much attention to anything apart from what we happen to be doing at a particular moment, and because life tends to be full of distraction in any case, it would therefore seem a reasonable assertion that the persistence of short-term memory is generally very brief, even if we cannot put a precise limit to it. Material in short-term memory must be dealt with as expeditiously as possible. Retaining something for longer than a fixation or two, for example, preempts attention that is required for the task on hand in reading and promotes a further loss of comprehension. The more a reader fills short-term memory with unrelated letters, bits of words, and other meaningless items, the more the letters and bits of words that the reader is currently trying to understand are likely to prove nonsense as well.

Long-Term Memory

Of course, memory is far more than whatever we happen to be thinking about at the moment. There is a vast amount that we know all the time, ranging from names and telephone numbers to all the complex interrelationships that we can perceive and predict among objects and events in the world around us, and only a minute part of all of this knowledge can be the focus of our attention at any one time. Anything that persists in our minds quite independently of rehearsal or conscious knowledge is long-term memory, our continuous knowledge of the world. Long-term memory has some distinct advantages over short-term memory, especially with regard to its relative capacity. Nevertheless long-term memory cannot be used as a dump for any overflow of information from short-term memory, for long-term memory also has its limitations.

Let us begin with the positive side. Where short-term memory is restricted in its capacity to barely half a dozen items, the capacity of long-term memory would appear to be infinite. No limit has been discovered to how much can be lodged in long-term memory. Nothing has to be lost or moved aside in long-term memory to accommodate something new. We never have to forget an old friend's name to make room for the name of a new acquaintance.

Similarly, there is no apparent limit to the persistence of long-term memory. No question of rehearsal here. Memories we may not even be aware that we had, recollections of a childhood incident, for example, can quite unexpectedly revivify themselves, triggered perhaps by a few nostalgic bars of music, an old photograph, or even a certain taste or smell.

But as everyone knows, the fact that there seems to be no ultimate limit to the capacity or persistence of long-term memory does not mean that its contents are constantly accessible. It is here that some failings of long-term memory begin to become apparent. Retrieval from long-term memory is by no means as immediate and effortless as retrieval from short-term memory.

Indeed, retention and retrieval seem quite different in long- and short-term memory. Short-term memory is like a set of half a dozen small boxes, each of which can contain one separate item, by definition immediately accessible to attention because it is attention that holds them in short-term memory in the first place. But long-term memory is more like a network of knowledge, an organized system in which each item is related in some way or another to everything else. The organization and operation of long-term memory—the theory of the world in the head—was discussed in Chapter 1. Whether or not we can retrieve something from long-term memory depends on how it is organized. The secret of recall from long-term memory is to tap one of the interrelationships.

Sometimes the effort to get hold of something in long-term memory can be most frustrating. We know something is there but cannot find a way to get to it. An illustration is provided by the "tip-of-the-tongue" phenomenon (Brown & McNeill, 1966). We know someone's name begins with an S and has three syllables—and we are sure it is not Sanderson or Somerset or Sylvester. Suddenly the name appears in the set of alternatives that our mind is running through, or perhaps when someone else mentions the name, and then we recognize it at once. It was in long-term memory all the time, but not immediately accessible.

Success at retrieving something from long-term memory depends on the clues we can find to gain access to it, and on how well it was organized in long-term memory in the first place. Basically, everything depends on the sense that we made of the material when we originally put it into memory. It is pointless to try to put an overflow of unrelated fragments from short-term memory into long-term memory—that is why rote learning is so often unproductive. It is not just that nonsense that goes in will be nonsense when it comes out, but that it is extremely difficult to get nonsense out at all.

But there is another reason why it is not feasible to accommodate an overflow from short-term memory in long-term memory, concerned with the rate at which long-term memory can accept new information. In contrast to the practically immediate input of half a dozen items into short-term memory, committing something to long-term memory is extremely and surprisingly slow. To put one item into long-term memory takes 5 seconds—and in that 5 seconds there is little attention left over for anything else at all. The telephone number that will tax short-term memory to its capacity is at least accepted as quickly as it is read or heard, but to hold the same number in long-term memory, so that it can be dialed the next day, will require a good half minute of concentration, 5 seconds for each digit.

Committing fragments of text to long-term memory is not something that can be attempted recklessly in reading to overcome limitations of the visual system or of short-term memory. Quite the contrary, efforts to cram long-term memory will have the effect of interfering with comprehension. Beginning readers with tunnel vision, who cannot hold in short-term memory more than the few letters they see in a single fixation, are even more confounded if they try to put isolated letters or bits of words into long-term memory.

Fluent readers can find reading impossible if they overburden long-term memory, even if they are trying to read material which they would find completely comprehensible if they relaxed and were content to enjoy it. This problem can be acute for students trying to read a novel or Shakespearean play and at the same time trying to commit to memory the unfamiliar names of all the characters and every trivial detail or event. Memorization interferes with comprehension by monopolizing attention and reducing intelligibility. Most readers have encountered the perverse textbook that is incomprehensible the day before the examination—when we are trying to retain every fact—yet transparently comprehensible the day after—when all we are reading for is to discover what we missed. If you are having difficulty comprehending what you are reading right now, it may be because you are trying too hard to memorize. On the other hand—as I shall demonstrate in a number of ways—comprehension takes care of memorization. If you comprehend what you read or hear, then long-term memory will reorganize itself so efficiently and effortlessly that you will not be aware that you are learning at all.

Long-term memory is in fact extremely efficient, but only if the acquisition and organization of new material is directed by what we know already. Once again we find that it is what we know already that tips the balance, that makes reading possible. It is time to look at how prior knowledge helps to overcome the limitations of both short-term and long-term memory.

OVERCOMING
MEMORY LIMITATIONS

There are some paradoxes to be resolved. The experimental evidence is that we can hold no more than half a dozen random letters in short-term memory, yet it is usually not difficult to repeat a sentence of a dozen words or more that we have just read or heard for the first time. It appears that we can put no more than one letter or digit into long-term memory every 5 seconds, yet we can commonly recall many of the larger themes and significant details that we have read in a novel or seen in a film.

To explain these discrepancies it is necessary to clarify some rather loose language that I have been using. I have been talking about retaining "material," or half a dozen "things" or "items," in short-term memory, and putting just one "item" into long-term memory. What are these "things" or "items"? The answer is that it depends on what you already know and the sense you are making of what you are reading or listening to. These "things" or "items" are units that exist in long-term memory already.

If you are looking for letters—or if you can only find letters in what you are looking at—then you can hold half a dozen letters in short-term memory. But if you are looking for words then short-term memory will hold a half a dozen words, the equivalent of four or five times as many letters.

It is a question of what you already know. Short-term memory is filled by a seven-digit telephone number, which also requires half a minute to put into long-term memory. But not if the number happens to be 123-4567 because that is a sequence that you already know. The number 1234567 will occupy just one part of short-term memory and will enter long-term memory within a few seconds because, in a sense, it is there already. Can you hold the letters *THEELEPELTJE* in short-term memory? Only if you recognize them as a word, which you will do if you can read Dutch. To put the same sequence of letters into long-term memory would require a good minute of concentration—and even then it is unlikely that you would be able to recall them all tomorrow—unless you already know the word, in which case you will commit it to memory as rapidly as the English word *teaspoon*, which is what the Dutch word happens to mean.

Psychologists refer to this process of storing the largest meaningful unit in short-term memory as *chunking*, which is a conveniently picturesque term but also a bit misleading. The term suggests that at the beginning we first attend to the small fragments (individual letters or digits) which we subsequently organize into larger units for efficiency in memory. But we are looking for the larger units all the time. When we move on to consider more specifically the processes of reading it will be seen that written words can be identified without any reference to letters, and meaning without reference to specific words. It is not that we perceive letters which we then—if we can—chunk into words, but that we can perceive words or meaning in the first place and never bother the visual system or memory with letters. The "items" that we commit to memory are the largest meaningful units we can find. In other words, what we put into short-term memory is determined by the largest units that we have available in long-term memory. It is what we know and are looking for that determines the content of short-term memory, which is the reason I present an alternative diagram of memory to that of Figure 5.1. In Figure 5.2, short-term memory is shown as part of long-term memory—the part that controls what we happen to be attending to at the time. Short-term memory is not an antechamber of long-term memory, but that part of long-term memory that we use to attend to, and make sense of, a current situation.

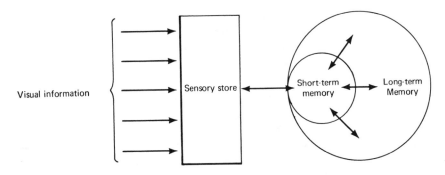

FIGURE 5.2.   An alternative representation of memory.

The arrow between short-term memory and sensory store is double-ended to acknowledge that the brain is *selective* about the visual information that it attends to, and the arrows between short-term and long-term memory are double-ended to represent their continual interaction.

One final elaboration must be made. We can hold in short-term memory a few letters, or a few words. But we can also put into short-term memory something far more mysterious—we can hold there large rich chunks of *meaning*. It is impossible to put a number to this—units of meaning cannot be counted the way we can count letters or words. But just as we can hold the letters contained in words in memory far more efficiently than letters that are unrelated to each other, so we can hold meaningful sequences of words in memory far more efficiently than we can hold individual unrelated words. The same applies to long-term memory; we can put an entire "meaning" away in just a few seconds—without any conscious awareness that we are doing so— even though that meaning might have been embedded in a dozen words or more. And by definition, any "meaning" that we put into long-term memory is going to be far easier to retain and retrieve because meaningfulness implies that the input is related to what we already know and makes sense to us.

We must get used to the notion that meaning does not depend on specific words. This crucial point is elaborated many times in this book. When we retain a meaningful sequence of words in memory—either short-term or long-term—we are not primarily storing the words at all, but rather the meaning that we attribute to them. "Meaning" is the largest and most efficient unit of analysis that we can bring to bear from what we know already to what we are trying to read (or hear) and understand. For the moment, I offer just one illustration of the fact that not only do we look for meaning, rather than specific words, when we comprehend speech or print, but also that this is the most natural thing to do.

I have said that we can hold a dozen or more words in short-term memory if they are in a meaningful sequence, whereas six or seven is the limit for words that make no collective sense, say, the same sequence of words in reverse. Try memorizing: *memory term short in words more or dozen a hold can we*. But in fact it is not the sequence of a dozen or so words that we are holding in short-term memory, but rather their meaning. Often, if you ask a person to repeat a sentence, you will get back the right meaning but not exactly the same words. The person who remembers is not so much recalling the same words as reconstructing the sentence from the meaning that was remembered. We do not in fact attend to words; we attend to meanings. So a substantial "mistake" might be made in repeating exact words—the word *automobile* might be recalled as the word *car*, for example—but there is rarely the substitution of a tiny word that makes a big difference to meaning, such as *not*. We shall see, incidentally, that "errors" of this kind, that preserve meaning, are committed by fluent readers and also by children learning to read who are in the process of becoming good readers. Reading involves looking for meaning, not specific words.

Memory Without Bottlenecks

Much of what we have considered so far might be called *contrived* memory—whether by experimenters or ourselves—where remembering is in effect put under external control. In memory research, subjects are usually told what they must remember and recall. When we make a deliberate effort to commit a particular thing to memory or to get a particular thing out, we usually come face to face with one of the frustrating bottlenecks I have been describing.

But most of the time there is no particular effort involved in remembering—and memory seems to be much more efficient. I have talked about how easily something goes into long-term memory provided we can make sense of it, provided it is relevant to what we are doing at the time. These are the occasions when memory could be said to be controlled "from the inside," by the way in which the brain is naturally operating on the world or making sense of it. It is sometimes surprising to discover how much has gone into memory without our awareness. I have more to say about this in the chapter on learning, in which I stress that efficient and effortless memorizing depends on how well it is integrated with the current organization of the brain, with its ongoing purposes and predictions, the operation of the dynamic theory of the world.

I have also talked in the present chapter about how easily things can be retrieved from long-term memory, provided they are "organized" in relationships with relevant parts of our current theory of the world. The most relevant kind of relationship is when what we need to remember is part of what we are actually involved in at the time.

I am referring to an aspect of memory that we rely on just about every moment of the day, that is incredibly efficient and rarely lets us down. It is memory that is not contrived in any way; it functions spontaneously, without premeditation or effort. Ironically, because of their predeliction for studying aspects of memory that can be brought under *control* in the laboratory, experimental psychologists have largely ignored this aspect of remembering, which takes place without the conscious contrivance of the experimenters or their subjects. Because of their rather narrow viewpoint, such researchers have even persuaded themselves and many educators that remembering is normally difficult, effortful, and frequently unsuccessful.

But most of the time we remember automatically and without strain, even without awareness that we are making demands on memory. We do not usually have difficulty remembering our own name, where we live, or our telephone number. We remember our birthday and that of a few other people as well, and we remember holidays. We remember our friends' names, and how they look, and where they live, and even some of their telephone numbers. We remember everything about the world that is familiar to us. We remember that trees are called "trees" and birds "birds," even though we may not remember the names of particular kinds. We remember the meanings of just about every word we know, how these words are pronounced, and how many of them are spelled as well. We not only remember facts, we remember *scenes, procedures, scenarios, scripts*—all of the cognitive *schemes* discussed in Chapter 1. We remember innumerable things. We do not remember these things all the time, of course. Our heads would be continually cluttered if we did. They come to mind just when it is appropriate for us to remember them, when they help us to make sense of the world we are in at the moment.

Psychologist George Mandler (1985) has termed this everyday aspect of memory *reminding*, although he does not want to say that it is different from any other facet of memory. In fact, Mandler suggests that apparent differences in kinds of memory are really only differences in the forms of tests, in the way memory is examined. If we look at the recall of something soon after it has come to our attention then we talk about "short-term memory." If we consider something over a longer period then we refer to "long-term memory." And instead of looking at particular things that we (or researchers) happen quite arbitrarily to be concerned with, if we consider what the brain remembers for its own purposes, then we have this continual phenomenon of "reminding."

And as with comprehension and with putting things into memory, the conditions that make reminding fluent and effortless are meaningfulness, relevance, and personal involvement. We remember most easily when what we need to recall is most relevant to what we are engaged in doing, and when we have no anxiety about not remembering. This is all part of the continually ongoing process of "thinking." Memory is not a special faculty of the brain that functions independently of everything else. Thinking and the "reminding" aspect of memory are inseparable.

Long-term memory is dynamic, it is generating predictions in the form of possible or potential worlds. Reminding is an inevitable and essential aspect of that continual interaction between possible and real worlds, when the brain is in control of the flow of events in which we are immersed.

When we are able to read with comprehension we are being reminded all the time. The events of the story (or the steps in the argument) carry us along as if we were experiencing them at first hand, and we rarely have to struggle to exercise our memory. We remember the meaning of particular words when we are reading those words, we recall what we have already read (and other aspects of nonvisual information) when it is appropriate to do so. And we are reminded of all manner of things that happen to be relevant to our understanding, and to our purposes in reading, at that particular time.

As a simple example, we are reminded of the appropriate meaning of the words (or we predict those meanings) in a sentence like *He wiped the tear from the child's eye,* but quite a different meaning in *He repaired the tear in the child's jacket.* Normally we would not even notice the word "tear" could have a different pronunciation and meaning than those that are appropriate for the context the word is in.

Of course, memory lets us down sometimes. We fail to remind ourselves to buy something at the store on the way home, or to make a telephone call that we had planned. Often there is an explanation of why we forget—we are distracted, or confused, or possibly we may not even want to remember and we somehow suppress the recall. If we fail to recall something it is usually not because we have suffered a permanent loss of memory. We just cannot get access for the moment (like the elusive word that stays on the wrong side of the tip of our tongue, but that we recognize the moment somebody mentions it). And sometimes memory is frustratingly difficult. Remembering becomes difficult when it is conscious, when we *contrive* deliberately to remember something that has not sprung to mind at once.

Easy and *difficult* remembering differ in the way they are invoked. Easy remembering occurs involuntarily, in the normal everyday course of events. Difficult remembering is the kind we engage in deliberately, because we "want" to remember something we have not conveniently reminded ourselves of, or because someone else wants us to remember something that is not part of our current frame of reference, our ongoing theory of the world. Remembering becomes difficult when we try to take charge of it "from the outside."

When we make a deliberate effort to remember something we are in a sense approaching it from the wrong end. Instead of allowing the memory to rise from the way the brain is currently making sense of the world, from the flow of thought, we try to dig down to it from the outside, where we have no frame of reference. Deliberate remembering is usually too contrived, too unrelated, to be successful. And the most deliberate and contrived efforts to manipulate memory occur when the control is in the hands of someone else— when we are *told* to bring something to mind. The worst conditions for memory are when someone else tells us precisely what we should remember.

Children do not need to be taught to use memory efficiently—to avoid overloading short-term memory and to refrain from forcing pointless detail into long-term memory. The way their brains are constructed prevents them from doing that. But reading instruction may make these natural efficiencies impossible. Anxiety while learning to read can force children into inefficient uses of memory. Reading, and therefore learning to read, depends on what you already know, on what you can make sense of. Reading teachers help to avoid overloading pupils' memories when they ensure that the material the children are expected to read makes sense to them, and then they are not required—

either by the material or by the instruction—to engage in extensive and point-less memorization.

SUMMARY

Short-term memory and **long-term memory** both have their limitations, but these are handicaps only to the readers who can make little sense of what they are doing in the first place. The differing characteristics of memory are summarized in Figure 5.3. When a reader can make sense of text, and does not strain to memorize, there is not even awareness of the bottlenecks of memory. Fluent readers are immediately **reminded** of what is relevant for their current situation and purposes.

	Short-term memory (working memory)	Long-term memory (permanent memory)
Capacity	limited	practically unlimited
Persistence	very brief	practically unlimited
Retrieval	immediate	depends on organization
Input	very fast	relatively slow

FIGURE 5.3.   Characteristics of short-term and long-term memory.

Notes to Chapter 5 begin on page 258, covering

Theories of memory
Chunking
Children's memory
Easy and difficult remembering

Chapter 6
LETTER IDENTIFICATION

The easiest route through complicated terrain may not be the most direct. Now that we are beginning an analysis of reading, an indirect approach is adopted. The point we are heading for is that fluent reading does not normally require the identification of individual letters or words, but the most convenient route to that point begins with a discussion of letter identification. Letter identification focuses on an aspect of reading where the issue can be concisely stated and specified: What is the process by which individuals who know the alphabet can discriminate and name any one of the 26 alternatives that is actually presented to them? I am talking about individual letters, not letters in sequences of any kind.

Unlike the reading of words, the question does not arise whether letters are read a bit at a time or all at once. Individual letters cannot be "sounded out" like words; their appearance has a purely arbitrary relationship to the way they are pronounced. And there can be little question about their meaning; we "comprehend" a letter when we can say its name, and that is that.

Yet despite this simplification, letter and word identification are alike in one important aspect—they both involve the discrimination and categorization of visual information. Later we shall see that the manner in which letters are identified may be of special relevance to an understanding of the identification of words.

Before we move ahead, a digression may be in order to explain the somewhat arbitrary use of the terms *identification* and *recognition* as labels for the process by which a letter or word (or meaning) is discriminated and allocated to a particular cognitive category. Dictionary definitions of the two words are tortuous but it is clear that they are not, strictly speaking, synonymous. *Identification* involves a decision that an object now confronted should be put into a particular category. There is no implication that the object being identified should have been met before. *Recognition,* on the other hand, literally means that the object now confronted has been seen before, although identification may not be involved. We *recognize* people when we know we have seen them before, whether or not we can put a name to them. We *identify* people when we put a name to them, whether or not we have met them before.

Experimental psychologists and reading specialists usually talk about letter and word *recognition,* but the use of the term seems doubly inappropriate. First, they would hardly consider a word to be recognized unless its name could be given; they would not consider that a child recognized a word if all the child could say about it was "That's the very same squiggle I couldn't read yesterday." Second, the skilled reader can very often attach a name to visual information that has never been met before. As a rather extreme case, do you "recognize" or "identify" the visual information *rEaDiNg* as the word "reading"? You almost certainly have never seen the word written that way before. The weight of evidence would seem to favor "identification," and the term is therefore used for formal purposes such as chapter headings. But having made a point of the distinction, we need not be dogmatic about it; "identify," "recognize," "categorize," "name," and even "read" will, in general, continue to be used interchangeably; it is the process we are concerned with at the moment, not the flexible way in which language is used.

It is, in fact, not strictly correct to refer to the visual information that the brain strives to identify on particular occasions as "letters"; this implies that the perceptual decision has already been made. Whether a particular mark on the page should be characterized as a letter depends on the intention of the perceiver (whether the reader or the writer). As we have seen, IO may be identified as two letters or two numbers. Prior to an identification decision, the visual information that is IO is merely a pattern of contrasting ink marks on paper, more precisely referred to as a *visual configuration,* a *visual array,* or even a *visual stimulus.*

THEORIES OF PATTERN RECOGNITION

Letter identification is a special problem within the broader theoretical area of *pattern recognition*—the process by which any two visual configurations are "cognized" to be the same. The process of recognition is of classical philosophical concern because it has been realized for over 2,000 years that no two events are ever exactly the same; the world is always in flux, and we never see an object twice in exactly the same form, from the same angle, in the same light, or with the same eye. A topic of very general interest to psychology is what exactly determines whether two objects or events shall be considered to be equivalent. The equivalence decision clearly rests with the perceiver and not in any property of the visual array. Are *J* and *ʃ* the same? Many might say yes, but a printer would say no. Are two automobiles of the same year, model, and color identical? Possibly to everyone except their owners. *It is the perceiver, not the object, that determines equivalence.* We organize our lives and our knowledge by deciding that some things should be treated as equivalent—these are the things that we put into the same category—and some as different. Those differences between objects or events that help us to place them in category systems may be called by a variety of names, such as *defining attributes* or *criterial attributes* or *criterial properties;* in essence, they are the differences that we choose to make *significant.* The differences that we choose to ignore, the ones that do not influence our decision, are often not noticed at all. Obviously it is more efficient to pay attention only to significant differences, particularly in view of the limited information-processing capacity of the human brain. It is, therefore, hardly surprising that we may overlook differences that we are not looking for in the first place, like the sudden absence of our friend's beard, or the pattern of his tie, or the misspelling in the newspaper headline. Human beings owe their preeminent position in the intellectual hierarchy of living organisms not so much to their ability to perceive the world in many different ways as their capacity to perceive things as the same according to criteria that they themselves establish, selectively ignoring what might be termed *differences that do not make a difference.* The intellectual giant is not the one who recognizes every individual animal in the zoological gardens, but the one who can look past the individual differences and group them into "equivalent" species and families on a more abstract and systematic basis.

The process that determines how particular letters or words are treated as equivalent has become a focus of theoretical attention because of its particular application to computer technology. There is an obvious economic as well as theoretical interest in designing computers that might be able to read. The construction of a computer with any fluent degree of reading ability is currently impossible for a number of reasons, one of which is that not enough is known about language to give a computer the necessary basic information. Language can be understood only if there is an underlying understanding of the topic to which the language happens to refer, and the ability of computers to "understand" any topic is very limited indeed. Computers can copy letters, and they can compare one letter with another. But it has not proved feasible to provide a computer with rules for identifying letters, let alone words or meanings, with anything like the facility with which humans can identify them. If we consider the problems of pattern recognition from the computer point of view, we may get some insights into what must be involved in the human skill.

There are two basic ways in which a computer might be constructed to recognize patterns, whether numbers, letters, words, texts, photographs, fingerprints, voiceprints, signatures, diagrams, maps, or real objects. The two ways are essentially those that appear to be open theoretically to account for the recognition of patterns by humans. The alternatives may be called *template matching* and *feature analysis,* and the best way to describe them is to imagine trying to build a computer capable of reading the 26 letters of the alphabet.

For both our models, for the template matching and the feature analytic devices, the ground rules have to be the same. We consider the computer to be equipped with exactly the same "input" and "output" mechanisms as a person. At the input end is an optical system or "eye" to examine visual information, and at the output end is a set of 26 alternative responses, the names of each of the letters of the alphabet. The aim, of course, is to construct a system between the input and output mechanisms to insure that when the visual array E is presented at the input end, "E" will be indicated by the output.

Template Matching

For a template-matching device, a series of internal representations must be constructed to be, in effect, a reference library for the letters that the device is required to identify. We might start with one internal representation, or "template," for each letter of the alphabet. Each template is directly connected with the appropriate response, while between the eye and the templates we shall put a "comparator" or matching mechanism capable of comparing any input letter with all of the set of templates. Any letter that comes into the computer's field of view will be internalized and compared with each of the templates, at least until a match is made. Upon "matching" the input with a template, the computer will perform the response associated with that particular template and the identification will be complete.

There are obvious limitations to such a system. If the computer is given a template for the representation A , what will it do if confronted with A or A not to mention H or even H or A ? Of course, some flexibility can be built into the system. Inputs can be "normalized" to iron out some of the variability; they can be scaled down to a standard size, adjusted into a particular orientation, have crooked lines straightened, small gaps filled, and minor excrescences removed; in short, a number of things can be done to increase the probability that the computer will not respond "I don't know" but will instead match an input to a template. But, unfortunately, the greater the likelihood that the computer will make a match, the greater the probability that it will make a mistake. This is the "signal detection" problem of Chapter 3. A computer that can "normalize" A to make it look like the template A will be likely to do the same with 4 and H. The only remedy will be to keep adding templates to try to accommodate all the different styles and types of lettering the device might meet. Even then, such a computer will be unable to make use of all the supporting knowledge that human beings have; it will be quite capable of reading the word HOT as AOT because it does not have any "common sense" to apply in the elimination of alternatives.

Critical limitations of template-matching systems, for both computer and human, lie in their relative inefficiency and costliness. A single set of templates, one for each category, is highly restricted in the number of inputs that it can match, but every increase in the number of templates adds considerably to the size, expense, and complexity of the system. The template-matching model does work, but the system copes with the diversity of input representations by cheating its way around the problem. Instead of providing the computer with templates to meet many different styles of character, it makes sure the computer eye meets only one style, like the "bankers' numbers" $5\ 2l0L$ that are printed on our checks.

Feature Analysis

The alternative method of pattern perception, *feature analysis*, dispenses with internal representations completely. There is no question of attempting to match the input with anything, but instead a series of tests is made on the input. The results of each test eliminate a number of alternatives until, finally, all uncertainty is reduced and identification is achieved. The "features" are properties of the visual array that are subjected to tests to determine which alternative responses should be eliminated. Decisions about which alternatives each test will eliminate are made by the perceivers (or computer programmers) themselves.

To clarify the explanation, let us again imagine constructing a computer for the identification of letters, this time using feature analysis. Remember, the problem is essentially one of using rules to decide into which of a limited number of categories might a very large number of alternative events be placed. In other words this is a matter of establishing equivalences.

At the receptor end of the system, where the computer has its light-sensitive optical scanner, we establish a set of "feature analyzers." A feature analyzer is a specialized kind of detector that looks for—is sensitive to—just one kind of feature in the visual information, and which passes just one kind of report back. For the sake of illustration, we might imagine that each analyzer looks for a particular "distinctive feature" by asking a question; one analyzer asks "Is the configuration curved?" (like C or O); another asks "Is it closed?" (like O or P); a third asks "Is it symmetrical?" (like A or W), and a fourth asks "Is there an intersection?" (as in T or K). Every analyzer is, in fact, a test, and the message it sends back is binary—either "yes" or "no," signal or no signal. Without looking too closely at the question of what constitutes a distinctive feature, we can say it is a property of visual information that can be used to differentiate some visual configurations from others. By definition, a distinctive feature must be common to more than one object or event, otherwise it could not be used to put more than one into the same category. But, on the other hand, if the feature were present in all objects or events, then we could not use it to segregate them into different categories; it would not be "distinctive." In other words, a feature, if detected, permits the elimination of some of the alternative categories into which a stimulus might be allocated.

As an example, a "no" answer to the test "Is the configuration curved?" would eliminate rounded letters such as a, b, c, d, but not other letters such as i, k, l, v, w, x, z. A "yes" answer to "Is it closed?" would eliminate open letters such as c, f, w, but not b, d, or o. The question about symmetry would distinguish letters like m, o, w, and v, from d, f, k, r. Different questions eliminate different alternatives, and relatively few tests would be required to distinguish among 26 alternatives in an alphabet. In fact, if all tests eliminated about half of the alternatives, and there was no test that overlapped with any other, only five questions would be needed to identify any letter. (The logic of the previous statement is set out in the discussion of information theory in the Notes.) No one would actually suggest that as few as five tests are employed to distinguish among 26 letters, but it is reasonable to assume that there need be many fewer tests than categories—that is one of the great economic advantages of a feature-analytic system.

With an input bank of say ten or a dozen feature analyzers built into the letter-identification device, a link has to be provided to the 26 responses or output categories; "decision rules" must be devised so that the results of the individual tests are integrated and associated with the appropriate letter names. The most convenient way to set up the rules is to establish a feature list for each category, that is, for each of the 26 letters. The construction of the feature lists is the same for every category, namely a listing of the analyzers that were set up to examine the visual configuration. The feature list for every category also indicates whether each particular analyzer should send back a "yes" or "no" signal for that category. For the category c, for example, the feature list should specify a "yes" for the "curved?" analyzer, a "no" for the "closed?" analyzer, a "no" for the "symmetrical?" analyzer, and so forth. Feature lists for a couple of the categories might be conceptualized as looking like Table 6.1 (The "+" sign indicates "yes.") Obviously, every category would be associated with a different feature list pattern, each pattern providing a specification for a single category.

TABLE 6.1.
Feature Lists for Letters

Category "A"	Category "B"
Test 1 −	Test 1 +
2 +	2 +
3 +	3 −
4 +	4 +
5 −	5 +
6 +	6 −
7 −	7 −
8 −	8 −
9 +	9 +
10 −	10 +

The actual wiring of the letter-identification device presents no problems—every feature analyzer is connected to every category that lists a "yes" signal from it, and we arrange that a categorizing decision (an "identification") is made only when "yes" signals are received for all the analyzers listed positively on a category's feature list. In a sense, a feature list is a *specification* of what the characteristics of a particular letter should be. *Descriptions* of a letter that is being looked at—the input—are compared with specifications of what the letter might be until a match is found.

And that, in a simplified and schematic form, is a feature-analytic letter-identification device. The system is powerful, in the sense that it will do a lot of work with a minimum of effort. Unlike the template model, which to be versatile requires many templates for every decision that it might make together with complex normalizing devices, the feature-analytic device demands only a very small number of analyzers compared with the number of decisions it makes. Theoretically, such a device could decide among over a million alternatives with only "20 questions."

Functional Equivalence and Criterial Sets

A considerable advantage of the feature-analytic model over template matching is that the former has very much less trouble in adjusting to inputs that ought to be allocated to the same category but which vary in size or orientation or detail, for example, A, *A*, x, *A*, and *H*. The types of tests that feature analyzers apply are far better able to cope with distortion and "noise" than any device that requires an approximate match. But far more important, very little is added in the way of complexity or cost to provide one or more alternative feature lists for every category. With such a flexibility, the system can easily allocate not only the examples already given, but also forms as divergent as *a* and *a* to the category "A." The set of alternative feature lists for a single letter response might then look something like Table 6.2. The only adjustment that need be made to the battery of analyzers is in wiring additional connections between them and the categories where the feature lists require positive tests, so that an identification will be made on any occasion when the specifications of any of the alternative lists are satisfied.

TABLE 6.2.
Functionally Equivalent Feature Lists

Category "A"			
Test 1	−	+	+
2	+	+	+
3	+	−	−
4	+	−	+
5	−	+	−
6	+	−	+
7	−	−	+
8	−	+	−
9	+	+	−
10	−	−	+

I shall call any set of features that meet the specifications of a particular category a *criterial set*. With the type of feature-analytic device being outlined, more than one criterial set of features may exist for any one category. Obviously, the more criterial sets that exist for a given device, the more efficient that device will be in making accurate identifications.

It is also useful to give a special name to the alternative criterial sets of features that specify the same category—we shall say that they are *functionally equivalent*. *A*, *a*, and *a* are functionally equivalent for our imagined device because they are all treated as being the same as far as the category "A" is concerned. Of course, the configurations are not functionally equivalent if they are to be distinguished on a basis other than their membership of the alphabet; a printer, for example, might want them categorized into type styles. But as I pointed out earlier, it is the prerogative of the perceiver, not a characteristic of the visual information, to decide which differences shall be significant— which sets of features shall be criterial—in the establishment of equivalences. Functional equivalence can be determined by any systematic or arbitrary method that the pattern recognizer follows. All that is required to establish functional equivalence for quite disparate visual configurations is alternative feature lists for the same category.

Another powerful aspect of the feature-analytic model of pattern recognition is that it can work on a flexible and probabilistic basis. If a single feature list specifies the outcomes of ten analyzer tests for the categorical identification of a letter of the alphabet, a considerable amount of redundant information must be involved. Redundancy, as I noted in Chapter 3, exists when the same information is available from more than one source, or when more information is available than is required to reduce the actual amount of uncertainty. Ten analyzer tests could provide enough information to select from over a thousand equally probable alternatives, and if there are only 26 alternatives, information from five of those tests could be dispensed with and there might still be enough data to make the appropriate identification. Even if analyzer information were insufficient to enable an absolutely certain selection between two or three remaining alternatives, it might still be possible to decide which of the alternatives is more likely, given the particular pattern of features that is discriminated. By not demanding that *all* the specifications of a particular feature list be satisfied before a category identification is made, the system can greatly increase its repertoire of functionally equivalent criterial sets of features. Such an increase significantly enhances the efficiency of the device at a cost of little extra complexity.

The fact that different criterial sets can be established within a single feature list provides an advantage that was alluded to in the previous paragraph—a feature-analytic system can make use of *redundancy*. Let us say that the system already "knows" from some other source of information that the configuration it is presented with is a vowel; it has perhaps already identified the letters *THR* . . . and it has been programmed with some basic knowledge of the spelling patterns of English. The device can then exclude from consideration for the fourth letter all those feature lists that specify consonant categories, leaving considerably reduced criterial sets for selection among the remaining alternatives. (Three tests might easily distinguish among five or six vowels.)

A final powerful advantage of the feature-analytic model has also already been implied; it is a device that can easily *learn*. Every time a new feature list or criterial set is established is an instance of learning. All that the device requires in order to learn is *feedback* from the environment. It establishes, or rejects, a new feature list for a particular category (or category for a particular feature list) by "hypothesizing" a relationship between a feature list and a category and testing whether that relationship is, in fact, appropriate.

You may have noticed that the feature-analytic discussion develops easily into such topics as "learning" and "thinking." It is evident that the more efficient and sophisticated we make our imaginary letter-identifying device, the more we are likely to talk about its realization in human rather than computer terms. It is time for the computer analogy to be discarded and to direct a more specific focus on the human pattern recognizer.

The Human Letter Identifier

The analogy is discarded; I intend to use feature analysis as a model for the process by which letters are identified by readers. We learn to identify the letters of the alphabet by establishing feature lists for the required 26 categories, each of which is interrelated to a single name "A," "B," "C," and so forth. The visual system is equipped with analyzers that respond to those features in the visual environment that are distinctive for alphabetic discriminations (and many other visual discriminations as well). The results of the analyzer tests are integrated and directed to the appropriate feature lists so that letter identifications can occur. The human visual perceptual system is biologically competent to demonstrate all the most powerful aspects of the feature-analytic model outlined in the last section—to establish manifold criterial sets of features with functional equivalence, to function probabilistically, to make use of redundancy, and to learn by testing hypotheses and receiving feedback.

Two aspects of letter identification can be distinguished. The first aspect is the establishment of categories themselves and especially the allocation of category names to them, such as "A," "B," "C." The second aspect of letter identification is the allocation of visual configurations to various cognitive categories—the discrimination of various configurations as different, as not functionally equivalent. The greater part of perceptual learning involves finding out what exactly are the distinctive features by which various configurations should be categorized as different from each other, and what are the sets of features that are criterial for particular categories. These are precisely the two aspects of object or concept learning involved in distinguishing one face from another, or cats from dogs. Categories must be established with unique names (like "cat" and "dog"), and rules must be devised for allocating particular instances to the appropriate categories.

To distinguish the two aspects of letter identification, we must ask how new categories might be established and associated with a particular response, such as the name of a letter of the alphabet. The first point to be made is that the association of a name with a category is neither necessary nor primary in the discrimination process. It is quite possible to segregate visual configurations into different categories without having a name for them. We can see that *A* and & are different, and know they should be treated differently, even though we may not have a category name, or even a specific category, for &. In fact, we cannot allocate a name to & unless first we acquire some rules for discriminating it from *A* and from every other visual configuration with which it should not be given functional equivalence. We will not learn a name for & if we cannot distinguish that particular visual configuration from *A*. The motivation for the establishment of a new category may come from either direction: either a configuration such as & cannot be related to any existing category, or a new name such as "ampersand" cannot be related to an existing category. The intermediate steps that tie the entire system together are the establishment of the first feature lists and criterial sets for the category so that the appropriate feature tests and the category name can be related.

Not only is the relating of a name to a category not primary; it is not difficult. The complicated part of learning to make an identification is not in remembering the name of a particular category but in discovering the criterial sets of features for that category. Children at the age when they are often learning to read are also learning hundreds of new names for objects every year—names of friends and public figures and automobiles and animals—as well as the names of letters and words. The person they learn from, the informal instructor, usually points to an object and says "That is an 'X,'" in effect, leaving the child with the problem. The instructor rarely tries to explain the "X"; it is left for the child to work out what the significant differences must be. The complicated part of learning is the establishment of functional equivalences for the categories with which names are associated.

The reason that "learning names" is frequently thought to be difficult is that the intermediate steps are ignored and it is assumed that a name is applied directly to a particular visual configuration. Of course, children may find it difficult to respond with the right name for the letters *b* or *d* (or for the words *house* and *mouse,* or for an actual dog or cat) but this is not because they cannot put the name to the configuration—that is not the way the visual system works. Their basic problem is to find out how two alternatives are significantly different. Once they can make the discrimination, so that the appropriate functional equivalences are observed, the allocation of the correct verbal label is a relatively easy problem because the label is related directly to the category.

The Letter Identifier in Action

We have come to the final question of the present chapter: Is there evidence to support the feature-analytic model of the human visual system? Some of the physiological evidence has already been indicated. There is no one-to-one correspondence between the visual information impinging on the eye and anything that goes on behind the eyeball. The eye does not send "images" back to the brain; the stammering pattern of neural impulses is a representation of discrete features detected by the eye, not the transfer of a "picture." In the brain itself, there is no way of storing a set of templates or even acquiring them in the first place. The brain does not deal in veridical representations; it organizes knowledge and behavior by shunting abstract information through its complex neural networks. It is true that one aspect of the brain's output, our subjective experience of the world, is generated in the form of "percepts" that might be regarded as pictures, but this experience is the consequence of the brain's activity, not something the brain "stores" and compares with inputs. Our visual experience is the product of the perceptual system, not part of the process.

Now we can examine evidence for the feature-analytic model from two kinds of letter-identification experiments. (Details are given in the Notes at the end of the book.) The basic assumption to be tested is that letters are actually conglomerates of features, of which there are perhaps a dozen different kinds. The only way in which letters can differ physically from each other is in the presence or absence of each of these features. Letters that have several features in common will be very similar, while letters that are constructed of quite different feature combinations will be quite dissimilar in appearance. How does one assess "similarity"? Letters are similar—they are presumed to share many features—if they are frequently confused with each other. And letters that are rarely confused with each other are assumed to have very few features in common.

Of course, we do not very often confuse letters, and when we do the character of the error is usually influenced by nonvisual factors. We might, for example, think that the fourth letter in the sequence *REQF*. . . is a *U* not because *F* and *U* are visually similar but because we normally expect a *U* to follow *Q*. However, large numbers of visual letter confusions can be generated by experimental techniques in which the stimulus letter is so "impoverished" that viewers cannot see it clearly, although they are forced to make a guess about what the letter probably is. In other words, the experimental subjects must make letter-identification decisions on minimal visual information. The experimental assumption is that viewers who cannot see the stimulus clearly must lack some vital information and thus be unable to make some feature tests. And if they are unable to make certain feature tests, then the tests they are able to make will not reduce all uncertainty about the 26 alternative responses. Viewers will still be left in doubt about a few possibilities that can be differentiated only by the tests that they have been unable to perform.

The actual method of impoverishing the stimulus is not important. The presentation may be a tachistoscopic brief presentation, or it may involve a stimulus that has very little contrast with its surroundings, projected by a lamp at a very low intensity, or printed on a page under several layers of tissue paper, or hidden behind a lot of visual noise, like ⍥ . As soon as viewers start making "errors," one can assume that they are not getting all the information that they need to make an identification. They are deciding on something less than a criterial set of features.

On the face of it, there are only two possibilities if viewers are forced to identify a letter on insufficient information; either their guesses will be completely random, or they will respond in some systematic way. If guesses are random, there can be no prediction of what the answer will be; they will be just as likely to respond with any of the 26 letters of the alphabet, whatever the letter that is presented. If we examine the record of "confusions," the occasions when a letter is reported incorrectly, we should find that each of the other 25 letters is represented about equally often. But if responses are systematic, there are two possibilities, both of which limit considerably the number of confusions likely to occur. One possibility, which is not very interesting, is that the viewers will always say the same thing if they cannot distinguish a letter; one might say "That's a 'k'," for example, whenever there is uncertainty. Fortunately, such a bias is easy to detect. The other and more interesting possibility is that the viewers will select only from those alternative responses that remain after the features that can be discriminated in the presentation have been taken into account. In such a circumstance, it is to be expected that the confusions will "cluster"; instead of 25 types of confusion, one for each of the possible erroneous responses, there will be only a few types.

The evidence can be summarized in a few words: Letter confusions fall into tightly packed clusters, and over two-thirds of the confusions for most letters can be accounted for by three or four confusion types. If a subject makes a mistake in identifying a letter, the nature of the erroneous response is highly predictable. Typical confusion clusters can be very suggestive about the kind of information the eye must be looking for in discriminating letters. Some typical confusion clusters are *(a, e, n, o, u)*, *(t, f, i)*, and *(h, m, n)* (Dunn-Rankin, 1968).

The specific conclusion to be drawn from the kind of experiment just described is that letters are indeed composed of a relatively small number of features. Letters that are easily confused, like *a* and *e*, or *t* and *f*, must have a number of features in common, and those that are rarely confused like *o* and w, or *d* and *y*, must have few if any features in common. The general conclusion that may be drawn is that the visual system is indeed feature-analytic. Letter identification is accomplished by the eye examining the visual environment for featural information that will eliminate all alternatives except one, thus permitting an accurate identification to be made.

There is a second line of experimental evidence supporting the view that letters are arrangements of smaller elements, and this is related to the fact that recognition is faster or easier when there are fewer alternatives for what each letter might be. The classic example of such evidence has already been described in the "tunnel vision" demonstration of Chapter 4, where it was shown that nonvisual information can be employed to reduce the amount of visual—or distinctive feature—information required to identify letters. There are other illustrations when the identification of words is considered in the next chapter.

WHAT IS A FEATURE?

The entire discussion of letter identification by feature analysis has been conducted without actually specifying what a feature is. The omission has been deliberate, because nobody knows what the distinctive features of letters are. Not enough is known about the structure of the human visual system to say exactly what is the featural information that the system looks for.

Of course, general statements about features can be made. There have been a number of attempts to do this, with statements like "The only difference between *c* and *o* is 'closed'; therefore, being closed must be a distinctive feature" or "The only difference between *h* and *n* is the 'ascender' at the top of *h;* therefore, an ascender must be a distinctive feature." This kind of deductive reasoning is quite illuminating, and it is true that one can make predictions about which pairs of letters might be confused on the basis of such analyses. But such features are proposed on the basis of logic, not of evidence, because we really do not know whether, or how, the eye might look for "closedness" or for "ascenders." It can be argued that these hypothesized features are really properties of whole letters, that we actually cannot tell whether something is closed or has an ascender until we see the letter as a whole, and it is far from clear how a property of the whole could also be an element out of which the whole is constructed. It is obviously a reasonable assertion that the significant difference between *h* and *n* has something to do with the ascender, but is an oversimplification to say that the ascender is the actual feature.

Another good reason for avoiding the specific question of what the features are is that one always has to make the qualification "It depends." The significant difference between *A* and *B* is not the same as the significant difference between *a* and *b*. In fact, one cannot predict what letters will be confused in an identification experiment unless one knows the typeface that is being used and whether the letters are upper or lowercase.

Fortunately, it is not necessary to know exactly what the features are in order to learn something about the identification process or to assist a child in discriminating letters. We can trust the child to locate the information required provided the appropriate informational environment is available. The appropriate informational environment is the opportunity to make comparisons and discover what the significant differences are. Remember, the primary problem of identification is to distinguish the presented configuration from all those to which it might be equivalent but is not; the configuration has to be subjected to feature analysis and put in the appropriate category. Presenting *h* to children 50 times and telling them it is "h" because it has an ascender will not help them to discriminate the letter. The presentation of *h* and other letters in pairs and groups, together with the feedback that they are *not* functionally equivalent, is the kind of information required for the visual system and brain to find out very quickly what the distinctive features really are.

SUMMARY

A feature identification model is proposed for letter identification. **Feature lists** are established to permit the allocation of visual information to specific cognitive categories, in the present case for letters. Feature lists are **specifications** of what visual information has to be like in order to be allocated to a particular category. The names of letters (and their relationships to sounds) are part of the interrelations among categories; they are not directly associated with particular visual configurations. To permit the identification of the same letter when it has different configurations, e.g., A, *a* , and *a* , **functionally equivalent** feature lists are established. For each feature list there will be a number of alternative **criterial sets** to permit identification decisions on a minimum of visual information, depending on the number and nature of the alternatives.

Notes to Chapter 6 begin on page 264, covering

Recognition versus identification
Theories of pattern recognition
Making letter identification easier

Chapter 7
WORD
IDENTIFICATION

The first chapter specifically concerned with reading was devoted to letter identification. In this chapter I show that word identification does not require the prior identification of letters. The present chapter is restricted to considering individual or unrelated words in isolation, where there is no extrinsic clue to their identity. I am still not focusing on anything which might normally be regarded as *reading*, where a meaningful purpose and context are involved. But this chapter is another step toward a demonstration that procedures permitting the identification of words without the prior identification of letters also permit comprehension without the prior identification of words.

THREE THEORIES OF WORD IDENTIFICATION

There are three broad classes of theory about word identification: whole word identification, letter-by-letter identification, and an intermediate position involving the identification of letter clusters, usually "spelling patterns." In effect, these three views represent three attempts to describe the manner in which a skilled reader is able to identify words on sight. They are accounts of what a reader needs to know and do in order to be able to say what a word is. One or another of the three views is apparent in practically every current approach to reading instruction.

116

Each of these traditional approaches to word recognition leaves more questions unanswered than it resolves. Nevertheless, each contains a kernel of truth about reading, otherwise it could not have survived to achieve a place in the folklore of the subject. In the following paragraphs I look a little more closely at which aspects of reading each theory appears particularly competent to illuminate and which aspects it leaves in the dark.

The *whole-word* view is based on the premise that readers do not stop to identify individual letters (or groups of letters) in the identification of a word. The view asserts that knowledge of the alphabet and of the "sounds of letters" is irrelevant to reading (although there is frequently a failure to indicate whether this stricture applies to fluent reading alone or to learning to read as well). One incontrovertible source of support for the whole-word view has already been alluded to—the fact that a viewer can report from a single tachistoscopic presentation either four or five random letters or a similar number of words. Surely if a word can be identified as easily as a letter, then it must be just as much of a unit as a letter; a word must be recognizable as a whole, rather than as a sequence of letters. Another unimpeachable piece of supporting evidence is that words may be identified when none of their component letters is clearly discriminable. For example, a name may be identifiable on a distant roadside sign, or in a dim light, under conditions that would make each individual letter of that name quite illegible if presented separately. If words can be read when letters are illegible, how can word recognition depend on letter identification? Finally, there is a good deal of evidence that words can be identified as quickly as letters. It has been shown that perception is far from instantaneous, and that successively presented random letters—or random words—cannot be identified faster than five or six a second (Kolers & Katzman, 1966; Newman, 1966). And if entire words can be identified as quickly as letters, how can their identification involve spelling them out letter by letter?

So much for some of the arguments in support of the whole-word point of view; now we can give equal time to the counterposition that, as a theory, it is most inadequate. One fundamental objection is that the view is not a theory at all; it has no "explanatory power" but merely rephrases the question that it pretends to answer. If words are recognized "as wholes," how are the wholes recognized? What do readers look for, and in what way is their prior knowledge of what a word looks like stored? It is no answer to say they have already learned what every word looks like, because that is the basic question: What exactly do readers know if they know what a word looks like? The qualification that words are identified "by their shapes" merely changes the name of the problem from "word identification" to "shape identification." Fluent readers are able to recognize at least 50,000 different words on sight (see Notes)—by what I shall call *immediate word identification*. Does that mean that readers have pictures of 50,000 different shapes stored in their minds, and that for every word they encounter in reading they rummage through a pack of 50,000 templates in order to find a match? In what way would they sort through 50,000 alternatives? Surely not by starting at the beginning and examining each internal representation until they find a match. If we are looking for a book in a library, we do not start at the entrance and examine every volume until we come across the one with a title that matches the title we are looking for. Instead we make use of the fact that books are categorized and shelved in a systematic way; there are "rules" for getting to the book we want. It would appear reasonable to suggest that word identification is also systematic, and that we make use of rules that enable us to make our decision quickly. We can usually find some explanation for any error that we make. We may misread *said* as "sail" or "send" (or even as "reported" in circumstances where the substitution would make sense), but never as "elephant" or "plug" or "predisposition." In other words, we obviously do not select a word from 50,000 alternatives, but rather from a much smaller number. An unelaborated whole-word point of view cannot account for this prior elimination of alternatives.

Besides, we have already discovered that 50,000 internal representations of shapes would be far from adequate to enable us to identify 50,000 different words. Even if we could identify *HAT* by looking up an internal representation, how could the same representation enable us to identify *hat* or *hat* or any of the many other ways in which the word may be written?

The *letter-by-letter* theory, which the whole-word view is supposed to demolish, itself appears to have quite substantial evidence in its favor. Readers are frequently sensitive to individual letters in the identification of words. The whole-word point of view would suggest that if viewers were presented with the stimulus *fashixn* tachistoscopically, they would either identify "the whole word" without noticing the *x*, or else fail to recognize the word at all because there would be no "match" with an internal representation. Instead, viewers typically identify the word but report that there is something wrong with it, not necessarily reporting that there is an *x* instead of an *o*, but offering such explanations as "There's a hair lying over the end of it" (Pillsbury, 1897).

Furthermore, readers are very sensitive to the *predictability* of letter sequences. Letters do not occur haphazardly in any language; in English, for example, combinations like *th*, *st*, *br*, and almost any consonant and vowel pair are more likely to occur than combinations like *tf*, *sr*, *bm*, *ae*, or *uo*. The knowledge that readers acquire about these differing probabilities of letter combinations is demonstrated when words containing common letter sequences are more easily identified than those with uncommon sequences. Readers can identify sequences of letters that are *not* English words just as easily as some English words, provided the sequences are "close approximations" to English—which means that they are highly probable letter combinations (Miller, Bruner, & Postman, 1954). The average reader, for example, hardly falters when presented with sequences like *vernalit* or *mossiant* or *ricaning*—yet how could these be identified "as wholes" when they have never been seen before? A letter-by-letter view might also seem to be somewhat more economical; instead of learning to recognize 50,000 words, one learns to recognize 26 letters and applies a few spelling rules, decoding every word on the spot.

A rather illogical argument is sometimes proposed to support the letter-by-letter view. In its most extreme form, this view seems to imply that because letters in some way spell out the sound of a word, therefore word identification *must* be accomplished by sounding out the individual letters. It would be about as compelling to suggest that we must recognize cars by reading the manufacturer's name on the back, simply because the name is always there to be read. Besides, the spelling of words is not a reliable guide to their sound. This question is so complex that "phonics" is given the next chapter to itself. For the moment we are not concerned with whether knowledge of letters can be used to identify words, but rather whether skilled readers normally and necessarily identify words "that they know" by a letter-by-letter analysis.

The intermediate position—that words are identified through the recognition of *clusters of letters*—has the advantage of being able to account for the relatively easy identifiability of nonwords such as *vernalit*. It argues that readers become familiar with spelling patterns, such as *ve* and *rn* and even *vern*, which are recognized and put together to form words. The larger the spelling patterns we can recognize, the easier the word identification, according to this view. The view is compatible with our normal experience that when a new word like *zygotic* or *Helsingfors* halts our reading temporarily we do not seem to break it down to the individual letters before trying to put together what its sound must be. But many of the arguments that favor the whole-word position over letter analysis also work against the letter-cluster view. It may be useful, occasionally, to work out what a word is by analysis of letters or syllables, but normal reading does not appear to proceed on this basis; in fact, it would seem impossible. There is no time to "work out" what words are by synthesizing possible sound combinations. Besides, as the letter-cluster argument is pushed to its extreme it becomes a whole-word approach since the largest and most reliable spelling patterns are words themselves.

The fact that the three traditional theories of word recognition continue to enjoy a wide acceptance obviously indicates that they rest on a fairly solid foundation of data, despite their shortcomings. No one can conclusively prove them wrong. Each approach, however, has inadequacies that are partly met by an alternative view, which would suggest that they are not mutually exclusive and that no one of them has any real claim to be the closest representation of the truth. In their place we need to find a theory of reading that will not be incompatible with any of the data, but that will also offer an explanation for inadequate aspects of the three traditional views. In short, any serious attempt to understand reading must be able to explain why it might sometimes appear that words are identified as wholes and at other times through the identification of component letters or groups of letters.

A Feature-Analytic Alternative

There is another point of view that would appear to overcome the major weaknesses of the three traditional theories without being incompatible with any of the evidence in their favor. Such a theory proposes that words are indeed identified "as wholes," but that the manner of their identification involves precisely the same procedures as the identification of letters, and in fact makes use of the same kind of visual information.

In the previous chapter, two models for letter identification were examined: feature analysis and template matching. The traditional whole-word theory that words are identified because of the familiarity of their "shape" is essentially a template-matching model, and arguments for its inadequacy have already been presented. The remainder of the present chapter considers the alternative, a feature-analytic model for word identification. It should be reiterated that the present chapter is concerned only with the *identification of individual words*, of words actually in isolation or effectively so because context is ignored. The identification of words in meaningful sequences—which is of course more representative of most reading situations—is considered in Chapter 9.

Basically, the feature-analytic model proposes that the only difference between the manner in which letters and words are identified lies in the categories and feature lists that the perceiver employs in the analysis of visual information. The difference depends on whether the reader is looking for letters or for words; the process of looking and deciding is the same. If the reader's objective is to identify letters, then the analysis of the visual configuration is carried out with respect to the feature lists associated with the 26 letter categories, one for each letter of the alphabet. If the objective is to identify words, then there is a similar analysis of features in the visual configuration with respect to the feature lists, or specifications, of a larger number of word categories.

What are the features of words? They obviously must include the features of letters, because words are made up of letters. The arrays of marks on the printed page that can be read as words can also be distinguished as sequences of letters, so the "distinctive features" of letters that constitute a significant difference between one configuration and another must also be distinctive features of words. For example, whatever visual information permits the brain to distinguish between *h* an *n* must also permit it to distinguish between *hot* and *not*. And precisely the same procedures that distinguish between *h* and *n* will accomplish the discrimination between *hot* and *not*. At first glance, many more discriminations and analyses of distinctive features would appear to be required to distinguish among tens of thousands of alternative words compared with only 26 alternative letters, but we shall see that the difference is not so great. In fact no more information—no more featural tests—may be required to identify a word in meaningful text than to identify a single letter in isolation.

If the distinctive features of the visual configurations of letters are the same as those for visual configurations of words, it might be expected that feature lists for letter and word categories would be similar. However, feature lists for word categories require an additional dimension to those for letters in that the analysis of word configurations involves *the position of features within a sequence*. The following examples, imaginary and quite arbitrary, compare four feature lists—two functionally equivalent lists for *H* and *h* in the letter category "h," and two functionally equivalent lists for the alternative forms *HORSE* and *horse* in the word category "horse." Each "test" represents information that could be received from an analyzer in the visual system about whether a particular feature is or is not present in the configuration being examined, and each + or − indicates whether a feature should or should not be present if the configuration is to be allocated to that particular category (see Table 7.1).

TABLE 7.1.
Feature Lists for Letters and Words

	Letter Category "H"		Word Category "Horse"									
	"H" Feature List	"h" Feature List	"HORSE" Feature List					"horse" Feature List				
			Position					Position				
			1	2	3	4	5	1	2	3	4	5
Tests 1	+	−	+	+	−	+	−	−	+	−	−	+
2	+	+	+	−	−	+	+	+	−	+	+	−
3	−	−	−	+	−	+	−	−	−	+	−	+
4	+	−	+	−	+	+	+	−	+	−	−	−
5	−	+	−	+	+	−	−	+	+	−	+	+
6	−	+	−	+	−	+	+	+	−	+	+	−
7	+	+	+	−	−	−	+	+	−	−	+	+
8	−	−	−	+	−	+	+	−	+	−	−	+
9	−	+	−	−	+	+	−	+	−	+	−	−
10	+	+	+	+	+	−	+	+	+	−	−	+

The number of "positions" in a word feature list indicates the number of times a particular feature could occur in the letter sequence that constitutes the word and obviously corresponds to the number of letters. Similarly, a feature test that will be applied only once for the identification of a letter may be employed several times in the identification of a word, the maximum number of tests depending on the number of letters in the word. A feature list for a word could, therefore, also be regarded as a set of specifications for its component letters, as in Table 7.1, where the features for the first position of *horse* are the same as the features for the letter *h*. This congruence between "position" and "letter" lists is inevitable because distinctive features of letters are also distinctive features of words, but it does not follow that letters must be identified in order for words to be identified. The term "position" is employed rather than "letter" to avoid any implication that a word is identified by its letters, rather than by the distribution of features across its entire configuration. A number of arguments are presented to show that the fact that feature test specifications for positions and letters might be identical is irrelevant to word identification.

(It should be added that there could be a few distinctive features of words that are not features of letters—for example, the relative height of different parts of the configuration or its length. As I have already noted, not enough is known of the visual system to assert what distinctive features actually are. The present discussion is restricted to presenting the view that words can be identified without the intervening identification of letters and does not claim to make precise statements about the actual features of letters or words.)

The feature-analytic view of *letter* identification asserts that because there is redundancy in the structure of letters—because there is more than enough featural information to distinguish among 26 alternatives—not all features of a letter need be discriminated in order to identify a letter. Therefore, a number of alternative *criterial sets* of features may exist within each feature list, information about the features within any criterial set being sufficient for an identification to be made. For example, Tests 1, 3, 4, 5, 7, and 8 or Tests 1, 2, 4, 5, 7, 9, or Tests 2, 3, 4, 6, 7, 9, 10 might constitute a criterial set of the *H* feature list for "*h*." Information about any of these combinations of features would be sufficient to eliminate all the 25 other alternative letters and permit the categorization—the identification—of a particular configuration as "*h*." Similar criterial sets would exist within the *h* feature list for the same category.

It would be expected that criterial sets also exist for *word* identification, except that now they would cover the second dimension and take into account feature combinations extending across the entire word. Criterial sets within the feature list for *HORSE* for example might include Tests 3, 4, 6, and 9 for Position 1; Tests 3, 7, and 9 for Position 3; Tests 4, 6, 7, and 8 for Position 4; and Tests 4, 6, 7, and 10 for Position 5. Three significant aspects of such a criterial set of features should be noted.

First, in no position are sufficient features tested to permit identification of a letter if that letter were standing in isolation. For example, feature tests 3, 4,

5, and 9 in Position 1 would not constitute a criterial set for the identification of *H* standing alone, although they are sufficient for the first position of *HORSE* (provided certain other features are tested in other positions). The explanation, of course, is that a criterial set for *H* alone would have to contain sufficient information to eliminate the 25 other letters of the alphabet while there are not that many alternatives that could occur in front of the sequence *-ORSE.* The difference between a criterial set for the first position of *Horse* and for the letter *H* in isolation illustrates the point that the "positions" in words should not be regarded as letters; word configurations are tested for feature information that leads directly to word categories, not to intermediate letter categories. Experimental evidence will be cited to show that words can be identified before any of their component letters are discriminable.

Second, the illustrative criterial set of features for *HORSE* does not include any features from the second position. The omission indicates that all of that particular part of the word (the letter *O*) could be blacked out and the word would still be identifiable because only one single letter can occur in that position. The ready identifiability of the sequence *H-RSE* is an example of the *redundancy* that exists within words, permitting the fluent reader to identify words on far less visual information than may be available in their configurations.

Third, the total number of features required to identify "horse" in the particular criterial set given as an example is far less than would be required to identify the letters, *H, O, R, S,* and *E* if they were presented in isolation, or in mixed-up order, or to a beginning reader or foreign-language speaker who could not recognize the whole word. Again, this economy is a consequence of redundancy within words.

If you recognize that the first letter of an English word is *T* and the second letter *H*, you do not get—or at least you do not need—as much information from the second letter as you did from the first. Knowing the first letter of a word provides information about the second. The first letter contains sufficient visual information to enable you to discard 25 out of 26 alternatives (assuming for the sake of argument that a word is equally likely to start with any of the letters of the alphabet). The second letter also contains enough visual information, or distinctive features, to distinguish among 26 alternatives because obviously you can distinguish it from all the other letters of the alphabet when it is standing alone. But you do not need featural information to distinguish the second letter from among 26 alternatives because there are not 26 letters that it could be. If the first letter of an English word is *T*, then there is a very high degree of probability that the second letter will be *H, R,* or one of the vowels; the number of possible alternatives for the second letter is fewer than 10. In fact, the more letters that are known of a word, the fewer alternatives there are on the average for what each additional letter could be. And because there is much less uncertainty about each letter, less and less featural information is required for their identification.

Knowledge of the way in which letters are grouped into words, or *orthographic information*, is located within the theory of the world of the fluent reader. It is an alternative nonvisual source of information to the *featural* or *visual information* that the eyes pick up from the page. To the extent that both of these sources of information reduce the number of alternatives that a particular letter might be, there is redundancy. Such duplication of information is also called *sequential redundancy* because its source lies in the fact that the different parts of a word are not independent; the occurrence of particular alternatives in one part of a sequence limits the range of alternatives that can occur anywhere else in the sequence.

The orthographic redundancy of English is enormous. If all 26 letters of the alphabet could occur without restriction in each position of a five-letter word, there could be nearly 12 million different five-letter words, compared with perhaps 10,000 that actually exist. An alphabet of seven letters would be sufficient to make that number of five-letter words distinguishable.

Redundancy Among Distinctive Features

I have been talking so far about the constraints that one letter places on the occurrence of *letters* in other parts of a word. But precisely the same argument can apply to *features*. Obviously, if we can say that the occurrence of the letter *T* in the first position of a word restricts the possibilities for the second position to *H, R, A, E, I, O, U,* and *Y,* then we can also say that the occurrence of *features* of the letter *T* in the first position limits the possible *features* that can occur in the second position. In fact, we can eliminate the mention of letters and specific positions altogether and say that when certain features occur in one part of a word, there are limits to the kinds of feature combinations that can occur in other parts of the word. A reader implicitly aware of such limitations is able to make use of *sequential redundancy among features*, the overlapping sources of information being the visual information that could eliminate all possible sets of alternative feature combinations and the reader's knowledge that many of the possible alternative sets do not in fact occur.

By virtue of sequential redundancy, the skilled reader can identify words with so little visual information that the identification of letters is completely bypassed. It is not necessary to identify letters in any part of a word in order to identify the entire word. Words may be identified before there is sufficient featural information in any position to permit the identification of a letter standing alone.

Here is a simple illustration of how featural redundancy might permit the identification of a two-letter word before either of the letters could be identified individually. Imagine that sufficient features could be discriminated in the first position of the word so that if we were looking at that position alone our alternatives would be reduced to either *a* or *e*—but that we could not make a final decision between the two. Suppose also that in the second position of the word we could detect sufficient features to reduce the alternatives to *f* or *t*, but not to make a final choice. From the four possibilities that might be constructed, *af*, *at*, *ef*, *et*, only one construction would be acceptable as a word. Because word categories do not exist for the other three possibilities, the configuration would be allocated to the category "at," identified as "at," and so perceived. If there was also a word (a category) "et" in the language, then a decision could not be made, and if "et" existed but not "at," then *et* is what would be seen.

Again, I am not suggesting that readers are *aware* of their knowledge of sequential redundancy, any more than they are aware of the decision-making process that is involved in reading or any other form of perception. But in the Notes some examples are given to show that the fluent reader must indeed be regarded as possessing such a knowledge of language.

Functional Equivalence for Words

Some remarks remain to be made concerning functional equivalence for word configurations. The notion of criterial sets permits a good deal of flexibility in the operation of a feature-analytic system. With letters, for example, ability to make an identification although information about one or two features may be absent from (or even contrary to) the total specification of a feature list need not prevent the categorization of a configuration. As a result, such diverse configurations as A, ⅄, Ⱥ, Ⱥ, and such impoverished forms as %⍏% and %⍉% might all meet the specifications of one or another of the criterial subsets of the feature list for *A*, and be allocated to the category "a." However, when alternative forms reach a particular level of featural dissimilarity such as *a* and *A*, there is the additional possibility available of setting up "functionally equivalent" feature lists for the same category. Within each such feature list a number of alternative criterial sets might exist.

Just as there may be functionally equivalent feature lists for various forms of the same letter, so alternative feature lists for functionally equivalent versions of the same word would be expected. Invented examples have been given of one feature list for *HORSE* and another for *horse*. However, it is not proposed that these two (and other) feature lists for the same word would exist completely independently, but rather that a visual configuration would be allocated to a particular category if tests of its parts satisfied positional specifications on any set of functionally equivalent feature lists. As an oversimplified example, it is not proposed that there must necessarily be a special feature list for the visual configuration *Horse*, because the first position of that configuration is congruent with the beginning of *HORSE* (and many other words) while the remainder is congruent with part of *horse* (and some other words). While tests of the configuration *Horse* will not satisfy a criterial set within the feature lists for *HORSE* or *horse* or any other word, it is only within the two functionally equivalent feature lists for the category "horse" that the configuration meets criterial requirements at both beginning and end. In other words, a configuration may be identified if it is congruent with nonoverlapping parts of two criterial sets of features, provided that these incomplete criterial sets are functionally equivalent for the same category. Such a view would suggest that a quite unfamiliar configuration like *HoRsE* should still be identifiable through meeting the criterial requirements for Positions 1, 3, and 5 for *HORSE* and Positions 2 and 4 for *horse*—and there is evidence that this is the case (Smith, Lott, & Cronnell, 1969).

It must be emphasized that we are still not talking about letters—I am not saying that *H, R,* and *E* are identified from one feature list and *o* and *s* from another. It is still proposed that the identification is being made directly to the category "horse" through the various equivalent feature lists for a word and not through the unrelated feature lists of individual letters.

To summarize, the difference between letter and word identification is simply the category system that is involved—the manner in which featural information is allocated. If the reader is examining an array of visual information in order to identify letters, the visual information will be tested and identifications made on the basis of the feature lists for the 26 categories. If the purpose is to identify words, the visual information will be tested with respect to the feature lists for words, and there will be no question of letter identification. It follows from the present argument that it should be impossible to identify a word and its component letters simultaneously, because one cannot use the same information to make two different kinds of decision.

Because letter and word identification involve the same featural information, it is not possible to identify a configuration both as a word and as a sequence of letters at the same time. We can see the configuration *cat* either as the letters *c, a, t* or as the word *cat,* but not as both simultaneously. Similarly, we can see the configuration *read* either as the word pronounced "reed" or as the word pronounced "red" but not as both at once; and *IO* can be seen either as a number or as letters but not as both. We cannot apply the same information to two categories simultaneously, just as we cannot use the same contour as part of two figures simultaneously—the center line of ⟩⟨ can be seen as part of a face on the left or as part of a face on the right, but the two faces can never be seen simultaneously.

It is easily shown that the limitation in the previous cases does not lie in an inability to allocate identical configurations to two different categories—we have little difficulty in seeing *IO IO* "ten eye-oh" or the two faces in ⟩⟨, or even *cat is cat* as "c, a, t is cat," or *"read read*" as if pronounced "red reed"—as in *I PICKED UP THE NOTE AND READ "READ THIS QUICKLY"*—provided that there is featural information for each of the two categories we are using. The impossibility is to use the *same* information for two purposes simultaneously.

LEARNING TO IDENTIFY WORDS

There are two aspects of learning to identify words which are analogous to the two aspects of learning to identify letters outlined at the end of the last chapter. One aspect is establishing criterial sets of functionally equivalent distinctive features for each category, the specifications for qualifying configurations, and the other is associating a name with a category. For letter identification it was asserted that relating the name to the category was not a problem; children learn names for visual configurations all the time. In word identification there may indeed be a problem in relating names to categories, not because children have particular difficulty in remembering the name for a category once they have found out what it is, but in finding out what the name of a category is in the first place. When children are beginning to discover written language, helpful adults usually act as mediators by saying what the printed words are, leaving to the child the more complex task of discovering how to distinguish one word from another. Someone says to them "There's a cat" or "Look at the dog." The process of finding out the name of a category may be termed *mediated word identification*, and is the topic of the next chapter. Word identification must be *mediated* when a word cannot be identified on sight by allocation to a category through an existing feature list. By contrast, I refer to word identification as discussed in this chapter as *immediate word identification*. The term "immediate" is used not in the sense of instantaneous, which we know is not the case, but to mean "not mediated," indicating that a word is identified directly from its features. The aspect of learning with which the remainder of this chapter is concerned is the establishment of appropriate visual feature lists for immediate word identification.

It will help if we consider a specific instance. A child is about to learn to recognize a particular written name, say *John*. The task confronting the child is to discover the rules for recognizing this event when it occurs again, which means finding out something about the configuration that will distinguish it from other configurations that should not be called "John." Assume that the child has already discovered that a reliable distinguishing characteristic for the configuration is not the color of the paper that it is printed on, or the color of the ink, both of which may be reasonable cues for other types of identification but which will sooner or later prove to be inadequate for the allocation of visual information to word categories. Also assume that the child at this time is not confronted by *John* in a number of different type styles. The ability to name any or all of the letters of the alphabet has no direct relevance in immediate word identification, although there will be an obvious (although by no means essential) advantage for children if they have learned to distinguish even a few letters, without necessarily being able to name them, because they will have begun to acquire cues about the features that distinguish words.

That is the problem for the child, to discover cues that will distinguish *John* from other configurations. The child may decide that a good cue lies in the length of the word, or the two upright strokes, or the shape of the "fishhook" at the beginning. In selecting a cue that will be the basis for recognition of the word, a child will establish the first tentative "distinctive features" to be looked for in the future when testing whether to allocate a configuration to the category "John."

Exactly what the first distinctive feature will be depends on circumstances; it depends on the other words from which the child tries to distinguish the configuration *John*. Until the child comes across another word that is not *John* there is no problem; the child applies the single test and calls every configuration that passes the test "John." But until the child comes across another word that is not *John*, there can be no learning. What brings a child to the beginning of the process of developing feature lists that will serve for *reading* is having to distinguish *John* from all the other configurations with which it is not functionally equivalent. The child will only really be able to identify *John* after learning not to apply that name to every other word configuration that is met. It is when the child is confronted by a configuration that should go into a different category that the soundness of the tentative discrimination is tested, and, of course, it is soon found to be wanting. If the hypothesized distinctive features were related to the length of the word, then the child would respond "John" to the configuration *Fred*. If the hypothesis involved the initial fishhook, the child would say "John" to *Jack* or *June* or *Jeremiah*. The more nonequivalent configurations—the more different "words"—children have to discriminate among, the more they will come to select as distinctive features those that will be appropriate to the eventual task of fluent reading. But until children can understand what they have to distinguish *John* from, they will never acquire an appropriate set of distinctive features for identifying that word.

The preceding statement does *not* mean that children must be able to *name* every other word they meet; not at all. All they have to do is see a representative sample of words that are not *John*, so that they can find out in what respects *John* is different. It does not matter if they cannot discriminate among all the other words (although in learning to identify *John* they will learn something about all other words); the beginning can be the establishment of only two categories: configurations that are "John" and configurations that are "not John." Attempting to teach "one word at a time"—writing a word on a variety of different surfaces and occasions and insisting "This is '*John*'; this is

'*John*' "—will not help children to learn the word because they will never learn how *John* may be distinguished from any other word. The notion that a child can learn to identify a word by the repetitious presentation of just that word is a template theory. Its inappropriateness is obvious as soon as we realize that there is no way in which a child can transfer a picture of what is presented to the eyes into a storehouse in the brain. Children do not need to be told interminably what a word is; they have to be able to see what it is *not*.

Acquaintance with a wide variety of nonequivalent alternatives is everything. Through growing familiarity with the written form of language, children learn not only to discriminate distinctive features, to establish feature lists, and to recognize functional equivalences, they also learn about redundancy. And by acquiring a pool of knowledge about the redundancy of words, they learn to identify words economically, on minimal quantities of visual information; they establish large numbers of alternative criterial sets.

It is perhaps a sobering thought that just about everything that a child learns, as described in the preceding paragraph, is never explicitly taught. Among the many positive things reading teachers can do—providing relevant demonstrations, collaboration, encouragement—they cannot include the provision of rules by which words are to be recognized. That part of learning must be left to the children themselves.

A POSTSCRIPT ABOUT WORDS

One of the inevitable consequences of examining closely a subject like reading, about which so much is taken for granted, is that it turns out to be far more complicated and less well understood than we thought it to be. An obvious first step in my discussion of word identification might have been to state clearly and precisely how many words the average fluent reader knows: This would give some useful knowledge about the dimensions of the problem. But the trouble with a simple request for a count of the words that a person knows is that the answer depends on what is meant by "word," while in any case there is no way to compute a reliable answer.

Consider first the matter of deciding what we want to call a word. Should *cat* and *cats*, or *walk* and *walked* be regarded as two different words or as two forms of the same word? Dictionaries usually provide entries only for the base or root form of words, refusing to count as different words such variations as plurals, comparatives, adjectival forms, and various verb tenses. If we want to call *cat* and *cats*, or *walk* and *walked* different words (and certainly we would not regard them as functionally equivalent visually), the number of words we know on sight might turn out to be three or four times greater than the number of words the dictionary-maker would credit us with. Furthermore, common words have many meanings as in "You can *bank* on the *bank* by the river *bank.*" But if the same spelling is to be regarded as (at least) three different words because *bank* has several meanings, should a preposition like "by," which has so many different senses, be counted as 40 words or more?

The next problem is to count. Obviously, it is not good enough simply to count the number of words that a person reads or hears or produces during the course of a day, for many words will be used more than once and others will occur not at all. To count the number of *different* words a person produces we have to look carefully in a torrent of very familiar words. But in how big a torrent shall we look? How can we ever be certain that we have given sufficient opportunity for all the words a person knows? Without a doubt, we shall find some new words in every additional sample of a thousand that we record, but surely a law of decreasing returns would apply. After analyzing, say, 100,000 words from one person, it would seem unlikely that many new ones would be produced. But such is not the case. Very many words with which we are quite familiar occur less than once in every million—and it may take anywhere from two months to two years for a person to produce that number of words. One very extensive analysis of nearly 5 million word occurrences in popular magazines (Thorndike & Lorge, 1944) found over 3,000 words that occurred an average of less than once in every million, and almost all of these words would fall under our category of "known." Here is a sample of words that occurred only once in every *5 million* words—*earthiness, echelon, echidna, eclair, effluence, egad, egotistic*—one or two may be a little unusual, but by and large they are words that we can recognize.

There is something a little eerie even to think about how we might acquire and retain familiarity with the relatively infrequent words. We meet them perhaps once a year, but it is not often we have to stop and wonder "Haven't I seen you before somewhere?" Obviously, it is not possible to "count" how many different words a person knows, so one has to make an estimate. And many estimates have been offered, varying from 50,000 to over 250,000, depending on the definitions used and assumptions made. This gives one good answer to the question of how many words a person might know—it is impossible to say.

SUMMARY

Words, like letters, can be identified directly from the distinctive features that are the visual information of print. **Immediate word identification** takes place when feature analysis allocates a visual configuration to the **feature list** of a word category in cognitive structure, without the intermediate step of letter identification. **Criterial sets** of features within **functionally equivalent** feature lists permit the identification of words on minimal information, for example, when the reader can employ prior knowledge of the **ortho-graphic redundancy** within words.

Notes to Chapter 7 begin on page 267, covering

Letter identification in words
Use of redundancy by children
Distributional redundancy among words

Chapter 8
PHONICS AND MEDIATED WORD IDENTIFICATION

The preceding chapter was concerned with *immediate* word identification, with the manner in which visual feature lists are established and used so that words can be recognized on sight, without "decoding to sound" or any other means of *mediated* word identification. In fact, the previous chapter argued that letter-by-letter identification is unnecessary and even impossible for word identification in normal reading, thus leaving no room for decoding to sound. Immediate word identification is illustrated in Figure 8.1.

But in the preceding chapter, I was talking about the identification of words where the "name" of the word—its pronunciation when read aloud—is either known to the reader or otherwise available to the learner. The learner does not need to figure out what the visual configuration "says," but only how it should be recognized on future occasions. This situation was compared with the cat-and-dog learning problem where the child is told that a particular animal is a cat and then left to discover how to recognize one another time.

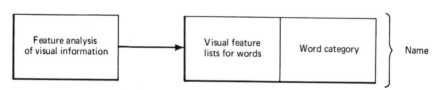

FIGURE 8.1. Immediate word identification.

Suppose, however, that the name of a word is not immediately available to the learner—that there is no one to identify an unfamiliar word, and there are no context cues, perhaps because the word is seen in isolation or as part of a list of unrelated words. Now the learner has a double problem, not only to discover how to recognize the word in the future, but to find out what the word is in the first place. This is the cat-and-dog problem without the learner being told whether the animal is in fact a cat or a dog. In such a situation in reading, a word obviously cannot be identified *immediately;* its identification must be *mediated* by some other means of discovering what it is. The present chapter is about the use of *phonics*—a set of relationships between letters and sounds—and other methods of mediated word identification. The use of phonic rules to mediate word identification is illustrated in Figure 8.2.

In particular this chapter examines the extent to which knowledge of the sounds associated with letters of the alphabet helps in the identification of words. For many, this process of decoding the spelling of words to their sounds is the basis of reading, a view that I do not think is tenable. It is not necessary to "say" what a written word is before we can comprehend its meaning. We no more need to say a written word is "cat" in order to understand it than we need to say that a particular animal is a cat in order to recognize it. Indeed, just as we cannot say that the animal is a cat unless we have already identified it, so the naming of a word normally occurs after the identification of its meaning.

This chapter is still not the whole story of reading, even as far as words are concerned. In both the preceding and the present chapters, the assumption is made that the word a reader is trying to identify already exists in the reader's spoken language vocabulary; its meaning is known. The reader's problem is to identify the word, to discover or recognize its "name," not to learn its meaning. The next chapter deals with the situation of words that are truly new, where the meaning must be discovered as well as the name or pronunciation.

THE AIMS AND COMPLEXITY OF PHONICS

Mediated word identification is not the most critical part of reading, and phonics is not the only strategy available for mediated word identification.

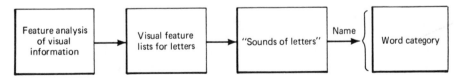

FIGURE 8.2.   Mediated word identification: The phonic model.

Nevertheless, phonics frequently plays a central role in reading instruction, and it will clear the air if we examine the nature and efficacy of phonics first of all.

Rules and Exceptions

The aim of phonics instruction is to provide readers with rules that will enable them to predict how a written word will sound from the way it is spelled. The value of teaching phonics depends on how many correspondences there are between the letters and sounds of English. A correspondence exists whenever a particular letter (or sometimes a group of letters) represents a particular sound (or absence of sound). Thus *c* is involved in at least four correspondences—with the sound /s/ as in *medicine*, with /k/ as in *medical*, as part of /ch/ as in *much*, and with no sound at all as in *scientist*. Alternatively, a correspondence exists whenever a particular sound is represented by a particular letter or letters, as /f/ can be represented by *f*, *ph*, and *gh*. Thus, the total number of "spelling-to-sound" correspondences must be the same as the total number of "sound-to-spelling" correspondences. But by now it is probably no surprise that any question related to language involving a simple "how many" leads to a very complicated and unsatisfactory evasion of an answer. Phonics is no exception.

Everything is wrong about the question. The first problem concerns our expectations about rules. If we expect a rule to mean a correspondence that has no exceptions, then we shall have a difficult task finding any rules in phonics at all. Here is a phonic rule that would appear to have impeccable credentials: Final *e* following a single consonant indicates that the preceding vowel should be long, as in *hat* and *hate*, or *hop* and *hope*. And here are two instant exceptions: *axe* has a single consonant but a short /a/, while *ache* has a double consonant but a long /a/. We have the choice of admitting that a familiar rule is not impervious to exceptions, or else we have to make a rule for the exceptions. One explanation that might be offered is that *x* is really a double consonant, *ks*, and that *ch* is really a single consonant, *k*. But then we are in the rather peculiar position of changing the notion of what constitutes a single letter simply because we have a rule that does not fit all cases. And if we have to say that the definition of what constitutes a letter depends on the pronunciation of a word, how can we say the pronunciation of a word can be predicted from its letters? Besides, what can we say about the silent *e* at the end of *have* or *love*, which is put there only because there is a convention that English words may not end with a *v?* Or the *e* at the end of *house*, which is to indicate that the word is not a plural? Or the *o* in *money* and *women*, which is there because early printers felt that a succession of up-and-down strokes, like *mun* and *wim*, would be too difficult to decipher?

Having made the point that phonic rules will have exceptions, the next problem is to decide what constitutes an exception. Some exceptions occur so frequently and regularly that they would appear to be rules in their own right. It is quite arbitrary how anyone decides to draw the line between rules and exceptions. We have a choice of saying that the sounds of written English can be predicted by relatively few rules, although there will be quite a lot of exceptions, or by a large number of rules with relatively few exceptions. Indeed, if we care to say that some rules have only one application, for example, that *acht* is pronounced /ot/ as in "yacht," then we can describe English completely in terms of rules simply because we have legislated exceptions out of existence.

If the concept of a rule seems somewhat arbitrary, the notion of what constitutes a letter is even more idiosyncratic. It is true that in one sense there can be no doubt about what a letter is—it is one of the 26 characters in the alphabet—but any attempt to construct rules of spelling-sound correspondence is doomed if we restrict our terms of reference to individual letters. To start with, there are only 26 letters compared with about 40 different sounds of speech, so many letters at least must do double duty. We find, of course, that many letters stand for more than one sound, while many sounds are represented by more than one letter. However, many sounds are not represented by single letters at all—*th, ch, ou, ue,* for example—so that we have to consider some combinations of letters as quite distinct *spelling units*— rather as if *th* were a letter in its own right (as it is in Greek, in two different forms for two different pronunciations). It has been asserted, with the help of a computer analysis of over 20,000 words (Venezky, 1967, 1970), that there are 52 "major spelling units" in English, 32 for consonants and 20 for vowels, effectively doubling the size of the alphabet.

The addition of all these extra spelling units, however, does not seem to make the structure of the English writing system very much more orderly. Some of the original letters of the alphabet are quite superfluous. There is nothing that *c* or *q* or *x* can do that could not be done by the other consonants. And many of the additional spelling units that are recognized simply duplicate the work of single letters, such as *ph* for *f,* and *dg* for *j.* There are also compound vowels whose effect duplicates the silent final *e,* like *ea* in *meat* compared with *mete.* Some combinations of letters have a special value only when they occur in particular parts of a word—*gh* may be pronounced as *f* (or as nothing) at the end of a word *(rough, through)* but is pronounced just like a single *g* at the beginning *(ghost* and *gold, ghastly* and *garden).* Often letters have only a relational function, sacrificing any sound of their own in order to indicate how another letter should be sounded. An obvious example is the silent *e,* another is the *u* that distinguishes the *g* in *guest* from the *g* in *gem.*

So for our basic question of phonics, what we are really asking is how many arbitrarily defined rules can account for an indeterminate number of correspondences between an indefinite set of spelling units and an uncertain number of sounds (the total and quality of which may vary from dialect to dialect).

Some aspects of spelling are simply unpredictable, certainly to a reader with a limited knowledge of word derivations, no matter how one tries to define a spelling unit. An example of a completely unpredictable spelling-to-sound correspondence is *th*, which is pronounced in one way at the beginning of words like *this, than, those, them, then, these* but in another way at the beginning of *think, thank, thatch, thong, theme*, and so on. There is only one way to tell whether *th* should be pronounced as in /this/ or as in /think/, and that is to remember every instance. On the other hand, in many dialects there is no difference between the sounds represented by *w* and *wh*, as in *witch* and *which*, so that in some cases it can be the spelling that is not predictable, not the sound.

Almost all common words are exceptions—*of* requires a rule of its own for the pronunciation of *f*, *was* for its *as*.

The game of finding exceptions is too easy to play. I give only one more example to illustrate the kind of difficulty one must run into in trying to construct—or teach—reliable rules of phonic correspondence. How are the letters *ho* pronounced, when they occur at the beginning of a word? And here are 11 possible answers; all, you will notice, quite common words: *hope, hot, hoot, hook, hour, honest, house, honey, hoist, horse, horizon*.

Of course, there are rules (or are some of them merely exceptions?) that can account for many of the pronunciations of *ho*. But there is one very significant implication in all the examples that applies to almost all English words—in order to apply phonic rules, *words must be read from right to left*. The way in which the reader pronounces *ho* depends on what comes after it, and the same applies to the *p* in *ph*, the *a* in *ate*, the *k* in *knot*, the *t* in *-tion*. The exceptions are very very few, like *asp* and *ash* which are pronounced differently if preceded by a *w*, and *f*, pronounced /v/ only if preceded by *o*. The fact that sound "dependencies" in words run from right to left is an obvious difficulty for a beginning reader trying to sound out a word from left to right, or for a theorist who wants to maintain that words are identified on a left-to-right basis.

In summary, English is far from predictable as far as its spelling-sound relationships are concerned. Just how much can be done to predict the pronunciation of a relatively small number of common words with a finite number of rules we see later. But before this catalog of complications and exceptions is concluded, two points should be reiterated. The first point is that phonic rules can only be considered as probabilistic, as guides to the way words might be pronounced, and that there is rarely any indication of when a rule does or does not apply. The rule that specifies how to pronounce *ph* in *telephone* falls down in the face of *haphazard*, or *shepherd*, or *cuphook*. The rule for *oe* in *doe* and *woe* will not work for *shoe*. The only way to distinguish the pronunciation of *sh* in *bishop* and *mishap*, or *th* in *father* and *fathead*, is to know the entire word in advance. The probability of being wrong if you do not know a word at all is very high. Even if individual rules were likely to be right three times out of four, there would still be only one chance in three of avoiding error in a four-letter word.

The second point is that phonic rules look deceptively simple when you know what a word is in the first place. I do not intend to be facetious. Teachers often feel convinced that phonic rules work because letter-sound correspondences seem obvious if a word is known in advance; the alternatives are not considered. And children may seem to apply phonic rules when they can recognize a word in any case—or because the teacher also suggests what the word is—thereby enabling them to identify or recite the phonic correspondences that happen to be appropriate.

The Efficiency of Phonics

One systematic attempt to construct a workable set of phonic rules for English was made by Berdiansky, Cronnell, and Koehler (1969). The effort had modest aims—to see how far one could go in establishing a set of correspondence rules for the 6,092 one- and two-syllable words among 9,000 different words in the comprehension vocabularies of 6- to 9-year-old children. (The remaining words, nearly one-third of the children's vocabularies, were all three or more syllables, adding too much complexity to the phonic analysis, though obviously not to the children's language understanding.) The words were all taken from books to which the children were normally exposed—they were the words that the children knew and ought to be able to identify if they were to be able to read the material with which they were confronted at school.

The researchers who analyzed the 6,092 words found rather more than the 52 "major spelling units" to which I have already referred—they identified 69 "grapheme units" that had to be separately distinguished in their rules. A group of letters were called a *grapheme unit*, just like a single letter, whenever their relationship to a sound could not be accounted for by any rules for single letters. Grapheme units included pairs of consonants such as *ch, th;* pairs of vowels such as *ea, oy;* and letters that commonly function together, such as *ck* and *qu*, as well as double consonants like *bb* and *tt*, all of which require some separate phonic explanation. The number of grapheme units should not surprise us. The previously mentioned 52 "major units" were not intended to represent the only spelling units that could occur but only the most frequent ones.

An arbitrary decision was made about what would constitute a rule: It would have to account for a spelling-sound correspondence occurring in at least 10 different words. Any distinctive spelling-sound correspondence and any grapheme unit that did not occur in at least 10 words was considered an "exception." Actually, the researchers made several exceptions among the exceptions. They wanted their rules to account for as many of their words as possible, and so they let several cases through the net when it seemed to them more appropriate to account for a grapheme unit with a rule rather than to stigmatize it as an exception.

The researchers discovered that their 6,000 words involved 211 distinct spelling-sound correspondences. This does not mean that 211 different sounds were represented, any more than there were 211 different grapheme units, but rather that the 69 grapheme units were related to 38 sounds in a total of 211 different ways. The results are summarized in Table 8.1.

Eighty-three of the correspondences involved consonant grapheme units, and 128 involved vowel grapheme units, including no fewer than 79 that were associated with the six "primary" single-letter vowels, *a, e, i, o, u, y*. In other words, there was a total of 79 different ways in which single vowels could be pronounced. Of the 211 correspondences, 45 were classified as exceptions, about half involving vowels and half consonants. The exclusion of 45 correspondences meant that about 10% of the 6,092 words had to be set aside as "exceptions."

The pronunciation of the remaining words was accounted for by a grand total of 166 rules. Sixty of these rules were concerned with the pronunciation of consonants (which are generally thought to have fairly "regular" pronunciations) and 106 with single or complex vowels.

The research that has just been outlined is important in a number of ways for understanding reading and the teaching of reading. Some conclusions that can be drawn are far-reaching in their implications. The first is very simply that phonics is complicated. Without saying anything at all about whether it is desirable to teach young children a knowledge of phonics, we now have an idea of the magnitude of the endeavor. We now know that if we really expect to give children a mastery of phonics, then we are not talking about a dozen or so rules. We are talking about 166 rules, which will still not account for hundreds of the words they might expect to meet in their early reading.

TABLE 8.1. Spelling-Sound Correspondences Among 6,092 One- and Two-Syllable Words in the Vocabularies of Nine-Year-Old Children

	Consonants	Primary Vowels	Secondary Vowels	Total
Spelling-sound correspondences	83	79	49	211
"Rules"	60	73	33	166
"Exceptions"	23	6	16	45
Grapheme units in rules	41	6	19	69

It is obvious that the most that can be expected from a knowledge of phonic rules is that they may provide a *clue* to the sound (or "name") of a configuration being examined.   Phonics can provide only approximations. Even if readers do happen to know the 73 rules for the pronunciation of the six vowels, they would still have no sure way of telling which rule applies—or even that they were not dealing with an exception.

There is still one issue to be considered concerning the *effectiveness* of phonics. Is the limited degree of efficiency that might be attained worth acquiring? Other factors have to be taken into account related to the *cost* of trying to learn and use phonic rules. There is the possibility that reliance on phonics will involve readers in so much delay that short-term memory will be overloaded, and they will lose the sense of what they are reading. A tendency to rely exclusively on phonic rules may create a handicap for beginning readers whose biggest problem is to develop speed in reading. Our working memories do not have an infinite capacity and reading is not a task that can be accomplished at too leisurely a pace. Other sources of information exist for finding out what a word in context might be, especially if the word is in the spoken vocabulary of the reader.

The Cost of "Reform"

The involved relation between the spelling of words and their sound has led to frequent suggestions for modifying the alphabet or for rationalizing the spelling system. To some extent both these intentions share the same misconceptions and difficulties. A number of contemporary linguists would deny that there is anything wrong with the way most words are spelled; they argue that a good deal of information would be lost if spelling were changed. Most of the apparent inconsistencies in spelling have some historical basis; the spelling system may be complex, but it is not arbitrary—it has become what it is for quite systematic reasons. And because spelling is systematic and reflects something of the history of words, much more information is available to the reader than we normally realize. (The fact that we are not *aware* that this information is available does not mean that we do not use it; we have already seen a number of examples of the way in which we have and use a knowledge of the structure and redundancy of our language that we cannot put into words.)

Spelling reform might seem to make words easier to pronounce, but only at the cost of other information about the way words are related to each other, so that rationalizing words at the phonological level might make reading more difficult at syntactic and semantic levels. As just one example, consider the "silent *b*" in words like *bomb, bombing, bombed,* which would be an almost certain candidate for extinction if spelling reformers had their way. But the *b* is something more than a pointless appendage; it relates the previous words to others like *bombard, bombardier, bombardment* where the *b* is pronounced. And if you save yourself the trouble of a special rule about why *b* is silent in words like *bomb*, at another level there would be a new problem of explaining why *b* suddenly appears in words like *bombard*. Remove the *g* from *sign* and you must explain where it comes from in *signature*.

Another argument in favor of the present spelling system is that it is the most competent one to handle different dialects, a matter relevant also to those who would want to change the alphabet. Although there is almost universal acceptance of the idea that words should be spelled in the same way by everyone, we do not all pronounce words in the same way. If the spelling of words is to be changed so that they reflect the way they are pronounced, whose dialect will provide the standard? Is a different letter required for every different sound produced in any dialect of English we might encounter? Phonics instruction becomes even more complicated when it is realized that in many classrooms teacher and students do not speak the same dialect and that both may speak a different dialect from the authorities who suggested the particular phonic rules they are trying to follow. The teacher who tries to make children understand a phonic difference between the pronunciation of *caught* and *cot* will have a communication problem if this distinction is not one that the children observe in their own speech. The teacher may not even pronounce the two words differently, so that while the teacher thinks the message to the child is "That word is not *cot;* it is *caught,*" the message coming across is "That word is not *cot;* it is *cot.*"

Spelling and Meaning

The manner in which words are spelled in English is seen as a problem primarily if reading is perceived as a matter of decoding words to sound, which it is not and could not be, and if the primary function of spelling is regarded as the representation of *sounds* of words. But in fact, spelling also represents meaning, and where there is a conflict between pronunciation and meaning it is usually meaning which prevails, as if even the spelling system of written language recognized the priority of meaning. For example, the plural represented by a simple *s* in written language may be pronounced in three different ways in speech—as the /s/ sound on the end of "cats," the /z/ sound on the end of "dogs," and the /iz/ sound on the end of "judges." Would writing be easier to read if the past tense of verbs were not indicated by a consistent -*ed* but rather reflected the pronunciation, so that we had such variations as *walkt* and *landid?* The reason that *medicine* and *medical* are spelled as they are is not because *c* is sometimes arbitrarily pronounced /s/ and sometimes /k/ but because the two words have the same root meaning, represented by *medic*. This commonality of meaning would be lost if the two words were spelled *medisin* and *medikal*. It should be noted, incidentally, that the consistent representation of the various pronunciations of the plural meaning by *s* or the past tense meaning by *-ed* rarely causes difficulty to readers, even beginners, provided they are reading for sense. It is not necessary for teachers to instruct children that *ed* is often pronounced /t/ (among other things). If a child understands a word, the pronunciation will take care of itself, but the effort to produce pronunciation as a prerequisite for meaning is likely to result in neither being achieved.

Of course, spelling is a problem, both in school and out, but it is a problem of *writing*, not of reading. Readers are not normally aware of spelling. They attend to the appearance of words, to their features, not to their individual letters. Knowing how to spell does not make a good reader because reading is not accomplished by the decoding of spelling. Good readers are certainly not necessarily good spellers; we can all read words that we cannot spell. I am not saying that knowledge of spelling is unimportant, only that it has a minimal role in reading, and that undue concern with the way in which words are spelled can only interfere with a child's learning to read.

There is a frequent argument that if spelling and decoding to sound are as irrelevant to reading as the preceding analyses indicate, why should we have an alphabetic written language at all? My view is that the alphabetic system is more of a help to the writer than to the reader. For a variety of reasons, including the memory load required to reproduce every word legibly in all its featural detail, writing is a much harder skill to learn and to practice than reading, at least if the writer is to be conventionally "correct" with respect to such matters as grammar, punctuation, neatness, and so forth. Spelling may be complicated for writers (especially if they have not been taught how spelling reflects meaning as well as sound), but it still makes writing much easier than if writers had to remember and reproduce thousands and thousands of non-alphabetic ideographic forms, like writers of Chinese.

A greatly underestimated advantage of alphabetic writing is that it enables readers and writers (and teachers) to *talk about* words. Instead of asking what the word is that looks like goal posts, a circle and a horizontal stroke with a vertical one beneath, a reader can simply say "What is the word that is spelled *h, o, t?*" Instead of having to say "Draw me (or describe to me) the shape of the word 'hot'," all the writer need ask is "How do you spell *'hot'?*" Indeed, the fact that words can be remembered as spellings rather than as complex shapes greatly facilitates writing and learning to write. For reading it is easier to *recognize* a shape, but for writing it is easier to *recall* and *reproduce* a series of letters.

The alphabetic system may have allowed more people to learn to write, but at a cost to readers. The Chinese ideographic system can be read by people from all over China, even though they might speak languages that are mutually unintelligible. If a Cantonese speaker cannot understand what a Mandarin speaker says, they can write their conversation in the nonalphabetic writing system they both share and be mutually comprehensible. This is something English and French speakers cannot do unless they employ the small part of their own writing systems that is not alphabetic, such as arithmetic symbols like $2 + 3 = 5$.

When we cannot remember or do not know how a word should be written, we have little recourse to anything but what we know about the spelling system. It does not help much in writing to look at the words before and after the one that is giving difficulty. But in reading we have some more effective alternatives before we need call upon phonics for help in identifying a word, and it is to these alternatives that we now turn.

STRATEGIES OF MEDIATED WORD IDENTIFICATION

To repeat, the problem with which we are concerned is that of a reader who encounters a word that cannot be recognized on sight, for which a visual feature list must be established, but where the reader does know what the word is to which the feature list will be assigned. The reader's problem is to identify the word by a mediated strategy.

Phonics, as we have seen, is one such strategy. But it is not the only one. An obvious alternative is simply being told what the word is. Before most children come to school, well-intentioned adults say to them "That word is 'John'," "That word is 'girls'," "That word is 'cereal'," just as on other occasions they say "That animal is a cat," in all cases leaving it to the child to solve the more complex problem of working out exactly how to recognize the word or animal in the future. But when the children get to school this support is frequently taken away from them, at least as far as reading is concerned. Another well-intentioned adult is likely to say to them: "Good news and bad news today, children. The bad news is that no one is ever likely to tell you what a word is again. The good news is that we are going to give you 166 rules and 45 exceptions so that you can work it out for yourselves."

Alternative Identification Strategies

Ask fluent readers what they do when they come across a word they do not recognize, and the most probable answer will be that they skip it. Passing over a word is a reasonable first strategy because it is not necessary to understand every word to understand a passage of text, and lingering to try to decipher a word may be more disruptive to comprehension than missing the word altogether. The second preferred strategy is to "guess," which again does not mean a reckless stab in the dark but making use of context to eliminate unlikely alternatives for what the unfamiliar word might be. The final strategy may be trying to work out what the word is from its spelling, but that is not so much likely to be decoding the word to sound with phonics as making use of what is already known about other words. The final strategy might be called "identification by analogy," because all or part of the unknown word is compared with all or part of words that are known.

Examine the same question with a child who is progressing in learning to read and again you are likely to get the same sequence of strategies. The best learners tend to skip unknown words (unless constrained by a teacher to "read carefully" and figure out every word). The second preference, especially if there is no helpful adult around to provide assistance, is to hypothesize what a word might be based on the meaning of the text, and the final choice is to use what is known about similar-looking words. Trying to sound out words without reference to meaning is a characteristic strategy of poor readers; it is not one that leads to fluency in reading.

What is the best method of mediated word identification? The answer depends on the situation a reader is in. Sometimes the best strategy will indeed be to ignore the unfamiliar word altogether, since sufficient meaning may be carried by the surrounding text not only to compensate for lack of understanding of the unknown word, but subsequently to provide critical cues to what the unknown word might be. For a child beginning to learn to read, or confronted by text where many words are familiar, the best situation is probably to have an adult or more competent young reader to turn to, if necessary by reading the entire passage to the child. But if the reader can understand enough of the passage to follow its sense, then a most effective strategy may be identification by analogy, making use of what is already known about reading.

The point is that phonics in itself is almost useless for sounding out words letter by letter, because every letter can represent too many sounds. But uncertainty about the sound of a particular letter diminishes as letters are considered not in isolation but as part of letter clusters or "spelling patterns." This has led a number of theorists to argue that the basic unit for word recognition should be regarded as the syllable rather than the individual letter. And indeed it is true; the pronunciation of syllables is far less variable than the pronunciation of the individual letters that make up syllables. The trouble is that it would take a reader years to learn to read by memorizing the pronunciation of hundreds of syllables, because syllables in themselves tend to be meaningless—there are relatively few one-syllable words—and the human brain has great difficulty in memorizing, and particularly in recalling, nonsense. What a reader can turn to for a ready-made store of syllabic information is *words* that have already been learned. It is far easier for a reader to remember the unique appearance and pronunciation of a whole word like *photograph*, for example, than to remember the alternative pronunciations of meaningless syllables or spelling units like *ph, to, gr* or *gra*, and *ph*. A single word, in other words, can provide the basis for remembering different rules of phonics, as well as the exceptions, since not only do words provide a meaningful way to organize different phonic rules in memory, they also illustrate the phonic rules at work. The 11 different ways of pronouncing *ho* cause no difficulty if one already has words like *hot, hoot, hope*, and so forth in one's sight vocabulary.

Identification by Analogy

The basis of the mediated word identification strategy of identification by analogy is looking for cues to a word's pronunciation and meaning from words that look the same. We do not learn to sound out words on the basis of individual letters or letter clusters whose sounds have been learned in isolation, but rather by recognizing sequences of letters that occur in words that are already known. Such a strategy offers an additional advantage to the reader because it does more than indicate possible pronunciations for all or part of unknown words; it can offer suggestions about meaning. As I pointed out earlier, English spelling in general respects meaning more than sound—words that look alike tend to share the same sense. And as I have reiterated throughout this book, the basis of reading and of learning to read is meaning. The advantage of trying to identify unknown words by analogy with words that are known already is not simply that known words would provide an immediately accessible stock of pronunciations for relatively long sequences of letters, but that all or part of known words can provide clues to meaning, which is always a far better clue to pronunciation than just the way in which an unknown word is spelled.

This is not to suggest that fluent readers cannot use their knowledge of spelling-sound correspondences to help identify unfamiliar words, or that the existence of such correspondences should be concealed from children learning to read. But there are three fundamental problems with spelling-sound correspondences: the total number of rules and exceptions, the time it takes to apply them in practice, and their general unreliability. The problem of the number of rules can be solved by not trying to learn (or teach) the rules in the abstract, independently of actual words. The easiest way to learn a phonic rule is to learn a few words that exemplify it, which means—another point that will bear some reiteration—that children master phonics as a result of learning to read rather than as a prerequisite for reading. The time problem is overcome by resorting to phonics in actual reading as infrequently as possible.

The problem of the unreliability of phonic generalizations is another matter. Phonic generalizations alone will not permit a reader to decode the majority of words likely to be met in normal reading simply because there are always too many alternatives. This is the reason that producers of phonic workbooks always prefer to work with strictly controlled vocabularies—there is not as much uncertainty of pronunciation with *The fat cat sat on the flat hat* as there is with *Two hungry pigeons flew behind the weary ploughman,* a sentence that makes more sense but defies phonic analysis.

Meaning Plus Phonics

But phonic generalizations can work if all they are required to do is reduce alternatives, without being expected to identify words completely or to decode them to sounds. To give an example, the use of phonics will never succeed in decoding *horse* if the word appears in isolation or is any one of thousands of alternatives. But if the reader knows that the word is either *horse, mule,* or *donkey* then the strategy will work effectively. It is not simply that minimal phonic analysis is required to know that *mule* and *donkey* could not begin with *h,* but that not much more can be expected of phonic rules in any case. This is why I have asserted that phonics is easy—for the teacher and the child—if they know what a word is in the first place. I am not suggesting that the word has to be known absolutely. In that case neither phonics nor any other mediated word identification strategy would be required. But if the reader has a good idea of what the word might be, if there is a prediction that includes what the word actually is among the likely alternatives, then the use of phonics will probably eliminate the remaining uncertainty.

Phonic strategies cannot be expected to eliminate all uncertainty when the reader has no idea what the word might be. But if the reader can reduce alternatives in advance—by making use of nonvisual information related both to reading and to the subject matter of the text—then phonics can be made most efficient. One way to reduce uncertainty in advance is to employ the mediating technique of making use of context. Understanding of the text, in general, will reduce the number of alternatives that an unknown word might be. The other way to reduce uncertainty in advance is to employ the alternative mediating technique of identification by analogy, comparing the unknown word with known words that provide hypotheses about possible meanings and pronunciations. The reason that we can so easily read nonwords like *vernalit, mossiant,* and *ricaning* is not because we have in our heads a store of pronunciations for meaningless letter sequences like *vern, iant,* or *ric* but because these close approximations to English are made up of parts of words or even entire words that are immediately recognizable, such as *vernal, lit, moss,* and so forth.

There is no simple answer to any question about the ideal method of mediated word identification. The three alternatives that have specifically been discussed—spelling-to-sound correspondences, prediction from context, and identification by analogy—are all likely to be inadequate when used alone. While all will reduce some uncertainty, none is likely to eliminate all alternatives by itself. But used in conjunction, the strategies complement each other. A reader using phonics will rarely identify an unfamiliar word without making sense of the passage as a whole, using this understanding to eliminate unlikely alternatives in advance. To ignore alternative means of reducing uncertainty is to ignore the redundancy which is a central part of all aspects of language.

And the prior elimination of unlikely alternatives is, after all, the foundation upon which reading takes place, according to the analysis of comprehension that was offered in Chapter 3. By this analysis, phonics is neither the basis of reading nor a strategy that a reader has to depend on wholly whenever an unfamiliar word is encountered. Rather, the use of phonic rules takes a supplementary and subordinate place in normal meaningful reading, occurring so rarely and effortlessly that the reader is not usually aware of the strategies employed as unfamiliar words are tentatively identified and feature lists established. Phonic rules function almost as a sentinels; they cannot decipher unknown words on their own, but they will protect the reader against making impossible hypotheses.

LEARNING MEDIATED WORD IDENTIFICATION STRATEGIES

The basis of all learning—and especially of language learning—is meaningfulness. It is pointless to expect a child to memorize lists of rules, definitions, even names, if these have no apparent purpose or utility to the child. Not only will learning be difficult, but recall will be almost impossible. The mediated word identification strategies that have been discussed can fall into the category of meaningless learning if a child is expected to acquire them outside of a context of meaningful reading. A child should not be expected to memorize phonic rules, or the pronunciation of isolated syllables and letter clusters, prior to learning how to read. Identification by analogy can also only be fostered after a child has begun to read.

Learning is self-directing and self-reinforcing when children are in a situation which makes sense to them, that can be related to what they know already. Rules that cannot be verbalized about many aspects of the physical world and of language are hypothesized and tested with little conscious awareness. Where a child can understand a relationship the child will learn the relationship, whether it is the relationship of a name to a word, of a meaning to a word, or of a spelling-sound correspondence.

What all this means is that *reading is basically a matter of increasing returns*. The more that children read, the more they will learn to read. The more they can recognize words, the easier they will be able to understand phonic correspondences, to employ context cues, and to identify new words by analogy. The more that children are able to read—or are helped to read—the more they are likely to discover and extend these strategies for themselves. There is no reason to conceal the existence of spelling-sound correspondences from children, but there is no point in impressing the rules upon an uncomprehending learner, or of concealing their limitations.

By acquiring an extensive "sight vocabulary" of immediately identifiable words, children are able to understand, remember, and utilize phonic rules and other mediated identification strategies. But such a summary statement does not imply that the way to help children read is to give them plenty of experience with flashcards and word lists. The easy way to learn words is not to work with individual words at all but with meaningful passages of text. We are considering only a limited and secondary aspect of reading when we restrict our attention to individual words. As we turn our attention to reading sequences of words that are grammatical and make sense, we find that word identification and learning are more easily explained theoretically and more easily accomplished by the child.

The time has come to complete the picture of reading by recognizing that words are rarely read or learned in meaningless isolation. Reading is easiest when it makes sense, and learning to read is also easiest when it makes sense. We are ready to view reading from a broader and more meaningful perspective.

SUMMARY

Mediated word identification is a temporary expedient for identifying unfamiliar words while establishing feature lists to permit immediate identification. Alternative strategies for mediated word identification include asking someone, using contextual cues, analogy with known words, and the use of **phonics** (spelling-sound correspondences). Attempting to decode isolated words to sound is unlikely to succeed because of the number, complexity, and unreliability of phonic generalizations. Phonic rules will help to eliminate alternative possibilities only if uncertainty can first be reduced by other means, for example, if the unfamiliar words occur in meaningful contexts. Spelling-sound correspondences are not easily or usefully learned before children acquire some familiarity with reading.

Notes to Chapter 8 begin on page 271, covering

The relevance of phonics
Phonological recoding
The alphabet

Chapter 9
THE IDENTIFICATION
OF MEANING

The preceding three chapters have been concerned with the identification of individual letters and individual words. They showed how the same system of feature analysis could be employed both for the identification of letters and for the direct identification of words. Word identification does not require the prior identification of letters, at least not the immediate word identification that readers accomplish when a word they are concerned with is familiar to them, a part of their "sight vocabulary." It is only when words cannot be identified immediately that the prior identification of letters becomes relevant at all, and then only to a limited extent depending on the amount of contextual and other information that the reader might have available. The alternatives are summed up in Figure 9.1.

Now I want to show that comprehension, which in this chapter will be referred to as the *identification* (or apprehension) of meaning, does not require the prior identification of words. The same feature-analytic process that underlies the identification of letters and words is also available for the *immediate* apprehension of meaning from visual information. Although *mediated* meaning identification may sometimes be necessary, because for some reason meaning cannot immediately be assigned to the text, attempting to make decisions about possible meaning by the prior identification of individual words is highly inefficient and unlikely to succeed.

In other words, I am asserting that immediate meaning identification is as independent of the identification of individual words as immediate word

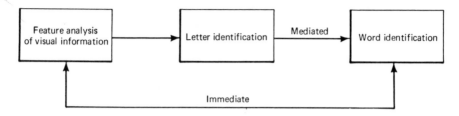

FIGURE 9.1. Immediate and mediated word identification.

identification is independent of the identification of individual letters. The alternatives are represented in Figure 9.2. The argument is presented in three steps:

1. Showing that immediate meaning identification *is* accomplished; that readers normally can and do identify meaning without or ahead of the identification of individual words.
2. Proposing how immediate meaning identification is accomplished.
3. Discussing how immediate meaning identification is learned.

In a final section I briefly discuss the mediated identification of meaning, or what a reader does when the direct apprehension of meaning is not possible.

USING MEANING IN READING

One demonstration has already been given that readers employ meaning to assist in the identification of individual words rather than laboring to identify words in order to obtain meaning. I am referring to the experiment showing that from a single glance at a line of print—the equivalent of about one second of reading—a reader can identify four or five words if they are in a meaningful sequence but scarcely half that amount if the words are unrelated to each other. The explanation in Chapter 4, when I originally described this classic study (Cattell, 1885), was that with meaningful text a reader could recruit

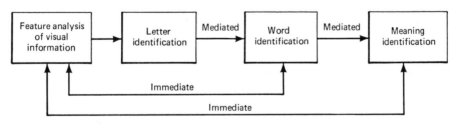

FIGURE 9.2. Immediate and mediated meaning identification.

9

nonvisual information to reduce alternatives so that the amount of visual information that the brain can handle in a second would go twice as far, to identify four or five words instead of a couple. The nonvisual information that the reader already possesses can only be meaning, or prior knowledge of the way in which words go together in language that is not only grammatical but makes sense.

A Constant Concern

It is important to understand that the reader in the situation just discussed is constantly making use of meaning; meaningfulness facilitates the identification of every word in the line. The reader does not first identify one or two words by a word identification strategy, as if they had nothing to do with the other words in the line, and then make an educated guess about the rest. Indeed, that same experiment shows that if two words had to be identified to give a clue about the others, then there would be no time left for the others to be identified. Two is the limit for words that have no meaningful relationships. Where a sequence of words does make sense, the identification of every word is facilitated, the first as well as the last, just as individual words can be identified in conditions in which none of their component letters would be individually discriminable. It is all a matter of the prior elimination of unlikely (and impossible) alternatives.

The demonstration just discussed is historic; it was first conducted and reported a century ago. But in a sense, the fact that meaning facilitates the identification of individual words is replicated every time we read, because reading would be impossible if we labored along, blindly striving to identify one word after another with no prior insights into what those words might be. Slow reading is not efficient reading because it tends to create tunnel vision, overload short-term memory, and leave the reader floundering in the ambiguity of language. Yet it is impossible to read quickly language that does not make sense, as you can experience for yourself if you try to read the following passage:

> Be might words those what into insights prior no with, another after word one identify to striving blindly, along labored we if impossible be would reading because, read we time every replicated is words individual of identification the facilitates meaning that fact the, sense a in but.

The words you have just tried to read are what I hope is a perfectly meaningful English sentence—because I used it myself in the previous paragraph—written backward. Any difference between the rate and ease with which you could read the backward and forward versions of that sentence can only be attributable to whether you were able to make sense of it. (If you had read the backward passage aloud, incidentally, you probably would have sounded very much like many "problem readers" at school, who struggle to identify words one at a time in a dreary monotone as if each word had nothing to do with any other. Such children seem to believe—and may well have been taught—that meaning should be their last concern; that sense will take care of itself provided they get the words right rather than that meaning facilitates the identification of words.)

Professional readers, for example broadcasters, know the importance of prior understanding of what they are about to read; that is why they like to scan through a script in advance. Looking ahead also helps the silent reading of novels and technical books—we can get a general idea of what will transpire and then go back where necessary to study particular points. The general comprehension comes out of fast reading, while the slow reading that might be necessary for memorization or for reflection upon detail can only be accomplished if comprehension has already been taken care of. Conversely, meaning can interfere with some reading tasks. Proofreaders tend to overlook misprints if they attend to the sense of what they read; they see the spellings and words that should be on the page rather than those that actually are there. Sometimes proofreaders will deliberately read backward in order to give all their attention to spelling and individual words, but then of course they will overlook anomalies of meaning. Their dilemma highlights the fact that attention to individual words and to meaning are alternative and not concurrent aspects of reading.

The prior use of meaning ensures that when individual words must be identified, for example, in order to read aloud, a minimum of visual information need be used. And as a consequence, mistakes will often occur. If a reader already has a good idea of what a word might be, there is not much point in delaying to make extra certain what the word actually is. As a result it is not unusual for even highly experienced readers to make misreadings that are radically different visually—like reading "said" when the word is actually *announced* or *reported* but which make no significant difference to the meaning. Beginning readers often show exactly the same tendency, demonstrating that children will strive for sense even when they learn to read (provided the material they are expected to learn from has some possibility of making sense in the first place). The mistakes that are made are sometimes called *miscues* rather than *errors* to avoid the connotation that they are something bad (Goodman, 1969). Such misreadings show that these beginning readers are attempting to read in the way fluent readers do, with sense taking priority over individual word identification. Of course, reading with minimal attention to individual words will sometimes result in misreadings that do make a difference to meaning, but one of the great advantages of reading for meaning in the first place is that one becomes aware of mistakes that make a difference to meaning. An important difference between children who are doing well in reading and those who are not is not that good readers make fewer mistakes, but that they go back and correct the mistakes that make a difference. Children who are not reading for sense have no chance of becoming aware of even important errors.

The Priority of Meaning

A unique illustration of the way in which the meaning takes priority over the identification of individual words was provided by Kolers (1966), who asked bilinguals fluent in English and French to read aloud from passages of text that made sense but where the actual language changed from English to French every two or three words. For example:

> His horse, followed de deux bassets, faisait la terre résonner under its even tread. Des gouttes de verglas stuck to his manteau. Une violente brise was blowing. One side de l'horizon lighted up, and dans la blancheur of the early morning light, il aperçut rabbits hopping at the bord de leur terriers.

The subjects in this experiment could read and understand such passages perfectly well, but when they had finished they often could not remember whether particular sentences or words were in English or French. Most significantly, they frequently substituted for a word in one language an appropriate word in the other. They might read "porte" when the word was *door* or "hand" when *main* was given, getting the meaning right but the language wrong. This does not mean that they were not looking at individual words at all—the passage was not completely predictable—but that they were looking at words and finding meanings, just as an English speaker might look at *2000* and understand "two thousand" while a French speaker would look at the same print and understand "deux milles."

An important and perhaps difficult point to understand from the preceding discussion is that it is possible to make meaningful decisions about words without saying exactly what the words are. In other words, we can *see* that the written word *door* means door without having to say aloud or to ourselves that the word *is* "door." Written words convey meaning directly; they are not intermediaries for spoken language. An obvious example is provided for English by words which have different spellings for the same sound, like *their* and *there*. It is easy to detect the spelling error in *The children left there books behind* because *there* represents the wrong meaning. The difference between *their* and *there*, and *read* and *reed*, and *so*, *sew*, and *sow*, is evidently not that the different spellings represent different sounds, because they do not, but that the different appearances of the words indicate different meanings. The visual appearance of each word indicates meaning directly.

The fact that readers can, do, and must read directly for meaning is similarly apparent with a written language like Chinese, which does not correspond to any particular sound system. It would be pointless to argue whether the written symbol 家 represents the Mandarin or the Cantonese word for "house" (or even whether the symbol represents the word "house" or the word "residence" in either spoken language) because it simply represents a *meaning*. My present assertion is that any written language is read as Chinese is read, directly for meaning. The fact that some written languages are also more or less related to the sound system of a spoken language is quite coincidental as far as the reader is concerned. As I suggested earlier, the alphabet could have originated purely for the convenience of writers. Certainly, there is no evidence that fluent readers identify letters in order to identify familiar words, and English spelling is, at best, an inadequate guide to the identification of words that are unfamiliar.

My final example that written language indicates meaning directly is rather poignant, since it comes from studies of brain-injured patients. People who are unable to find the exact word have been reported, for example, as reading the isolated word *ill* as "sick," *city* as "town," and *ancient* as "historic" (Marshall & Newcombe, 1966). Or *injure* as "hurt," *quiet* as "listen," and *fly* as "air" (Shallice & Warrington, 1975). In a remarkable "misreading" one patient identified *symphony* as "tea," presumably first visually confusing the written word with *sympathy*.

COMPREHENSION AND THE REDUCTION OF UNCERTAINTY

I have tried to show that meaning can take priority over the identification of individual words in two ways, both for fluent readers and for beginners. In the first case, the meaning of a sequence of words facilitates the identification of individual words with relatively less visual information. In the second case, written words can be understood without being identified precisely. Usually both aspects of meaning identification occur simultaneously; we comprehend text using far less visual information than would be required to identify the individual words, and without the necessity of identifying individual words. Both aspects of meaning identification are, in fact, reflections of the same underlying process—the use of minimal visual information to make decisions specific to implicit questions (or predictions) about meaning on the part of the reader.

I am using a rather awkward expression "meaning identification" as a synonym for comprehension in this chapter to underline the fact that the way in which a reader makes sense of text is no different from that by which individual letters or words may be identified in the same text. I could also use the rather old-fashioned psychological term *apprehension* to refer to the way meaning must be captured, but that would cloud the similarities between comprehension and letter and word identification. What is different about comprehension is that readers bring to the text implicit questions about meaning rather than about letters or words. The term *meaning identification* also helps to emphasize that comprehension is an active process. Meaning does not reside in surface structure. The meaning that readers comprehend from text is always relative to what they already know and to what they want to know. Put in another way, comprehension involves the reduction of a reader's uncertainty, asking questions and getting them answered, which is a point of view already employed in the discussion of letter and word identification. Readers must have *specifications* about meanings.

A passage of text may be perceived in at least three ways: as a sequence of letters from a certain alphabet, as a sequence of words of a particular language, or as an expression of meaning in a certain domain of knowledge or understanding. But in fact a passage of text is none of these things, or at least it is only these things potentially. Basically, written text is a lot of inkmarks on a page, variously characterized as visual information, distinctive features, or surface structure. Whatever readers perceive in text—letters, words, or meanings—depends on the prior knowledge (nonvisual information) that they happen to bring and the implicit questions they happen to be asking. The actual information that readers find (or at least seek) in the text depends on their original uncertainty.

Consider, for example, this sentence that you are reading at this moment. The visual information in the sentence can be used to make decisions about letters, for example, to say that the first letter is "c," the second "o," the third "n," and so forth. Alternatively, exactly the same visual information could be used to decide that the first word is "consider"; the second word, "for"; the third word, "example"; and so forth. The reader employs the same visual information, selects from among the same distinctive features, but this time sees words, not letters. What readers see depends on what they are looking for, on their implicit questions or uncertainty. Finally, exactly the same visual information can be employed to make decisions about meaning in the sentence, in which case neither letters nor words would be seen individually. It is not easy to say precisely what is being identified in the case of meaning, but that is due to the conceptual difficulty of saying what meaning is, not because the reader is doing anything intrinsically different. The reader is using the same source of visual information to reduce uncertainty about meaning rather than about letters or words.

As we have already seen, the amount of visual information required to make letter or word identification depends on the extent of the reader's prior uncertainty, on the number of alternatives specified in the reader's mind (and also the degree to which the reader wants to be confident in the decisions to be made). With letters it is easy to say what the maximum number of alternatives is — 26 if we are considering just one particular typeface in upper- or lowercase in the English alphabet. It is similarly easy to show that the amount of visual information required to identify each letter goes down as the number of alternatives that the letter might be (the reader's uncertainty) is reduced. The fewer the alternatives, the faster or easier a letter is identified, because fewer distinctive features need to be discriminated for a decision to be made. It is not so easy to say what the maximum number of alternatives is for words, because that depends on the range of alternatives that the reader considers in the first place, but again it is not difficult to show that the amount of visual information required to identify a word goes down as the reader's uncertainty is reduced. A word can be identified with fewer distinctive features when it comes from a couple of hundred alternatives than from many thousands. Finally, it is quite impossible to say how many alternative meanings there might be for a passage of text, because that depends entirely on what an individual reader is looking for, but it is obvious that reading is easier and faster when the reader finds the material meaningful than when comprehension is a struggle. The less uncertainty readers have about the meaning of a passage, the less visual information is required to find what they are looking for in the passage.

The Use of Nonvisual Information

In each of the preceding cases nonvisual information can be employed to reduce the reader's uncertainty in advance and to limit the amount of visual information that must be processed. The more prior knowledge a reader can bring to bear about the way letters go together in words, the less visual information is required to identify individual letters. Prediction, based on prior knowledge, eliminates unlikely alternatives in advance. Similarly, the more a reader knows about the way words go together in grammatical and meaningful phrases—because of the reader's prior knowledge of the particular language and of the topic being discussed—the less visual information is required to identify individual words. In the latter case, meaning is being used as part of nonvisual information to reduce the amount of visual information required to identify words. An example may be given in the form of a demonstration (based on a study reported by Tulving & Gold, 1963).

First, as a kind of pretest, I ask whether you can identify a word, or any of the letters, in the minimal visual information ᴧʟᴧʟᵢᴧ . Now we can proceed with the illustration. Because of the syntactic redundancy of language, a sentence like *After dinner let's go to the*———is almost certain to end with a noun rather than a verb or adjective or preposition, a piece of grammatical prior knowledge that reduces considerably the number of alternatives that the word in the final position might be. In addition there are semantic (meaning) constraints that go even further in reducing the number of alternatives. In fact, just one word has a much higher probability of being put into the blank position in the sentence than any other—the word "theater." "Theater," however, is not the most probable word in all contexts; at the end of a sequence such as *We agreed that he would meet me at the* ———, the word "station" or "airport" has a very much higher probability of occurring than "theater" and a number of other words.

We can now test our hypothesis that prior knowledge results in the reduction in the number of visual features required to identify a word in a meaningful context. We flash the two words onto a screen, and ask two groups of people to try to identify them. For one group we flash the word "theater" after they have been told the other words of the first sentence, and the word "station" after they have been given the words of the second sentence. For the other group we reverse the order, flashing "station" after the first sentence and "theater" after the second. You will notice, of course, that both words are equally feasible in each context. There is nothing nonsensical about going to the station after dinner or arranging to meet at the theater. It is just that these combinations are less likely. Our experimental assumption is that if more people manage to identify a word from a brief exposure on one occasion than on another, then they must be identifying it on less visual information; they are making use of other sources of information.

The result of the experiment should come as no surprise at this point. A much greater proportion of viewers is able to recognize the word "theater" from a brief flash if it follows the first sentences than if it follows the second. And more people identify the word "station" after the second sentence than after the first. It must be noted that the viewers are not guessing; they are making use of visual information because they do not respond "theater" when *station* is presented. But the amount of information required to identify either word depends on the sequence of words that it follows, on the sense that the reader can predict.

To nail down the point, let us see once more if you can identify the elements printed in our pretest ᴄʟᴏᴛ̣ɪᴏɴ . You probably can now. If you cannot, then you should have no difficulty in the context "There was a happy reunion at the ᴄʟᴏᴛ̣ɪᴏɴ ."

Many people can follow the meaning of a novel or newspaper article at the rate of a thousand words a minute, which is four times faster than their probable speed if they were identifying every word, even with meaning to help them. There is a prevalent misconception that for this kind of fast reading the reader must be identifying only one word in every four and that this gives sufficient information at least for the gist of what is being read. But it is very easy to demonstrate that identifying one word in four will not contribute very much towards the intelligibility of a passage. Here is every fourth word from a film review: *Many——been——face——business——sour——If—— to. . . .* The passage is even less easy to comprehend if the selected words are in groups, with correspondingly larger gaps between them. It is somewhat easier to comprehend what a passage is about if every fourth *letter* is provided rather than every fourth word, and, of course, my argument is that reading at a thousand words a minute is possible only if the omissions occur at the *featural* level. A skilled reader may need to discriminate only a fraction of the features available in every word, but not if these features are all concentrated in a single letter.

It should not be thought from the preceding discussion that there is a special kind of distinctive feature for meaning in print, different from the distinctive features of letters and words. There is no "semantic feature," for example, that *house* and *residence* physically have in common that we should expect to find in the inkmarks on the page. What makes visual features distinctive as far as meaning is concerned is precisely what makes them distinctive for individual letters and words as well—the particular alternatives that already exist in the reader's uncertainty. The same features that can be used to distinguish the letter *m* from the letter *h* will also distinguish the word *mouse* from the word *house* and the meaning of *we went to the mill* from the meaning of *we went to the hill*. It is not possible to say what the specific features are that readers employ to distinguish meanings; this would depend upon what the reader is looking for, and, in any case, it is not possible to describe the features of letters ,or words either. The situation is only additionally complicated by the fact that we cannot say what a meaning is.

Capturing "Meaning"

As pointed out in Chapter 2, in the discussion of the chasm between the surface structures and the deep structure of language, meaning lies beyond words. One cannot *say* what meaning is in general, any more than one can say what the meaning of a particular word or group of words is, except by saying other words that are themselves surface structure. The meaning itself can never be exposed. This inability to pin down meaning is not a theoretical defect or scientific oversight. We should not hope that a marvelous discovery will be made one day to enable us all to say what meanings are. Meaning, to repeat myself, cannot be captured in a net of words.

A reader does not comprehend the written word *table* by saying the spoken word "table" either aloud or silently, any more than the spoken word "table" can itself be understood simply by repeating it to oneself. (Would you understand the Spanish word *"mesa"* by saying it to yourself if you did not understand the language?) And neither the written nor the spoken word *table* is understood by saying silently to oneself "a four-legged flat-topped piece of furniture," or whatever other definition might come to mind, because of course the understanding of the definition would itself still have to be accounted for. There can be no understanding and no explanation unless the web of language is escaped. The actual *words*, written or spoken, are always secondary to meaning, to understanding.

We are normally unaware of *not* identifying individual words when we read because we are not thinking about words in any case. Written language (like speech) is *transparent*—we look through the actual words for the meaning beyond, and unless there are noticeable anomalies of meaning, or unless we have trouble comprehending, we are not aware of the words themselves. (When we deliberately attend to specific words, for example in the subtle matter of reading poetry, this is a consequence of asking a different kind of question in the first place. The sounds that we can give to the words do not so much contribute to a literal interpretation as establish a different—a complementary or alternative—kind of mood or meaning.)

Reading Aloud and Silently

Of course, word identification is necessary for reading aloud, but as I have tried to show, the identification of words in this way depends upon the identification of meaning. The voice lags behind the understanding, and is always susceptible, to some extent, of diverging from the actual text. The substitution of words and even phrases with appropriate meanings is again not something that the reader will be aware of; the reader's main concern, even in reading aloud, must be with the sense of the passage. Misreadings would have to be pointed out by a listener following both the text and the reading. Misreadings of this kind are not normally made when words are not part of meaningful text, but rather words in isolation or in lists, but then there is no way that meaning could be sought or utilized in any case. Besides, in such circumstances readers usually have the leisure to scrutinize sufficient visual information to identify individual words precisely (giving the words a label rather than a meaning) because nothing is lost by reading slowly.

Subvocalization (or reading silently to oneself) cannot in itself contribute to meaning or understanding any more than reading aloud can. Indeed, like reading aloud, subvocalization can only be accomplished with anything like normal speed and intonation if it is preceded by comprehension. We do not listen to ourselves mumbling parts of words or fragments of phrases and then comprehend. If anything, subvocalization slows readers down and interferes with comprehension. The habit of subvocalization can be broken without loss of comprehension (Hardyck & Petrinovich, 1970). Besides, most people do not subvocalize as much as they think. If we "listen" to ascertain whether we are subvocalizing, subvocalization is bound to occur. We can never hear ourselves not subvocalizing, but that does not mean that we subvocalize all the time. Why do we subvocalize at all? The habit may simply be a holdover from our younger days, perhaps when we were expected to real aloud. A teacher knows that children are working if their fingers are moving steadily along the lines and their lips are moving in unison. Subvocalization may also have a useful function in providing "rehearsal" to help hold in short-term memory words that cannot be immediately understood or otherwise dealt with. But in such cases subvocalization indicates lack of comprehension rather than its occurrence. There is a general tendency to subvocalize when reading becomes difficult, when we can predict less.

Prediction and Meaning

Readers do not normally attend to print with their minds blank, with no prior purpose and with no expectation of what they might find in the text. Readers normally look for meaning rather than strive to identify letters or words. The way readers look for meaning is not to consider all possibilities, nor to make reckless guesses about just one, but rather to predict within the most likely range of alternatives. In this way readers can overcome the information-processing limitations of the brain and also the inherent ambiguity of language. Readers can derive meaning directly from text because they bring expectations about meaning to text. The process is normally as natural, as continuous and effortless as the way we bring meaning to every other kind of experience in our lives. We do not go through the world saying "There's a chair; there's a table; a chair is something I can sit on," struggling to make sense of every bit of information our sensory systems direct towards the brain. Instead we look out for those aspects of our environment that will make the world meaningful to us, especially with respect to our particular purposes and interests. Comprehension is not a matter of putting names to nonsense and struggling to make sense of the result, but of operating in the realm of meaningfulness all the time.

LEARNING TO IDENTIFY MEANING

The remarks that concluded the preceding discussion should have made the present discussion largely unnecessary. There is no need for a special explanation about how children learn to apprehend meaning from print because no special process is involved. Children will naturally try to bring meaning to print. For them there is no point in language that is not meaningful, whether spoken or written. They perceive spoken language by looking for meaning, not by focusing on the sounds of words.

The Expectation of Sense

There is a classic illustration of the priority that meaning takes as children learn to talk. Even when children try to "imitate," it is meaning that they imitate, not meaningless sounds. McNeill (1967) reported an exchange between mother and child which went like this:

Child: Nobody don't like me.
Mother: No, say "Nobody likes me."
Child: Nobody don't like me.
(eight repetitions of this dialogue)
Mother: No, now listen carefully, say *"Nobody likes me."*
Child: Oh! Nobody don't likes me.

Even when children are asked to perform a language exercise, they expect that it will make sense. Like the child in the above example, it takes them a long time to understand the task if they are required to attend to surface structure, not to meaning. Children do not need to be told the converse, to look for sense; that is their natural (and only) way of learning about language in the first place. Indeed, they will not willingly attend to any noise that does not make sense to them.

Just as children do not need to be told to look for meaning in either spoken or written language, so they also do not need to learn special procedures for finding meaning. Prediction is the basis of meaning identification, and all children who can understand the spoken language of their own environment must be experts at prediction. Besides, the very constraints of reading—the constant possibility of ambiguity, tunnel vision, and memory overload—can only serve as reminders to learners that the basis of reading must be prediction.

Certainly there is no need for a special explanation of how comprehension should be *taught*. Comprehension is not a new kind of skill that has to be learned for reading but is the basis of all learning. Rather it may happen at school that children are taught the *reverse* of comprehension, being instructed instead to take care to "decode" correctly and not to make "guesses" if they are uncertain. They may even be expected to learn to read with materials and exercises specifically designed to discourage or prevent the use of nonvisual information.

Of course, there is a difference between the comprehension of written language and the comprehension of speech or of other kinds of events in the world, but these are not differences of process. The differences are simply that the reader must use the distinctive features of print to test predictions and reduce uncertainty. Children need to become familiar with these distinctive features for print and with how they are related to meaning. This familiarity and understanding cannot be taught, any more than the rules of spoken language can be taught, but formal instruction is similarly unnecessary and in fact impossible. The experience that children require to find meaning in print can only be acquired through meaningful reading, just as children develop their speech competence through using and hearing meaningful speech. And until children are able to do meaningful reading on their own account, they are clearly dependent on being read to, or at least on being assisted to read.

The Right to Ignore

A final point. It is not necessary for any readers, and especially not for beginners, to understand the meaning of *everything* that they attempt to read. Whether adults are reading novels and other lengthy texts or menus or advertisements, they always have the liberty to skip quite large passages and certainly to ignore many small details, either because they are not comprehensible, or simply because they are not relevant to their interest or needs. Children, when they are learning spoken language, seem able and willing to follow adult conversations and television programs without comprehending every word. A grasp of the theme, a general interest, and the ability to make sense on the basis of a few comprehensible parts can be more than sufficient to hold a child's attention. Such partially understood material is indeed the basis for learning; no one will pay attention to any aspect of language, spoken or written, unless it contains something that is new. For children, a good deal that is not comprehensible will be tolerated for the opportunity to explore something that is new and interesting. But children are rarely given credit for their ability to ignore what they cannot understand and to attend only to that from which they will learn.

Unfortunately, the right of children to ignore what they cannot understand may be the first of their freedoms to be taken away when they enter school. Instead, attention may be focused on what each child finds incomprehensible in order to "challenge" them to further learning. Anything a child understands may be set aside as "too easy." Paradoxically, many reading materials are made intentionally meaningless. Obviously, in such cases there is no way in which children will be able to develop and profit from their ability to seek and identify meaning in text.

MEDIATED MEANING IDENTIFICATION

Reading usually involves bringing meaning *immediately* or directly to the text without awareness of individual words or their possible alternative meanings. There are occasions, however, when the meaning of the text or of particular words cannot be immediately comprehended. On these occasions, mediated meaning identification may be attempted, involving the identification of individual words before comprehension of a meaningful sequence of words as a whole. The discussion is divided into two parts, the first concerned with the mediated meaning identification of entire sequences of words, such as phrases and sentences, and the second concerned with the mediated identification of the meaning of occasional individual words.

I have already argued that the first is rarely possible. The meaning of a sentence as a whole is not understood by putting together the meanings of individual words (Chapter 2). Individual words have so much ambiguity—and usually alternative grammatical functions as well—that without some prior expectation about meaning there is little chance for comprehension even to begin. In addition, limitations of visual information processing and memory are difficult to overcome if the reader attempts to identify and understand every word as if it had nothing to do with its neighbors and came from many thousands of alternatives. So although some theories of reading and many methods of reading instruction would appear to be based on the assumption that comprehension of written text is achieved one word at a time, the present analysis leaves little on this topic to be discussed. To attempt to build up comprehension in such a way must be regarded as highly inefficient and not likely to succeed.

But the second sense of mediated meaning identification—where the passage in general is comprehensible and perhaps just one word is unfamiliar and not understood—is a more general and useful characteristic of reading. In this case the question is not one of trying to use the meanings of individual words to construct the meaning of the whole, but rather of using the meaning of the whole to provide a possible meaning for an individual word. And not only is this possible; it is the basis of much of the language learning that we do. The bulk of the vocabulary of most literate adults must come from reading (Nagy, Herman, & Anderson, 1985). It is not necessary to understand thousands upon thousands of words to begin to learn to read—basically all that is required is a general familiarity with the words and constructions in the written material from which one is expected to learn, and then not all of those. And it seems highly unlikely that our understanding of many of the words that we have learned as a result of reading should be attributed to thousands of trips to the dictionary or to asking someone else what the word might be. We learn the meaning from the text itself.

Informal evidence that we quite coincidentally learn new words while reading comes from those words whose meaning or reference we know well but which we are not sure of pronouncing correctly, so there is no way we could have learned about them from speech. I am referring to words like *Penelope* (Penny-loap?), *misled* (mizzled? myzelled?) and *gist* (like guest or gest?), and perhaps *slough* and *orgy*, not to mention innumerable foreign words, names and places. There is what I like to call the *facky-tious* phenomenon (*tious* to rhyme with "pious") after the occasion when the mother of a friend commented that one did not often hear the word "facky-tious" these days. My friend confessed that he could not remember the last time he heard the word and asked what it meant. "A little sarcastic or supercilious," he was told. Something clicked.

"You mean *facetious*," he said. "No," replied his mother thoughtfully, "though the two words do have a similar meaning. Come to think of it," she added, "I don't think I've ever seen the word *facetious* in print."

The question, of course, is where she got the correct meaning of facky-tious which she had never heard in speech and had obviously never asked anyone about. And the answer must be that she learned it the way most of us learn the meaning of so many of the words that we know—by making sense of words from their context, using what is known to comprehend and learn the unfamiliar. Mediated meaning identification from context is something that fluent readers probably do frequently without awareness and is the basis not just of comprehension but of learning.

Learning new words without interference with the general comprehension of text is another example of the way in which children—and all readers—can continually learn to read by reading. The vocabulary that develops as a consequence of reading provides a permanent basis of knowledge for determining the probable meaning and pronunciation of new words. If you know both the meaning and the pronunciation of *auditor* and *visual*, you will have little difficulty in comprehending and saying a new word like *audiovisual*. The larger your capital, the faster you can add to it—whether with words or material wealth. The best way to acquire a large and useful sight vocabulary for reading is by meaningful reading. If the text makes sense, the mediation and the learning take care of themselves.

SUMMARY

Comprehension, the basic objective of reading, also facilitates the process of reading in two ways. Immediate meaning identification makes unnecessary the prior identification of individual words, and **comprehension** of a passage as a whole facilitates the comprehension and, if necessary, the identification of individual words. **Mediating meaning identification** increases the probability of tunnel vision, memory overload, and ambiguity caused by overreliance on visual information.

Notes to Chapter 9 begin on page 276, covering

Effects of meaningful context
Learners and context
Eye movements
Subvocalization

Chapter 10
READING, WRITING, AND THINKING

So far this book has been primarily concerned with topics much broader than reading—like language, comprehension, or memory—or with small aspects of reading—like letter or word identification. In this chapter the focus can finally be fixed on reading itself, on the specific act, when something meaningful is in front of a reader's eyes, and the reader is looking at it for a purpose. What does it mean to read? What can be said to be happening? And what do readers need to know?

Reading is never an abstract, purposeless activity, although it is frequently studied in that way by researchers and theorists, and regretably still taught in that way to many learners. Readers always read *something*, they read for a *purpose*, and reading and its recollection always involve *feelings* as well as knowledge and experience.

In other words, reading can never be separated from the purposes of readers and from its consequences upon them. This chapter is mainly concerned with what reading means to readers. Reading also cannot be separated from writing or thinking, although this book is not specifically directed to either of these large topics. But their relevance cannot be ignored, so the chapter ends with brief comments on writing and thinking. The final chapter is concerned with learning to read (which also will be found inseparable from the act of reading itself).

On Definitions Of Reading

Books on reading often attempt to define their terms with formal statements like "reading is extracting information from print." But such assertions do not provide any insight into reading or the way it is being discussed, and can lead to contentious debates. A definition does not justify its author using a common word differently from anyone else. Formal definitions are useful only if there is a reason for using words in a specialized, narrow, or otherwise unpredictable way, and even then they can cause more trouble than they are worth because readers prefer to interpret familiar words in familiar ways. (Philosopher Karl Popper, 1976, pointed out that precision can only be achieved at the cost of clarity). As I have already discussed, common, easily understood words tend to have a multiplicity of meanings, and what usually gives a word an unambiguous interpretation is neither prior agreement nor fiat but the particular context in which it happens to be used. As Popper also said, it is better to *describe* how a word is used than to define it.

Take the question of whether "reading" necessarily involves comprehension, an issue sometimes discussed at great length. But the question asks nothing about the nature of reading, only about the way the word is used on particular occasions. And the only possible answer is that sometimes the word "reading" implies comprehension, and sometimes it does not. When we suggest that someone should read a particular book, we obviously include comprehension in our recommendation—it would be redundant if not rude to say "I think you ought to read and comprehend this book." But on the other hand, our friend might reply "I've already read it, but I didn't understand it" now obviously excluding comprehension from the meaning of the word reading. Everything depends on the general sense in which words are used, even in the same conversation, in two successive sentences. If there is doubt, it is better to provide a more complete description of how the word is being used, than to attempt a general definition.

Consider, for example, the differences between reading a novel, a poem, a social studies text, a mathematical formula, a telephone directory, a recipe, the formalized description of some opening moves in chess, or an advertisement in a newspaper. Novels are usually read for the *experience*, for involvement in a situation, not unlike watching a play or movie or participating in actual events, where we are caught up with the characters and motivations of individual people, and with how circumstances will deal with them. To read a novel is to participate in life. A poem may involve a much more intense experience, especially emotionally, involving a particular mental attitude and a sensitivity to the sounds as well as to the meanings of words, akin in many ways to listening to music. The social studies text may lack the direct emotional and aesthetic connection of a novel or poem, but involve more detailed analytic thought—thinking that is more "off the page" and general than the details directly presented in the print. The mathematical formula is a tool, to be lifted (with understanding) from its position in the text and used elsewhere, whereas the telephone directory is like a collection of keys, each of which will open the lock on a particular connection. A recipe is a description of a set of actions for the reader to follow, chess notation involves participation in a game, and a newspaper advertisement is a device for persuading readers to act in particular ways.

These descriptions are pathetically inadequate for the richness that is reading. My aim in attempting a list was to illustrate the richness by demonstrating the inadequacy. And even then, I oversimplified. There is not one kind of novel or one kind of advertisement, and the same texts can be read in different ways. A novel can be read like a social studies text, and a social studies text like a novel. A newspaper advertisement may be read like a poem. Moreover, each of these different ways of reading texts is more like other forms of behavior or experience that do not involve reading than they are like other forms of reading. I equated reading a novel with watching a play, not with reading a play, and reading a recipe is obviously more like cooking a meal than like reading about any other kind of activity. There is no one activity that can be summed up as *reading;* no description that can be summarized as the "process" that is involved.

The meaning of the word "reading" in all these senses depends on everything that is going on—not just on what is being read, but on why a particular reader is reading. It might be said that in all of the examples I have given, answers are sought to questions that vary with the person asking them. And the only thing that makes all of these different activities "reading" is that the answers are being sought in print.

Because of the limitations on the amount of visual information from the text that the brain can deal with, the location and nature of the answers must to some extent be predictable. Thus the reader must have relevant expectations about the text. All questions must be couched within a prediction, a range of possible alternatives. This leads to a very broad description that I have already offered—that comprehension of text is a matter of having relevant questions to ask (that the text can answer) and of being able to find answers to at least some of those questions. To use a term I introduced earlier—reading depends on the relevance of the reader's *specification* of the text.

The particular questions can range from the implications of a single word to matters related to the style, symbolism, and world view of the author. I have avoided any attempt to list and characterize all these different questions because of their very specific—and sometimes specialized—nature. Instead, I have focused on three kinds of questions that all fluent readers seem able to ask and answer in most reading situations, related to the identification of letters, words, and meanings. These three kinds of questions are alternatives, all three cannot be asked simultaneously, and it is unnecessary for the reader to attempt to ask them in sequence. Reading is not a matter of identifying letters in order to recognize words in order to get the meaning of sentences. Meaning identification does not require the identification of individual words, just as word identification does not require the identification of letters. Indeed, any effort on the part of a reader to identify words one at a time, without taking advantage of the sense of the whole, indicates a failure of comprehension and is unlikely to succeed. In the same way any endeavor to identify and perhaps "sound out" individual letters is unlikely to lead to efficient word identification.

From this perspective it does not make sense to ask whether print basically consists of letters, words, or meanings. Print is discriminable visual contrasts, inkmarks on paper, that have the potential of answering certain questions—usually implicit—that readers might ask. Print is *visual information*, in which readers can select *distinctive features* and make decisions among the alternatives in which they are interested. Readers find letters in print when they ask one kind of question and select relevant visual information; they find words in print when they ask another kind of question and use the same visual information in a different way; and they find meaning in print, in the same visual information, when they ask a different kind of question again. It should be rare for a reader to ask questions about specific letters (except when letters themselves have a particular relevance, for example, as a person's initials or as a compass direction *N, S, E,* or *W*). It should also be rare for a reader to attend specifically to words, unless again there is a particular reason to identify a word, for example, a name.

Comprehension, as I have said, is relative; it depends on getting answers to the questions being asked. A particular meaning is the answer a reader gets to a particular question. Meaning therefore also depends on the questions that are asked. A reader "gets the meaning" of a book or poem from the writer's (or a teacher's) point of view only when the reader asks questions that the writer (or teacher) implicitly expected to be asked. Disputes over the meaning of text, or the "correct" way to comprehend text, are usually disputes over the questions that should be asked. A particular skill of accomplished writers (and of accomplished teachers) is to lead readers to ask the questions that they consider appropriate. Thus, the basis of fluent reading is the ability to find answers in the visual information of written language to the particular questions that are being asked. Written language makes sense when readers can relate it to what they know already (including those occasions when learning takes place, when there is a comprehensible modification of what readers know already). And reading is interesting and relevant when it can be related to what the reader *wants* to know.

READERS AND WRITERS

Readers must bring meaning to texts, they must have a developing and constantly modifiable set of expectations about what they will find. This is their specification of the text. But obviously writers make a contribution too. They must have their own specifications. And there must be a point at which readers and writers interact. That point is the text, and this section is about the interaction, about readers, writers, and the text.

Global and Focal Predictions

So far throughout this book I have talked as if predictions are made and dealt with one at a time. But predictions are usually multiplex, varying widely in range and significance. Some predictions are overriding; they carry us across large expanses of time and space. Other predictions occurring concurrently are far more transient, arising and being disposed of relatively rapidly. Our predictions are layered and interleaved.

Consider the analogy of driving a car. We have a general expectation that we will reach a certain destination at a certain time, leading to a number of relatively long-range predictions about landmarks that will be met along the route. Call these predictions *global*, because they tend to influence large parts of the journey. No matter how much our exact path might have to be varied because of exigencies that arise on the way, swerving to avoid a pedestrian or diverting down a side street because of a traffic holdup, these overriding global predictions tend to bring us always toward our intended goal.

But while global predictions influence every decision until our intended goal is reached, we simultaneously make more detailed predictions related to specific events during the course of the journey. Call predictions of this nature *focal*, because they concern us for short periods of time only and have no lasting consequence for the journey as a whole. Focal predictions must be made, usually quite suddenly, with respect to the oncoming truck or the pedestrian or as a consequence of a minor diversion. In contrast to global predictions, we cannot usually be specific about focal predictions before the journey begins. It would be futile to try to predict before starting the specific location of incidents that are likely to occur on the way. Yet while the occasion for a focal prediction is likely to arise out of particular sets of local circumstances, the prediction itself will still be influenced by our global expectations about the journey as a whole. For example, the modified focal predictions that will result if we have to make an unexpected detour will still be influenced by our overriding expectation of eventually reaching a particular destination.

We make similar global and focal predictions when we read. While reading a novel, for example, we may be concerned with a number of quite different predictions simultaneously, some global that can persist through the entire length of the book, others more focal that can rise and be disposed of in a single fixation.

We begin a book with extremely global predictions about its content from its title and from what perhaps we have heard about it in advance. Sometimes even global predictions may fail—we discover that a book is not on the topic we anticipated. But usually global predictions about content, theme, and treatment can persist throughout the book. At a slightly more detailed level there are likely to be still quite global expectations that arise and are elaborated within every chapter. At the beginning of the book we may have such predictions about the first chapter only, but in the course of reading the first chapter expectations about the second arise, the second leads to expectations about the third, and so on to the end. Within each chapter there will be rather more focal predictions about paragraphs, each paragraph being a major source of predictions about the next. Within each paragraph there will be predictions about sentences and within each sentence predictions about words.

Lower level predictions arise more suddenly; we will rarely make focal predictions about words more than a sentence ahead of where we are reading, nor predictions about sentences more than a paragraph ahead, nor predictions about paragraphs more than a chapter ahead. The more focal the prediction, the sooner it arises (because it is based on more immediate antecedents) and the sooner it is disposed of (because it has fewer long-range consequences). In general, the more focal a prediction, the less it can be specifically formulated in advance. You would be unlikely to predict the content of the present sentence before you had read the previous sentence, although the content of the paragraph as a whole was probably predictable from the previous paragraph. On the other hand, predictions at the various levels inform each other. While focal-level predictions are largely determined by the particular situation in which they arise, they are also influenced by our more global expectations. Your focal predictions about my next sentence will depend to some extent on your comprehension of the present sentence but also on your expectations about this paragraph, this chapter, and the book as a whole. Conversely, the global predictions that we make at the book and chapter level must be constantly tested and if necessary modified by the outcomes of our predictions at more focal levels. Your comprehension of one sentence could change your view of a whole book. The entire process is at once extremely complex and highly dynamic, but in Figure 10.1, I try to illustrate the framework of it with a considerably simplified and static diagram.

In general, the expectations of Figure 10.1 should be regarded as developing from left to right; the past influences our expectations for the future. But it can occasionally help at all levels of prediction in reading to glance ahead. The sequence of reading does not have to follow the page numbering of the book. Similarly, there should perhaps be diagonal lines all over the diagram as the

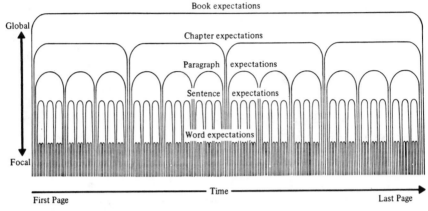

FIGURE 10.1.   Layers of prediction in reading a book.

outcomes of local predictions have their effect on global predictions and the global expectations exert their constant influence on specific focal predictions. At any moment, the character of our existing expectations about the book, chapter, paragraph, sentence, and word is our ever-changing specification of the text.

Do not take the diagram too literally. It is not necessary to predict at every level all of the time. We may become unsure of what a book as a whole is about and, for a while, hold our most global predictions to the chapter or even to a lower level while we try to grasp where the book might be going. Sometimes we may have so much trouble with a paragraph that we find it impossible to maintain predictions at the chapter level. At the other extreme we may find a chapter or paragraph so predictable, or so irrelevant, that we omit predictions at lower levels altogether. In plain language, we skip. It is only when we can make no predictions at all that a book will be completely incomprehensible. It should also not be thought that there are clearly defined boundaries between the different levels of prediction; the global-focal distinction does not describe alternatives but rather the extreme ends of a continuous range of possibilities.

The Writer's Point of View

I consider now the intentions of writers using the framework just employed to analyze the predictions of readers. To some extent, the patterns of predictions and intentions can be seen as reflections of each other.

Writers of books usually begin with only global intentions of what the book as a whole will be about and of the way the subject will be treated. These global intentions, in due course, then determine lower level intentions for every chapter. Within each chapter will arise more focal intentions about every paragraph, and within each paragraph quite detailed focal intentions regarding sentences and words. And just as the more focal predictions of the reader (or the driver) tend to arise at shorter notice and to be dispensed with more quickly, so the more focal intentions of the writer extend over a shorter range in both directions. What I want to say in the present sentence is most specifically determined by what I wrote in the previous one and will, in turn, place a considerable constraint upon how I compose the next sentence. But these focal constraints are at the detailed level. My intention in every sentence that I write is also influenced by the more global intentions for the paragraph as a whole, and of course my intention in every paragraph reflects the topic I have selected for the chapter and more generally for the book.

The intentions of writers can in fact be represented by exactly the same framework that I have used to represent the predictions of readers in Figure 10.1. The only difference would be that now the diagram should be captioned "Layers of intention in writing a book," with the word "intentions" replacing "expectations" at every level from global to focal. The same qualification would also apply about not taking the diagram too literally. Authors may at times be fairly sure about their global intentions at book, chapter, and even paragraph levels but be lost for focal intentions concerning particular sentences and individual words. At other times the words may flow without any clear indication of where they are going, the paragraph and other more global intentions remaining obscure.

It is from the overlapping perspectives of predictions and intentions that one can perhaps best perceive the intimate relationship between readers and writers. From the writer's point of view it might be said that a book is comprehended when the reader's predictions mirror the writer's intentions at all levels. Certainly one important aspect of writing is the intentional manipulation of the reader's predictions. A textbook writer must try to lead readers in a Socratic sense so that the answers to one set of predictive questions set up the succeeding predictions that the readers should make. In a more dramatic context an author may strive for tension by maintaining a particular degree of uncertainty in the reader's predictions at all levels throughout a book. And in a mystery story an author might quite deliberately lead readers into inappropriate predictions so that the inevitable consequence of predictions that fail— surprise—becomes a part of the reading experience.

But readers should also have intentions of their own. When we read a book purely for its literary or even entertainment merit we may willingly submit our expectations to the control of the author or poet, the willing suspension of disbelief. But with textbooks—like the present one, for example—readers should not only be pursuing certain pathways of ideas for their own particular ends, quite independently of the author, they should constantly be on guard against having their expectations entirely controlled by the author's arguments. Critical thinkers always reserve some questions of their own.

Global and Focal Conventions

The cascading diagram of Figure 10.1 can be used for a third time, to tie together much of what I have said so far about readers needing to predict what writers intend and writers needing to anticipate what readers will predict. First I used Figure 10.1 to represent the reader's point of view, the texture of *predictions*. Then with a slight modification of labeling it was used from the writer's point of view, as a network of *intentions*. Finally it can be employed as a representation of the text itself, the meeting ground of writer intentions and reader expectations.

In what way do writers manifest their various intentions, and what is it that readers predict at the various global and focal levels? As argued in Chapter 2, the answer is *conventions*. Conventions exist in every aspect of language; they correspond to every kind and level of intention and expectation. In considering the written language of books, Figure 10.1 needs simply to be relabeled "Layers of convention in a book," with the word *convention* replacing "expectations" (or "intentions") at every level. There are global conventions for books as a whole—these are *genre schemes, story grammars,* and the conventions of *register*. There are conventions for the way paragraphs are arranged into chapters and chapters into books—these are the *discourse structures*. There are conventions for the way sentences are organized into paragraphs—these are the conventions of *cohesion*. There are the conventions for the organization of words in sentences, the conventions of *grammar* and of *idiom*. And there are conventions for the words themselves, the conventions of *semantics,* and for the physical representation of those words, the conventions of *spelling*.

Intentions, predictions, and conventions—all have their relatively global levels and all have their focal. The same diagram can represent all three with just the slightest change in wording. There is just one critical difference. When labeled for conventions, Figure 10.1 is, I think, one reasonably appropriate way to characterize an entire text. Texts are static, they do not change their structure from moment to moment (unless someone is working on them). But the figure offers only *a way of thinking about* readers and writers; I do not want to suggest that such a structure ever exists in its entirety or in a stable form in anyone's head. We can inquire into particular global and focal intentions or predictions in writer's and reader's minds at particular times, but we should never expect to find a complete or unchanging set of them the way the diagram might suggest, the way conventions exist in a text. Instead we would find that writers and readers, each in their own way, have in their minds a *specification of a text*, a specification of global and focal elements far less complete and detailed than Figure 10.1, but far more dynamic and changing.

The Specification of a Text

Consider the matter first from the writer's point of view. What does a writer have in mind (a) before a text is begun to direct the writing that will be done, (b) while the text is being written to ensure that it follows the writer's developing intentions, and (c) when the text is done so that the writer can say "That is what I intended to write"? My answer each time is a *specification*.

The specification of a text is similar in many ways to the specification of a house. Such a specification is not the house itself, nor is it the plans for a house. It is a cluster of intentions and expectations, of constraints and guidelines, which determine what the plans and ultimately the house will be like. Specifications are never complete—we would not say to the architect "This is *exactly* how we want the house" because in that case we would not need the architect. Specifications will have gaps, they may even be internally inconsistent, and during the designing of the plans we or the architect may find a need for the specifications to be changed. Indeed, specifications should be expected to change as the execution of the plans develops, so that eventually there is a match between the plans (and house) and the specifications, between the aim and its fulfillment, partly because the house was designed around the constraints of the specifications but also because the specifications were changed and developed to meet the contingencies of actually designing and building the house. A different architect might have designed a different house, but we would still say "That is what we wanted" if the design is in accordance with our final specifications.

So with the writer. The book (or any other kind of text) that the author plans will initially develop in conformity with certain specifications which do not contain all the details of the text. And as the text develops the specifications will change, partly as the demands of the text change but also as a consequence of what has already been written. Details will be developed in the specifications as focal concerns arise and are then set aside and even forgotten because they are no longer relevant. Revisions will be made to the text with reference to the specifications and the specifications will be revised in the course of writing and revising the text. And at the end, if the final text is compatible with the final specification, the author will say "That is what I wanted to write," even though the constantly changing specification at no time spelled out exactly what the book would contain at all of its global and focal levels, even though a different book might have been written to the same initial specifications on a different occasion.

So too with readers. We begin with a sketchy specification of the text ("This is a book about reading") which develops in the course of our reading, consolidating in terms of what we have read so far and elaborating when necessary for the prediction of what is to come. Focal aspects of the specification are developed to make sense of detail as we come to it but then discarded as we move on to the next detail. Apart from the occasional quotation or specific idea which might lodge in our mind, we shall in general be far more concerned with the persisting global aspects of our specification than with the transient focal ones. And at the end we will have a specification that is still not the book itself but that is our ultimate comprehension of the book (just as the specification we can put together a week or a month later is our memory of the book at that time).

Texts exist independently of writers and readers. At no time does the text in its entirety exist in either the writer's or the reader's head. But before the interaction with the text (the writing or the reading), the specification determines what the writer or reader will do. And the developing interaction with the text changes the specification and contributes to what writers and readers finish up believing they have done.

How we comprehend when we read is a matter of the richness and congruence of the specification that we bring to the text and of the extent to which we can modify the specification in the course of reading the text. What we comprehend, and what we are left with in memory as a consequence of the reading, are the consequence of how our experience with the text modifies our specification. Subsequent reflection may change the specification even more, of course, which is the reason that we often cannot distinguish in memory what we read *in* a text from what we read *into* it.

Little research has yet been done specifically into the specifications of readers and writers as they move through texts from their particular perspectives. But recent investigations into story grammars, discourse structures, and event knowledge could lead toward an understanding of how readers and writers interact with texts, not from the static point of view of the texts themselves but from the dynamic point of view of the constantly changing and developing specifications in readers' and writers' minds.

Fluent Reading and Difficult Reading

This section was originally headed "Fluent Reading and Beginning Reading," to contrast the fluent manner in which experienced readers read with the stumbling, less proficient behavior of learners. But the distinction is not valid. It is usually possible to find something any beginning reader can read easily, even if it is only one word. And it is always possible to find something an experienced reader cannot read without difficulty. The advantage of a competent reader over a neophyte lies in *familiarity* with a range of different kinds of text, not in the possession of *skills* that facilitate every kind of reading.

For beginners and experienced readers alike, there is always the possibility of fluent reading and the possibility of difficult reading. There is no sudden transition from beginning reading, when nothing can be read without difficulty, to fluent reading, when all reading is easy. The more we read, the more we are able to read. Learning to read begins one word and one kind of text at a time, continues a word and a text at a time, and the learning never stops. Every time a reader meets a new word, something new is likely to be learned about the identification and meaning of words. Every time a new text is read, something new is likely to be learned about reading different kinds of text. Learning to read is not a process of building up a repertoire of specific skills, which make all kinds of reading possible. Instead, experience increases the ability to read different kinds of text.

Even experienced readers have difficulty in reading some texts—because of the way the texts are written, or because of inadequate nonvisual information on the reader's part, and sometimes because of pressures or anxieties involved in the particular act of reading. And when otherwise "competent" readers experience difficulty in reading, they tend to read like beginners. By the same token, when beginners find easy material to read, they tend to read like experienced readers.

In other words, the critical difference is not between experienced and beginning reading, or even "good reading" and "poor reading," but between fluent reading, which even beginners can do in the right circumstances, and difficult reading, a situation in which even experienced readers can sometimes find themselves. The problem for children learning to read is that everything they might attempt to read is likely to be more difficult.

Experienced readers (when they are reading fluently) can easily identify individual words if they have to. They use nonvisual information in order to comprehend, and are less dependent on the identification of individual words in the text or on the surrounding words. They "take control" of the text through the four characteristics of meaningful reading—their reading is purposeful, selective, anticipatory, and based on comprehension. Inexperienced readers, on the other hand, have more trouble identifying individual words— and ironically, more need to identify them. They depend more on the actual words in the text when they read because they can bring less prior knowledge to bear. They are less in control of their reading, more dominated by the text, lacking purpose, selectivity, appropriate anticipation, and comprehension. Experienced readers who are having difficulty reading have the characteristics of inexperienced readers.

Fluent reading involves pursuing a complex and ever changing set of objectives in order to make sense out of print in ways that are relevant to the purposes of the reader. Neither individual letter identification nor individual word identification are involved unless they are relevant to the particular requirements of the reader. Nor is every potential "meaning" on a page examined unless it has some bearing on the reader's purposes. Fluent reading is based upon a flexible specification of intentions and expectations, which change and develop as a consequence of the reader's progression through a text. Thus fluent reading demands knowledge of the conventions of the text, from vocabulary and grammar to the narrative devices employed. How much conventional knowledge is required depends on the purposes of the reader and the demands of the situation. Knowledge need not be complete, in fact provided there is sufficient comprehension to maintain the reader's attention, learning is likely to take place where specific knowledge is lacking.

The eyes of experienced readers (when they are reading fluently and intently) tend to fixate on every word in a text—or at least on every content word (Just & Carpenter, 1980), although not necessarily in order to identify the words. Obviously, meaning must have already been taken into account in order for content words to be focused on. Beginning readers may pay particular attention to the sounds of the words they read (Stanovich, 1986)—a phenomenon known as *phonological awareness*. This attention to sound is probably not exhibited by beginners in order to name unfamiliar words, but rather in an effort to ascertain their meaning from known words in spoken language vocabulary.

The Consequences of Reading

Reading is more than just a pleasant, interesting, and informative experience. It has consequences, some of which are the typical consequences of any kind of experience we might have. Other consequences are uniquely particular to reading.

General consequences of experience are an increase in specific memories and knowledge. I have not found any studies of how much individuals normally remember from what they read (outside of artificial experimental situations looking at how much can be recalled of items determined by the researcher). But common observation would suggest that individuals remember as much about books that they find interesting and readable as they do about "real life" experiences in which they are involved. Many anecdotal reports indicate remarkable memories on the part of readers for the appearance, titles, authors, characters, settings, plots, and illustrations of books that were important to them, often extending back to childhood. With books, as with every other kind of experience, we remember what we understand and what is significant to us.

There are also specific consequences. Experience always results in learning. Experience in reading leads to more knowledge about reading itself. Not surprisingly, students who read a lot tend to read better (Anderson, Hiebert, Scott, & Wilkinson, 1985). They do not need to read better in order to read a lot, but the more they read, the more they learn about reading. The same researchers reported that students who read more also tended to have larger vocabularies, better "comprehension skills," and generally did better on a range of academic subjects. In other words, reading makes people smarter.

Other things are learned through reading. I have argued at length (Smith, 1983b) that it is only through reading that anyone can learn to write. The only possible way to learn all the conventions of spelling, punctuation, capitalization, paragraphing, even grammar, and style, is through reading. Authors teach readers about writing.

In the next two chapters I describe learning in metaphorical terms as the *membership of clubs*. By joining the club of readers, individuals can learn to become readers and writers. But reading also opens the doors to any club that can be the topic of a book, which probably means most of the clubs in the world, and certainly many clubs that could not exist in the world as we know it. Reading is the club of clubs, the only possibility of many experiences of learning.

And finally, there are emotional concomitants and consequences of reading. Reading, like everything else, inevitably involves feelings. On the positive side, reading can provide interest and excitement, it can stimulate and alleviate curiosity, console, encourage, arouse passions, relieve loneliness, assuage tedium or anxiety, palliate sadness, and on occasion anaesthetize. On the negative side, reading can bore, confuse, and generate resentment. The emotional response to reading is treated insufficiently in most books about literacy (not excluding the present volume), although it is the primary reason most readers read, and probably the primary reason most nonreaders do not read.

Because of the range and depth of feelings involved, attitudes toward reading become habitual. Reading can become a desired activity or an undesirable one. People can become inveterate readers. They can also become inveterate nonreaders, even when they are capable of reading. One of the great tragedies of contemporary education is not so much that many students leave school unable to read and to write, but that others graduate with an antipathy to reading and writing, despite the abilities they might have. Nothing about reading or its instruction is inconsequential.

Reading and Thinking

The heading may be a trifle misleading. Reading is thinking, as I hope I have demonstrated throughout this chapter. And the thinking we do when we read, in order to read, is no different from the thinking we do on other occasions. Just as we cannot talk without thinking, or understand what someone is saying without thinking, or make any sense of the world without thinking, so it is impossible to read and not think. (If we sometimes say that we have spoken without thinking, we mean that we did not consider all the implications of what we were about to say.) Reading is thinking that is partly focused on the visual information of print; it is thinking that is stimulated and directed by written language. The only time we might attempt to read without thinking is when the text we are trying to read is meaningless to us, a situation unlikely to persist in normal circumstances.

It is true that we may read a story or magazine "to relax," in order not to think about particular things—but we obviously have to think enough about whatever we are reading in order to be distracted from other thoughts. If we fail to read every story with the intensity and acumen of a literary critic, it is probably not because we cannot think, but because we are not interested in reading like a literary critic.

The thought in which we engage while we are reading is like the thought we engage in while involved in any kind of experience. Fulfilling intentions, making choices, anticipating outcomes, and making sense of situations are not aspects of thinking exclusive to fluent reading. We must draw inferences, make decisions, and solve problems in order to understand what is going on in situations that involve reading and situations that do not. Reading demands no unique forms or "skills" of thought.

Thought that transpires as a consequence of reading is similarly no different from the reflection that can occur after any experience. We reconstruct an experience we have had, sometimes just for the pleasure of having it again, we wonder why events transpired the way they did, and whether they could have transpired differently. Reading can facilitate further thinking. We can join the clubs of authors, or of characters in books, who think in different ways about matters we might never otherwise contemplate, and as a consequence become more versatile and efficient thinkers ourselves. On the other hand, if we are generally not disposed to think critically in particular circumstances, or if we do not feel we have the authority to think critically about what certain "experts" are asserting, then we are unlikely to think critically when we read. The failure of children—or adults—to "think" in certain ways when they read may be less a matter of inadequate skill than of expectations about the manner in which they should think on any occasion.

An enormous advantage of reading over thinking in other circumstances is the *control* that it offers over events. Readers can pause in the middle of an experience for reflection. Readers can relive experiences, as often as they wish, and examine them from many points of view. Readers can even skip over experiences they are not interested in having, or that would disrupt their flow of thought. Readers have *power*.

Reading is no different in essence from any other manifestation of thoughtful activity—but it may be the most natural and satisfying form of thinking available to us. As Harold Rosen (1986) and others have often pointed out, the human brain is essentially a narrative device. It runs on stories. The knowledge that we store in the brain, in our "theory of the world," is largely in the form of stories. Stories are far more easily remembered and recalled than sequences of unrelated "facts." The most trivial small episodes and vignettes are intrinsically more interesting than "data." We cannot see random patterns or dots (or clouds or stars) without putting faces or figures to them. We cannot even observe small points of light moving randomly against a dark background without seeing them "interact" with each other in a narrative fashion (Michotte, 1946).

Thinking thrives on stories, on the construction and exploration of patterns of events and ideas, and reading often offers greater scope for engaging in stories than any other kind of activity.

SUMMARY

Reading—like writing and all other forms of thinking—can never be separated from the purposes, prior knowledge, and feelings of the person engaged in the activity, nor from the nature of the text being read. The **conventions** of texts permit the **expectations** of readers and the **intentions** of writers to meet. **Global** and **focal** expectations and intentions form a personal **specification** that readers and writers develop and modify as they proceed through a text. The fluency of reading depends as much on characteristics of the text and reader as on reading ability. Experienced readers who find a text difficult may read like beginners (who are likely to find most reading difficult).

Notes to Chapter 10 begin on page 281, covering

Comprehension—and thinking
Reading speed
Comprehension and context
Other aspects of reading
Reading and writing

Chapter 11
LEARNING ABOUT THE WORLD AND ABOUT LANGUAGE

This chapter, which introduces the topic of learning, is not specifically concerned with learning to read, a matter postponed to the next and final chapter. But this chapter is concerned with the *manner* in which children learn to read, because this is the same as the manner in which children achieve mastery of spoken language and, even earlier, begin learning about the world in general through their first elaborations of a theory of the world.

The present chapter provides an appropriate link with many of the preceding chapters, with their emphasis on comprehension in reading, because it attempts to show that the basis of all learning, including learning how to read, is comprehension. Children learn by relating their understanding of the new to what they know already, while modifying or elaborating their prior knowledge. Learning is continuous and completely natural, and it is not necessary to propose separate "processes" of motivation and reinforcement to sustain and consolidate learning (nor should it be necessary for teachers to regard motivation and reinforcement as separate concerns that can be grafted onto reading instruction). Children may not always find it easy or even necessary to learn what we try to teach them, but they find the state of not learning anything at all intolerable.

CONSTRUCTING A THEORY OF THE WORLD

Chapter 1 discussed the complex yet precise and accurate theory of the world that we all have lodged in our brains. Obviously, we were not born with such a theory. The ability to construct a theory of the world and to predict from it may be innate, but the actual contents of the theory, the specific detail underlying the order and structure that we come to perceive in the world, is not part of our birthright. But equally obviously, very little of our theory can be attributed to instruction. Only a small part of what we know is actually *taught* to us. Teachers and other adults are given altogether too much credit for what we learn as children.

The Cat and Dog Problem

Consider for example what it is that we know that enables us to tell the difference between cats and dogs. What were we taught that has given us this skill? It is impossible to say. Just try to write a description of cats and dogs that would enable a being from outer space—or a child who has never seen cats and dogs before—to tell the difference. Anything you might want to say about some dogs, that they have long tails or pointed ears or furry coats, will apply to some cats and not to other dogs. The fact is that the difference between cats and dogs is *implicit* in our heads, knowledge that cannot be put into words. Nor can we communicate this knowledge by pointing to a particular part of cats and dogs and saying, "That is where the difference lies."

Differences obviously exist between cats and dogs, but you cannot find and do not need language to distinguish them. Children without language can tell the difference between cats and dogs. Cats and dogs can tell the difference between cats and dogs. But if we cannot say what this difference is, how can we teach it to children? What we do, of course, is point out to children examples of the two kinds of animal. We say, "That is a cat" or "There goes a dog." But pointing out examples does not teach children anything; it merely confronts them with the problem. In effect, we say "There is something I call a cat. Now you find out why." The "teacher" poses the problem and leaves the child to discover the solution.

The same argument applies to just about everything we can distinguish in the world, to all the letters of the alphabet, to numbers, chairs and tables, houses, foodstuffs, flowers, trees, utensils, and toys, to every kind of animal, bird, and fish, to every face, every car and plane and ship, thousands upon thousands of objects that we can recognize not only by sight but by other senses as well. And when did anyone tell us the rules? How often has anyone told us "Chairs can be recognized because they have four legs and a seat and possibly a back and arms"? (You can see how inadequate a description that would be.) Instead, somebody once said, "There is a chair" and left us to decide not only how to recognize chairs on other occasions but also to discover what exactly the word "chair" means, how chairs are related to everything else in the world.

With reading we do not even need someone to pose the problem in the first place. Reading at the same time presents both the problem and the possibility of its solution. Just by virtue of being a reader, every one of us has acquired a sight vocabulary of at least 50,000 words, words that we can identify on sight the way we recognize familiar faces and houses and trees. How did we acquire this enormous talent? Fifty thousand flashcards? Fifty thousand times a teacher wrote a word on a board and told us what it was? Fifty thousand times we blended together the sound of a word through phonics? We have learned to recognize words by reading.

Not only can we recognize 50,000 words on sight—and also, of course, by sound—we can usually make sense of all of these words. Where have all the meanings come from? Fifty thousand trips to the dictionary? Fifty thousand lessons? We have learned all the conventions of language through using language, by speaking it, reading it, and making sense of it. What we know about language is largely implicit, just like our knowledge of cats and dogs. So little of our knowledge of language is actually taught, we underestimate how much of language we have learned.

Our language is full of rules that we were never taught. You would think it odd if I wrote *I have a small wooden blue sailing boat* or *a blue wooden small sailing boat*. There is only one way to say what I want to say—*I have a small blue wooden sailing boat*—and just about every English speaker over the age of five would agree. There is a rule for how we do this, but it is not a rule that most of us can put into words. It is not a rule that we were taught.

Most of our theory of the world, including most of our knowledge of language, whether spoken or written, is not the kind of knowledge that can be put into words; it is more like the implicit cat-and-dog kind of knowledge. Knowledge which no one can put into words is not knowledge that can be communicated by direct instruction.

How, then, do we acquire and develop the theory of the world we have in our heads? How does it become so complex and precise and efficient? There seems to be only one answer: *by conducting experiments*.

Learning by Experiment

Children learn by testing hypotheses and evaluating feedback. For example, a child might hypothesize that the difference between cats and dogs is that cats have pointed ears. The child can then test this hypothesis in experiments, by saying, "There is a cat" or "What a nice cat" or "Hi cat" when any animal with pointed ears passes by, and "There is a dog" (or "That's not a cat") for any animal without pointed ears. Relevant feedback is any reaction that tells the child whether the hypothesis is justified or not. If someone says something like, "Yes, there's a pretty cat" or accepts the child's statement by making no overt response at all, then the child has received feedback that the hypothesis has worked, on this occasion at least. The child's theory can be tentatively modified to include a rule that cats are animals with pointed ears. But if the feedback is negative, if someone says to the child, "No, that's a dog" or even something as rude as, "Think again, stupid," then the child knows that the hypothesis has failed. Another hypothesis must be selected and tested. Clearly more than one experiment will be required; it will take a lot of experience with cats and dogs before a child can be reasonably certain of having uncovered the true differences between them (whatever the differences may be). But the principle is always the same: stay with your theory for as long as it works; modify your theory, look for another hypothesis whenever it fails.

Note that it is essential for the child to understand the problem in the first place. Children will not learn to recognize cats simply by being shown cats; they will not know what to look for. Both cats and dogs must be seen in order for the hypothesis about their relevant differences to arise. Children learn each letter of the alphabet by seeing them all; they must see what the alternatives are.

There is an intimate connection between comprehension and learning. The children's experiments never go beyond their theories; they must comprehend what they are doing all the time they are learning. Anything that bewilders a child will be ignored; there is nothing to be learned there. It is not nonsense that stimulates children to learn but the possibility of making sense; that is why children grow up speaking language and not imitating the noise of the air conditioner. Children do not learn by being denied access to problems. A child learning to talk must be immersed in spoken language, and it is far better that a beginning reader having difficulties should be helped to read than be deprived of reading.

This process of hypotheses testing goes on instinctively, below the level of awareness. If we were aware of the hypotheses we test, then we could say what it is that enables us to tell the difference between cats and dogs. We are no more conscious of the hypotheses that underlie learning than we are of the predictions that underlie comprehension or of the theory of the world itself. Indeed, there is basically no difference between comprehension and learning; hypotheses are simply tentative predictions.

LEARNING ABOUT LANGUAGE

When does all this experimentation take place? I think that for young children there is only one answer: They are testing hypotheses all the time. Their predictions are always tentative. This assertion is best illustrated with respect to the topic with which we are most concerned, namely language.

Bringing Meaning to Speech

Consider for example the relatively well-researched procedures by which infants gradually master rules that enable them to produce grammatical utterances in the language spoken around them (Brown, 1973; McNeill, 1970). No one could spell out these rules with sufficient precision to attempt to teach them to a child, nor is there any indication that children could produce comprehensible utterances as a result of being given instruction in these rules. Instead, infants "invent grammar." They hypothesize rules for the formation of utterances as and when they require them, and test the adequacy of these hypotheses by putting them to use to represent a meaning. And infants progressively modify these hypothesized rules in the light of the feedback that they receive from the speakers of the language to whom their utterances are addressed. Adults elaborate in adult language the meaning that infants try to express in their own tentative way. The critical focus of this interaction is on the meaning that is shared; the adult must be able to comprehend what the infant is talking about. Adults do not know the rules by which infants form their early utterances, but they can make sense of these utterances by their prior understanding of the infants and of the situations in which the utterances are made. As a consequence, the infants can get on with the problem of working out how the surface structure and deep structure are related.

Children who have just begun to talk frequently make statements that are completely obvious. A child looking out of a window with you will say something like "See big plane" although you may even have pointed the plane out in the first place. Why then should the child bother to make the statement? The answer is because the child is learning, conducting an experiment. In fact, a child could be conducting no fewer than three different experiments at the same time in that one simple situation.

The child could be testing the hypothesis that the object you can both clearly see in the sky *is* a plane, that it is not a bird or cloud or something else unidentified. When you say, "Yes, I see it," you are confirming that the object is a plane: positive feedback. Even silence is interpreted as positive feedback, since the child would expect you to make a correction if the hypothesis were in error. The second hypothesis that the child might be testing concerns the sounds of the language, that the name "plane" is the right name for the object, rather than "pwane," "prane," or whatever else the child might say. Once again the child can assume that if you do not take the opportunity to make a correction, then there is nothing to be corrected. A test has been successfully conducted. The third hypothesis that the child may be testing is linguistic, whether "See big plane" is a grammatically acceptable and meaningful sentence in adult language. The feedback comes when the adult says, "Yes, I can see the big plane." The child learns to produce sentences in your language by using tentative sentences for which you both already know the meaning, *in a situation which you both comprehend.*

The same principle of making sense of language by understanding the situation in which it is used applies in the other direction as children learn to *comprehend* adult speech. At the beginning of language learning, infants must be able to understand what adults say before they can understand adult language. Does that statement sound paradoxical? What I mean is that children do not come to understand sentences like "Would you like a drink of juice?" or even the meaning of single words like "juice," by figuring out the language or by having someone tell them the rules. Children learn because initially they can hypothesize the meaning of a statement from the situation in which it is uttered. An adult is usually carrying or pointing to a drink of juice when a sentence like "Would you like a drink of juice?" is spoken. This language is situation-dependent speech. From such situations a child can hypothesize what might happen the next time someone mentions "juice." The situation provides the meaning and the utterance provides the evidence; that is all a child needs to construct hypotheses that can be tested on future occasions. Children do not learn language to make sense of words and sentences; they make sense of words and sentences in understanding how language is used (Macnamara, 1972).

There is an interesting role for the eyes to play in these first experiments with language. Newson and Newson (1975) have noted that the sharing of meaning is facilitated by a convergence of gaze. When a parent offers an infant a drink of juice, they are probably looking not at each other but at the cup that the adult is offering. When a parent says, "Ah, there's a diaper pin" to a baby who does not understand a word of speech, the gaze of parent and baby are likely to converge on the diaper pin. By bringing a possible meaning to the utterance the infant can hypothesize a relationship between the two, and thus test, confirm, or modify provisional rules about this relationship—a highly efficient procedure that will work only if the infant can make sense of the purpose of adult language.

I know of no research on how much language children might learn simply by observation. But if a baby can hypothesize and test a potential meaning when offered a cup of juice, there is no reason why the child could not test a similar hypothesis by overhearing one adult offer another a cup of coffee, provided the entire situation can also be seen. The child could again compare probable meaning with utterance. There are obvious limits to the number of language interchanges in which infants are directly involved, and which in any case may be in the pseudo "baby talk" of adults that cannot be of much use to children trying to learn adult language. It might at least seem possible that most infants overhear far more language than is actually addressed to them, though again there is no research on the issue. And by and large much of this overheard domestic language would be situationally meaningful; it would have functions and outcomes that are both predictable and testable.

It is in fact the functions of language, the uses to which it is put, which are the key to infant language learning. As the linguist Halliday (1973) has pointed out, children learn language and its uses simultaneously. They do not learn language, either spoken or written, which they then use for various purposes. The learning comes with the use of language and with the understanding of its uses. Language learning is in fact incidental. Children do not learn about language as an abstraction, as an end in itself, but in the process of achieving other ends, like getting another drink of juice, learning to distinguish cats from dogs, or striving to enjoy a story from a book. The basic insight that must enable a child to make sense of speech is that its sounds are not random, they are not arbitrarily substitutable. By this I mean that the sounds of speech make a difference, they are there for a purpose. An adult cannot produce the sounds "There's a truck" when the intended meaning is "Let's go for a walk."

THREE ASPECTS OF LEARNING

Learning is the modification or elaboration of what is already known, of cognitive structure, the theory of the world in the head. What exactly is modified or elaborated? It can be any of the three components of the theory: the category system, the rules for relating objects or events to categories (sets of distinctive features), or the complex network of interrelations among categories.

Children are constantly required to establish new categories in their cognitive structure and to discover the rules that limit the allocation of events to a new category. They have to learn that not all animals are cats and dogs but that some animals are. Children learning to sight-recognize the printed word *cat* have to establish a visual category for that word, just as they must have a category for actual cats, distinguished from other categories for dogs, and so forth. Skilled readers develop categories for every letter of the alphabet and also for every word that can be identified on sight, together, possibly, with lists for frequently occurring syllabic groups of letters. This process of learning to establish categories involves hypothesizing what are the significant differences—the only reason to establish a new category is to make a new differentiation in our experience, and the learning problem is to find the significant differences that should define the category.

Each category that we distinguish must be specified by at least one set of distinctive features. Every time children succeed in learning to recognize something new, they must have established a new set of distinctive features. But usually they go further and establish *alternative* sets of features for specifying the same categories. They learn that an *a, ɑ* , or even an *A* should be categorized as a letter "a" just as many different-looking animals must be categorized as a cat. Any set of features that will serve to categorize an object is a *criterial set,* and alternative sets for the same category are *functionally equivalent.* As children learn, they discover more and more ways in which to make the decision that a particular object or event should be categorized in a certain way. The number of functionally equivalent criterial sets gets larger. Learning is also involved in the ability to make use of less and less featural information to comprehend text. We ran into many examples of the use of functionally equivalent criterial sets of features in our discussion of the processes of reading. Most skilled readers can identify words that have had large parts (many features) obliterated, such as HAPPINESS , and can make sense of text that has even more features obliterated. All this is possible because we have learned to make optimal use of the information that is available, both visually and from our acquired knowledge of the language.

Finally, children constantly learn new interrelationships among categories, developing their ability to make sense of language and the world. Understanding how words go together in meaningful language makes prediction possible and, therefore, comprehension. As I have tried to show, these interrelationships, the transformational rules of language, are also not taught. But a child can learn new interrelationships by the same process of hypothesis testing. Comprehension is the basis of a child's learning to read, but reading, in turn, contributes to a child's growing ability to comprehend by permitting elaboration of the complex structure of categories, feature lists, and interrelationships that constitute every child's theory of the world.

LEARNING ALL THE TIME

Learning is a continual and effortless process, as natural as breathing. A child does not have to be especially motivated or rewarded for learning; in fact the thrust is so natural that being deprived of the opportunity to learn is aversive. Children will struggle to get out of situations where there is nothing to learn, just as they will struggle to escape from situations where breathing is difficult. Inability to learn is suffocating.

There is no need to worry that children who are not constantly driven and cajoled will "take the easy way out" and not learn. Young children who read the same book 20 times, even though they know the words by heart, are not avoiding more "challenging" material in order to avoid learning; they are still learning. It may not be until they know just about every word in a book that they can get on with some of the more complex aspects of reading, such as testing hypotheses about meaning and learning to use as little visual information as possible.

Underestimating Learning

It is because children learn continuously and effortlessly that adults generally fail to give them credit for the amount of learning that they do. It is a widespread adult belief that learning is a difficult and even painful activity, that it involves grappling with something which you do not understand, and therefore necessarily leaves its marks of effort and strain. But in fact, the sight of a child struggling to learn is a clear sign that learning is not taking place, that the child is confronted by something incomprehensible. When learning does occur it is normally inconspicuous, an intrinsic but incidental part of doing something else that makes sense in its own right.

Because of this common myth that learning is effortful, many adults believe that they themselves do not learn often or without strain. They regard learning as struggling to make sense of a textbook or set of exercises, not as something that takes place whenever they relax to read a magazine or enjoy a film on television. But the next day they can relate a large part of what interested them in the magazine and recall a surprising amount of detail from the movie, detail which may stay with them for months or years afterward. If we can remember we must have learned, and it is pointless to argue that this was not learning because there was no conscious effort to remember. For reasons already set out in Chapter 5, the conscious effort to memorize the magazine or movie would probably have interfered with both the comprehension and the memorization. The "making sense" and the learning go on—or are destroyed—together.

Children will not willingly stay in any situation in which there is nothing for them to learn. They are equipped with a very efficient device that prevents their wasting time in situations where there is nothing to learn. That device is called *boredom*, and boredom is something all children want to escape. A child who is bored in class is not demonstrating ill will or inability or even cussedness; boredom should convey just one very clear message for the teacher. There is nothing in the particular situation for the child to learn.

Unfortunately, there are two reasons why there might be nothing for a child to learn in a particular situation, and hence two reasons for boredom, that arise from quite different sources. One reason why children might have nothing to learn is very simple—they know it already. Children will not attend to anything they already know. Nature has equipped them not to waste time in this way. But children will also suffer and exhibit the same symptoms of boredom because they cannot make sense of what they are expected to learn. Teachers might see quite clearly that a certain exercise will improve a child's useful knowledge or skills, but unless the child can see some sense in the exercise, the instruction is a waste of time.

The Risk and Rewards of Learning

There is one other reason why children might turn their faces against learning, and that is its risk. In order to learn you must take a chance. When you test a hypothesis, there must be a possibility of being wrong. If you are certain of being right, there can be nothing to learn because you know it already. And provided there is a possibility of being wrong, you learn whether you are right or not. If you have a hypothesis about what constitutes a cat, it makes no difference whether you say "cat" and are right or say "dog" and are wrong. In fact, you often get the most useful information when you are wrong because you may be right for the wrong reason, but when you are wrong you know you have made a mistake.

Many children become reluctant to learn because they are afraid of making a mistake. If the previous statement seems even slightly improbable, consider the relative credit children are given in and out of school for being "correct" and for being "wrong."

There should be no need for special inducements to motivate a child to learn. Children are in a condition to learn whenever they are confronted by something which seems meaningful and purposeful to them, something which should be part of their own theory of the world or repertoire of skills, provided they feel there is a chance that they can learn. They learn language, basically, because it is part of the world around them; because they see other people using it, because it makes sense. Irrelevant inducements—sometimes called extrinsic reinforcement—become necessary only when a child is confronted with something that does not make sense. And forcing a child to attend to nonsense is a pointless enterprise in any case. Bewilderment is aversive.

Nor does learning need to be extrinsically rewarded. The final exquisite virtue of learning is that it provides its own reward. Learning is satisfying, as everyone knows. Deprivation of learning opportunities is boring, and failure to learn is frustrating. If a child needs "reinforcement" for learning, then there is only one conclusion to be drawn: that the child does not see any sense in attempting the learning in the first place.

THE CONDITIONS OF LEARNING

I want to recapitulate and elaborate upon what has been said about learning in a rather different way. Learning is a continuous process, a natural state of the brain, and children therefore are likely to be learning all the time. I can see no other explanation for the enormous amount of unsuspected learning of the conventions of language that takes place. What then are the conditions under which these ever-learning brains succeed in learning as much about language as they do? In what kind of circumstance do children learn to read? And why is it that learning sometimes fails, as it sometimes fails for all of us, so that something which even the learner wants to master remains unlearned? Three constituents seem to determine what is learned, when it is learned, and whether indeed learning will take place at all. These may be termed *demonstrations*, which are learning conditions existing in the world around us; *engagement*, which is the interaction of the brain with a demonstration; and *sensitivity*, the learning state of the brain.

Demonstrations

The first essential constituent of learning is the opportunity to see what can be done and how. Such opportunities may be termed *demonstrations* because they literally show a potential learner "This is how something is done." The world continually provides demonstrations, through people and through their products, by acts and by artifacts.

Every act is a cluster of demonstrations. A parent saying to a child "Here's your juice" is demonstrating the meaning of the word juice and the language with which juice is presented. A parent who says "There's a pretty dog" is demonstrating that there is a category of objects called dogs, that "dog" is the name of that category, and that the animal being referred to is a member of that category with all the appropriate distinctive features. A teacher who stands before a class demonstrates how a teacher stands before a class, how a teacher talks, how a teacher dresses, how a teacher feels about what is being taught and about the people being taught. A tired teacher demonstrates how a tired teacher behaves, a disinterested teacher demonstrates disinterest. Enthusiasm demonstrates enthusiasm. What kinds of things are demonstrated in classrooms? The fact that children are learning all the time is a time bomb in every classroom. What kind of reading do children see teachers doing? What do teachers demonstrate about their interest in reading?

Every artifact is a cluster of demonstrations. Every book demonstrates how pages are put together, how print and illustrations are organized on pages, how words are set out in sentences, and how sentences are punctuated. A book demonstrates the appearance and meaning of every word in that book. It demonstrates a particular genre scheme, discourse structure, and perhaps a story grammar too. What kinds of things do our artifacts in the classroom demonstrate? Is it possible that those ever-learning brains are exposed to demonstrations that books can be incomprehensible, that they can be nonsense?

An important category of demonstrations is self-generated, like those we can perform in our imagination. We can try things out in the mind—in the world in the head rather than in the world around us—and explore possible consequences without anyone actually knowing what we are doing. How much opportunity do children have for such private demonstrations?

The world is full of demonstrations, although people and the most appropriate demonstrations may not be brought together at the most appropriate times. And even when there is a relevant demonstration learning may not take place. There has to be some kind of interaction so that "This is how something is done" becomes "This is something I can do."

Engagement

The term *engagement* was chosen deliberately for the productive interaction of a brain with a demonstration, because my image is of the meshing of gears. Learning occurs when the learner *engages* with a demonstration, so that it becomes, in effect, the learner's demonstration. Two examples follow.

Most people are familiar with the experience of reading a book or magazine and stopping suddenly, not because of something they did not understand, but because their attention was engaged by a spelling they did not know. They did not start to read to have a spelling lesson, nor could they have predicted the unfamiliar spelling that they actually met, but when they encountered it— perhaps a name that they had only previously heard on radio or television— they stopped and in effect said, "Ah, so that's the way that word is spelled." At such a moment we can catch ourselves in the act of learning; we have not simply responded to a spelling, we have made it a part of what we know. Sometimes it is not a spelling that stops us, but a particularly interesting fact, or the answer to a question which has been puzzling us for some time.

The second example is similar. Once again we find ourselves pausing while we read, this time not because of a spelling or some other piece of information, and certainly not for lack of understanding, but simply because we have just read something that is *particularly well put*, an interesting idea appropriately expressed. This time we have engaged not with a spelling or an interesting new item of information, but with a style, a tone, a register. We are learning about language vicariously, learning how it is used from the way someone else is using it.

The two examples given were necessarily of situations in which we might actually be consciously aware of a learning moment. But such moments are rare. Perhaps we catch ourselves engaging with a new spelling or idea because it is a relatively rare event in our lives, because we have learned most of the things we want or expect to learn by now. New information is surprising. But children learning the sounds, meanings, and written appearance of scores of new words every day of their lives are hardly likely to be stopped, like an adult, by the novelty of actually meeting something new. Instead, most of their learning must be like adults learning from the newspapers and the movies, an engagement so close and persistent that it does not intrude into consciousness.

Learning by engaging in the demonstrations of others is a particularly efficient and economical way for children to learn, because it limits the possibility of mistake and uncertainty. You are not likely to be in error if you let the demonstrator do your learning trials for you. This is learning by conducting experiments, where the other person (who can do it) conducts the experiment. It is hypothesis-testing where the appropriate hypothesis is easily available in the skilled performance of the demonstrator.

Children engage with particular kinds of demonstrations because "that is the kind of person they are," because they take it for granted with their ever-learning brain that these are the kinds of things they should and could know. Obviously children can learn by doing things themselves. With engagement they can assimilate the demonstration of another (in an act or artifact) and make it vicariously an action—and learning act—of their own. What I still must account for is what makes us all the kinds of persons that we are; what determines whether or not engagement takes place.

Sensitivity

What makes the difference in whether we learn or do not learn from any particular demonstration? The answer cannot be motivation, a grossly overrated factor, especially in schools where it is sometimes used to cover a multitude of other possibilities. For a start, learning of the kind described in this chapter usually occurs in the absence of motivation, certainly in the sense of a deliberate, conscious intention. It makes no sense to say an infant is motivated to learn to talk, or that we are motivated to remember what is in the newspaper, unless the meaning of motivation is made so general that it cannot be separated from learning.

On the other hand, motivation does not ensure learning. No matter how much they are motivated to spell, or to write fluently, or to learn a foreign language, many people still fail to learn these things. Desire and effort do not necessarily produce learning. Indeed, the only relevance of motivation to learning that I can see is that it puts us in situations where appropriate demonstrations are particularly likely to occur, and learning will certainly not take place if there is motivation *not* to learn.

Closer to the truth is that we learn when we expect to learn, when learning is taken for granted. But a *conscious* expectation is not precisely what is required. Infants may take learning to talk for granted, but not in the sense of consciously expecting it. Rather, what seems to make the difference is absence of the expectation that learning will not take place.

This is how I propose to define *sensitivity*, the third constituent of every learning situation: the absence of any expectation that learning will not take place, or that it will be difficult. Where does sensitivity come from? Every child is born with it. Children do not need to be taught that they can learn; they have this implicit expectation which they demonstrate in their earliest learning about language and about the world—they believe they are omnipotent. Experience teaches children that they have limitations, and unfortunately, experience often teaches them this unnecessarily.

Why is learning to walk usually so much easier than learning to swim? Walking must surely be the more difficult accomplishment. Infants have scarcely any motor coordination and on two tottering feet they must struggle against gravity. Little wonder walking takes several months to master. Swimming, on the other hand, can be learned in a weekend—if it is learned at all. It is learned when the learner has much better motor coordination and is in a supportive element—water. And it must be as "natural" as walking. So why the difference? Could it be that difficulty and failure are so often anticipated with swimming and not with walking?

Why is learning to talk generally so easy while learning to read is sometimes so much harder? The answer cannot be the intrinsic difficulty of reading. Infants learning to talk start with essentially nothing; they must make sense of it all for themselves. Despite the remarkable speed with which they are usually credited with learning about language, it still takes them two or three years to show anything approaching mastery. Reading should be learned very much quicker, as it has so much language understanding to support it. And when children do learn to read, whether they learn at three years of age, six, or ten, they learn—in the observation of many teachers—in a matter of a few weeks. The instruction may last for years, but the learning is accomplished in weeks. What is the difference? I can only think that with reading an expectation of failure is frequently communicated to the child.

The apparent "difficulty" cannot be explained away on the basis of age. Teenagers are expected to learn to drive cars—surely as complicated a matter as learning to swim, if not to read—and lo, they learn to drive cars. In fact, for anything any of us is interested in, where the learning is taken for granted, we continue to learn throughout our lives. We do not even realize we are learning, as we keep up to date with our knowledge of stamp collecting, astronomy, automotive engineering, spelling, world affairs, the television world, or whatever—for the "kind of person" we happen to be.

Engagement takes place in the presence of appropriate demonstrations whenever we are sensitive to learning, and sensitivity is an absence of expectation that learning will not take place. Sensitivity is obviously related to two factors I mentioned in earlier chapters regarding willingness to engage in critical thinking, namely disposition and authority. Individuals who do not feel competent to think critically on particular occasions, because of the way they perceive themselves or the way others perceive them, could be said to lack sensitivity for critical thinking. If they do not feel it is appropriate or possible for them to behave in a particular way, they will also feel that it is inappropriate (and probably impossible) for them to learn to behave in those ways. Lacking the disposition and authority to learn, they will decline opportunities for the necessary engagement.

Sensitivity does not need to be accounted for; its absence does. Expectation that learning will not take place is itself learned. The ultimate irony is that the brain's constant propensity to learn may in fact defeat learning; the brain can learn that particular things are not worth learning or are unlikely to be learned. The brain is indiscriminate in its learning—the time bomb in the classroom—and it can learn things which it would really do much better not learning at all. Learning that something is useless, unpleasant, difficult, or improbable may be devastatingly permanent in its effect. These are the risks of learning discussed earlier in this chapter.

LEARNING—A SOCIAL EVENT

So far learning has been discussed as if it were the entire responsibility of the learner, a matter of individual effort. But this is not the case. Whether or not learning takes place usually depends more on people around learners than on the learners themselves. Personal effort does not guarantee learning, nor does conscious motivation. Learners often need do nothing in order to learn. Someone else does something, and the learner learns. Neither the learner nor the people around the learner need know that learning is taking place. Learning is usually inconspicuous.

Family and friends are generally unaware of how much even the youngest children learn of spoken language, for example. Infants do not practice talking, they say something—and usually they are right first time. They occasionally make mistakes, of course, and when they do, parents tell their friends and regard the mistakes as cute. But most of the time parents find themselves saying "Where did the child learn to say that?". Learning inconspicuously and effortlessly continues into adulthood. How else would we all learn the meanings of the scores of thousands of words that we know, and to talk the way we do? Where does it all come from?

The typical absence of evident error might seem to provide problems for the hypothesis testing, learning-by-experimenting point of view adopted earlier in this chapter. If children test hypotheses in order to learn, they must get the hypotheses right most of the time. And right or wrong, where do the hypotheses come from?

The answer to all of these questions must be—from other people. Much of what children (and adults) learn, they learn when they are not trying to learn, but when they are interested in something someone else is doing. To use a term I have already employed, children learn when they are *engaged* in an activity that someone else may actually be doing. They learn as if they were doing it themselves. The learning is vicarious.

Learning From Other People

George Miller (1977) recognized the importance of other people in the title of his book *Spontaneous Apprentices: Children and Language.* He argued that infants learn to talk and to understand speech by apprenticing themselves to adults, or to more competent children. And they learn to talk just like the people they apprentice themselves to. Children do not even learn to talk like the people they hear talking most. (Once they get to school, children hear their teachers talking more than anyone else, but they do not grow up talking like teachers—unless they are going to become teachers themselves.)

No *modeling* is involved. It is not a matter of infants saying "I want to be like that person," and studying and practicing the other person's behavior. Instead, the child seems effortlessly to learn what the other person does. The other person is an unwitting surrogate for the child's learning. If this is trial and error learning, other people conduct the trial, and because they can already do what they are doing, there are very few errors.

A baby babbles, someone else puts the utterance into conventional language—"You want a drink of juice?", and the child has learned something about drinks of juice, without practice, without error. One adult says to another "Pass the salt"—it could be babble as far as the infant is concerned— but their behavior allows the infant to hypothesize the meaning of the utterance. If the salt is passed, the child has learned by hypothesis testing, without error and without anyone knowing that learning has taken place.

We learn when we comprehend. (A struggle to learn is always a struggle to comprehend.) Other people help us to learn by helping us to understand. That is essentially the social nature of learning, even when we are learning from books, when it is the author's responsibility to facilitate the reader's comprehension.

Joining the Spoken Language Club

An alternative metaphor for explaining how infants learn about language (and everything else) is that they join a club (Smith, 1987a). Infants join communities of people they see themselves as being like, who accept the infants as being like them, and the infants learn to be exactly like other members of the club. They learn not to be like members of the clubs they do not belong to.

A spoken language club is probably the first club most infants join, but it has exactly the same advantages as any other club they might join later in life. First, more experienced members disclose the nature of the club's activities. These are the *demonstrations* I talked about earlier in this chapter. In the spoken language club, members show the child what spoken language can be used for, how it helps to fulfil intentions in a variety of ways.

Second, when new members of the club themselves want to engage in club activities—when they want to use spoken language to fulfil their own intentions—more experienced members of the club help. They do not give newcomers *instruction* from which learning is supposed to take place, they provide *collaboration*. To be specific, other members help the infant to say what the infant is trying to say, and they help the infant to understand what the infant is trying to understand. The learner is totally involved because everything centers on the learner's intentions and interest—this is the *engagement* to which I referred earlier.

Children finish up talking exactly like their friends, the other members of the spoken language club they eventually affiliate with. They learn to dress and ornament themselves exactly like their friends—like the kind of person they see themselves as being. They learn the other club members' ways of perceiving the world, their attitudes, their values, their dislikes, their imperatives. They learn a *culture*—not by practice or by trial and error, but by imperceptibly yet inevitably coming to be exactly like the kind of person they see themselves as being. In other words, the clubs they join become their identity.

If we see ourselves as members of a club, and the club members do not exclude us, then we cannot help becoming like the other members because of the demonstrations and collaboration we receive. But if we are rejected by a club, or if we decide to exclude ourselves, then we not only fail to become like the club members, we often become as different from them as we can be. As I said earlier, we lose our *sensitivity*—and it is usually almost impossible to get it back. It is as if we do not want to be mistaken for members of the club—except that none of the learning or failure to learn is under conscious control. Everyone fails, in one way or another, to become members of clubs of people who have mastered things like statistics, automobile engines, computer programming, algebra, identifying constellations—or reading or writing. This has nothing to do with motivation or effort—the most conspicuous things most of us have failed to learn are things we have been most motivated to learn, and that we have spent the most "time on task" trying to learn.

The social nature of learning has been most influentially urged in recent years through the work of Lev Vygotsky. In *Mind and Society*, Vygotsky (1978) outlines his theory of *the zone of proximal development*. He demonstrates that everyone can do things with assistance that they cannot do alone, and what they can do with collaboration on one occasion they will be able to do independently on another. It is within the zone of proximal development, Vygotsky argues, that learning takes place; it should be the area on which educational effort is focused. Successful teachers collaborate with learners in enterprises in which the learners want to be engaged, in the zone of proximal development.

SUMMARY

Most of what individuals know about language and the world is not formally taught. Instead, children develop their theory of the world and competence in language by testing **hypotheses,** experimenting in meaningful and purposeful ways with tentative modifications of what they know already. Thus the basis of learning is **comprehension.** Children learn continuously, through **engagement** in **demonstrations** that make sense to them, whenever their natural **sensitivity** for learning is undamaged. Learning is a social activity. Children learn from what other people do, and help them to do.

Notes to Chapter 11 being on page 288, covering

Language learning
Vocabulary
Learning as a social event
Motivation
An alternative perspective

Chapter 12
LEARNING TO USE
WRITTEN LANGUAGE

This book is primarily about reading, therefore this chapter is primarily about learning to read. But nothing a child learns about reading—whether about letter identification, word identification, or the comprehension of print—will make any sense unless the child has an understanding of what written language does. Hence the title of this chapter. The first insight every learner must have in order to become a reader (or a writer) is that written language itself makes sense—an insight not always easy to achieve in educational settings.

The Importance of Nonvisual Information

There is only one way to summarize everything that a child must learn in order to become a fluent reader, and that is to say that the child must learn to use nonvisual information, or prior knowledge, efficiently when attending to written language. (And an understanding of the purposes and conventions of texts is a central part of nonvisual information.)

Learning to read does not require the memorization of letter names, or phonic rules, or a large vocabulary, all of which are in fact taken care of in the course of learning to read, and little of which will make sense to the child without some experience of reading. Nor is learning to read a matter of application to all manner of exercises and drills, which can only distract and perhaps even discourage a child from the business of learning to read. And finally, learning to read is not a matter of a child relying upon instruction, because the essential skills of reading—namely the efficient uses of nonvisual information—cannot be explicitly taught. But they can be demonstrated to the child.

In a general sense, learning to read is very much like the cat-and-dog problem for children. No one can teach explicitly the relevant categories, distinctive features, and interrelationships that are involved. Yet children are perfectly capable of solving the problem for themselves provided they have the opportunities to generate and test their own hypotheses and to get appropriate feedback. In quite a literal sense, learning to read is like learning spoken language. No one can even begin to explain to infants what essential features and conventions of speech should be learned, let alone construct a course of study for infants to follow; yet even this complex problem is solved by children, without any apparent strain or difficulty, provided again that they have the opportunity to exercise their innate learning ability. All that children require to master spoken language, both to produce it themselves and more fundamentally to comprehend its use by others, is to have experience of *using* language in a meaningful setting. Children easily learn about spoken language when they are involved in its use, when it has the possibility of making sense to them. And in the same way children will try to understand written language by being involved in its use, in situations where it makes sense to them and they can generate and test hypotheses.

It should not be a cause for dismay that we cannot say with exactitude what a child has to learn in order to read, or that a foolproof method of instruction cannot be found to direct a child's progress in learning to read. It was not possible to specify the content or course of a child's learning spoken language either (or the difference between cats and dogs for that matter). But it is possible to specify the *conditions* under which a child will learn to read, and these are again the general conditions that are required for learning anything—the opportunity to generate and test hypotheses in a meaningful, collaborative context. And to reiterate the constant theme, the only way a child can do all this for reading is to read. If the question arises how children can be expected to learn to read by reading before they have learned to read, the answer is very simple. At the beginning—and at any other time when it is necessary—the reading has to be done for them. Before children acquire any competence in reading, everything will have to be read to them, but as their ability expands they just need help, the opportunity to engage in reading demonstrations.

One of the beautiful things about written language that makes sense (to the child) is that to a growing extent it will itself provide learning assistance to the child. Authors can take over teaching children to read. Meaningful written language, like meaningful speech, not only provides its own clues to meaning, so that children can generate appropriate learning hypotheses, but it also provides the opportunity for tests. If a child is not sure about the likely meaning of what is being attended to, the context (before *and* after) can provide clues. And the subsequent context will provide the feedback about whether the child's hypotheses were right or wrong. Reading text that makes sense is like riding a bicycle; children do not need to be told when they are falling off.

Let me list the advantages a child gains from reading meaningful written language—building vocabulary, making sense of letter-sound relationships, developing mediated meaning and word identification ability, acquiring speed, avoiding tunnel vision, preventing memory overload, relying on sense, acquiring familiarity with such relevant conventions as the appropriate discourse structure, grammar, and register—in short, increasing relevant nonvisual information and experience in using it more efficiently. And always the child will be the best guide to learning in the most efficient manner, because children will not willingly limit their vision, overload memory, or tolerate nonsense. Children also will not tolerate *not learning,* so just as there is no reason to expect that they will be satisfied with what has become simple for them, so also they should not be expected to remain in situations where no learning or comprehension is possible at all.

It is also easy to list the conditions required for children to take advantage of the learning opportunities that reading meaningful text provides. There are only four: access to meaningful and interesting reading material (ideally the child's own choice), assistance where needed (and only to the extent that it is required), a willingness to take the necessary risks (anxiety increases the proportion of visual information a reader needs), and freedom to make mistakes.

I have said little about motivation because it is not something that can be artificially promoted or maintained, certainly not by means of extrinsic "reinforcers" such as irrelevant material rewards, improved grades, or even extravagant praise. None of these is necessary for a child to learn spoken language. All the satisfaction that a child requires is in the learning itself, in the utility and understanding that result. And the impetus in the first place? Why do children set themselves the enormously time-consuming task of learning spoken language? Not, I think, in order to communicate. Children cannot understand this use of language until they have got some. And certainly not to get their material needs fulfilled or to control the behavior of others. Children are never so well looked after as before they can use language; afterwards they can be told to wait, to do without, or to do it themselves. When language fails, even adults can feel the urge to revert to earlier, nonlanguage, and more assertive ways of trying to get their way. I think there can be only one reason why children apply themselves to learning spoken language—because it is *there,* a functioning part of the world around them. They learn when its sense, its utility, and its meaningfulness is demonstrated to them. And because language is meaningful, because it changes the world and is not arbitrary or capricious, not only do children succeed in learning it, but they want to learn it. Children will not stop learning anything that is meaningful to them, unless the learning becomes too difficult or too costly for them, in which case the learning itself becomes meaningless. The child's sensitivity for reading is destroyed.

Children will endeavor to understand, and engage in, anything they see adults doing, provided the adults demonstrate enjoyment and satisfaction in doing it. If meaningful written language exists in the child's world, and is visibly used with satisfaction, then the child will strive to master its mystery; that is in the nature of childhood. There is no need for special explanations about why children should want to learn to read, only for why they might come to the conclusion that it is pointless or too costly.

All this has been very general. No special theories of learning are required for how and why children learn to read. There is nothing unique about reading, whether from the point of view of the language skills involved (no different in principle from those of spoken language comprehension), the visual skills involved (no different from discriminating any aspects of the visual world), or of the situations in which learning takes place. There are, however, two special insights that children must have in order to learn to read. These insights are fundamental, in the sense that children who do not have them are bound to find reading instruction nonsensical, and will not therefore succeed in learning to read. Yet not only are these insights not taught in school, much of what constitutes formal reading instruction might be seen as contrary to these insights, and thus likely to inhibit them. The insights, which I shall discuss in turn, are first, that print is meaningful, and second, that written language is not the same as speech.

Insight 1: Print Is Meaningful

There is no need to belabor why the insight that print is meaningful is an essential precondition for learning to read. Reading is a matter of making sense of print, and meaningfulness is the basis of learning. For as long as children see no sense in print, for as long as they regard it as arbitrary or nonsensical, they will find no reason to attend to print. They will not learn by trying to relate letters to sounds. Written language does not work in that way, and it is not something that can make any sense to children.

Research has offered abundant evidence that children are as much immersed in written language as they are in speech, and they respond to it with similar intelligence. I am not referring to school, nor to those overrated books that are supposed to surround and somehow inspire some privileged children to literacy. I refer instead to the wealth of situation-dependent print to be found on every product in the bathroom, on every jar and package in the kitchen, in the television guide (and in television commercials), in comics, catalogs, advertising fliers, telephone directories, on street signs, store fronts, gas stations, bill-boards, at fast-food outlets, supermarkets, and department stores. All of this print is meaningful; it makes a difference. We no more predict cereal in a package labeled *detergent* than we expect candy in a store advertising *cleaning* or a concert in a television program announced as *football.*

For those not blind to it (which experienced readers are inclined to be), our visual world is an ocean of print, most of it (check your supermarket) literally right in front of our eyes. Even children who cannot yet read pay attention to it. I have told of a 3½-year-old boy who obviously could not read the words *luggage* and *footwear* on signs in a department store (because he got both of them wrong) but who nevertheless asserted that the first said "cases" and the second said "shoes" (Smith, 1976). Here was one child who could bring meaning to print long before he could read the actual print, and who therefore had acquired the insight that differences in print are meaningful.

There is only one way in which such an insight might be achieved, and that is when a child is being read to or observes print being responded to in a meaningful way. At this point, I am not referring to the reading of books or stories, but to the occasions when a child is told "That sign says 'Stop'," "That word on the door is 'Boys'," or "This is the jar for cookies." Television commercials may do the same for a child—they not only announce the product's name, desirability, and uniqueness in spoken and written language, but they even demonstrate the product at work. And just as with the spoken language of the home, there is a great deal a child might learn from this situation-dependent written language by hypothesizing a likely meaning and seeing if the hypothesis is confirmed. Children can test hypotheses about the meaning of the printed word *toys* in a store, not because anyone reads it to them, but on the basis of whether the sign does in fact indicate the location of the toy department. There is a consistency between the print and its environment. The print that normally surrounds children is potentially meaningful, and thus provides an effective basis for learning.

There may be very little meaningful print in school, in the sense that it would not be possible to substitute one word for another. A teacher writes the words *table* or *chair* on the board but could just as well write *horse* or *cow.* The words in word lists, or the sentences in many "stories," could be changed without any child noticing anything "wrong." Teachers may believe there are good reasons for a particular exercise or element of instruction, but if children cannot see the sense of the enterprise, then it can reasonably be regarded as incomprehensible. A brief list of fundamentally incomprehensible aspects of reading instruction to which children may be exposed would include:

1. The decomposition of spoken words to "sounds." The spoken word "cat," in some contexts, can make sense, but the sounds "kuh," "a," "tuh" do not.
2. The decomposition of written words to letters. The printed word *cat,* in some contexts, can make sense—when it refers to a real or imaginary animal with

which children can meaningfully interact. But the letters *c*, *a*, and *t* are arbitrary visual symbols that have nothing to do with anything else in the child's life.

3. The relating of letters to sounds. For a child who has no idea of reading to be told that some peculiar shapes called letters—which have no apparent function in the real world—are related to sounds that have no apparent independent existence in the real world must be the purest jabberwocky.

4. Meaningless drills and exercises. There are so many candidates for this category, ranging from deciding which of three ducks is facing the wrong way to underlining silent letters in words, that I shall not attempt to make a list. Children may learn to score high on repetitive and nonsensical tasks (especially if they happen to be competent readers), but such a specialized ability will not make readers of them.

The preceding kinds of activity may, through their very incomprehensibility, make learning to read more complicated, arduous, and nonsensical than need be. It is not until children have begun reading that they have a chance of making sense of such activities at all. Children who do not have the insight that written language should make sense may never achieve it, while children who have it may be persuaded that they are wrong.

Insight 2: Written Language
Is Different from Speech

The first insight was concerned primarily with written language in the form of single words (or small groups of words) like labels and signs. These kinds of print function very much like the everyday situation-dependent spoken language of the home in that cues to meaning (and constraints on interpretation) are provided largely by the physical situation in which they occur. Now I want to consider context-dependent *text*, where constraints on substitutability and interpretation are placed not by the physical environment but by the syntax and semantics of the text itself. As discussed in Chapter 2, the conventions of written and spoken language are evidently not the same, and probably for very good reason, including the fact that written language has especially adapted itself for being read.

Children who expect written language to be exactly the same as speech are likely to have difficulty in predicting and comprehending its conventions and thus in learning to read. They must be familiar with how written language works. It does not matter that theorists cannot say with any precision what exactly the differences are between spoken and written language. They cannot list all the rules of spoken language; yet children learn to make sense of speech. Immersion in functional language, the possibility of making sense, a plentiful experience, and the opportunity to get feedback to test hypotheses would seem to be just as easily met with written language as with speech. In fact, written language might seem to have several advantages, since a number of tests can be conducted on the same piece of material, a second hypothesis tried if the first one fails. By virtue of its internal consistency the text itself can provide relevant feedback about the correctness of hypotheses.

How might children who cannot yet read acquire and develop the insight that speech and written language are not the same? Only by being read to, or at least by hearing written language read aloud. When a child's predictions of written language fail because they are based on knowledge of spoken language, then the occasion exists for the insight to arise that spoken and written language are not precisely the same. And a similar process of engagement as written language is heard and comprehended will develop an understanding of the particular conventions of written language, considerably augmented, of course, as children become able to do more and more of their own reading.

The kind of reading that would most familiarize children with written language is coherent *stories*, ranging from items in newspapers and magazines to traditional fairy tales, ghost and adventure stories, history, and myth. All of these types of story are truly written *language*—produced for a purpose in a conventional medium and distinguishable from most school texts by their length, sense, and semantic and syntactic richness. There is no evidence that it is any harder for children to understand complex texts (when they are read to them) or when they can explore them for themselves than it is difficult for children to understand the complex adult speech that they hear around them and on television.

Children at school may not be provided with complex written material as part of their reading instruction for the obvious reason that they could not be expected to read it by themselves. Because most of the material in which children are likely to be interested—and from which they would be likely to learn—tends to be too difficult for them to read by themselves, less complex material is found or produced in the expectation that children will find it "simpler." And when these specially tailored-for-children texts also seem to confound beginners, the assumption may be made that the fault lies with the children, or with their "language development."

And indeed, it may be the case that the language of such texts is unfamiliar to many children. But this inadequacy need not have its roots in the particular kind of spoken language with which the child is familiar nor even in the possibly limited experience of the child with print. The reason is more likely to be associated with the child's unfamiliarity with the artificial language of school books, whether of the truncated "Sam the cat sat on the mat" variety or the more florid "Down the hill, hand in hand, skipped Susie and her friend." This is also so different from any other form of language, spoken or written, that it is probably safest to put it into an exclusive category of "school language."

Of course, such material tends to be quite unpredictable for many children who consequently have enormous difficulty understanding it and learning to read from it. And ironically it may be concluded that written language is intrinsically difficult for children who would be better off learning from "spoken language written down." The text is then based on the intuition of a professional textbook writer or classroom teacher about what constitutes spoken language—or more complex still, a dialect of that language or even children's language. All of these are problems that would confound a professional linguist. The result is quite unlike written language yet has none of the advantages of speech, since it will have to be comprehended out of context. Children may learn to recite such print, but there is no evidence that it will make them readers. Any insight they might have in advance about the nature of written language is likely to be undermined, and worse, they might become persuaded that the print which they first experience in school is a model for all the written language that they will meet throughout their lives—a conviction that would be as discouraging as it is misleading.

On Instructional Methods

I have not said anything about the best (or the worst) programs, methods, or materials for teaching children to read. This was intentional, because the conclusion to which all my analysis, research, and experience with teachers and with children in schools has led is that children do not learn to read from programs. In particular, they cannot learn from the more structured, systematic "reading skills" programs where every supposed learning step is predetermined for the child; they cannot acquire or maintain the two basic insights just discussed. A program cannot demonstrate to a child the many things that can be done with written language, from getting yourself a hamburger to enjoying an interesting story or poem. Only people can demonstrate how written language is *used*. Programs cannot help children to do these things for themselves, since they cannot anticipate what a child will want to do or know at a particular time. They cannot provide opportunities for engagement. And anything a program teaches that is irrelevant to a child will be learned, if it is learned at all, as something that is irrelevant.

No "method" of teaching will take care of all the contingencies. Nor should the development of a foolproof method be expected, despite the millions of dollars that have been spent in its pursuit. While some methods of teaching reading are obviously worse than others (because they are based on very weak theories of the nature of reading), the belief that one perfect method might exist to teach all children is contrary to all the evidence about the multiplicity of individual differences that every child brings to reading.

Research is of little help in the selection of appropriate methods. Research tells us that all methods of teaching reading appear to work for some children but that none works for all. Some teachers seem to succeed whatever the method they are formally believed to employ. We must conclude that the instructional method is not the critical issue. (Researchers recognize this point and have to control in their studies for the "variability" introduced first by the different abilities of children and second by the varying influences of teachers.) It might not be particularly unfair to say that many children learn to read—and many teachers succeed in helping them—despite the instructional method used.

Millions of children learned to read before the systematic and objectivized reading programs that are being developed or promoted today, often on the basis of unsupported or unsophisticated theories of learning or reading. Many children of 2 and 3 years of age have learned to read, and so have many illiterate adults. Children from the poorest homes have learned to read and so have children from all cultures. Children who are not very smart have learned to read (while many otherwise bright children, even from "privileged" homes, have failed). A good deal more research is required before we can hope to spell out exactly what helped those millions to read, sometimes despite substantial difficulties. It is likely to have less to do with precise instructional programming than with stories and the labels on doors and cookie jars.

The analysis I have made cannot be translated into a system for teaching, though it can indeed be translated into an environment for learning. In fact, the analysis explains environments in which children do learn to read, whether or not there is a program that is supposed to be teaching the child to read at the same time. These are environments in which written language makes sense, and in which an autonomous program-independent teacher has a critical role.

The Place of Computers

Two basic theories of how children learn to read have been contrasted in these pages. One point of view, which this book obviously reflects, is sometimes termed "psycholinguistic," the "meaning" approach, or "whole language." The opposing point of view, which relies heavily on phonics and other exercises and drills, is generally called the "skills" approach.

For anyone who believes that there are basic skills that children must master in order to become readers and writers, and that repetitious exercises, corrections, tests, and grading are essential for learning those skills, computers constitute an ideal educational technology. With sophisticated graphics (like the video arcade games), tightly controlled instructional sequences and loops, constant testing, immediate feedback of results, and ability to remember and compare every score, computer-based literacy programs offer systematic instruction in a form that can appeal to everyone. Children enjoy them because they make "fun" out of previously tedious ritual, like the Saturday morning television cartoons. Parents like the computer programs, because the technology is contemporary and labeled "educational." Teachers may like them because they plot a path for every student and keep them on track. And administrators can find the promises and control that computer-assisted instruction offers irresistible.

Such computer programs must be questioned about what they demonstrate to learners about literacy. Yet many major publishers of reading and writing programs, from kindergarten through high school, have now invested in elaborate computer programs. The worksheet activities and tests contained in their print materials are now presented on the computer screen in seemingly endless profusion and variety. And the same claims of instructional efficacy are made. There is no evidence that such computer programs have succeeded in making children literate, and no convincing theories that they could succeed. Such programs could rapidly give children a totally false idea of the purposes and possibilities of literacy (Smith, 1986).

This does not mean that computers have no place in the literacy classroom. As word processors, computers have helped the youngest children to become writers, by assisting them in the physical act of writing, and also in such writerly activities as drafting, editing, and preparing clean and legible copies of their texts. And when used in these and a variety of other practical ways—in simulations, games, design activities, communication links, drama, art, and music—computers seem able to stimulate children to talk more, plan more, think more, and write and read more. The issue is not whether computers should be in classrooms, but how they should be used.

TEACHING READING

The primary role of reading teachers can be summed up in very few words—to ensure that the children have adequate demonstrations of reading being used for evident meaningful purposes, and to help children to fulfill such purposes themselves. Where children see little relevance in reading, then teachers must show that reading is worthwhile. Where children find little interest in reading then teachers must create interesting situations. No one ever taught reading to a child who was not interested in reading, and interest cannot be demanded. Teachers must themselves be conspicuous practicing users of written language.

Where children have difficulty in reading, teachers must see that they are helped to read what they would like to read. In part, this assistance can be given by developing the confidence of children to read for themselves, in their own way, taking the risk of making mistakes and being willing to ignore the completely incomprehensible. Even bizarre personal interpretations are better than none at all; children find out soon enough the mistakes that make a difference. But children will also from time to time look for help from others, either in answering specific questions or in assisting with reading generally. Such reading on behalf of the child can be provided by the teacher, an aide, by other children, or by recordings.

The Child's Point of View

Children themselves must judge whether materials and activities are too difficult or too dull. Anything children would not listen to or understand if it were read to them is unsuitable material for them to be expected to read. A child's preference is a far better yardstick than any readability formula, and grade levels have no reality in a child's mind. Teachers need not be afraid that children will engage in reading so easy that there is nothing to learn; that would be boring. Children learn about reading as long as they read, but they can never learn to read by not reading.

There is no simple formula to ensure that reading will be comprehensible, no materials or procedures are guaranteed never to interfere with a child's progress. Instead teachers must understand the factors that make reading difficult, whether induced by the child, the teacher, or the task. For example, the concentration on visual detail that will cause tunnel vision; the overloading of short-term memory by attention to fragments of text that make little sense; logjams in long-term memory as the child strives to be ready to answer questions afterward, or to write "reports"; attempts to sound out words at the expense of meaning; slow reading; anxiety not to make a mistake; lack of assistance when a child needs it for sense or even word identification; or too-insistent "correction" that may be irrelevant to the child and that may in the long run inhibit the self-correction that is an essential part of learning. All of these ways in which reading can be made harder can be characterized as limitations on the extent to which children can use nonvisual information.

And conversely, what makes reading comprehensible for children is the teacher's facilitation of the use of nonvisual information. Not only should a child come into every reading situation with relevant nonvisual information—equipped with, in plain English, an adequate prior understanding—but also the child must feel free to use it. A child's fund of knowledge and confidence should be constantly developed, but this will occur as a consequence of reading. Not only should the teacher try to avoid materials or activities that are nonsense to the child, there should be active encouragement for the child to predict, to understand, to enjoy. The worst habit for any learner is to treat text as if there were no sense to be found in it. Where there is a mismatch, where there is little likelihood that a child will comprehend the material, then the preference should be to change the material rather than to try to change the child. For older children teachers may be reluctant to change material because a certain content is expected to be learned, but they still have a choice. Students cannot learn two things at the same time; they cannot simultaneously learn to read and to master an unfamiliar subject matter like history or math. If the teacher's intention is to improve reading, then students must have material they can easily understand. If the intention is to extend subject matter knowledge—which will in turn make reading easier—then until the student can read it with some fluency the subject matter must be taught in some other way, by lecture, film, board work, or individual tuition. The two can be taught *concurrently*—the math need not wait for the reading competence any more than the reading need wait for the math skills—but they cannot be learned simultaneously.

Teaching the Hard Way

Teachers sometimes try to resolve problems the hard way, for example in expecting poor readers to improve while they are doing less reading than better readers. When children have trouble understanding text they may be given isolated word drills, while problems with word identification may provoke attention to letter identification and sound blends. But letters (and their phonic interrelations) are recognized and learned best when they are parts of words, and words are recognized and learned more easily when they are in meaningful sequences. Good readers tend to be good at letter and word identification and at phonic drills, but these more specific skills are a consequence, not a cause, of good reading (Samuels, 1971). Good readers tend also to understand the technical jargon of reading such as *letter, word, verb, sentence, paragraph,* but this again is a result of being able to read. Practice with definitions does not make readers (Downing & Oliver, 1973–74).

An understanding of the language that is used in talking *about* written language, such as the terms given at the end of the previous paragraph, is sometimes called *metacognitive* (or *metalinguistic*) *awareness,* or *cognitive clarity* (Downing & Leong, 1982). It is occasionally asserted that this metalinguistic and metacognitive knowledge is essential for learning to read. But of course, many children have learned to read and write without ever having heard of such words. Knowledge of these words is necessary only if they are made a focal part of the instruction, if it is necessary for children to understand the words in order to be allowed to get on with the business of learning to read and write. The lack of specialized knowledge can be made confusing, but not because it is an essential prerequisite for literacy.

Children may also be confounded by instruction that is as unnecessary as it is futile, often as a consequence of a theoretical vogue among specialists. When, for example, Noam Chomsky popularized transformational linguistics as a technical method of analyzing language, many people thought children would not learn to read unless they became miniature linguists themselves, and made children spend a lot of time doing transformational exercises that made no apparent difference to their language ability. After psychologists became interested in the theoretical notion of distinctive features there were several efforts to teach children the distinctive features of letters, although no one could convincingly demonstrate what these features might be. Children who had difficulty with the alphabet or with these exercises were sometimes diagnosed as having poor feature discrimination, although they had no reported difficulty with knives and forks or dogs and cats. Phonic-based reading programs and materials have flourished whenever linguists have become particularly interested in the spelling-sound correspondences of language, and more recently there have been moves toward teaching "prediction" as if it were something foreign to most children's experience. In all of these cases, concepts that scientists have found useful as hypothetical constructs in their attempts to understand their discipline have become, with little justification, something a child must learn as a prerequisite for learning to read. (How children learned to read before these concepts were devised is not explained.) There is a growing acknowledgment today of the importance of comprehension as the basis of learning, but at the same time there is a feeling that comprehension itself must be taught, that it can be broken down into a series of "comprehension skills" that presumably can be taught without comprehension.

I am not saying that it is not useful for children to know the alphabet, to build up sight vocabularies, or even to understand the relationships between the spelling of words and their sounds. But all of these are by-products of reading that make more sense as reading itself is mastered and understood. It is pointless for teacher and child to labor over activities that will not facilitate learning to read and that will become easy once reading experience develops. It is certainly not the case that teachers should never correct or make suggestions. But correction or advice may be offered too soon. A child pauses while reading aloud and half the class shouts out the next word, although the reader may be thinking about something else six words behind or ahead. Problems arise when corrections and explanations sap children's confidence or stop them in their tracks for what might be quite extraneous reasons. The teacher should always ask "What is causing the confusion here?"

The First Steps

Children begin to read with the first written word they are able to recognize. Nonvisual information is so important that reading potential is enhanced with every expansion of a child's knowledge of the world or of spoken language. (But there is no particular need for extensive prior knowledge of the world or of spoken language for a child to begin to read; just enough to make sense of the first print that will be read. Much of the knowledge and language skills of fluent readers is again a consequence of literacy rather than its cause.)

There is no "best age" for learning to read. Many children have learned to read, often spontaneously, as young as 3 years of age (Clark, 1976), and it is equally well documented that adult illiterates can learn in a few months provided their sensitivity has not been blunted by years of failure with formal reading instruction (Freire, 1972). Many of the early readers who have been studied did not have above-average intellect or any particular social or cultural privileges, they simply found reading something that was useful and straightforward to learn, usually without any particular consciousness of what they were doing. Whether a child will learn to read is not something that can be determined with reference to a calendar or the learner's "mental age."

Similarly, there is no unique mental condition of "reading readiness." Children are ready to learn to read whenever they have a purpose and intelligible opportunity for reading, not in terms of settling down to a concentrated period of systematic instruction but in an explorer's interest in signs and labels, in telephone directories and catalogs, and in stories. In educational contexts, "reading readiness" is often related more to the form and demands of instruction than to reading itself. Obviously, if instruction emphasizes knowledge of letter names—another example of "metalinguistic awareness"—then a child who cannot grasp the nature of the alphabet is not ready. If instruction requires detailed attention to the sound patterns of a particular spoken language dialect, then a child who cannot do this is not ready. But none of this has anything to do with reading itself. It is difficult to see what kind of special physical, emotional, intellectual, or cultural status is required for learning to read, except the two basic insights I have already discussed.

Reading is not intrinsically different from other activities; it should blend smoothly into all the other visual and linguistic and intellectual enterprises of a learner's life. There is no magical day when a 'pre-reader" suddenly becomes a "learner," just as there is no landmark day when learning is completed and a reader graduates. No one is a perfect reader, and we all continue to learn every time we read.

None of this is to say that all children will easily learn to read; there has always been evidence that such is unlikely to be the case. But failure need not be attributed to *dyslexia*, a disease that only strikes children who cannot read, and that is invariably cured when they can read. I have argued that there is nothing unique about reading, either visually or as far as language is concerned. There are no evident visual defects that are specific to reading, but this does not mean that there are no general visual anomalies that will interfere with learning to read. Children who need glasses will not find reading easy until their sight is corrected. The few children who have difficulty learning to understand speech, or learning anything, may also find learning to read difficult.

But there is no convincing evidence that children who can see normally, with or without glasses, and who have acquired a working competence in the language spoken around them, might be physically or congenitally incapable of learning to read. It cannot be denied that some children who seem "normal" and even bright in all other respects may fail to learn to read. But there can be other reasons for this failure that do not presuppose any organic dysfunction on the part of the child. Children do not learn to read who do not want to, or who see no point in doing so, or who are hostile to the teacher, or to the school, or to the social or cultural group to which they perceive the teacher and the school as belonging. Children do not learn to read who expect to fail, or who believe that learning to read will be too costly, or whose preferred image of themselves, for whatever reason, is that of a nonreader. Children do not learn to read if they have the wrong idea of the nature of reading, if they have learned—or been taught—that reading does not make sense.

Tests

It is in the context of failure that brief reference should be made to the effects on young readers of the contemporary mania for constant testing and evaluation, and especially on those having difficulty in making sense of the way reading is taught.

Tests are primarily an administrative convenience. They are devised and administered for a variety of bureaucratic and political reasons to classify children and to evaluate teachers. But no reading test ever helped a child learn to read. And there is nothing in tests themselves to indicate why a child might not be succeeding in learning to read.

Problems arise in two ways. The first is that it is widely believed that the content of reading tests (or of comprehension or readiness tests) indicates what a child needs to know in order to learn to read. This is a fallacy. Tests may provide indicators of what children are able to do as a consequence of learning to read, so that children who are good readers tend to do well on tests (though not invariably) and children who are poor readers do not. But trying to teach a child to score well on individual items on a test will not teach a child how to read. Counting the number of times a child voluntarily visits the library might be a relatively sensible test indicator of reading ability, but training the child to visit the library more often would not in itself improve reading ability, though it would raise the test score. If anything, tests measure how well children have been able to make sense of formal reading instruction, to work their way through programs.

The reason for the close affinity of tests and programs is that they are both forced to treat reading in the same arbitrary and artificial way. Because someone outside the classroom must determine what is appropriate for children to do and know (and that can be measured), and because for reasons of control and standardization it is necessary to break reading down into fragmented and predetermined sequences, tests and instructional programs both tend to become concerned with the same superficial and isolated aspects that are supposed to be "components" of reading.

Thus the first problem with tests is that they give teachers and children a distorted idea of the nature of reading and of what must be done to teach a child to read (or to satisfy some outside authority that the child is being taught to read). This is perhaps not too much of a handicap for a child who is indeed learning to read, who does reasonably well on the tests, and whose exposure to meaningful reading is not limited as a consequence. But tests can be devastating for children who do not do well on them, partly because they may then have the opportunity to read meaningfully withdrawn from them (in favor of exercises and drills that they have already demonstrated that they do not understand) and also because of the inevitable consequence for their self-esteem. The second major problem with tests is that they do nothing positive for the sensitivity of children who do badly on them.

Teachers do not need "off the shelf" tests to discover if their students are learning or if they are confused. Every teacher can tell (or should be able to tell) if a child has made progress in reading, just by talking with the child. Learning to read does not inch along one item of information after another; there should be no difficulty in determining whether a child has progressed in ability and interest over a period of a few months. If the method of instruction is such that neither teacher nor child can tell whether progress is being made without recourse to a standardized test, that is a certain sign that the instruction itself is essentially meaningless.

The best tests are "homemade," constructed on the spot to reassure the teacher that whatever a particular child is supposed to be learning at a particular time is making sense. Good teachers do this intuitively, and because such tests are a natural part of whatever activity the child is engaged in, they are both relevant and inconspicuous.

Tests of "readability" should also be treated with caution. Teachers should always be able to tell whether children in their classes would be likely to find a particular text comprehensible and interesting; they should know the children. But mechanical calculations of readability can only be interpreted *negatively*. The fact that a readability analysis indicates that a text has a "vocabulary level" and "syntactic complexity" appropriate for a particular grade may well mean that children below that grade might have difficulty with it. (Although it is not necessarily the case that children find shorter sentences easier than long ones or minimal vocabularies easier than rich ones.) But a readability level cannot be taken to indicate that a text *should be* comprehensible to children of a particular age, and that children who cannot read such a text have something wrong with their reading ability. Texts should not be constructed by formula, and compliance with a formula will not guarantee readability, comprehensibility, or interest.

The situations that I have characterized as making reading more difficult, and thus likely to interfere with children's learning to read, are a fact of life in many classrooms that many teachers feel they can do little about. Tests must be administered; instruction must be directed toward the tests; the "language arts" are arbitrarily and artificially fragmented; children are categorized and streamed; teachers must be accountable; certain curricula must be followed;

parents and trustees must be assuaged; work must sometimes be graded; competition and anxiety are unavoidable. Much of a teacher's time is necessarily directed to classroom management, many activities are engaged in to satisfy guidelines or other demands laid down by external sources, and few teachers can find the time or the resources to provide an ideal learning environment for children all the time.

A theory of reading will not change all this (although it might provide ammunition for anyone who tries to make a dent). The kind of change that will make a difference in schools will not come with better theories or with better materials or even with better-informed teachers, but only with individuals taking action toward change. The problem of improving reading instruction, in the long run, is a political question. But whether teachers can change their world or not, they will still be better off to the extent that they understand about reading and about how children learn to read. Teachers who cannot relieve children of the disruptions of irrelevant demands and activities may at least protect them by pointing out that the activities have little to do with reading or with the child's learning ability. Children understand that meaningless tasks are often given to them simply to keep them occupied and quiet, but they are not helped by being led to believe that such tasks are an important part of learning to read.

The Literacy Club

There is increasing evidence that children know a great deal about literacy before they come to school (Ferreiro & Teberosky, 1982; Goelman, Oberg, & Smith, 1984). They may not have learned to read and to write, but they know how literacy is used in the community to which they belong. If their family reads books and newspapers, they know about books and newspapers. If their family consults the television guide, they know about television guides. If they leave each other messages on the refrigerator door, they know about messages on refrigerator doors. If their friends read comics, or consult catalogues, they know about comics and catalogues. They know about signs, labels, lists, letters, greetings cards, telephone directories, and everything else that might be part of their personal written language environment. They also know roughly how written language works, that it consists of symbols written on lines, that it is laid out in various conventional ways. Before they can spell, they know there are rules of spelling. They have ideas of why people read, even before they can read themselves. They pretend to read and to write in their games.

There are no kits of materials or systematic exercises for teaching children how the world uses written language. They learn—usually without anyone being aware that they are learning—by participating in literate activities with people who use written language. It can all be summed up in a metaphor. Children learn about reading and writing by "joining the literacy club." They are given demonstrations of what written language can be used for, and they receive collaboration when they become interested in uses of written language themselves. The assistance is usually completely casual, when someone points out that an approaching sign says "Stop" or "Burgers," the way one might say to a child "Look, there's a horse." Someone helps them to read what they are interested in reading, and helps them to write what they would like to write.

Membership of the literacy club offers the same advantages as the spoken language club that I discussed in the previous chapter, and all the other clubs children might join. Children in the literacy club have opportunities to see what written language can do, they are encouraged and helped to do those things themselves, and they are not at risk of exclusion if they make mistakes, or display a passing lack of interest. They learn to be like the other members of the club. (And if they learn from other demonstrations that reading and writing are boring activities, or that they do not belong to the club, then they learn not to be like people who read and write.)

This does not mean that children are lost to literacy if they have not learned about reading and writing out of school. But it becomes all the more crucial that every child has the opportunity to belong to the literacy club in school. For children who are not interested in reading and writing, it is even more important that activities in the classroom are made interesting and accessible for them. They need more demonstrations that there are worthwhile uses of literacy, and more collaboration in engaging in those uses themselves. And in any case, children who have joined the club before they come to school should not then risk rejection because school definitions of literacy or perceptions of literate activities are different.

There is no need to fear that reading to learners, or writing for them, will make them passive and dependent. They will not always expect other people to do their reading and writing for them. No child has that much patience. The moment children feel they can read or write well enough to do what they want to do for themselves—often long before adults might think they are ready to do so—they reject the helping hand. It is no different when children learn to ride a bicycle. Children never want to be pushed when they can pedal away for themselves (except when the going is uphill).

Margaret Spencer (1987) has described how the authors of children's books *teach* children how to read. These are the authors of the books that children love to read, time and time again. The children already know the stories before they open the books—or the stories are so predictable that they know what is on a page before they turn it. The children know the story, according to Spencer, and the author shows them how to read it.

Jane Torrey (1969) has described how the authors of labels and television commercials might also help children to learn to read by themselves. Spontaneous self-admission into the literacy club may even explain how children succeed in learning to read when subjected to intensive classroom regimes of phonics and other worksheet activities (which then get the credit for the achievement).

Someone must do the learners' reading for them until they are able to read a few things for themselves, and they are ready to learn to read by reading. Reading to children need not take long—only until they can read enough for authors to take over. Very little actual reading ability is required for this to occur, if the right kinds of interesting and familiar materials are available (for details of such materials, ask a child). Indeed, for a child to know the stories in advance by heart may be enough to turn the child over to the authors. What matters is for the learner to be reading known or familiar texts like an experienced reader.

The role of the teacher is to support the reading and writing of all children until authors, and the children's own interest and self-perception, ensure their continued membership in the literacy club. For teachers who are themselves committed readers and writers, the opportunity to develop new club members should be a pleasure as well as a privilege.

SUMMARY

Learning to read depends on two basic insights—that written language is meaningful, and that it is different from spoken language. Learners must rely on the visual information of print as little as possible. Teachers help children learn to read by stimulating interest and facilitating written language use to a degree that formal instructional programs, with their necessarily limited objectives, cannot achieve. Teachers must ensure that all children receive the demonstrations and collaboration necessary to maintain membership of the "literacy club."

Notes to Chapter 12 begin on page 296, covering

Learning to read
Reading to children
Literacy and schooling
Teachers and programs
Metalinguistic awareness
Dyslexia and learning disabilities

NOTES

NOTES TO PREFACE AND
INTRODUCTION, pp. i-5.

Psycholinguistics

The term *psycholinguistics* as used in the subtitle and other places in this book refers to an overlapping area of specialized fields of psychology and linguistics, a common ground where psychologists (who study human behavior) and linguists (who study language) meet to explore the ways in which human language is actually learned and used.

In reading education, however, "psycholinguistics" has become something of a battlecry (or term of opprobrium, depending on which side you are on). A heavily phonic approach to teaching reading has long been called "the linguistic method," and "psycholinguistic" became adopted in the early 1970s as the emblem of the opposing point of view (which has also been called the "meaning approach"—or even the "reading approach"—to teaching reading).

There are two radically divergent points of view about the nature of reading. I have broadly characterized these theoretical perspectives as "inside-out" and "outside-in" (Smith, 1979), depending on where the control is presumed to originate in reading, with the reader or with the text. More generally these opposing positions have become known as "top-down" or "bottom-up" (because metaphors taken from the jargon of computer technology have a cachet of being more scientific). Top-down is roughly equivalent to my inside-out, implying that the reader determines how a text will be approached, dealt with, and interpreted. The bottom-up view is outside-in, putting the text in charge, with the letters on the page the first and final arbiters of the reader's responses. The present book, I should perhaps add, could be regarded as strongly representative of the inside-out view.

Naturally there have been attempts at compromise (or at carving out a third position), arguing for "interaction" theories which are both top-down and bottom-up at the same time. But no top-downer would want to claim that reading is not an interaction with the text in any case. Just because meaning has to be brought by the reader does not mean that *any* meaning will do (just as there may be many different ways to walk through a forest, but the forest itself puts a limit on how varied those ways might be). And as K. Goodman (1981) has pointed out, many interaction theories tend to be bottom-up in disguise; they sound more liberal but they still tend to give the basic power to the print.

Words can be promiscuous when used as labels for points of view, and "psycholinguistic" has had a particularly wayward career in education. Initially—in the late 1960s and early 1970s—the term primarily connoted academic studies into the nature of language and the manner in which infants learn to use it, focussing on the critical role of meaning and constructive thought. In education, the psycholinguistic perspective implied a similar focus on meaningfulness in literacy learning.

Kenneth Goodman and I once tried to stave off the inevitable in an article arguing that there could never be a "psycholinguistic method" of teaching reading (F. Smith & K. Goodman, 1971), a contradiction in terms which would make about as much sense as a "culinary method" of boiling eggs. Of course, we failed. "Psycholinguistics" became a rallying call for an approach to teaching reading which renounced fragmentary prepackaged "skills-based" materials and activities. But publishers quickly produced "psycholinguistic materials" (or relabeled old materials as "psycholinguistic"). The principal successor to the psycholinguistic perspective in education is today known as "whole language." Once again, this was originally a term connoting a philosophy of learning, opposed to artificial decontextualized exercises and drills. But as whole language has gained influence and prominence in education, the perspective has become distorted, the theory has become a method, and publishers have begun to produce "whole language materials."

In the academic world the term psycholinguistics has also been changing its connotations—and provoking some territorial disputes. Many researchers into language learning who originally called themselves psycholinguists employed "naturalistic" methods—they *observed* how children learned or used language in natural settings, rather than experimentally manipulating learning situations. Since the mid-1970s, however, numbers of language researchers have joined forces with computer and artificial intelligence specialists in the new sub-discipline called *cognitive science*. This new breed of "psycholinguists" frequently has a distinctly experimental and prescriptive attitude to instruction, leading to some discussion about whether they aren't misusing the term "psycholinguistics." From a purely semantic point of view, of course, any student of language and learning is entitled to claim the occupational category of "psycholinguist," because it pertains to an area of study not an educational commitment. But given the way the term has been widely employed, the excess connotations are probably unavoidable.

Nevertheless I have retained the word in the title of the present edition, partly because that was the way *Understanding Reading* was titled when it first came out in 1971, but also to indicate constraints I have continued to observe in the contents of the book. The primary concern is with what readers need to know and do in order to make sense of written language. The book does not delve deeply into *sociolinguistic* issues, such as the particular social circumstances in which literacy is employed and learned (though it does not ignore the latter completely), nor into the extent and consequences of illiteracy, into types of literate behaviors, literacy criticism, semiotics, or cultural differences.

Research

Research into the nature of reading and reading instruction peaked in the early 1970s with the support of enormous federal grants aimed at the eradication of illiteracy. The goal was never reached, largely because (I would argue) the research and instructional efforts were largely predicated on fragmented and decontextualized outside-in theories of reading and instruction (Smith, 1986). And with the failure, the bulk of available financial support and the focus of attention have tended to shift, first to writing and more recently to thinking (without however a significant change in the general theoretical approach).

Despite these changes, and a universal diminution of support funds, reading research continues to be a thriving minor industry. The International Reading Association's *Annual Summary of Investigations Related to Reading* has abstracted well over a thousand studies annually since 1980—without claiming to catch them all. Many of these studies are byproducts of the obligatory theses or dissertations produced by graduate students, many of whom will never engage in research again. Other reports, often even more pedestrian, are generated by academics requiring publications for promotion, or by the beneficiaries of research centers and other granting agencies who depend on publications to justify their existence. There is a heavy experimental emphasis in the majority of these studies, which are far removed from the realities of actual reading or classroom situations.

Barr (1986), for example, notes that only a quarter of the reports in the International Reading Association's flagship journal *Reading Research Quarterly* from 1980 to 1985 focused on instruction, and about 80% of those were experimental. She observed that the majority of the instructional studies involved "manipulating a single or limited number of conditions, such as teaching method and/or materials . . . controlling other relevant conditions by experimental or statistical design." This approach, Barr contends, "does not consider conditions shown to be central for the instructional process, such as the number of stories actually read, the amount of time available and used, the composition of the class, and the management skills of the teacher."

On the other hand, there has been a growing amount of research into comprehension in reading. The methodologies of much of this research, reviewed by Keiras and Just (1984), tend to regard comprehension as a rather mechanical process. A popular technique (employed also in many other studies of thinking) requires subjects to say aloud what they are thinking (or think they are thinking) while they read. Some studies of comprehension focus more on eye movements, which can be measured, than on a reader's knowledge and aims, which are less amenable to experimental control. More general research into comprehension over the ten years up to 1984 has been documented and assessed in a federal research project conducted by Jerome Harste, Pamela Terry, and Philip Harris at Indiana University. Their reports (Crismore, 1985; Harste and Stephens, 1985) conclude that no general statements can be made from all this effort—reading and learning are too complex, and everything depends on the individual reader, text, situation and intentions. There is more discussion of such research in the Notes to Chapter 1.

I have obviously not attempted in this volume to summarize all of the research done in the name of reading. That would be impossible. Instead I have drawn primarily from what helps me to construct a coherent picture of reading and of learning to read. People with an alternative point of view could be similarly selective in order to reject my conclusions. Research in the behavioral sciences rarely resolves disputes of a fundamentally philosphical nature. Occasionally I make reference to alternative points of view, at least to set out the arguments, but this book does not attempt to be eclectic.

On Not Being Eclectic

One aspect of eclecticism is the view that science is an incremental activity— that every bit of research is valid and worthwhile, adding a nugget of truth to an always-growing accumulation of knowledge and understanding. Such a view rests on a rosy belief that researchers never start from false assumptions or finish with unreliable conclusions. All reported findings are supposed to fit together like pieces of a jigsaw puzzle, no matter how contradictory they might be. Educational textbooks are frequently pastiches of this nature, covering immense amounts of ground without the provision of navigable pathways. The alternative point of view is that scientific research is based on conceptual *paradigms*, or ways of seeing the world, which frequently conflict. They are subjectively adopted and emotionally retained. A paradigm is rarely abandoned by its adherents unless they find it totally worthless and have another to replace it with (Kuhn, 1970). The research that is done, the evidence gathered and conclusions reached all depend on the researcher's beliefs and expectations.

Another common form of eclecticism, conspicuous in education, shuts its eyes to the possibility that conventionally-held positions might have been discredited, and attempts instead to assimilate alternative points of view into established or "official" lines of thinking. Such conceptual dilution is frequently found in reviews of research produced by committees or by bureaucratic institutions. A recent example is *Becoming a Nation of Readers: The Report of the Commission on Reading,* published by the Center for the Study of Reading at the University of Illinois (Anderson, Hiebert, Scott, & Wilkinson, 1985). This report cites—and even recommends—a variety of irreconcilable points of view about how reading is learned and should be taught, rather like arguing that vegetarianism has been shown to be good for you, but you should still eat plenty of meat.

Finally, there are eclectic approaches to teaching reading, which entail using a little bit from every prominent theorist or instructional proponent. According to such an undiscriminating view, every "authority" is probably a little bit right, and it is difficult to make decisions, so every point of view should be given its turn. Nonjudgmental approaches to instruction fail to recognize that inappropriate theories and methods can mislead the people most in need of a reliable and coherent understanding of the nature of reading, namely children trying to learn and teachers trying to teach them. It is necessary to take a position. Some current views about reading and reading instruction must be wrong.

Changes in the Fourth Edition

The most significant differences between this edition and its predecessors, both in organization and content, lie in an added emphasis on comprehension and learning. The importance of "experience" as well as "meaningfulness" is now stressed, and I have completed the move begun in the previous edition away from the notion of reading as "the reception of transmitted information." There have consequently been changes in the order of chapters at both ends of the book, with a concentration of attention on comprehension at the beginning and on learning at the end.

Chapter 1 in the third edition, "Perspective and Preview," has been relegated to the status of an Introduction, shortened, and completely revised. "Knowledge and Comprehension," which was the former Chapter 5, has been revised and advanced to become Chapter 1 in the present edition, reflecting the organizational emphasis on experience and comprehension. "Language: Spoken and Written" (formerly Chapter 6), is now revised as Chapter 2. The present Chapter 3, contrasting "Experience and Information" in reading, picks up the information theoretic parts of the old Chapters 1 and 2, but is otherwise new. The present Chapter 4, "Between Eye and Brain," is a revised version of the former Chapter 3 (with the same title) plus parts of the former Chapter 2. "Bottlenecks of Memory" (the former Chapter 4) is now expanded into Chapter 5. The chapter "Learning about the World and about Language" (formerly Chapter 7) has been expanded and transferred to the end of the book (new Chapter 11), where it more conveniently introduces the topic of learning to read.

After the "general" discussions of the five opening chapters, Chapters 6 through 9 in the present edition are the former Chapters 8 through 11, on letter identification, word identification, phonics and mediated word identification, and the identification of meaning. Apart from some updating of research citations, these chapters are largely unchanged. The former Chapter 12, "Reading and Learning to Read," however, has been split and expanded. The "reading" section becomes part of a new Chapter 10 on "Reading, Writing and Thinking," while the "learning to read" section is expanded into a chapter in its own right at the end of the book.

The last two chapters in the present edition concentrate on learning. Chapter 11, "Learning about the World and About Language," as I have already noted, is basically the former chapter 7. And Chapter 12, "Learning to Use Written Language," consists of new material as well as "learning to read" passages from the old Chapter 12. The present Chapter 12 also includes passages on learning from the former Chapter 13 on "The Teacher's Role," which has otherwise been discarded as gratuitous or redundant.

Acknowledgments

I am pleased to acknowledge helpful suggestions and support from three reviewers, Kathleen L. Daly, of the University of Wisconsin-River Falls; Diane E. DeFord, Ohio State University; and Jerome C. Harste, Indiana University. As with all my writing, Mary-Theresa Smith provided invaluable intellectual and editorial collaboration.

NOTES TO CHAPTER 1, KNOWLEDGE AND COMPREHENSION, pp. 6-23.

Theories of Comprehension

Comprehension is not a topic that attracted a great deal of attention among psychologists until the 1970s, with the notable exception of Piaget. The notion that everyone's brain contains a structure of knowledge concerning the world, into which all experience is assimilated, was a central aspect of Piaget's theorizing. Piaget's writings are voluminous and not always transparent; one might begin with *The Construction of Reality in the Child* (Piaget, 1954) or one of his collaborative efforts, such as Piaget and Inhelder (1969). Alternatively there are many useful general introductions to Piaget's thought, for example Rotman (1977), Phillips (1981), and Liben (1983).

Paradoxically, the computer has provided a great impetus to many psychologists interested in comprehension, not necessarily because the brain is conceptualized as a kind of computer (although such a notion does seem to underlie some theorizing) but because the computer has proved a convenient tool for simulating knowledge structures and memory processes. Some experimentalists believe that theories about mental events "lack rigor" unless they can be simulated on a computer to prove that they are at least feasible, while others find such claims constricting if not misleading. I shall talk more critically of these matters in the Notes to Chapter 3.

Some ingenious though limited models of cognitive activities have been explored through computer simulations; for examples see Norman and Rumelhart (1975), Meyer and Schvaneveldt (1976), Kintsch (1974), and Smith, Shoben, and Rips (1974), as well as some of the memory theorists listed in the Notes to the next chapter. There is a large degree of overlap between studies of memory and those of the structure of human knowledge. All agree that the basis of comprehension, whether of language or of the world in general, must be some internal organization of knowledge (or beliefs) about the world. An earlier, classic book on the interaction between world and brain, presaging computer analogs but remaining readably untechnical, is Miller, Galanter, and Pribram (1960). For a brief but thought-provoking paper about the knowledge background of comprehension, see Attneave (1974).

Karl Popper is a philosopher who argues for an active process of comprehension and learning similar to the discussions of the present volume; he suggests that the knowledge that each of us (and of our cultures) has accumulated is a record of the problems we have had to solve. Popper tends to be repetitive and fairly heavy going in his technical writing (e.g., Popper, 1973), but his views are expressed more concisely in an engaging autobiography (Popper, 1976) and even more clearly in a biography (Magee, 1973). Popper also points out that the brain is not the only place where knowledge can be found. Knowledge exists in books and films, in maps and diagrams, in tools and other artifacts. For someone who had never seen one, a bicycle could itself "explain" how bicycles are used. Popper thinks all of this knowledge is so substantial and so important—because it persists without necessarily being in any individual's head—that he gives it the name of "World 3," to distinguish it from the world of objective events and the world of subjective mental states. Computers, obviously, are part of World 3. Knowledge in World 3 is remarkably inert and sterile, however, until someone comes on the scene to "read" and comprehend it. On the other hand, we can all have knowledge in the head (in World 2)—for example in the form of memorized "facts"—which is meaningless to us, and might just as well be in an encyclopedia. Knowledge is useless without comprehension, wherever it is located.

Boulding (1981) argues from an economist's as well as a behavioral scientist's point of view that human knowledge is a special system, unlike other information systems like libraries, computers, or the "real world." Human knowledge constitutes a world in itself and is not simply a combination of the "real world" and a brain. In other words—as I interpret it—we live in a world that the brain creates, rather than in some concrete world that exists independently of us. I argue that reading can provide actual experiences in real worlds, not mere replicas of experiences in "representations" of the world. The world in the head is the basis of all our reality.

Yates (1985) analysed the contents of momentary awareness—what we happen to be aware of at any particular moment—and found that though fragmentary it is always part of a complete world. Our thoughts and perceptions are never unrelated to the world as a whole. They are always capable of anticipating or simulating future events, and thus provide a basis for the formulation of appropriate action. Such complex awareness, Yates argues, must reflect an underlying model of the world—a theory of the world in the head.

Basic ideas in this and later chapters on comprehension and learning are presented at greater length in F. Smith (1975). Miller and Bruner are perhaps the two psychologists who have written most on a wide variety of topics relevant to comprehension. For examples of their investigations into the organization of human knowledge, see Bruner (1973) and Miller and Johnson-Laird (1975). For examples of computer-based approaches to comprehension see Just and Carpenter (1977). For schema theory, see J. Mandler (1984) and G. Mandler (1985). For thinking, see McPeck (1981), Bruner (1986), and Vygotsky (1978). Gardner (1983) presents a different point of view about thinking. Flavell (1981) is a key source on metacognition. Two recent texts on cognitive psychology generally are Anderson (1980) and Eysenck (1984).

Prediction

Prediction as I have discussed it in this chapter is not a topic that has been widely explored, although there is an extensive psychological literature on the consequences of expectancy, for example in word recognition (Broadbent, 1967) and in pattern recognition (Garner, 1970). Bruner (1957) wrote an influential paper on "perceptual readiness," and Neisser (1977) explores the notion that perception is based on anticipated information from the environment, and that our schemes (see below) are continually restructured through prediction and experience. Our cognitive structures are anticipations. Wildman and Kling (1978/79) discuss "semantic, syntactic and spatial anticipation" in reading, and the effect of anticipation (or of its absence) on comprehension and recall has been investigated experimentally by Glynn and DiVesta (1979), Anderson and Pichert (1978), and Anderson, Reynolds, Schallert, and Goetz (1977). Everyone is familiar with the "double-take" reaction to unexpected semantic anomaly—like reading "he spread the warm bread with socks." Kutas and Hillyard (1980) have shown that encountering such a sentence actually produces a measurable surge in certain electrical potentials of the brain.

The standard reference on not having direct access to the knowledge stored in our heads is Polanyi (1966); see also Nisbett and Wilson (1977). We do not know what we know, unless we put it to use in some way, for example by saying something, or imagining saying something. We similarly do not have immediate access to thought. We can be aware of a decision that we have made, but attempts to reconstruct the "process" by which we came to that decision are inventions, even if we can hypothesize about the factors that might have weighed upon us. Normally we are only aware of thought when it has problems, when we find it difficult to make a decision, just as the only time we are normally aware of comprehension is when it is absent, when we are confused. Most of the time the brain seems able to take care of our affairs very well, without our having to become consciously involved.

Categories

There is considerable debate about the exact nature of the categories constructed in the brain. In particular, the hard-edged category boundaries implied by descriptions such as the one given in this chapter have been challenged. It is not always the case that something either belongs in a category or it doesn't. Some things have a greater claim to being in a category, they are more "typical," while others have only a tenuous membership, regardless of any distinctive features they might possess. Rosch and Lloyd (1978), for example, report that robins are usually regarded as more typical birds than chickens, with eagles somewhere between. Penguins and emus are much closer to the boundaries between categories, which can be quite fuzzy. Rosch proposes that there are certain "natural" categories that form themselves around prototypical members, like carrots for vegetables and football for sports. The prototypical class members provide the main features of the category. Other possibilities achieve membership of the category to the extent that they share "family resemblances" with the prototypes. In a challenging and wide-ranging book taking off from Rosch's prototype theory, Lakoff (1987) rejects classical categorization theories (going back to Aristotle) and proposes instead what he calls *experiential realism*. We perceive the world in terms of holistic "basic level" categories and bodily proportions, functions and purposes, which provide metaphors for understanding the world. This is a compelling and scholarly book, technical in parts but reiterating insistently and persuasively that the brain is not an information processing or symbol manipulating device, but a creative and imaginative organ.

Schemes

It is infrequent for isolated cognitive categories to play a significant role in human thought or behavior. We usually function on the basis of much larger conceptual structures, the schemes or schemas that are constructed out of complex and often dynamic organizations of categories. The English word "schemes" is becoming the standard term for the various kinds of abstract mental structure that enable us to make sense of the world, and participate appropriately in it, but the area of study is still known as "schema theory," perpetuating the Latin term introduced by Bartlett (1932).

One of the pioneers of schema research, Jean Mandler (1984), distinguishes three broad categories of schemes: (a) *scenes,* or spatially organized knowledge, (b) *events,* like the scripts and scenarios I have mentioned in this chapter, and (c) *stories,* which have their own "grammars" of plots, characters, settings, episodes, motives, goals, and outcomes. Some theorists—myself included—would go further to argue that stories are the primary basis of all our perception and understanding of the world. The way we perceive, comprehend and remember events is in the form of story structures that we impose upon them, even though events may not present themselves to us in such ways.

Demonstrations that story schemes are known and employed in reading, by adults and by children, include Bower (1976), Stein and Glenn (1978), J. Mandler (1978), and J. Mandler and Johnson (1977). All basically show that comprehension requires more than just a knowledge of the world and of the language in which a text is written. Comprehension requires sharing knowledge with the author about the manner in which such a text is conventionally constructed. There is more on the structure of texts in Chapter 2 and its Notes.

Analogous to the notion that we have general conceptual frameworks in our heads that enable us to make sense of specific texts that we happen to meet (Norman & Rumelhart, 1975) is the view that we have *frames* (Minsky, 1980; Rumelhart & Ortony, 1977), *scenarios,* or *scripts* (Schank & Abelson, 1977) underlying all our routine interactions with the world. Such patterns of expectation and behavior enable us to apply general procedures for behaving appropriately in specific situations, such as finding our way around a department store or ordering a meal in a restaurant. Schemes are abstract descriptions of events or situations with "slots" for specific detail, which we try to fit in when we want to do or understand something. Comprehension, according to Rumelhart and Ortony (1977), is the confirmation of a tentative hypothesis about what schemes are relevant by finding the slots into which the details of events fit. Rumelhart (1980) sees schemes as the building blocks of cognition, comparing them with the scripts of plays that can be performed by different groups of actors in different settings. Schank (1980) provides a critical but constructive book review entitled "What's a schema anyway?"

A more general point of view is provided by Katherine Nelson (1986) and her colleagues in many research papers and in a book entitled *Event Knowledge*. They show that children are skilled at expressing ideas in "generic," abstract representations rather than as descriptions of concrete events. Asked to describe a birthday party, for example, they talk about cakes, games and gifts, about expected behavior and events, rather than about specific occurrences on a particular occasion. They speak impersonally—"you" get presents—about events with no specific location in time and place. They tell a *story*.

The Narrative Brain

The brain is a narrative device, continuously and inevitably creating stories to explain and understand the world and our role in it, to remember and to anticipate events, to create worlds that might not otherwise exist. This urge to create narratives is so compelling that we impose them on otherwise meaningless situations. We strain to find objects in blurred patterns of color and shade (Potter, 1975), we detect faces and figures in clouds and other amorphous forms, and we impose structure on random sequences of letters or numbers (Restle, 1970; Klahr, Chase, & Lovelace, 1983). When people are shown flashing points of light in a dark room, they see dramas, with objects moving to meet or to avoid each other (Michotte, 1946). When the brain is in charge of its own affairs, in the flow of its own narratives, comprehension, memory and learning all seem to take care of themselves, as I try to show throughout this book. When the flow is broken, when comprehension, memory and learning are manipulated from the outside, they may seem to be very difficult indeed. Often in these contrived situations, where the brain has no control, there is only boredom and bewilderment. The narrative nature of children's thought has been demonstrated by van Dongen (1987).

Rosen (1986) has argued most consistently that the brain is a narrative device. If this is correct, then reading and writing must be very fundamental human activities. Sadowsky (1983) has demonstrated that reported *imagery* improves both comprehension and recall of stories, and Black, Freeman, and Johnson-Laird (1986) have shown the same for *plausibility*. The less plausible we find a tale, the less we are likely to understand and remember it. In other words, we understand and remember best when we can engage our imagination. Other research would no doubt show that drama, excitement, personal relevance, and familiar settings and characters are conducive to increased comprehension and recall (unless they are so familiar that they are boring). It seems unlikely to me that these are all separate avenues for coming to grips with texts or with the world; rather I would regard them as varied reflections of the more general fact that the closer an experience is to what the brain conceives to be a coherent story, the more likely it is to be understood and remembered.

Thinking

An intriguing recent book, stressing the creative and constructive nature of thought and also the brain's narrative mode of functioning, is Jerome Bruner's (1986) *Actual Minds, Possible Worlds.* In *Mind in Society,* Lev Vygotsky (1978) underlines the social nature of thought, which he sees as internalized action. (Bruner would be more likely to see action as externalized thought.) Vygotsky also says profound things about the social nature of learning, which will become prominent in later chapters of this book. Some research on intelligence is really research on thinking, because it regards intelligence as just about everything that goes on in the mind. Sternberg (1983, 1985), for example, inquires into the relationships between intelligence and the "internal world" of the individual, the external world of the individual, and the individual's experience. Sternberg's (1985) article in *Science* is a particularly concise and readable review of the variety of ways in which psychologists have thought about these relationships. Gilhooly (1982) and Gellatly (1986) are accessible and comprehensive on contemporary approaches to thinking.

In a review article on research into metacognition, Bransford, Stein, and Vye (1982) make the typical summary observation that less successful students fail to "activate knowledge" that can help them to understand and remember new information. One might argue whether being unable to "activate knowledge" (which in less esoteric language means to make sense) is a cause of failure or simply a description of the condition such students find themselves in. The researchers also say that less successful students are less able to assess their own level of comprehension. But comprehension is a state rather than a process, and so is inability to comprehend. One can hardly be unaware of whether one is comprehending or confused—that is like asserting that we might be aware of whether or not we feel hungry. Of course, we can believe we understand something when we are in error, just as we might feel hungry without needing food. But to make a mistake is not a failure of metacognition, of being out of touch with our own thought processes. It is simply a matter of being wrong.

NOTES TO CHAPTER 2, LANGUAGE: SPOKEN AND WRITTEN, pp. 24-48.

Surface Structure and Deep Structure

There is one significant exception to the statement that surface structure is the part of language which physically exists and can be measured in the world around us. That exception is the private *subvocal speech* which we "hear in our heads" when we talk to ourselves or "listen to ourselves" reading silently. It would be a mistake to believe that such an inner voice is deep structure, or indeed that it is some special but (to ourselves) observable quality of thought. Subvocal speech is just as much a *product* of thought as overt speech, the only difference being that it is uttered for our own benefit rather than anyone else's. But subvocal speech *could be* uttered aloud, just as the voice we hear in "silent" reading could be made audible to others. The inner voice is surface structure, with all the surface structure characteristics of vocabulary and grammar (albeit a little telegraphic at times). There must still be a deep structure underlying the utterances of the inner voice, a deep structure of meaning, which does not consist of sequences of words and sentences but of intangible concepts, global interrelationships, and propositions. (There is more on subvocalization in Chapter 9 and its notes.)

Rosenberg and Simon (1977) demonstrate experimentally that there is a single underlying semantic representation, different from but common to "information" presented in a variety of ways, in French and in English, in sentences and in pictures. McNeill (1985), reflecting on the nature and origins of language, sees parallels between speech and gesture in function, development, use, and even loss with different kinds of aphasia. In a long and rather abstruse article entitled "Against Definitions," Fodor, Garrett, Walker, and Parkes (1980) argue that sentences are not understood by recovering definitions of words. We do not understand the statement that someone is a bachelor by understanding that he is an unmarried man. "Bachelor" and "unmarried man" are not representations of each other but rather alternative representations of the same underlying meaning. Anderson and Ortony (1975) also show that the interpretation of a sentence, its "mental representation," is always much richer than the words in the text literally entail.

Gibbs (1984) argues against the notion that sentences usually have "literal meanings" in the context in which they occur (a view which he says dominates theories of language). He cites some experimental evidence that listeners do not necessarily "compute" the literal meaning of an utterance before understanding it. Golden and Guthrie (1986) show that ninth graders respond quite differently to the same short story, in the way in which they empathize with particular characters or react to events in the text, depending on their prior beliefs about what is right and natural. It is, of course, unlikely that any two people could ever experience any complex series of events, written or "real," in the same way, or come away with the same understanding of what took place.

For arguments that writing is an independent language system, not derivative of speech, see Olson, Torrance, and Hildyard (1985), especially the Kolers chapter, also Vachek (1973). For arguments that written language can on occasion be spoken, and spoken language written, see Tannen (1982a, 1982b).

For discussions of conventions generally, see Douglas (1968). Halliday and Hasan (1976) is the essential sourcebook for the conventions of cohesion in English, and Gregory and Carroll (1978) elucidate register. For more about the conventions of writing, see F. Smith (1982). Baldwin and Coady (1978) argue that punctuation rules are "empty" conventions, explaining nothing and ignored by above-average fifth grade readers.

Linguistic Theories

Noam Chomsky's influential theory of *generative transformational grammar* is in fact a theory of the way language functions in the human mind, an attempt to describe the kind of knowledge that underlies language skills. The theory has been through a number of modifications, by Chomsky and others, since its first publication (Chomsky, 1957), and has continually provoked dissent as well as enthusiasm. Chomsky's basic notion is that grammar is the bridge between surface structure and deep structure. These latter terms are employed in a variety of ways by different theorists. In this book I am using them in their most contrastive sense—regarding surface structure as the observable sounds of speech or inkmarks of print and deep structure as meaning, beyond the realm of language itself. Chomsky keeps deep structure as part of language, lodged securely within his system of grammar, the input to an underlying semantic (meaning) system which "interprets" the abstractions of deep structure. Similarly, surface structure for Chomsky is another intangible abstraction at the opposite pole of his grammatical system, the input to a phonological (sound) system, which "interprets" surface structures into actual speech. Other linguists, like the generative semanticists whom I shall discuss, propose that there must be several layers of depth in language, with abstract forms of sentences going through a number of hypothetical changes as they rise from the abysses of meaning to the surface of realized sound.

Chomsky's view, then, is that the link between deep and surface structures, and ultimately between meaning and sound (or print), is *grammar*, which consists of two components: (a) a *lexicon*, or "dictionary" of *lexical entries* (roughly speaking words); and (b) a *syntax*, or set of *rules*, for the selection and ordering of lexical entries. These syntactic rules are not to be confused with the traditional "rules of grammar" which are classroom precepts for "correct" language use; they constitute a dynamic language system that Chomsky sees in everyone's head, producing and comprehending sentences.

Chomsky's grammar is a device that *generates* sentences. With only a few rules and a small number of words it can produce an infinite number of utterances, all "grammatical" (according to the built-in syntactic rules), and all potentially new to the language user. Thus the theory offers a description of how individuals might be able to produce sentences they have never heard before. I shall give a very simple illustration to show the potential productivity and creativity of even the smallest generative grammar. This grammar will consists of just three syntactic rules and a lexicon of eight words. The syntactic component is always in the form of "rewrite rules," indicated by the single arrow → which means that a symbol on the left side of the arrow must be replaced or "rewritten" by the symbols on the right. Here are three rewrite rules:

1. $S \rightarrow NP + VP$
2. $VP \rightarrow V + NP$
3. $NP \rightarrow D + N$

The actual choice of letters as symbols is purely for convenience; they could be called X, Y, and Z but instead S is used for "sentence," NP for "noun phrase," VP for "verb phrase," N for "noun," V for "verb," and D for "determiner."

The eight lexical entries might be chosen as follows:

$N \rightarrow$ *dog, cat, man*
$V \rightarrow$ *chases, frightens, ignores*
$D \rightarrow$ *the, a*

To produce a grammatical sentence, we simply put the grammar to work, starting at the beginning with S (because we want a sentence) and following the instructions of the rewrite rules. Rule 1 says that we erase S and replace it with $NP + VP$; rule 2 changes VP to $V + NP$, giving us $NP + V + NP$, and rule 3 (applied twice) rewrites each NP as $D + N$, giving us a "terminal string" of the symbols $D + N + V + D + N$. Then we enter the lexicon, where we can exercise choice. For the first D we might perhaps select *the*, and for the first N *dog*. V can be rewritten as *chases*, the second D as *a* and the second N as *cat*, giving us the sentence *the dog chases a cat*. Eminently grammatical, you will agree. With different lexical selections we could have produced *a man frightens the cat* or *the cat ignores the dog* or indeed a total of no fewer than 108 sentences ($2 \times 3 \times 3 \times 2 \times 3$ alternatives), all of them grammatical. Add a few more rules (Chomsky estimated about a hundred) for alternative sentence structures, and a larger lexicon, and you would have—theoretically—a grammar with the productive power of the human mind.

Some of the additional rules would be *transformational* rather than *generative*, which is the reason Chomsky's grammar is sometimes called by one or other of the two labels alone and sometimes by the two together. A transformational rule operates on entire sequences of symbols on the left of the arrow instead of taking them one at a time like a generative rule. The transformational arrow has a double shaft, $\Leftrightarrow$. Thus a transformational rule might take a sequence like the $D_1 + N_1 + V + D_2 + N_2$ that we just produced (the subscripted numbers are required to keep track of the different Ds and Ns) and reorganize it as follows:

$$D_1 + N_1 + V + D_2 + N_2 \Leftrightarrow D_2 + N_2 + \text{is} + V + \text{by} + D_1 + N_1$$

Thus *the dog chases a cat* would be "transformed" (with an additional slight modification of the verb which I have ignored for the sake of simplicity) into *a cat is chased by the dog*—a perfectly grammatical passive sentence. Similarly *a man frightens the cat* would by the same rule be transformed into *the cat is frightened by a man*. In fact every active sentence that our original generative grammar produced could be transformed into a passive by this simple transformation rule, at one stroke doubling the number of sentences that the grammar could produce. A second transformational rule, say for negatives, would quadruple the total number of possible sentences (active positives, active negatives, passive positives, passive negatives) while a third transformational rule, say for interrogatives, would give eight times the power, permitting sentences as complex as *Isn't a cat chased by the dog?* Three generative rules, eight lexical entries, and three transformational rules, producing a total of $108 \times 8 = 864$ possible sentences. Other transformational rules permit combinations of sentences *(the dog chases a cat, the cat is limping $\Leftrightarrow$ the dog chases a limping cat)* making the grammar's potential output infinite, because there is no theoretical limit to the length of sentences.

All this is simplified in the extreme. To experience the complexity of unadulterated Chomsky you should sample his work directly (e.g., Chomsky, 1957, 1965, 1972, 1975), and also N. Chomsky and Halle (1968) which makes some comments on spelling relevant to reading. A brief and clear explanation of Chomsky's theoretical positions, and their radical changes, in 1957 and 1965, together with a discussion of related psycholinguistic research, can be found in an excellent paperback by Greene (1972). A more recent critical and technical review is provided by Katz (1980) who argues that three versions of Chomsky's theory have still failed to account satisfactorily for the issue of meaning. For a fascinating debate between Piaget and Chomsky, see Piattelli-Palmarini (1980).

A frequent criticism of Chomsky's theory concerns his treatment of meaning. In fact Chomsky ignores meaning, at least as far as his grammar is concerned. He claims that grammar works without reference to meaning. But there are many sentences whose grammar cannot be decided if the meaning is unknown. Even the noun "dog" in our eight-word illustrative lexicon could have been a verb. A sentence like *the child opens the door* cannot involve the same generative rules as *the key opens the door*, since you could not say *the child and the key open the door* (and *the door opens* is another case again). But you can only explain the difference between what the child does to open the door and what the key does by reference to meaning, not to grammar. Similarly the sentence *Sarah was soaked by the fountain* is passive (a transformation of *the fountain soaked Sarah*) but *Sarah was seated by the fountain* is not passive (it is not a transformation of *the fountain seated Sarah*), although the same syntactic markers might appear to be present. In these and many other quite familiar kinds of sentence, meaning must be comprehended before the grammar can be determined; grammar is not the bridge to meaning.

Moreover, Chomsky's grammar might be considered too productive. Any rules that will generate a sentence like *the runaway car frightens the angry invalid* will also generate nonsense like *the runaway invalid frightens the angry car*. But Chomsky's theory is not concerned with sense. It does not explain how we usually finish up with a sentence that more or less expresses the meaning we want to convey, nor how meaning is brought to words that are not labeled "noun" or "verb" in advance. It is not easy to see how the system works in reverse for comprehension. While Chomsky's grammar may *describe* the grammatical competence of language users, it does not convincingly explain how particular sentences are produced or comprehended on particular occasions, nor indeed does it claim to.

Generative semantic theories, by contrast, are solely concerned with how language develops out of meaning. These theories consider syntax to be subordinate to meaning or taken care of by meaning altogether. Sentences are seen not as arrangements of syntactic structures but as expressions or *propositions*, related of course to the intentions of whoever produces them. Propositions may be analyzed in terms of *case relations* between the various nouns in a sentence, whether expressed or understood, and the verb. For example, the deep structure (meaning) of a particular sentence might be centered on the verb *open*, which has different "case" relations to such nouns as *child* (the agent of the opening), *key* (instrument of the opening), *door* (the object of the opening), and so forth. These and other relations are represented in the diagram on page 234.

The diagram represents meaning, not surface structure. Each relationship (indicated by arrows) is a case relationship, of which there are perhaps a score altogether, their names and number depending on the particular theorist. The actual surface structure of an utterance will result from various transformations applied to the base structures (or case relations). In English, for example, the agent and object of a proposition are usually indicated by word order while the instrumental case may be represented by a preposition such as *with* or *by*, the locative case by *at* or *on* or *in*, manner by *with (with stealth)* or by an adverb *(stealthily)*. You will notice that there are often alternatives—the choice will depend on the particular statement the language producer wishes to make— and that some forms are ambiguous; they can represent more than one case relation. It is not necessary for all underlying case relationships actually to be expressed. When we read, *the window broke* we usually assume that there was an agent (someone) who broke the window and perhaps an instrument too (a stone). In *John was anxious to leave*, John is the deep structure subject, while in

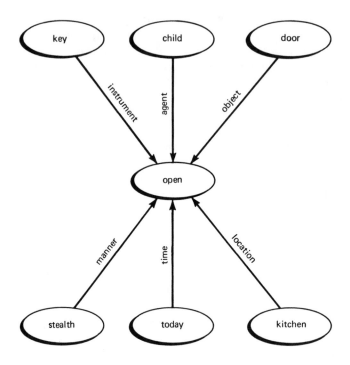

John was asked to leave, despite the similarity of surface structure, John is the deep structure object and a subject is implied (someone asked John to leave).

Generative semantic theories have little trouble with explaining how we usually manage to produce sentences that seem (to the producer at least) to express the intended meaning, because of course they arise out of meaning. And it is not necessary for such theories to run in reverse for comprehension provided the listener or reader is able to make predictions; the listener or reader will start from roughly the same meaning base as the producer of a sentence and be as unlikely as the producer to be aware of potential ambiguity.

A classic article on generative semantics is called "The Case for Case" (Fillmore, 1968), and there is more elaborate exposition in Fillmore and Langendoen (1971). Case grammar has been extended across sequences of sentences in paragraphs by Grimes (1975). Other rather technical discussions are provided by Perfetti (1972) and Chafe (1970). Excellent reviews of case grammars and their concepts generally are provided coincidentally by Brown (1973) and Slobin (1979) in their volumes on child language learning, and by Anderson and Bower (1973) in a book about memory. Many introductory books on semantics have relatively nontechnical discussions of generative theories (e.g., Palmer, 1976; see also Carroll & Freedle, 1972). A rather longer discussion of the topics of these notes so far, and their relation to the theory of comprehension that I have presented, will be found in F. Smith (1975).

Another alternative to transformational grammar, influential in the United Kingdom, is termed *systemic* (or *functional*) grammar (Halliday, 1985; Butler, 1985). The emphasis is on meaning, but from a social point of view, influenced by the anthropological theories of Firth and Malinowski. Not concerned at all with language "in the head," systemic grammar argues that every aspect of language is maintained by activity in social contexts, and must be studied in those contexts. By contrast, Johnson-Laird (1982), in a system known as *procedural semantics*, proposes two stages of "mental models" in the interpretation of sentences. The first stage generates propositions at a superficial sentence level, the second stage takes into account what the listener or reader knows. The system is claimed among other things to be able to account for inferences based solely on meaning, without recourse to the constraints of logic. Lakoff (1987), cited in the Notes to Chapter 1, also rejects all "objectivist grammars"—and there are many of them—which relate language to the world, in favor of a "cognitive grammar" relating language to our experiential perception of the world. From a different, evolutionary point of view, Lieberman (1984) also rejects conventional theories of language.

Many of the topics in this chapter are elaborated, from various points of view, in introductory textbooks on psycholinguistics, such as Wanner and Gleitman (1982), Taylor (1976), Glucksberg and Danks (1975), and Slobin (1979). Elementary texts on linguistics include Fromkin and Rodman (1983) and Steinberg (1982). Ortony (1979) is an edited volume on metaphor and thought. Mayor and Pugh (1987) contains excellent chapters on systems of communication and the power of literacy. Among many basic texts on semantics, see the two volumes of Lyons (1977) and also Fodor (1977). A classic text on the relationship between language and thought is Vygotsky (1962); see also Beveridge (1982).

For general discussions about the context of language and its uses, see Wilkinson (1971), Halliday (1973), Olson (1972), and F. Smith (1977b). For discussions of the consequences of writing systems and literacy, see Havelock (1976), Goody and Watt (1972), and Olson (1977).

There are of course other kinds of theory about language, notably that of B. F. Skinner (1957), who sees language production and comprehension in terms of stimulus-response connections. A lively critique of Skinner's views is in a classic review by N. Chomsky (1959), and there is a little more about Skinner in the Notes to Chapter 11.

Several linguists have proposed that every sentence in a meaningful context contains some information that is old and some new. Chafe (1970) refers to information carried from one sentence to another as "foregrounding"; see also Halliday (1970), Bates (1976), and Clark and Clark (1977), the latter being an important general reference on many aspects of language.

Nystrand (1986) argues that written language is not "context-free" or "situation-independent," but that the context of texts is their "potential use." In other words, readers' understanding of the purposes for which texts were written can make the texts more predictable.

Semiotics

Semiotics is an abstruse and frequently opaque science that studies all manner of "signs," or communicative conventions, and their relationships to whatever it is they signify. Classic sources in semiotics are Morris (1946), Peirce (1931-58), and more recently Eco (1984). None are particularly easy to read, nor is it immediately clear how their theories contribute to an understanding of why people read and write, and of how they learn to do these things. Relatively clear introductions to semiotics generally are provided by Culler (1981) and Deely (1982). The educator who has tried the most to make semiotics relevant to an understanding of reading and writing is Jerome Harste (see Harste, Woodward, & Burke, 1984). One aspect of semiotics to which Deely and Harste draw attention is concerned with major forms of logic and their relevance to thinking and learning generally. Two of the three forms are widely known, if not always well understood. The first is *deduction*, when known ideas or interpretive procedures are employed to develop new ideas or procedures, such as deducing what the "result" or consequence will be from a rule and an instance of that rule. Mathematics and the formal syllogisms of classical logic are examples of deductive reasoning. The second category, *induction*, relates to the inferring of cases and rules from a result, for example through the "scientific method," or hypothesis testing. Less well-known and possibly more interesting is the third category, *abduction*, when a new rule or explanation is hypothesized from a particular result or state of affairs. Such creative thinking is not normally considered part of either logic or science, but it may better characterize much of human thought, including that involved in reading or writing.

Discourse Analysis

Texts are more than simple collocations of words, arranged sequentially according to the conventions of grammar and the desire to tell a story or to explain ideas. Texts have layer upon layer of interwoven texture, and these layers are not unravelled independently of each other. One theorist, de Beaugrande (1981), proposes seven interconnected systems or "standards" in texts which both writers and readers must respect. The seven are *cohesion* (the way sentences are interlocked), *coherence* (of the parts to the whole), *intentionality*, *acceptability* (of expression and interpretation), *informativity*, *situationality* (or relevance), and *intertextuality* (relationships to texts already written or read).

Readers, according to de Beaugrande, create "textual worlds" as they read, organized around over 30 different kinds of semantic relationship and over 40 types of semantic network, the four most important of which pertain to events, actions, objects and situations. See also de Beaugrande and Dressler (1981). On the other hand, van Dijk (1980) is concerned less with all the detailed "microstructure" of texts than with "macrostructures" that involve large areas of text and reader knowledge. Kintsch and van Dijk (1975, 1978) have frequently collaborated to examine how texts, and readers' interpretations of texts, can be analyzed in terms of a "propositional text base", a tissue of connected assertions about states of affairs. A different point of view proposed by Meyer (1985) is that text structures involve a variety of relationships among the predicates of propositions. All of this is very complex, abstract, technical, and permeated with specialized jargon, related not just to texts but to every aspect of written and spoken language. Almost all theories of discourse analysis claim some experimental evidence that readers are sensitive to the kinds of structures the theorist believes exist in texts, but it is difficult to see how any particular theory could be disproved. Their most practical value may be in suggesting ways in which knowledge might be organized and employed on computers by experts in artificial intelligence, which is the area from which the theories originally derived. Claims that the theories are important for instruction—that students should be made aware of them—are vigorously disputed (e.g., Eisner, 1982). Probably everyone who can read and write today learned to do so without the benefit of such specialized knowledge, which could obviously put great stress on the attention-capacity and interest of beginners. What is clear is the importance of shared knowledge of the content of the text and experience of the manner in which different kinds of text are conventionally written.

For a general discussion of discourse analysis and comprehension, see Tierney and Mosenthal (1982), and more technically Stubbs (1982), Britton and Black (1985), and Halliday (1985).

Text Organization and Comprehension

Meyer (1985) has proposed a method of "scoring" texts in order to predict how much readers will be able to comprehend and recall. Texts that are difficult to understand because of the way they are written are sometimes referred to as "inconsiderate" texts (Armbruster & Anderson, 1984). There is no doubt that texts can often be improved. Beck, McKeown, Omanson, and Pople (1984) revised two basal reader stories to make them more coherent without altering their plots, enhancing the comprehension of both skilled and less skilled readers. The length of the two stories was increased from 782 and 811 words to 900 and 957 words, but comprehension went up by a grade level for both second- and third-grade readers. Readability formulas based on word counts and sentence length have been generally discredited (e.g.

MacGinitie, 1984). "Simplifying" reading material by fragmenting it into short sentences can greatly interfere with comprehension and recall. See also Slater (1985).

Hundreds of studies have been conducted and reported since the mid-1970s demonstrating that texts are better understood and remembered if readers (of all ages and ability) are familiar with the relevant story grammars, e.g. Bower (1976), Bower, Black, and Turner (1979), Fredericksen (1975), Mandler and Johnson (1977), Reder (1980), Stein and Glenn (1979), and Walker and Meyer (1980). McGee (1982) showed that third- and fifth-grade readers were aware of text structures and used them in recall, even the poor readers (though they did so less well than better readers, who might reasonably be expected to have had greater familiarity with stories). Mandler and Goodman (1982) found that reading speed dropped when story structures were not congruent with reader's expectations, and also that second sentences were read faster than the first sentences in chapters, when readers had gained an idea of what the chapter was about. Anderson and Pearson (1984) theorize about the relevance of schemes in reading comprehension. See also Grimes (1975) and Applebee (1977).

Piper (1987) has some cautions about teaching students the explicit structures of story grammar, which he sees as no different from more traditional modes of analysis which have not fared well in education. Consciousness of structure does not necessarily promote understanding, he argues, and the theories also assume that there is just one interpretation for every text. Durkin (1981) also looks critically at the significance of the "new interest" in comprehension for education. Beers (1987) argues that schema theory—and cognitive science generally—are inappropriate approaches to reading because of their underlying "machine metaphor."

Some Technical Terms

One might think that there could not be too much complication about the fact that the basic elements of language are sounds. The word "bed," for example, is made up of three distinctive sounds /b/, /e/, and /d/ (it is a useful convention that the sounds of language are printed between oblique // strokes). With a few perverse exceptions, each sound of the language is represented by a particular letter of the alphabet, so the number of alternative sounds in English must be about 26. Unfortunately, none of the preceding statements is correct.

English has rather more functionally different sounds than it has letters in the alphabet, about 40. These sounds have the special name *phonemes*. A variety of letters can represent a single phoneme and a variety of phonemes can be represented by a single letter or letter combination. It is necessary to be tentative in making statements about the total number of phonemes because it depends on who is talking and when. All dialects have roughly the same number of phonemes, but not always the same ones, so that words that are individually distinguishable in some dialects, such as "guard" and "god" may not be distinguishable in others unless in a meaningful context. We often think we make distinctions between words when in fact we do not—redundancy in context is usually sufficient to indicate which alternative we intend. Many literate speakers do not have phonemes to distinguish among "Mary," "marry," and "merry," or "cot," "caught," and "court." Say these words one at a time and ask a listener to spell what you have just said. You may find that the listener cannot observe all the differences you think you are making. Phonemes often drop out of casual or colloquial speech.

A phoneme is not so much a single sound as a collection of sounds, all of which sound the same. If that description seems complicated, a more formal definition will not appear much better—a phoneme is a class of closely related sounds constituting the smallest unit of speech that will distinguish one utterance from another. For example, the /b/ at the beginning of the word "bed" distinguishes "bed" from words like "fed" and "led" and "red," the /e/ in the middle distinguishes "bed" from "bad" and "bide" and "bowed," and the /d/ distinguishes the word from such alternatives as "bet" and "beg." So each of the three elements in "bed" will serve to distinguish the word from others, and each also is the smallest unit that can do this. Each is a *significant difference*. It does not matter if the /b/ pronounced at the beginning of "bed" is a little different from /b/ at the beginning of "bad," or if the /b/ in "bed" is pronounced in different ways on different occasions. All the different sounds that I might make that are acceptable as the sound at the beginning of "bed" and "bad," and that serve to distinguish them from "fed" and "fad," and so forth, qualify as being the same phoneme. A phoneme is not one sound, but a variety of sounds any of which is acceptable by listeners as making the same contrast. The actual sounds that are produced are called *phones*, and the sets of "closely related" phones that all serve as the same phoneme are called *allophones* of each other (or of the particular phoneme). Allophones are sounds that the listener learns to treat as equivalent and to hear as the same.

When electronic equipment is used to analyze sounds heard as the same, quite marked differences can be found, depending on the sound that follows them. For example, the /d/ in "dim" is basically a high-pitched rising sound, while its allophone at the beginning of "doom" is much lower pitched and falling (Liberman, et al., 1957). A tape recorder will confirm that the two words have no /d/ sound in common. If they are recorded, it is impossible to cut the tape in order to separate the /im/ or /oom/ from the /d/. Either one is left with a distinct /di/ or /doo/ sound, or else the /d/ sound disappears altogether, leaving two quite different kinds of whistle. Other phonemes behave in equally bizarre ways. If the first part of the tape-recorded word "pit" is cut and spliced at the front of the final /at/ of a word such as "sat" or "fat," the word that is heard is not "pat," as we might expect, but "cat." The /k/ from the beginning of "keep" makes "top" when joined to the /op/ from "cop" and makes "poop" when combined with the /oop/ from "coop."

There is a simple way to demonstrate the sounds that we normally hear to be the same can be quite different. Say the word "pin" into the palm of your hand and you will feel a distinct puff of air on the /p/; however, the puff is absent when you say the word "spin." In other words, the /p/ in "pin" is not the same as the /p/ in "spin"—and both are different from the /p/ in "limp." If you now pay careful attention to the way you say the words, you can probably detect the difference. Usually the difference is ignored, because it is not significant. Other word pairs provide a similar demonstration—for example, "kin" and "skin," or "team" and "steam." You may also be able to detect a difference between /k/ in "cool" and /k/ in "keen," a difference that is allophonic in English and phonemic in Arabic, or in the /l/ at the beginning and end of "level." Japanese often have difficulty in distinguishing between English words such as "link" and "rink" because there is no contrast at all between /l/ and /r/ in their language. In short, a phoneme is not something present in the surface level of spoken language—it is something that the listener constructs. We do not hear different sounds when we are listening to speech, but instead we hear significant differences, phonemes instead of phones. The preceding distinctions may be further illustrated by reference to writing, where a comparable situation holds. Just as the word "sound" is ambiguous in speech, since it can refer to a phone or a phoneme, so the word "letter" is ambiguous in writing. We call "a" one letter of the alphabet, as distinguished from "b", "c", "d", etc., but we also talk about *a*, A, *a*, etc. as being letters, although they all in a way represent the same "letter." In the first case, the letter of the alphabet "a" is really a category name for a variety of written symbols such as a, A, *a*. The 26 category names for the letters in the English alphabet may be called *graphemes*, the written symbols (which are innumerable in their various forms) may be called *graphs*, and the graphs that constitute alternatives for a single grapheme are known as *allographs*.

The same defining framework can now be used for the basic elements of speech and writing. A *phoneme (grapheme)* is a class of closely related *phones (graphs)* constituting the smallest significant differences in speech (writing) that will distinguish one meaningful unit from another. The set of functionally equivalent *phones (graphs)* constituting a single *phoneme (grapheme)* are termed *allophones (allographs)*. Allographs may not seem to have as much in common as allophones; in fact, some allographs, such as *a*, and *A*, or *g* and *G*, would appear to have nothing in common at all. But they do have a *functional equivalence* in that their differences are not significant for reading, any more than the differences between allophones are significant for comprehending speech.

Linguists make several other distinctions along the same lines. A *morpheme* is the smallest meaningful part of a word. A word may consist of one or more morphemes, some "free" like *farm* or *like* because they can occur independently, and some "bound," like *-er* (meaning someone who does something) and *-s* (meaning plural) or *un-* (meaning negative), which have to be joined to a free morpheme. Thus *farmers* is three morphemes, one free and two bound, and so is *unlikely*. Different *morphs* may represent the same morpheme—thus for plurality we can have not only *-s* but *-es*, *-en*, and a lot of quite odd forms like the vowel change in *man-men* or even nothing at all, as in the singular and plural *sheep*. Morphs that constitute the same morpheme are called *allomorphs*. Meaning itself may be considered in the form of elements sometimes called *sememes*. "Bachelor," for example, comprises sememes related to maleness, age, marriage, and negation. Words in a dictionary—earlier referred to as "lexical entries"—may similarly be termed *lexemes*.

More About Words

A number of my observations about the ambiguity of words are derived from the work of the linguist Fries (1945), who calculated that the 500 most common words of our language have an average of 28 distinct dictionary meanings each. The most detailed analyses of the relation between word frequencies and their different meanings are by Zipf (1960), and there are interesting and more readable summaries in Miller (1951). Miller points out that the 50 most common words of our language do the bulk of our communicative work, constituting 60 percent of talk and 40 percent of writing. A mere seven words constitute 20 percent of our language—*the, of, and, a, to, in* and *is*. The 10 most common French words—*à, de, dans, sur, et, ou, que, ne, pas,* and *y*—constitute 25 percent of that language.

The eye-voice span phenomenon shows that when reading aloud we do not say the words we are looking at; the eye roves ahead over meaningful stretches of words and the brain deals in units that make sense. There is a flurry of small studies of the eye-voice span every decade or so; a recent review is included in Gibson and Levin (1975), and earlier in Geyer (1968).

NOTES TO CHAPTER 3, INFORMATION AND EXPERIENCE, pp. 49-63.

Measuring Information and Uncertainty

Mathematics plays only a small part in this book. But a brief introduction to some elementary techniques of information theory measurement will allow some numbers to be put to the rate at which the brain can deal with visual information from the eyes (its "channel capacity"). The same techniques also permit quantification of the uncertainty or redundancy of letters and words of English (or any other language) in differing circumstances.

It is necessary to be a little circumlocutionary to putting actual figures to information and uncertainty because although both are measured with respect to alternatives, the measure is not simply the number of alternatives. Instead, information is calculated in terms of a unit called a *bit*, which always reduces by half the uncertainty on any particular occasion. Thus the card player who discovers that an opponent's strongest suit is red (either diamonds or hearts) gets one bit of information, and so does a child trying to identify a letter who is told that it comes from the second half of the alphabet. In the first case two alternatives are eliminated (the two black suits) and in the second case 13 alternatives are removed (and 13 still remain). In both cases the proportion of uncertainty reduced is a half and therefore the amount of information received is regarded as one bit.

The uncertainty of a situation in bits is equal to the number of times a "yes or no" question would have to be asked and answered to eliminate all uncertainty if each answer reduced uncertainty by a half. Thus there are two bits of uncertainty in the card-playing example because two questions will remove all doubt, for example: *Q1. Is it a black suit? Q2. If yes, is it clubs? (If no, is it hearts?)*, or *Q1. Is it spades or diamonds? Q2. If yes, is it spades? (If no, is it hearts?)*.

You can see it does not matter how the questions are posed, provided they permit a yes-no answer that will eliminate half the alternatives. The final qualification is important. Obviously, a single lucky question such as "Is it clubs?" will eliminate all alternatives if the answer is "yes," but will still leave at least one and possibly more questions to be asked if the answer is "no." The most efficient way of reducing uncertainty when the answer can only be "yes" or "no" is by a binary split, that is, by partitioning the alternatives into two equal sets. In fact the word *bit*, which may have sounded rather colloquial, is an abbreviation of the words *b*inary dig*it*, or a number representing a choice between two alternatives.

The uncertainty of the 26 letters of the alphabet lies somewhere between four and five bits. Four bits of information will allow selection among 16 alternatives, not quite enough, the first bit reducing this number to 8, the second to 4, the third to 2, and the fourth to 1. Five bits will select among 32 alternatives, slightly too many, the first eliminating 16 and the other four removing the rest of the uncertainty. In brief, x bits of information will select among 2^x alternatives. Two bits will select among $2^2 = 4$, three bits among $2^3 = 8$, four bits among $2^4 = 16$, and so on. One question settles only $2^1 = $ two alternatives, and no questions at all requires that you have only one alternative to begin with ($2^0 = 1$). Twenty bits ("twenty questions") are theoretically sufficient to distinguish among $2^{20} = 1,048,576$ alternatives. There is a mathematical formula that shows that the theoretical uncertainty of 26 letters of the alphabet is almost precisely 4.7 bits, although, of course, it is not easy to see how one could ask just 4.7 questions. (The formula is that the uncertainty of x alternatives is $\log_2 x$, which can be looked up in a table of logarithms to the base 2. $\log_2 26 = 4.7$, since $26 = 2^{4.7}$. Can you calculate the uncertainty in a deck of 52 playing cards? Since 52 is just twice 26, the uncertainty of the cards must be one bit more than that of the alphabet, or 5.7 bits.)

Measuring Redundancy

It will be helpful to pursue the matter of redundancy a little more deeply, partly because of the importance of the concept of redundancy to reading, but also because the discussion of how *bits* of uncertainty or information are computed contained an oversimplification that can now be rectified. We shall consider two aspects of redundancy, termed *distributional* and *sequential*.

Distributional redundancy is associated with the relative probability that each of the alternatives in a particular situation can occur. Surprising as it may seem, there is less uncertainty when some alternatives are less probable than others. And because there is less uncertainty when alternatives are not equally probable, there is redundancy. The very fact that alternatives are not equally probable is an additional source of information that reduces the uncertainty of the set of alternatives as a whole. Redundancy that occurs because the probabilities of alternatives are not equally distributed is therefore called distributional redundancy.

Uncertainty is greatest when every alternative has an equal chance of occurring. Consider a coin-tossing game where there are only two alternatives, head or tail, and there are, in fact, equal chances of a head or tail turning up. The informativeness of knowing that a particular toss of the coin produced a head (or a tail) is one bit, because whatever the outcome uncertainty is reduced by a half. But now suppose that the game is not fair, and that the coin will come down head nine times out of ten. What is the uncertainty of the game now (to someone who knows the coin's bias)? The uncertainty is hardly as great as when the odds were 50–50, because then there was no reason to choose between head and tail while with the loaded coin it would be foolish knowingly to bet tail. By the same token, there is likely to be far less information on being told the outcome of a particular toss of the loaded coin. Not much uncertainty is removed if one is told that the coin has come down head because that is what was expected all the time. In fact the informativeness of a head can be computed to be about .015 bit compared with one bit if the game were fair. It is true that there is much more information in the relatively unlikely event of being told that a toss produced a tail—a total of 3.32 bits of information compared with the one bit for a tail when heads and tails are equally probable—but we can expect a tail to occur only once in every 10 tosses. The *average* amount of information available from the loaded coin will be nine-tenths of the .015 bit of information for head and one-tenth of the 3.32 bits of information for tail which when totaled is approximately .35 bit. The difference between the one bit of uncertainty (or information) for the 50–50 coin, and the .35 bit for the 90–10 loaded coin, is the distributional redundancy.

The earlier statements that every bit of information halves the number of alternatives, and that the number of bits of uncertainty is the number of yes-no questions that would have to be asked and answered to eliminate all the alternatives, hold only when all the alternatives are equally probable. If some alternatives are less probable than others, then an *average* amount of uncertainty or information has to be computed, taking into account both the number of alternatives and the probability of each. Because uncertainty and information are at their maximum when alternatives are equally probable, the average uncertainty of situations where this does not occur is necessarily less than the maximum, and redundancy is present.

The statement that the uncertainty of letters of the English language is 4.7 bits is perfectly true for any situation involving 26 equally probable alternatives—for example, drawing a letter from a hat containing one instance only of each of the 26 letters of the alphabet. But the letters of English do not occur in the language with equal frequency; some of them, such as *e, t, a, o, i, n, s*, occur far more often than others. In fact *e* occurs about 40 times more often than the least frequent letter, *z*. Because of this inequality, the average uncertainty of letters is somewhat less than the maximum of 4.7 bits that it would be if the letters all occurred equally often. The actual uncertainty of letters, considering their relative frequency, is 4.07 bits, the difference of about .63 bit being the distributional redundancy of English letters, a measure of the prospective informativeness that is lost because letters do not occur equally often. If letters were used equally often, we could achieve the 4.07 bits of uncertainty that the 26 letters currently have with a little over 16 letters. We could save ourselves about nine letters if we could find a way (and agree) to use the remainder equally often.

Words also have a distributional redundancy in English. One of the oldest and still least understood findings in experimental psychology concerns the "word-frequency effect," that more common words of our language can be identified on less visual information than less frequent words (Broadbent, 1967; Howes & Solomon, 1951). Computations of the distributional redundancy of letters and words in English are contained in Shannon (1951) and are discussed in Cherry (1978) and Pierce (1961).

Sequential redundancy exists when the probability of a letter or word is constrained by the presence of surrounding letters or words in the same sequence. For example, the probability that the letter *H* will follow *T* in English words is not 1 in 26 (which would be the case if all letters had an equal chance of occurring in any position) nor about 1 in 17 (taking distributional redundancy into account), but about 1 in 8 (because only eight alternatives are likely to occur following T in English; namely, R, H, or a vowel). Thus the uncertainty of any letter that follows T in an English word is just three bits ($2^3 = 8$). The average uncertainty of all letters in English words is about 2½ bits (Shannon, 1951). The difference between this average uncertainty of 2½ bits and a possible uncertainty of 4.07 bits (after allowing for distributional redundancy) is the *sequential redundancy* of letters in English words. An average of 2½ bits of uncertainty means that letters in words have a probability of about 1 in 6 instead of 1 in 26. This figure, of course, is only an *average* computed over many readers, many words, and many letter positions. There is not a progressive decline in uncertainty from letter to letter, from left to right, in all words. An English word beginning with q, for example, has zero uncertainty about the next letter u, an uncertainty of about two bits for the four vowels that can follow the u, and then perhaps four bits of uncertainty for the next letter, which could be one of over a dozen alternatives. Other words have different uncertainty patterns, although in general the uncertainty of any letter goes down the more other letters in the word are known, irrespective of order. Because of constraints in the spelling patterns of English—due in part to the way words are pronounced—there is slightly more uncertainty at the beginning of a word than at the end, with slightly less in the middle (see Bruner & O'Dowd, 1958).

The orthographic (spelling) redundancy of print to which I have referred comprises both distributional and sequential redundancy for letters *within* words, while syntactic (grammar) and semantic (meaning) redundancy are primarily sequential redundancy *between* words.

Signal Detection Theory

As I said in the chapter, observers (whether radar operators or readers) always have a choice between reducing the number of their absolute errors while increasing "misses" or of achieving maximum hits while increasing the number of "false alarms." In effect, observers can place themselves at any point along a curve ranging from zero false alarms (but zero hits) to 100 percent hits (but a maximum of false alarms). This curve is called a *receiver operating characteristic*, or ROC curve, and varies with every individual and situation. At any one time an observer can choose where to be placed on the ROC curve—the criterion level selected depending on the perceived relative costs of hits, misses, and false alarms. But to shift the ROC curve as a whole—to improve the ratio of hits, misses, and false alarms—requires an improvement in the clarity of the situation (e.g., better illumination) or in the ability of the observer (e.g., more skill). Encouragement or success has the effect of moving an observer up an ROC curve, just as anxiety will move the observer down, but only a change in ability—or, for example, an increase in the availability of nonvisual information—will shift the ROC curve in its entirety.

There is an interesting example of the ability of human observers to penetrate noise and extract information-carrying signals in what Cherry (1977) calls the *cocktail party problem*. The example illustrates a point frequently made in this book that the prior knowledge of the perceiver contributes so much to comprehension. The problem is this: How can listeners in a crowd of people all talking loudly at the same time manage to follow what one person is saying, and tune out everything else? The communication channel to each listener's ear is full of noise (both literally and technically), yet the individual can select from within the noise the information coming from one source only. And this "selected" voice is the only one that is heard—unless someone else happens to say something particularly relevant personally, such as the listener's name, in which case it is demonstrated that the listener has really been monitoring all the conversations all the time, "listening without hearing." No one has yet been able to devise a machine that, using the same communication channel, could unscramble more than one voice at a time. Yet the human receiver can separate intermingled messages, and not because they come in different voices or from different directions (it has been shown experimentally that we can follow one message even if successive words are produced by different voices), but by following the sense and syntax of the message being attended to. Such a feat can be accomplished only if listeners draw upon their own knowledge of language to extract a message from all the irrelevant noise in which it is embedded.

Further Reading

For communication theory and information theory generally, see Pierce (1961) and Cherry (1978). Attneave (1959) discusses specifically applications of information theory to psychology. Miller (1964) reprints useful brief articles on both information theory and signal detection theory. An introductory psychology text that employs concepts from both theoretical domains is Lindsay and Norman (1977). Garner (1962, 1974) also develops psychological descriptions from an information theory point of view. A classic article on signal detection theory is Swets, Tanner, and Birdsall (1961); at a more popular level see Swets (1973) and, more technically, Pastore and Scheirer (1974).

Limitations of Information Theory and of "Information"

The first practical application of information theory was in measuring the efficiency of communication systems like telephone lines and radio links. The measure was related to the proportion of words emitted by the "transmitter" at one end of a communication channel that the "receiver" at the other end could correctly identify. Information theory had a brief but spectacular decade of influence in psychology in the 1950s and 1960s, primarily due to the erudition of George Miller (1956) in an article that referred to limits on human "capacity for processing information." For many psychologists this was a brand new and seductive way of talking about the brain.

Information theory became influential at a time when reading was primarily considered to be a matter of identifying letters and words. The text could be regarded as a transmitter, the reader as a receiver, and the visual system as a communication channel. The efficiency or "capacity" of this channel could be computed from the proportion of letters and words that the reader correctly identified under various conditions. The perspective and techniques were useful theoretically and enabled all kinds of interesting comparisons to be made, as I tried to indicate in the opening sections of the present Notes. They helped to demonstrate in a quantifiable way that the visual system has limitations—it can't see everything that is in front of the eyes. The theory also offered some useful concepts, notably that of redundancy.

However, information theory itself has severe limitations, with respect to texts and to brains. It can measure "information" in its own narrow terms of reducing uncertainty among known sets of alternatives, but it can do nothing about "meaning." It cannot say how meaningful a text is, or how much understanding there might be in the brain. Outside the experimental laboratory, readers usually read for meaning rather than for information—or they get their information enveloped in meaning. And when readers do "receive information", it is usually not in the constricted sense of information theory. Statements like "More than a thousand kinds of brown algae exist" may be informative, but there is no way of saying how much uncertainty they reduce. Redundancy in spelling patterns can be calculated, but not redundancy in short stories. Information theory loses its utility once we get inside the head.

Besides, information does not seem to be what the brain is primarily concerned with (Smith, 1983a). The brain deals with understanding rather than information. Either information becomes understanding when it gets into the brain, part of the interlocked theory of the world in the head, or it remains an isolated fact, at best potential meaning, like a fact in an encyclopedia. Information can be derived from experience in the same way that vitamins can be obtained from food, but information is no more experience than vitamins are food. I now have some concern about the terms "visual information" and "nonvisual information" which I coined in the first edition of this book. The first term may be appropriate for tasks restricted to letter and word recognition, but once we get behind the eyeballs, in the "nonvisual" domain, then "knowledge" might be a better term than "information." I quietly introduced such a modification in Chapter 1 of the present edition, although I obviously think the original distinction still has some expository usefulness.

The semantic problems are compounded by the fact that in contrast with the narrow sense in which the word "information" is employed in information theory, its general use these days is positively indiscriminate. Everything is information—the content of every book, journal, and television program, the entire educational curriculum, anything on a computer, even junk mail.

Rosenblatt (1978), in her distinction between reading for information and reading for experience, doesn't use the word information in either the narrow information theory sense or the catch-all general sense. To her, information means "facts." Perhaps because the terms "information" and "experience" have such broad general uses she actually employs quite uncommon terms for what she wants to explain. Informational reading she describes as *efferent*, meaning "carrying outward" from the text, and the alternative she terms *aesthetic*, implying involvement in the text through the senses.

In cognitive science and science computer jargon, information is always "processed" rather than "understood." Almost everything now is a process in the educational research literature—and in disquisitions on teaching as well. It is rare to read of unadulterated reading, writing, comprehension, learning, or teaching, but always of the reading process, the writing process, the comprehension process, the learning process, and the teaching process. And according to my dictionary, the word "process" has broad mechanical connotations—it entails a succession of actions or operations in a specific or prescribed sequence (much like the manner in which a computer is programmed). Among cognitive scientists, reading and comprehension are now both "text processing." Writing is "word processing." Thinking is "ideas management" or "the organization of knowledge." Information processing is no longer something done by computers alone.

Perhaps to underline the growing influence of computer-based ways of thinking, there are signs that the word "information" is beginning to be superseded by "data" (a plural word which, like "media," is commonly used in the singular). Knowledge is becoming a "data-base." "Process" may also be losing ground to "procedures," an artificial intelligence term, and even to "instructions," which are what computers run on. The "schemas" and "scenarios" that our brains might (metaphorically) be said to contain (Chapter 1) are becoming seen as procedures rather than as narratives. "Procedural" knowledge is contrasted with "propositional" knowledge (Anderson, 1980). Larsen (1986) even argues that there is a need today for "procedural literacy," which is not the same thing as "computer literacy," but rather the ability to produce and understand sequences of instructions for the organization of knowledge.

Cognitive Science

I have referred several times already to cognitive scientists—the theorists and researchers who are concerned with knowledge systems in both humans and computers. Many cognitive scientists are cognitive psychologists or psycholinguists (who used to regard the brain as something unique). But now they share ideas and language with experts in advanced computer systems and artificial intelligence. They are concerned with "systems" that can organize information and make "rational" decisions. A prominent cognitive scientist, Roger Schank (1982), has published a book entitled *Reading and Understanding: Teaching from the Perspective of Artificial Intelligence.* In the book he describes how he taught his daughter to read, and how he is teaching computers to read, by step-by-step procedures. The purpose of reading, he asserts, is to remember the information in the text, which the reader accomplishes by encoding "representations of meanings." Comprehension is important for Schank because it facilitates remembering. Two other cognitive scientists, Bransford and Stein (1984), base their "guide for improving thinking, learning, and creativity" on "insights from artificial intelligence."

A large number of studies of comprehension (or comprehension processes) from a cognitive science perspective are contained in an edited volume by Kieras and Just (1984). Olson, Duffy, and Mack (1984), for example, analyse what they term "real-time comprehension processes," in which they treat comprehension as a reader's ability to repeat what is said in the text (not what the reader might feel about the text). Reading adds to the reader's "knowledge base." Other chapters in the same volume describe computer simulations of reading, or rather of superficial characteristics of reading, such as the length of time eye fixations rest on particular words.

For more general discussions of cognitive science, see Anderson (1980), Simon (1980), Sternberg (1983, 1985) and Eysenck (1984). Mandler (1985) discusses the subject from a more humanistic point of view. The basic assumption underlying the cognitive science approach is perhaps most strongly expressed by Goldstein and Papert (1977), who declare that human beings and computers are involved in organizing and using knowledge in similar ways. They believe that artificial intelligence will "deeply transform the theory and practice of education, not just because of more intelligent machines, but by helping students understand their own thought." Lawler and Yazdani (1987) is an edited volume relating artificial intelligence to education, and Friedman, Klivington, and Peterson (1986) relate cognitive science and education with particular consideration to neuroscience. Spiro, Bruce and Brewer (1980) consider the contribution of artificial intelligence to reading comprehension. More general studies of the rise of cognitive science are Gardner (1987) and Baars (1986). See also a review of Baars by Levin (1987).

It can be argued that cognitive science has become an elaborate behavioristic stimulus-response system, despite the fact that it calls itself "cognitive." Individuals are perceived as totally under the control of an environment, which is the source of "data" or "information" rather than of stimuli and contingencies of reinforcement. There are no intentions, feelings or values except for what something outside the system has put into it. This is not my argument, but that of the foremost exponent of behaviorism, B. F. Skinner (1985), who claims that the only difference between cognitive science and his own theory is in the language that is used.

There are critics of cognitive science among cognitive psychologists. Neisser (1983) debates Sternberg's (1983) attempt to decompose mental states into parts, quoting J. R. R. Tolkien: "He that breaks a thing to find out what it is has left the path of wisdom." Neisser argues that the elements of Sternberg's analysis "are not separate elements in any genuine mental process; they are more like chapter headings in books on how to think." (There is a response by Sternberg in the journal in which Neisser's critique appears.) In an important article on the semantic nature of reading, Kolers and Roediger (1984) also contend that information-processing "models of mind"—full of little boxes, processes, and stages—"don't work." Information-processing models become more and more elaborate but have led to little cumulative knowledge about how information flows through supposed information systems. Kolers and Roediger recommend studying instead how the mind creates, transforms and manipulates symbols, transferring them to new occasions. They take reading as a particular example—we remember the way we understand, and how we understand depends on what we look for. See also Beers (1987).

Computers

The discussion of cognitive science is inseparable from discussion of the relationship of computers and the brain, a complex, philosophical topic. Computers don't do anything unless told what to do and how to do it, so they are not like the human brain unless you believe that is what humans are like. Computers may do things that we can't do—like calculate thousands of prime numbers, or scrutinize complex landscapes, or generate elaborate designs—but nevertheless they are following instructions that humans give them (or instructions which the computers develop as a consequence of earlier instructions that humans have given them). And there is no guarantee that the procedures computers follow are those used by the brain when humans make mathematical calculations, study a landscape, or paint a picture; they almost certainly are not. A computer doesn't have plans and intentions, except those it is given. It doesn't have wishes or feelings or values. These characteristics may be simulated on computers, but this does not give them human characteristics. Computers are born with nothing, not even needs. They don't have experiences. They don't understand sarcasm, or irony, or affection. They don't understand *anything*. Programming a computer is not the same thing as teaching it, and being programmed is certainly not the same thing as learning. Computers are said to have learned when they perform differently. Human beings do not necessarily behave differently as a consequence of learning, and can change their behavior without learning anything.

Among many vehement arguments that computers cannot provide appropriate metaphors or models for human thought and behavior are a number by computer experts. Terry Winograd designed a renowned program (called SHRDLU) that enabled computers to make statements and answer questions about objects of different colors and shapes on a table-top. But computers don't really understand even that "carefully-constrained world," says Winograd (1981). Their procedures are inadequate representations of reasoning. Dreyfus and Dreyfus (1986) maintain that computers can't be "intelligent" like humans because they can't replicate intuition. "Logical precision" is not enough. Computers can't even recognize patterns like human beings, say Dreyfus and Dreyfus—and they advise educators not to get involved with artificial intelligence. In a densely philosophical article entitled "Tom Swift and his procedural grandmother," Fodor (1978) sets out why computers cannot provide a theory of what it is to know the meaning of a word. Natural language can't be reduced to computer language (or to anything else—once you say that "bachelor" means "unmarried man" there is not much more to be said). There is no way to reduce "meaning" further to "procedures" or "instructions." Boulding (1981) says that human knowledge is not like any other "system," whether in a library or a computer, because human knowledge is inseparable from the world in which we are located. See also Jones (1986) on the inability of computers to construct the social realities that determine human thought and Hausman (1985) on whether computers can create.

NOTES TO CHAPTER 4, BETWEEN EYE AND BRAIN, pp. 64-86.

Vision and Information

For vision generally, Gregory (1966) is a brief, easily read and well-illustrated introduction. Gregory (1970), Oatley (1978), and Hochberg (1978) all deal rather more technically with the constructive nature of perception. Bronowski (1978) points out picturesquely that there is no little man in the brain looking at pictures sent from the eyes (or listening to the sounds of speech transmitted from the ears). Rock (1983) insists that perception is intelligent, and based on operations similar to those which characterize thought. There are several psychology texts with a cognitive basis to their discussions of visual perception, notably Neisser (1967), Lindsay and Norman (1977), Calfee (1975), and Massaro (1975).

That there is a limit to how much print can be identified at any one time, varying according to the use a reader can make of redundancy, is not exactly a recent discovery. The illustration in this chapter of how much can be identified from a single glance at a row of random letters, random words, and meaningful sequences of words, is derived directly from the researches of Cattell (1885, republished 1947) and of Erdmann and Dodge (1898). Descriptions of many similar experimental studies were included in a remarkably broad and insightful book by Huey (1908, republished in 1967) which remains relevant today and is the only classic in the psychology of reading. A good deal of recent research on perception in reading is basically replication of early studies with more sophisticated equipment; nothing has been demonstrated to controvert them. Yet the pioneer research was neglected by experimental psychologists for nearly half a century and is still widely unknown in education, partly because behaviorism inhibited psychologists from studying "mental phenomena" and partly because "systematic" or "operationalized" piecemeal approaches to reading instruction have concentrated on decoding and word attack—the "tunnel vision" extreme—at the expense of comprehension.

Cattell's findings have not all been proved easily replicable by contemporary researchers. Baumann and Schneider (1979) found that a group of 24 graduate students could identify from a single 40 msec tachistoscopic exposure 3.7 random letters or 2.0 unrelated words (9.3 letters), which corresponds reasonably closely to Cattell's reported results, but a less dramatic increase to 2.4 words (11.5 letters) for words in context. However, a table showing the average results of their top, middle, and bottom eight subjects shows that while there were only relatively slight differences among the three groups in the random letter and unrelated word conditions (my calculations show means of 5.6, 5.0, and 4.0 random letters for the top, middle, and bottom groups, respectively, with 13.7, 11.4, and 9.7 for letters in unrelated words) the top group showed a marked advantage in the words in context condition, an average of 18.2 letters (about 4 words), compared with 13.7 letters for the middle group and 11.3 letters for the bottom. Baumann and Schneider note that the better subjects in their study also made the most errors, especially in the word conditions, supporting the view that fluent reading involves risk-taking, the willingness to make mistakes. Willingness to take a chance is of course a difficult variable to take into account in laboratory investigations of reading, and may account for the difficulty of replicating earlier studies.

Other contemporary researchers using sophisticated equipment to open or narrow a "window" through which subjects can read have shown a "perceptual span" of between 21 and 31 characters (letters or spaces) in a single fixation, up to 15 on each side of the point of fixation (den Buurman, Roersma, & Gerrissen, 1981; McConkie & Rayner, 1975). Krueger (1975) summarizes a number of studies showing that familiar letters, words, and other visual configurations are identified more rapidly and accurately than less familiar ones.

Information Theory and Reading

The mathematics of information theory (Chapter 3 Notes) can be applied directly to the Cattell findings to show that readers identifying just four or five random letters, a couple of random words, or a meaningful sequence of four or five words, are each time processing the same amount of visual information. The differences among the three conditions can be attributed to the varying amounts of nonvisual information that readers are able to contribute, derived from distributional and sequential redundancy within the print.

The random letter condition suggests that the limit for a single glance (the equivalent of a second of processing time) is about 25 bits of information. The calculation is based on a maximum of five letter identifications of about five bits of uncertainty each (2^5 bits $= 32$ alternatives). In random sequences of letters, of course, there is no distributional or sequential redundancy that a reader can utilize. That 25 bits per second is indeed a general limit on the rate of human information processing has been argued by Quastler (1956) from studies not only of letter and word identification but of the performance of piano players and "lightning calculators" as well (see also Pierce & Karlin, 1957).

How is it possible then to identify two random words, consisting on the average of 4.5 letters each, with just 25 bits of visual information? Nine or ten letters at five bits each would seem to require closer to 50 bits. But as I pointed out in the Chapter 3 Notes, because of distributional and sequential redundancy the average uncertainty of letters in English *words* is about 2½ bits each (Shannon, 1951) making a total average uncertainty for letters in two random words of something under 25 bits. From a different perspective, random words taken from a pool of 50,000 alternatives would have an uncertainty of between 15 and 16 bits each ($2^{15} = 32,768$, $2^{16} = 65,536$), but due to distributional redundancy among words—and probably also because unusual words are unlikely to be employed in reading studies—we can probably again accept the estimate of Shannon that the average uncertainty of English words without syntactic or semantic constraints (sequential redundancy) is about 12 bits per word. So whether we look at the random word condition from the point of view of letter uncertainty in words (about 2½ bits per letter) or of isolated word uncertainty (about 12 bits per word) the result is still that the reader is making the identification of about 9 or 10 letters or two words with roughly 25 bits of visual information. The fact that both the number of letters identified and the effective angle of vision double in the random word condition compared with the four or five letters that can be perceived in the random letter condition reflects the use that the reader can make of redundancy. In other words, the viewer in the isolated word condition contributes the equivalent of 25 bits of nonvisual information to enable twice as much to be seen in a single glance. Anyone who did not have the relevant nonvisual information would have had to rely on visual information alone and therefore have seen only half as much.

In meaningful and grammatical passages of English there is considerable sequential redundancy among the words themselves. Speakers and authors are not free to choose any word they like whenever they please, at least not if they expect to make any sense. From statistical analyses of long passages of text and also by a "guessing game" technique in which people were actually required to guess letters and words, Shannon calculated that the average uncertainty of *words* in meaningful sequences was about seven bits (a reduction over isolated words of about a half) and that the average uncertainty of *letters* in meaningful sequences was only slightly over one bit (again reducing by half the uncertainty of letters in isolated words). On this basis, one would expect viewers in the meaningful word sequences condition to see twice as much again compared with isolated words, which is of course the experimental result. A phrase or sentence of four or five words can be seen in one glance, a total of 20 letters or more. This is four times as much as can be seen in the random letter condition, but still on the basis of the same amount of visual information; four or five random letters at about five bits each, or 20 letters in a meaningful sequence at just over one bit each. Put in another way, when reading sequences of meaningful words in text the reader can contribute at least three parts nonvisual information (in the form of prior knowledge of redundancy) to one part visual information so that four times as much can be perceived.

For a more detailed discussion of the preceding argument, see Smith and Holmes (1971). Other examinations of uncertainty and redundancy in English are included in Garner (1962, 1974) and in Miller, Bruner, and Postman (1954), the latter using carefully constructed "approximations to English." McNeill and Lindig (1973) demonstrate that what listeners perceive in spoken language also depends on how much they are looking for—individual sounds, syllables, or entire words.

The Rate of Visual Decision-Making

Seventy years after the demonstrations of a limit to how much can be seen in a single glance, other tachistoscopic studies showed that the limit cannot be attributed to any restriction on the amount of visual information that the eye can gather from the page, nor because viewers forget letters or words that have already been identified before they can report them. Rather the bottleneck occurs as the brain labors to process what is transiently a considerable amount of raw visual information, organizing "seeing" after the eyes have done their work. Perceptual decision-making takes time, and there is a limit to how long visual information sent back by the eyes remains available to the brain.

Subjects in the kind of tachistoscopic experiment that I have described often feel that they have potentially seen more than they are able to report. The brief presentation of visual information leaves a vaguely defined "image" that fades before subjects are fully able to attend to it. The validity of this observation has been established by an experimental technique called *partial recall* (Sperling, 1960) in which subjects are required to report only four letters out of a presentation of perhaps 12 so that the required report is well within the limits of short-term memory (see Chapter 5). However, the subjects do not know *which* four letters they must report until after the visual presentation, so they must work from visual information that remains available to the brain after its source has been removed from before the eyes. At one stroke the experimental technique avoids any complication of memory by keeping the required report to a small number of items, while at the same time testing whether in fact viewers have information about all 12 items for a brief time after the eyes' work is complete.

The experimental technique involves presenting the 12 letters in three rows of four letters each. Very soon after the 50-msec presentation is ended, a tone is sounded. The subject already knows that a high tone indicates that the letters in the top row are to be reported, a low tone calls for the report of the bottom row, while an intermediate tone indicates the middle line. When this method of partial recall is employed, subjects can normally report back the four required letters, indicating that for a short while at least they have access to raw visual information about all 12 letters. The fact that subjects can report any four letters, however, does not indicate that they have identified all 12, but simply that they have time to identify four before the visual information fades. If the cue tone is delayed more than half a second after the end of the presentation the number of letters that can be reported falls off sharply. The "image" is unprocessed visual information that decays by the time about four letters have been identified.

Other evidence that visual information remains available in a "sensory store" for about a second, and that the entire second is required if a maximum of four or five letters is to be identified, has come from the "masking" studies described in this chapter (e.g., Averbach & Coriell, 1961; Smith & Carey, 1966). If a second visual array is presented to the eye before the brain has finished identifying the maximum number of letters that it can from the first input of visual information, then the amount reported from the first presentation declines. The second input of visual information erases information from the first presentation.

However, it can be as disruptive for reading if visual information reaches the eye too slowly as if it is too fast. Kolers and Katzman (1966), Newman

(1966), and Pierce and Karlin (1957) have shown an optimum rate of about six presentations a second for receiving visual information about individual letters or words; at faster rates the brain cannot keep up and at slower speeds there tends to be a greater loss of earlier items through forgetting. These studies and the earlier calculations of Quastler (1956) all tend to support the view that the "normal reading rate" of between 200 and 300 words a minute (Tinker, 1965; S. Taylor, 1971) is an optimum; slower reading is more than inefficient, it is almost certainly disruptive to comprehension.

There is another historic strand of evidence leading to the same conclusion that perception is a judgmental process that takes time, with the amount of time required depending on the number of alternatives among which the brain must choose. These are the studies of *reaction times,* or of the *latency* between the presentation of visual information to a subject and the identification response. Latency always increases with the number of alternatives within a category. For example, it took subjects an average of 410 msec to name a letter of the alphabet (out of 26 alternatives) but only 180 msec to say whether a light was flashed (a simple yes-no choice). Interestingly, short words could be identified faster (388 msec) than single letters—and no one has ever satisfactorily explained why this should be the case. I have taken these figures from a long and interesting section on vision and eye movements in Woodworth and Schlosberg's compendious *Experimental Psychology* (1954); even more basic detail about early studies of reading is included in the original Woodworth (1938) edition.

Eye Movements in Reading

Classic studies of the nature of eye movements and rate of fixation changes in reading are reported in Tinker (1951, 1958). S. Taylor, Frackenpohl, and Pettee (1960) report the stabilization of fixation rates by Grade 4. Llewellyn-Thomas (1962) discusses the eye movements of speed readers, who sample visual information over such a broad area that they break free of the constraint of moving their fixations along lines of type and rather move down and even up the center of pages (without, however, increasing their rate of fixations). More recent studies of eye movements in reading, involving sophisticated equipment and theorizing, are provided by Hochberg (1978), Rayner (1977, 1978), Just and Carpenter (1980), and Spragins, Lefton, and Fisher (1976). Hochberg has been influential among a number of experimental psychologists with his development of the view that reading is a highly selective process as the brain determines in advance the best place for each fixation to fall. More generally and very technically, Treisman (1969) has argued that perception is most efficient when the viewer is in control of what the eyes will look for. Garner (1966) has also summarized a number of experiments demonstrating the selective nature of perception.

Under the laboratory conditions of most experimental studies of "reading," subjects do not have control of where they fixate their gaze or of how long fixations may last. The experimenter makes these decisions for them. In many tachistoscopic and eye-movement studies, subjects are not even free to move their heads, which are constrained by chin rests or even bite plates. Yet head movements are a conspicuous part of normal reading. To avoid head movement constraints, some reading researchers have gone to another extreme by providing helmets equipped with electronic gadgetry for their subjects to wear while looking at a computer screen.

It might be asked why the most general and most efficient fixation rate in reading seems to be about four fixations a second when the information from a single glance persists for a second or more and at least one second is required for analyzing all the information that can be acquired from a single fixation. Why do readers normally fixate on every word—or at least every content word (Just & Carpenter, 1980)—when they can see four or five words at a glance? There has not been a good research answer to this question, but my conjecture is that the brain is less concerned with squeezing the last bit of information from each fixation than with receiving a smooth inflow of selected visual information as it builds up a coherent understanding of the text. Obviously, readers are not simply progressing from word to word. They must already have a good idea of where to fixate if their gaze rests primarily on content words. Potter (1984) shows that limitations on the speed of eye-movements may be a factor in slowing down reading.

On Seeing Backwards

Moyer and Newcomer (1977) argue and demonstrate that reversals are not caused by perceptual deficits but by inexperience with directionality.

Hemispheric Specialization

A basic article about functional differences in the cerebral hemispheres, and about the occasionally bizarre consequences of their being superficially disconnected, is provided by one of the earliest researchers in the area, Sperry (1968). See also Gazzaniga (1970). More recent discussions of the relationship between the hemispheres and language are included in several chapters in Caplan (1980). A readable presentation of the nature of hemispheric asymmetry, followed by some remarkable speculations about the origins of consciousness itself, can be found in Jaynes (1976, 1986). Careful research reviews leading to the conclusion that hemispheric specialization should not be considered an explanation of reading difficulties in children are reported in Naylor (1980), Young and Ellis (1981), and in the chapter by Bryden in Underwood (1978).

NOTES TO CHAPTER 5,
BOTTLENECKS OF MEMORY, pp. 87-100.

Theories of Memory

One of the earliest and most coherent attempts to distinguish short-term and long-term characteristics of memory was by Norman (1969), revised and expanded into a comprehensive analysis of the processes and contents of memory (Norman, 1976). The underlying perspective also pervades the Lindsay and Norman (1977) introductory psychology text. A more technical basic paper is Baddeley and Patterson (1971) and there are useful reviews by Shiffrin (1975) and Schneider and Shiffrin (1977), who particularly emphasize the relationship between short-term memory and attention. There are of course alternative points of view. Craik and Lockhart (1972; see also Cermak & Craik, 1979) have proposed an influential *levels of processing* model, arguing that the different short-term and long-term "stages" of memory are in fact reflections of different "levels" or "depths" to which processing is done. From their point of view, the additional processing required to identify words rather than letters, or meanings rather than words, accounts for evidence often used to account for stage theories. On the other hand, it is not clear that word identification *is* a deeper level of perception or memory, or that it involves more processing, than letter identification; short-term and long-term memory effects can be found with both letters and words. The argument is not really about the evidence, but about the way it is most usefully interpreted.

Lewis (1979) has also critically reviewed the short-term and long-term memory distinction, proposing that most forgetting is retrieval failure rather than storage loss and suggesting instead an active and inactive memory distinction with active memory part of the greater inactive one (similar to my Figure 5.2). A rather different view, that memory is founded on *descriptions* of varying degrees of precision and complexity, is proposed by Norman and Bobrow (1979).

Tulving (1985a, 1985b) has proposed that there are *three* different memory systems, which he terms *episodic, semantic,* and *procedural*. He associates each with a different kind of consciousness (or absence of consciousness). Tulving's basic memory system is *procedural;* it is also the most primitive, the only one that animals have. It is also the only one of the three systems that can be completely independent of the other two. Procedural memories require overt action to become established, and are not accessible to consciousness. Tulving calls this condition *anoetic* (literally, "without knowledge"). We can never be aware of what we know procedurally (except by actually doing something, possibly in the imagination). Such a memory system may be fundamental, but it is not trivial. It is probably the aspect of our memory containing the "rules" of language, which are not learned consciously (Krashen, 1985). Tulving's *semantic* memory is a subset within the procedural, and it makes possible representations of states of the world not perceptually present (i.e., which we can imagine). Semantic memory includes facts—but not in any particular order. Most people, for example, know that both John F. Kennedy and Charles de Gaulle are dead, but they cannot immediately say who died first. Semantic memory "describes" events and situations for us—it brings them to consciousness. Tulving calls this *noetic*. Finally *episodic* memory, which is nested within the semantic system, is "self-knowing," or *autonoetic*. It is our awareness of the order or sequence of events, the only conscious form of memory that includes temporal relationships. Earlier papers by Tulving and his colleagues citing research that distinguishes episodic and semantic memory include Tulving and Thomson (1973) and Tulving and Watkins (1975). See also Friendly (1977).

Tulving stresses something that few cognitive psychologists would dispute these days, that the quality of a particular memory depends on the manner and circumstances in which it was originally learned. Kolers (1975) frequently argued for a "procedural" memory, also studied experimentally by Masson and Sala (1978). See also Minsky (1980) and Anderson (1980).

A great deal of laboratory research is being done into the nature of the actual brain processes underlying memory, but much more remains to be done before there is complete understanding, or indeed, an idea of what such an understanding might be like. It is clear that certain biochemical changes take place during learning, when memories are established, and that chemical interventions can apparently destroy memories, and in some circumstances possibly enhance them. But these studies fall far short of explaining how an entire statement like "July 4 is Independence Day" might be represented in the chemical composition of the brain, let alone how its meaning and comprehension might. It is not even clear how such questions should be put. For a recent comprehensive review of research into mechanisms of memory in the brain, including arguments for the possible locations of short-term and long-term memory, and procedural and propositional knowledge, see Squire (1986). From a practical educational point of view, it is difficult to see how a more refined (but still very gross) understanding of the neurological structures and chemical events underlying reading could add to improvements in how it is taught.

Another distinction frequently drawn is between *recognition* and *reproduction* memory. It is usually (but not always) easier to recognize a face or a place (or an object or symbol) then it is to draw it. We recognize correct spellings easier than we can produce them. At any age we can understand more of language than we can produce ourselves. This should not be taken as implying that we have two entirely different kinds of memory—that we go to one "store" for recognition and another for reproduction. It is not that we have a collection of pictures (or "images") in the brain that we can refer to for recognition. Mental images themselves have to be constructed, and we can usually recognize faces and other things easier than we can imagine them. There is probably a simple explanation—that we usually need to produce less detail for recognition than for reproduction. To recognize a face, or even a word, we may need to see only a part of it, while reproduction means that we have to generate it all, without omission or error. For factual matters, a similar distinction is frequently made between *recognition* and *recall* memory. We may be able to agree that a certain actor starred in a particular movie, yet be quite unable to think of the actor's name if asked who the star of the movie was. Once again, it is probably more complex cognitively to construct or to complete what we think is a true statement than simply to recognize the statement as true when it is produced by someone else (see Anderson, 1980).

The nature and role of imagery in memory is much debated. Pylyshyn (1973, 1979) vigorously rejects any suggestion that images can be stored like pictures in the brain, for inspection by "the mind's eye." Kosslyn (1980) proposes that mental images can be represented in two ways. The first possibility is indeed a form that can be viewed mentally, but this is simply transient imagination. Such images do not persist. Instead they must be constructed on the basis of "deeper" representations that are not pictures but more like descriptions (or specifications) from which mental images can be constructed. All this is part of a more general notion that the brain must have its own language in order to make sense of every aspect of the world. The meaning of a sentence can't be a paraphrase of that sentence, because we would then need the meaning of the paraphrase. But similarly, the meaning of a picture can't be another picture. There must be something, possibly quite inexplicable to us intellectually, which enables us to understand anything—or to feel that we understand it. The notion that the brain has its own language is argued from a linguistic point of view by Fodor (1979) and neurophysiologically by Pribram (1971).

The idea that memory is constructive, or reconstructive, rather than a simple recall of original information, also has a long history in psychology, with its own classic by Bartlett (1932). Other arguments that present perspectives influence recall of past events are offered by Cofer (1973) and J. Mandler and Johnson (1977).

Klatzky (1980) provides a relatively nontechnical introduction to the highly technical area of memory, and there is a good summary in Calfee (1974), embedded in a discussion of reading somewhat different from the approach taken in this book. For the organization or contents of memory see an early paper by G. Mandler (1967), as well as G. Mandler (1985). For the structure or contents of memory, there are useful reviews as well as some idiosyncratic points of view in Puff (1977), Anderson, and Bower (1973), and Crowder (1976). By contrast there is a very easy to comprehend paper by Jenkins (1974) relating his conversion from a traditional *associationistic* view of memory to a more meaningful cognitive approach, entitled, "Remember that old theory of memory? Well, forget it!" For a general discussion of children's memory, see Kail (1979). Because memory—at least the long-term aspect of it—and the theory of the world in the head are alternative descriptions of the same thing, many of the general references in the Notes to Chapter 1, on knowledge and comprehension, apply to the present chapter also and could be consulted.

Chunking

The two apparent bottlenecks of memory—the limited capacity of short-term memory and the slow entry into long-term memory—can both be circumvented by the strategy known as *chunking*, or organization of information into the most compact (most meaningful) unit. For example, it is easier to retain and recall the sequence of digits 1491625364964 as the first eight square numbers, or the letters JFMAMJJASOND as the initials of the months of the year, than to try to remember either sequence as a dozen or so unrelated elements. But it is a mistake to think that we normally perceive first and chunk afterward; we no more read the letters *h, o, r, s,* and *e* which we then chunk into the word *horse* than we perceive a particular nose, ears, eyes, and mouth which we then chunk into a friend's face. Chunking research and instruction both tend to get things backwards, starting with arrays of ostensibly unrelated elements which the individual is supposed to group together in some meaningful way. In practice, prior knowledge and expectation of the larger grouping leads to the perception of elements in a chunked manner—if we recognize a word we don't see the individual letters. The size or character of a chunk is determined by what we are looking for in the first place (the "levels of processing" issue again). The word "chunk" became something of a minor fad term in education, with some teachers asking, "How can we teach children to chunk?" or even, "What do I do about a child who can't chunk?" But chunking is not something you learn to do, rather it is a simple consequence of what you already know; if you can recognize *horse* as a word there is no chunking problem in the first place. Chunking also has its own classic paper in the psychological literature, written with the flair suggested by its title, "The magical number seven, plus or minus two" (Miller, 1956). Another readable and informative paper on the same topic is by Simon (1974).

A remarkable report of how a college student increased his short-term memory span from 7 to 79 digits with 230 hours of chunking practice over 20 months is contained in Ericsson, Chase, and Falcon (1980).

One important and common means of chunking is to employ imagery to remember; there is a substantial literature demonstrating the unsurprising fact that our recall of particularly graphic sentences that we have heard or read is more likely to be related to scenes that we imagine from the descriptions provided by the words than to the words themselves (Barclay, 1973; Bransford & Franks, 1971; Bransford, Barclay, & Franks, 1972; Sachs, 1974). These papers are relevant to larger arguments that meaning lies beyond words in any case; whenever possible everyone, including children, tends to remember the meaning of words rather than the words themselves. But while we remember some sequences of words in terms of the pictures they conjure up, we also often remember scenes or pictures in terms of their descriptions. We recall a scene of birds flying over a town but not whether they were seagulls or pigeons, nor how many there were. There is nothing remarkable about any of this: We naturally try to remember in the most efficient manner possible. If a scene is easiest to remember, or most efficiently remembered, in terms of a description, because perhaps we are interested in particular things rather than in the scene as a whole, then the memorization will proceed accordingly. Not only is our recall influenced by the way we learned or perceived in the first place, but the manner of memorization will tend to reflect the most probable way in which we shall want to recall or use the information in the future. For important discussions of the role of imagery in memory, see Paivio (1971) and Brooks (1968), and for a technical analysis of the relationship of words to images see Reid (1974).

Children's Memory

There is no evidence that children have poorer or less well-developed memories than adults. Simon (1974) argues that children have the same memory capacity as adults but do not chunk as efficiently; however there is probably an adult bias behind the notion of chunking "efficiently" in the first place. We tend to chunk—or to perceive and remember in rich meaningful units—that which is most rich and meaningful to us. Recall of strings of unrelated letters and digits, which is the test by which children are usually judged to have inferior memories to those of adults, is not the most meaningful of tasks, for children especially. The number of digits a child can repeat after a single hearing increases from an average of two at the age of 2½ to six at the age of 10 (and eight for college students). But rather than suppose that children's memory capacity grows with their height and weight, one can argue that the younger children have had little experience, and see little sense, in repeating sequences of numbers, especially before they have become accustomed to using the telephone. The memory span of adults can be magically increased by teaching them little tricks or strategies, for example, to remember strings of numbers not as single digits (2, 9, 4, 3, 7, 8 . . .) but as two-digit pairs (29, 43, 78 . . .). Adults are so familiar with two-figure numbers through their use of dollars and cents that separate digits, like 2 and 9, can become chunked into a single unit, 29. Practice improves performance on any memory task, but does not seem to improve memory beyond the particular skill into unrelated areas or activities. The best aid to memory for anyone of any age is a general understanding of the structure and purpose behind the required memorization. Skilled chess players can recall the layout of most or all of the pieces on a board after just a couple of glances while beginners can remember the positions of only a few pieces—but only if the pieces are arranged as part of an actual game. If the pieces are organized randomly then the skilled player can remember no more than the beginner, because then the skilled player's experience of hundreds of games and positions is of no relevance or utility.

Baer and Wright (1975) argue that children's memory is not inferior to adults' but that they *encode* (or organize memory) differently. Huttenlocher and Burke (1976) refer to the additional difficulty (lesser experience) of children in identifying items and especially information about order in memory tasks. Paris and Carter (1973) report that children use imagery in remembering sentences just like adults (see also G. Olson, 1973). Hudson (1986) demonstrates that "events" comprise the core of children's memory.

Easy and Difficult Remembering

As noted in the chapter, Mandler (1985) has pointed out that the fluent "easy" remembering that the brain does so efficiently most of the time—he calls it "reminding"—has been largely neglected by experimental psychology. It is in fact due to such neglect that memory, comprehension, and learning have come to be widely regarded as difficult things to do, requiring instruction, practice, and effort. The problem is that the aspects of memory, comprehension, learning, and thinking generally that experimental psychologists have tended to study *have been* difficult, because the exigencies of experimental design demand control of all variables. The most difficult variables to control are those related to individual differences, especially in interest and prior knowledge. Not surprisingly, the more interest and knowledge we have of something, the easier it is to learn, understand, remember and think about it. The experimental solution to such unpredictability has usually been to construct tasks that remove all possibility of interest and prior knowledge, usually achieved by the employment of nonsense materials in quite artificial situations. When different individuals are required to commit nonsensical matters to memory, or to recall them, they usually do badly in very predictable ways (which have become the basis of psychology's "Laws of Learning"). Unfortunately, educators looking for theories on which to base instructional techniques have tended to turn to psychology for what are essentially theories of difficult and artificial learning, comprehension and remembering. The story is spelled out in an article entitled *How Education Backed the Wrong Horse* (Smith, 1987b).

NOTES TO CHAPTER 6, LETTER IDENTIFICATION, pp. 101-115.

Recognition versus Identification

G. Mandler (1980) makes a similar distinction to that made in this chapter between *identification* (putting a name to something) and *recognition* (deciding that something is familiar). He proposes a general theory of word recognition relevant to Chapter 9 of this book. Benton (1980) discusses the remarkable human ability to recognize patterns (in this case, faces) years after perhaps only a single partial glimpse.

Theories of Pattern Recognition

Problems and theories of pattern recognition are discussed in the texts by Neisser (1967) and Lindsay and Norman (1977); there are more technical expositions in Kolers and Eden (1968) and Selfridge and Neisser (1960). Selfridge has proposed an intriguing "pandemonium" metaphor in which each analyzer is regarded as a "demon" looking out for its own particular feature, with the brain making letter-identification decisions based on the loudness of the combined shouts of recognition of the collective demons for particular letters. More recent reviews—with a substantial neurophysiological emphasis—are Marr (1982) and Spoehr and Lehmkuhle (1982). Pinker (1984) is a basic but technical examination of contemporary theories of visual perception, including template, feature and other more complex models, including a discussion of the nature and role of imagery. Pinker points out that there are problems with all theories—a horse, for example, would seem to consist of too many lines and curves to be easily recognized by "features" alone, yet it is inadequate to say that a horse must therefore be recognized by body parts like hooves, because the parts themselves would have to be recognized by features. The current alternative (employing computer jargon that may in fact be a closer representation of how the brain works), is to rely on "massively parallel" models, which search concurrently for numbers of features and for interrelationships among them. Rarely acknowledged is that prior knowledge and expectation must be equally massive to support such complex perceptual mechanisms. On the other hand, perhaps to show that pattern recognition should not be complicated and mystified out of proportion, Blough (1982) has shown that pigeons can easily be taught to distinguish the letters of the alphabet. When shown a particular letter on one side of a screen, they had to distinguish it from two incorrect alternatives elsewhere on the screen (by pecking at the correct alternative). The pigeons, which were hungry, were rewarded with 3 seconds of eating mixed grain for every 4 successive correct answers they gave in 2700 test-trials over four days. When they made mistakes, the birds demonstrated the same confusions as humans, e.g. C–G–S, M–N–W, and D–O–Q.

It is not suggested that we have visual analyzers that function solely to collect information about letters of the alphabet. Information used in letter identification is received from analyzers involved in many visual activities, of which those concerned with reading are only a small part. The same analyzers might contribute information in other circumstances to the identification of words, digits, geometric forms, faces, automobiles, or any other set of visual categories, as well as to the apprehension of meaning. The brain makes a variety of specialized uses of very general receptor systems; thus statements can be made about analyzers "looking for" alphabetic features without the implication that a benign destiny has "prewired" mankind to read the alphabet. We all have a "biological inheritance" that enables us to talk and read, to ride bicycles and play pianos, not because of some specific genetic design, but because spoken and written languages, bicycles and pianos, were progressively developed by and for human beings with precisely the biological equipment that humans are born with.

Readers should resist any temptation to figure out what might be the particular features or tests specified in my illustrative list. They should not try to deduce what feature should be marked − on Test 1 for "A" and + on Test 1 for "B". The examples are quite arbitrary and imaginary. For an attempt to specify possible features of English letters, see Gibson (1965).

Incidentally, it is just as appropriate to talk about distinctive features of speech as it is to refer to distinctive features of written language. In fact, the feature model for letter identification that was developed in the 1960s was inspired by a feature theory of speech perception published in the 1950s (Jakobson & Halle, 1956). In both theories a physical representation, acoustic or visual, is scanned for distinctive features which are analyzed in terms of feature lists that determine a particular categorization and perceptual experience. The number of physical features requiring to be discriminated will depend on the perceiver's uncertainty and other sources of information about the language (redundancy) that can be utilized.

Just as the basic elements of the written or printed marks on a page are regarded as distinctive features smaller than letters, so elements smaller than a single sound are conceptualized as distinctive features of speech. Distinctive features of sounds are usually regarded as components of the process by which a phoneme is articulated, such as whether or not a sound is *voiced* (whether the vocal chords vibrate as for /b/, /d/, /g/ compared with /p/, /t/, /k/), whether the sound is *nasal* (like /m/ and /n/), the sound's duration, and the position of the tongue. Each distinctive feature is a significant difference, and the discrimination of any one feature may eliminate many alternatives in the total number of possible sounds (the set of phonemes). Every feature cuts the set of alternatives in a different way, so that theoretically a total of only six distinctive features could be more than enough to distinguish among 40 alternative phonemes ($2^6 = 64$). There are many analogies between the distinctive features of print and those of speech. The total number of different features is presumed to be much smaller than the set of units that they differentiate (26 for letters, about 40 for sounds). The number of features suggested for phonemes is usually 12 or 13 (note again the redundancy). Phonemes can be confused in the same manner as letters, and the more likely two sounds are to be confused with each other, the more distinctive features they are assumed to share. Some sounds, such as /b/ and /d/, which probably differ in only one feature, are more likely to be confused than /b/ and /t/, which differ in perhaps two, and /t/ and /v/ which may differ in three features. Spoken words may also differ by only a single feature. "Ban" and "Dan," which have only a single feature's difference, should be rather more likely to be confused than "ban" and "tan," and much more likely than "tan" and "van"; experimental evidence suggests that assumptions of this kind are correct (Miller & Nicely, 1955).

Many people involved in the complexities of reading tend to think that the identification of spoken words is somehow more spontaneous and instantaneous and holistic—almost as if the ears detect whole words rather than patterned soundwaves that the brain has to analyze and interpret. Yet the perception of speech is no less complex and time consuming than that of reading; what we hear is the end product of a decision-making procedure that leads to the identification (the categorization) of a sound or word or meaning prior to the perceptual experience. We rarely "hear" words and then identify them; the identification must precede the hearing, otherwise we would just hear noise. And we do not hear distinctive features of sound any more than we see distinctive features of writing; the unit that we are aware of discriminating is determined by the sense that the brain is able to make, the kind of question that it is asking. Usually we are aware only of meaning for both spoken and written language. Occasionally we may attend to particular words, but only rarely and in special circumstances will we be aware of the surface structure phonemes or letters. The features themselves evade our attention completely.

Making Letter Identification Easier

Letter identification as I have described it in this chapter is not the easiest task for any reader. Asking someone to identify a random letter flashed on a screen or even written on a chalkboard or piece of paper is in fact the most difficult task possible, given a constant size of type, duration of exposure, clarity of view, and so forth. The task is the most difficult in the given physical circumstances because there is no redundancy; the particular letter to be identified could be any one of the 26 alternatives in the alphabet, so the viewer requires a maximum of visual information and has no check if in fact an identification is incorrectly made. Letters are much easier to identify, and to learn, when they come from a smaller set of alternatives, or when they are not equally probable; in other words, when the viewer can make use of redundancy. As pointed out in the Notes to Chapter 3, there is a marked reduction in the overall uncertainty of letters if they are selected at random from English text rather than drawn from a set of 26 equiprobable alternatives. The viewer can make use of the *distributional* redundancy of English letters if the particular letter to be identified is taken from a preselected point in a book, say the third letter of the fourth word of the seventeenth line of the eightieth page, in which case the nonvisual information that the letter is 40 times more likely to be *e* than *z* can be used, with all the other letters ranked between. Distributional redundancy reduces uncertainty from the 4.7 bits for 26 equiprobable letters to about 4.07 bits, the equivalent of about 17 equiprobable alternatives, a considerable saving even without the sequential redundancy that becomes available from other letters or words in a sequence. The sequential redundancy of letters within English words is enormous. If all 26 letters of the alphabet could occur independently in each position of a five-letter word, the number of five-letter words there could be would be $26^5 = 11,881,376$, compared with perhaps 10,000 that actually exist. Even if permissible letter combinations are restricted to alternate consonants and vowels (CVCVC or VCVCV) there would still be a quarter of a million alternatives. And not only is it harder for viewers to identify letters without redundancy cues, it is far less familiar as an activity since the redundancy with which language is permeated is something which every language user capitalizes upon.

The identification of random letters is so uncharacteristic of reading and of so little relevance outside the specialized literature of experimental psychology that I can find no additional references on the topic sufficiently interesting to include as further reading, a section that must remain in abeyance for the next chapter or two while the discussion is at such a detailed level.

NOTES TO CHAPTER 7, WORD IDENTIFICATION, pp. 116-131.

Anderson and Dearborn (1952) include a basic discussion of traditional assumptions underlying most theories of word identification (or more often, theories of teaching the identification of words) prior to the development of the feature-analytic view. For more recent general discussions of word recognition research, see the three "cognitive psychology" texts I have already mentioned, Anderson (1984), Keiras and Just (1984), or Eysenck (1984). Goodman (1982) has some general criticism of researchers who focus on words (or letters) in their analyses of reading.

Letter Identification in Words

There is one type of experiment which might at first sight appear to indicate that words are *not* identified more easily than letters, but which actually provides an additional demonstration that words are indeed processed on a featural basis with the reader making use of sequential redundancy. One experimental method (Smith, 1969) involves projecting letters or words at such a low intensity that there is barely any contrast with the screen on which they are shown, and then to increase the contrast slowly, gradually making more and more visual information available until observers are able to identify the word. Under this procedure the observers are not constrained by time or memory limitations and may choose to make either word or letter identifications with the information available at any moment. They typically identify letters within words before they say what an entire word is, although the entire word may still be identified before any of its letters could be identified in isolation. While this finding is not inconsistent with the classical evidence that words can be identified before any of their component letters in isolation it does make clear that words are, in fact, not recognized all-or-none "as wholes" but by analysis of their parts. The sequential redundancy among features that exists within the word configuration permits identification of the letters on fewer features than would be required if they were presented in isolation. Put in another way, criterial sets of features for words need not include sufficient information in any one position for the unique identification of an individual letter if all sequential redundancy were removed, but when sequential redundancy is present it may facilitate the identification of one or more letters even before the word as a whole can be identified. The letter *h* requires fewer features to identify if presented in the sequence *hat* than if presented alone, even if the reader identifies the *h* before the *at*. The additional information that enables the earlier letter identification to be made in words is based on orthographic redundancy in the spelling of words, reducing the uncertainty of letters from over four bits to less than three (about seven alternatives), as discussed in the Notes to Chapter 3. Even if a reader has not discriminated sufficient features in the second and third positions of the configuration *hat* to identify the letters *at* there is still some featural information available from those positions which, when combined with nonvisual information about featural redundancy within words, permits identification of the letter in the first position on minimal visual information.

There is other evidence that although words are identified "as wholes," in the sense that featural information from all parts may be taken into account in their identification, they are by no means identified on the basis of the familiarity of their shape or contour. Examples were given earlier in this chapter of the ease with which quite unfamiliar configurations like *rEaDiNg*, would be read. Entire passages printed in these peculiar configurations can be read about as fast as normal text (Smith, Lott, & Cronnell, 1969). In fact if the size of the capital letters is reduced slightly so that they do not interfere with the discriminability of the lower case letters, for example *rEaDiNg*, then there is no difference at all in the rates at which such words and normal text are read. The result is perhaps not surprising when we reflect on the ease with which practiced readers can adapt to quite distorted forms of typography or handwriting. Indeed, the facility with which we can read passages of handwriting when individual letters and even words would be indecipherable is further evidence that reading does not depend on letter identification.

It is obviously a gross oversimplification to talk about the relative "discriminability" of individual letters of the alphabet or to assume that letters difficult to identify when standing alone must be difficult to perceive when in words. (This argument applies especially to the question of "reversals" of letter pairs like *b* and *d*, which are particularly bothersome to some children—and to adults in constrained circumstances, and now, apparently, to pigeons. Reversals were specifically considered in Chapter 4.) The criterial features of letters are not fixed and immutable. The amount of visual information required to identify a letter has relatively little to do with the physical characteristics of the actual stimulus but depends much more on the reader's experience and the context in which the letter occurs. And precisely the same kind of argument applies to words. Children learning to read can often identify words in context that they cannot identify in isolation (Pearson & Studt, 1975). It is misleading to talk of children's word identification ability in terms of their "sight vocabulary" or word attack skills.

There is an extensive technical literature on the identification of letters in words, including Reicher (1969), Wheeler (1970), Meyer and Schvaneveldt (1971), Rumelhart and Siple (1974), Johnson (1975), and Cosky (1976). Silverman (1976) shows that words can be identified as integrated perceptual units, a point also made by Santa, Santa, and E. Smith (1977). Brand (1971) shows that distinctions can be made between letters and digits without the identification of specific letters or digits (underlining the featural aspect of identification), and an article subtitled "Seek not and ye shall find" (Johnston and McClelland, 1974) describes how letters are sometimes more easily identified in words if they are not specifically looked for. Another neatly titled paper, "Forest Before Trees," by Navon (1977), shows that letters within larger visual configurations do not intrude in the recognition of the larger unit, but that the larger will interfere with the perception of the smaller. Further arguments for the priority of words over letters (and of meaning over individual words) are in Kolers (1970) and F. Smith and Holmes (1971). For an opposing point of view, Massaro and Klitzke (1977) claim that letters always have a function in word identification (although no one argues that letter information cannot be used when the word as a whole cannot be recognized).

In a pair of complex and detailed theoretical articles, McClelland and Rumelhart (1981) and Rumelhart and McClelland (1981), two cognitive scientists, present a model for "parallel processing structures on the fly" by means of feature detectors of letters that are differentially activated or inhibited by visual information, depending on the context the letters are in, words or nonwords. This combination of neurophysiological jargon and computer methodology has produced a computer system which they claim can identify 1200 4-letter words in the same way that humans do (with word frequency effects, and letters easier in words than in nonwords). There is a summary of this work in a somewhat broader conceptual framework in McClelland (1985). See also Ellis (1984). Golden (1986), in another recent review, proposes a *spatial* feature analytic word recognition model sensitive to letters in specific positions, to between-letter interconnections, and also to "spatial redundancy." Words need not be recognized letter-by-letter, he concludes—and he has constructed a computer model based on these suppositions which he claims performs like humans on letter-identification tasks in both words and nonwords.

Haber and Haber (1981) show that the outline shape of a common word is usually sufficient visual information for the unique identification of the word in a meaningful context. Haber, Haber and Furlin (1983) showed that college students could use information about both length and shape to identify missing words in context, each kind of clue adding about 10 per cent to the probability of a correct identification, and each interacting with other contextual cues. Doggett and Richards (1975) demonstrated that longer words are more difficult to identify only if the words are unfamiliar.

Use of Redundancy by Children

There is no evidence that children need to be trained to seek or use redundancy in any way; indeed, part of the argument of this book is that all of perception depends on the use of prior knowledge and that the youngest of children demonstrate ability to limit uncertainty by eliminating unlikely alternatives in advance. Studies with young readers have found ability to use sequential redundancy very early (Lott & Smith, 1970). First-grade children who had had a limited amount of reading instruction in kindergarten were shown letters in isolation and in simple three-letter words that they could normally identify easily. The children showed themselves able to identify letters in words on less visual information than when they were presented alone. For children in fourth grade the difference between the information on which letters were identified in words and that on which the same letters were identified in isolation was equal to that of skilled adult readers, indicating that for familiar three-letter words at least, fourth-graders could make as much use of sequential featural redundancy as adults. Krueger, Keen, and Rublevich (1974) subsequently confirmed that fourth-grade children may be as good as adults in making use of redundancy among letter sequences in words and nonwords.

Distributional Redundancy Among Words

The sequential redundancy that exists among words in text—which has a critical role in making reading possible—is discussed in later chapters. But there is also a *distributional* redundancy among words, reflecting the obvious fact that some words are used far more often than others. The distributional redundancy of English words has not been formally calculated, but is probably related to the maximum theoretical uncertainty of between 15 and 16 bits for a set of about 50,000 alternatives and the actual 12-bit uncertainty of isolated words computed by Shannon (1951) and discussed in the Notes to Chapter 5. Distributional redundancy among words complicates experimental studies of word identification because more frequent words are usually identified faster, more accurately, and on less visual information than less frequent words. The precise reason for this "word frequency effect" is itself the subject of a long and inconclusive debate in the technical literature (Broadbent, 1967; Broadbent & Broadbent, 1975; Howes and Solomon, 1951). See also the McClelland and Rumelhart references above. The standard reference for relative word frequencies has long been the list of Thorndike and Lorge (1944), with a more recent complication by Carroll, Davies, and Richman (1971).

NOTES TO CHAPTER 8, PHONICS AND MEDIATED WORD IDENTIFICATION, pp. 132-147.

The Relevance of Phonics

The analysis I have given of the relationship between the spelling of written words and the sounds of speech is mainly derived from the work of a group of researchers (Berdiansky, Cronnell, & Koehler, 1969) associated with the Southwest Regional Laboratory (SWRL), a federally sponsored research and development center in California. SWRL researchers have not only endeavored to analyze the maze of spelling-to-sound correspondences in English, based largely on the work of Venezky (1967, 1970), but also to devise instructional programs to teach these correspondences to children, both native speakers and others, in the expectation that it will make them better readers and spellers. The fifteen-year history of this enterprise is recorded in a number of technical reports published by SWRL.

The fifty-eighth in the series of SWRL technical reports (Rhode & Cronnell, 1977) provides an analysis of a 10,000-word lexicon which they consider to be the basis of a kindergarten through sixth grade communication skills program. This time words of three or more syllables are included, a total of 27 percent of the 10,000. Ninety-nine grapheme units are distinguished, 77 related to 225 spelling-to-sound correspondence "rules" and 22 to 32 "exceptions." Eighty of the rules are associated with 48 consonant grapheme units, 111 with the six primary vowels (a/e/i/o/u/y), and 34 with 23 secondary vowel units (ai/au/etc.).

The best that computers can do, with absolute knowledge of every rule considered to be relevant (because it is programmed into them), is described in a brief news items in the November 1980 issue of *The Reading Teacher* (Vol. 34, *2*, p. 159). Apparently the "latest reading machine" for the visually impaired can employ its optical character recognition device to transform printed letters into "relatively natural speech quality," thanks to a pronunciation based on over 1,000 linguistic rules and 1,500 exceptions to these rules. And it is still not explained what the device does with the 200 or more *homographs* in the English language, common words like *wind, wound, tear, read,* and *live,* whose pronunciation varies with their meaning but not with their spelling.

The relevance of phonics instruction is the topic of a frequently cited volume by Chall (1967) entitled *Learning To Read: The Great Debate,* although her discussion is more about how reading is taught than how it is learned, and the conclusions may not be thought to follow inevitably from the evidence presented. A vigorous British proponent of "new phonics," based on the Venezky analysis and including 396 correspondences ("all the necessary facts"), is Morris (1974, 1982). The alternative point of view, that phonics interferes with reading, is presented by Goodman (1982); see also Sebasta (1981). Carol Chomsky (1970), drawing extensively from her own experience and from the theorizing of Noam Chomsky (N. Chomsky & Halle, 1968), argues that spelling does not so much represent sound as the underlying meaning structure of language. C. Chomsky (1971, 1979) recommends an early introduction to writing because it may help beginning readers make sense of phonics instruction. This view should not be confused with the occasional argument that children must be taught phonics to learn how to spell. Children who spell words the way they are pronounced, as most children do at the beginning (Read, 1971), spell poorly. Spelling by rule is not an efficient strategy for spelling most common words (Brown, 1970). Although clues may be obtained from known words with similar meanings, the main requirement for good spelling is to *remember* individual spellings (Smith, 1982), a requirement that is not relevant to reading and which may, if allowed, complicate learning to read. Gillooly (1973) argues that there is no justification for attempts to change the current spelling of English, which he says increases reading speed and is nearly optimum for learning to read.

The belief that phonics must be an indispensable part of learning to read is curiously upheld by a number of researchers despite their own demonstrations of its difficulty and limited relevance to fluent reading—for example, Smith and Kleiman (1979) in an article showing how words are recognized and understood without recourse to letters or sound, Weaver and Shonkoff (1978) in demonstrating the arbitrary and conflicting complexities of syllabication rules, and Liberman and Shankweiler (1979) on the difficulty children have with phoneme segmentation. (Children may have difficult recognizing, for example, that *bet* has three phonemes but *best* four, even though they can easily hear and see the difference between the words.) All of these difficulties are in fact *metalinguistic*—they do not involve language itself (as a means of expression or communication) but rather the ability to talk abstractly about language. Downing (1979) refers to mastery of many metalinguistic aspects of reading as "cognitive clarity," which he appears to regard as a prerequisite for learning to read," although it might also be seen simply as familiarity with the jargon of various forms of reading instruction.

A small but noteworthy controversy developed out of a demonstration by Rozin, Poritsky, and Sotsky (1971) that poor readers who failed to learn through conventional phonics instruction could succeed when the Chinese characters for English meanings were substituted for the English spelling. After showing clearly that readers could extract meaning directly from written text, without the mediation of phonics, the authors rather remarkably concluded that reading would therefore best be taught by a syllabic method. Gleitman and Rozin (1973a) elaborated upon this notion of teaching reading through a syllabary, and responded vehemently (Gleitman & Rozin, 1973b) when K. Goodman (1973) commented that their proposal seemed to him to be another easy way to make learning to read difficult. The latter three articles are all contained in one lively issue of *Reading Research Quarterly*. On the relative ease with which children can learn to read in nonalphabetic written language, see also Makita (1968, 1976) for research with Japanese children. Steinberg and Yamada (1978/79) also discuss Japanese. Park and Arbuckle (1977) compare alphabetic and ideographic aspects of Korean, while Liberman and Shankweiler (1979) observe that learners still have reading problems with the highly phonetic Serbo-Croat script. Seidenburg (1985) demonstrates that in both Chinese (logographic) and English writing systems, large numbers of high frequency words—or "familiar" words—are recognized "visually," immediately, without phonological mediation. Slower responses for less frequent words are made only by slower readers (who are presumably less experienced). Dunn-Rankin has demonstrated that readers of English are able to identify large numbers of syllables on sight. (He had noticed how familiar certain three-letter combinations had become when they caught his eye on the license plates of cars he drove behind on freeways.) Dunn-Rankin calculated that about 1500 syllables accounted for 95% of English words, and "appear suited to represent both the visual and phonetic aspects of speech." Obviously this is not a system to be taught, although it is required in the course of reading. Dunn-Rankin also notes that experienced readers are flexible and adaptable in the use of any clues to word identification that are available. Fraisse (1984) has observed that experienced readers can often name written words flashed on a screen quicker than they can identify drawings of the referents of those words.

Phonological Recoding

McCusker, Hillinger, and Bias (1981) provide a recent and technical review of research into the question of whether *phonological recoding* (the mediated identification of written words through the sounds represented by their letters) is always a necessary or even alternative means of identification. For a typical argument that word identification has to be mediated through the identification of letters and their sounds, see Liberman and Shankweiler (1979). Mosberg (1978) critically reviews research claiming that such recoding is done "automatically." Glusko (1979) argues that even unfamiliar words or nonsense syllables (like *tave* or *heaf*) are pronounced more by analogy to known words with similar spellings (like *have* and *deaf*) than by spelling-to-sound rules as such. The notion that phonics is primarily useful for discarding orthographically unlikely alternatives in meaningful situations where contextual cues eliminate most of the semantic and syntactic uncertainty in advance is supported by evidence that children who successfully attempt to use phonics look primarily at the first letters of words (Marchbanks & Levin, 1965), which happen to be the most informative (Bruner & O'Dowd, 1958), and also where the phonics (especially for consonants) is least reliable (Broerse & Zwaan, 1966).

Walters, Komoda, and Arbuckle (1985) provide experimental evidence that phonological recoding plays a very small part in skilled reading (for gist), and that it is unnecessary unless there are detailed memory demands. They also demonstrate that words have to be identified before they are named. Other evidence for phonological (or phonemic) recoding *after* words have been recognized is reviewed by Ellis (1984) and Besner, Davelaar, Alcott, and Parry (1984). Steinberg, Harada, Tashiro and Harper (1980) describe teaching deaf children to read, obviously without decoding to sound. Evidence from deaf readers is also discussed by Mattingly (1985), who also argues that hearing readers can discover the pronunciation of words when ascertaining their meaning (from an internal "lexicon"), without having to decode the sounds of the letters. Baron (1973, 1979) has demonstrated experimentally that decoding to sound is not necessary for comprehension, and conversely Calfee, Arnold, and Drum (1976) have disputed the frequent but undocumented assertion that it is possible for children to "decode" in the absence of comprehension.

An ostensible "dual process" or "dual route" point of view asserts that readers identify some words immediately (or "directly") but other words by decoding through the letters. The difference becomes one of degree. Obviously all readers must employ alternative methods of identifying unfamiliar words. Ehri and Wilce (1985) take an opposing point of view and argue that beginning readers may begin by identifying whole words on sight, but that they move from "visual cue processing" to "phonetic cue processing" in order to read larger numbers of words. Therefore, they argue, beginning readers should be made familiar with letters and their sounds, even perhaps before they have the opportunity to read words. It could be argued, however, that it was their young readers' familiarity with words that enabled them to make sense of the instruction they were given about letters and sounds. For reviews of dual process theories, see Henderson (1984b), and also Baron and Strawson (1976).

The Alphabet

Consideration of the complexity and unreliability of spelling-to-sound correspondences (and the reverse) leads me to conclude that the alphabet may be just as misleading for writers as for readers if its primary purpose is seen as representing in print the sounds of spoken language. Instead, I conjecture that the great advantage of the alphabet—and it is an enormous one—for readers, writers, teachers, and all kinds of administrators and bureaucrats, is that it permits written words to be talked about (Smith, 1982). The alphabet offers a highly economical way of *describing* and *ordering* the visual characteristics of words. All you need know is the names and appearance of 26 letters and you can describe uniquely many thousands of written words, asking how they should be pronounced (for readers) or how they should be visually represented (for writers). Knowledge of how to *draw* the 26 letters enables the writer to reproduce any word in our language legibly, compared with the knowledge of thousands of entire word forms required to produce ideographic text. The fact that alphabetically written words can be constructed from a relatively small number of discrete characters also has the great technological advantage of making keyboards possible, for typewriters, computers, and printing machines. And the fact that the alphabet is easily given a conventional order makes possible dictionaries and every kind of bureaucratic organization. The Chinese scholar Lin Yutang succeeded in compiling the first practical English-Chinese dictionary in the 1970s only by arbitrarily imposing an "alphabetical order" on 33 basic stroke formations in Chinese script. The alphabet is preeminently an instrument of *control*, from many points of view. Interestingly, one of the few times that public opinion in China was able to modify a national policy of Mao Tse-tung was when he tried to introduce an alphabet into Chinese writing, based on European and Russian letters (Barlow, 1981). The peasants successfully resisted this purely administrative decree on the sound linguistic ground that the new script would prevent them from reading traditional ancient Chinese writings.

The classic book on writing systems is Gelb (1963), although it reflects an occidental bias for crediting the Greeks with the sole discovery of an alphabet. A good case can also be made for the independent and alphabetic Sanskrit writing system devised about 3000 B.C. It all depends on whether you want to say that an alphabet must have vowel symbols that are separate from but equal to those for consonants. See also Vachek (1973). Taylor and Taylor (1983) and Henderson (1984b) present interesting discussions of writing systems, in general volumes presenting different views of reading from the present author's. Other recent works on alphabets and writing systems include Stevenson (1983) and Sampson (1985).

NOTES TO CHAPTER 9, THE IDENTIFICATION OF MEANING, pp. 148-163.

Effects of Meaningful Context

Meaningfulness clearly has a substantial role in facilitating the identification of words in reading, reducing their uncertainty from at least 12 bits (the equivalent of 4,096 equiprobable alternatives) for words in isolation to fewer than eight bits (256 alternatives) for words in context (Chapter 4 Notes). It is really irrelevant to talk of letters at this stage—letters are not usually a concern when meaningful text is read. But as a yardstick, it is interesting to recall from the Chapter 4 discussion of the Cattell (1885) experiment that the uncertainty of letters falls from 4.7 bits to scarcely one bit when context is meaningful, enabling the brain to perceive four times as much of a line of print. Not only can twice as many words be identified in a single glance when they are in a meaningful context, thus overcoming bottlenecks of information processing and memory, but problems of ambiguity and the gulf between surface structure and meaning are removed by the prior elimination from consideration of unlikely alternatives. Context has its effect not because it exists but because it can be *meaningful* and contribute information that reduces the uncertainty of individual words through sequential redundancy. Context places constraints on what each individual word might be.[1] These constraints constitute sequential redundancy, usable only if it is reflected in prior knowledge, or nonvisual information, that the reader can bring to bear. That is why I stress the context

---

[1] The present concern is with *language* context, the body of words in a text. But as outlined in Chapter 2, words can also be constrained by more general *situational* contexts; for example, there is a very small and highly predictable set of alternative words likely to occur on a toothpaste tube. There is also an important context in the receiver's expectations. As Olson (1970) has pointed out, words are selected and get meaning from what the listener or reader needs to know.

must be *meaningful*, with all the relative connotations of that word. If a particular context is not comprehensible to a reader, or if for one reason or another the reader is reluctant to take advantage of the redundancy and reduce the amount of visual information required for any aspect of reading, then the context might just as well be nonsense, a random arrangement of marks on the page.

Meaningful context as I have been using the term exercises its constraints on word occurrence in two ways, syntactic and semantic. These are two types of restriction upon the particular words an author can select—or a reader predict—at any time. (There are other constraints on authors, such as the limited set of words a reader might be expected to understand.) Choice of words is always limited by what we want to say (semantics) and how we want to say it (syntax). I have not tried to separate the effects of syntax and semantics in this discussion for the simple reason that I have not found a good way to do so. The theoretical analysis of Chapter 2 argued that the two are inseparable; that without meaning it is pointless to talk about grammar. Treisman (1965) attempted to unravel the two experimentally and concluded that in normal language the syntactic component is subordinate to the semantic.

There is no shortage of research demonstrating the powerful facilitatory effect of meaningful context on word identification. Indeed, there is no evidence to the contrary. But before I begin to cite this research, a fundamental point must be reiterated: *Reading does not usually involve or rely upon word identification*. Banal though it may sound, the basic point about meaningful context is that it makes reading for meaning possible and word identification unnecessary. The fact that meaningful context makes individual words easier to identify is basically as irrelevant as the fact that individual letters are easier to identify in words; the research evidence is merely a demonstration of the effect of meaningful context. Even when reading aloud is involved, so that the accurate identification of words is required, the prior apprehension of meaning is an important prerequisite. Reading aloud is difficult if prior comprehension is limited, and if word identification is given priority there will be interference with comprehension (Howe & Singer, 1973). Sharkey and Mitchell (1985) show that word recognition in meaningful contexts is frequently minimal and not very predictable, especially when the context is itself a predictable "script"—when it is a familiar narrative, in other words.

Levy (1978) reported that changing the wording but not the sense of written language did not affect a short-term memory task—meanings not specific words are retained whenever possible, even for brief periods. Sometimes context leads us astray, evidence again for the potency of meaning and prediction. Carpenter and Daneman (1981) give several examples of "garden path" texts where context misleads rather than facilitates, such as "Cinderella could not go to the ball. There were tears in her dress." Marcel (1978) even demonstrates a "subliminal" effect of what he calls "unconscious reading"—people acquiring information when they were not aware that any text had been presented (because it was flashed so briefly and then "masked"). But in a sense all reading except the most difficult and artificial is "unconscious"; we may be aware of what we read but not of the fact of reading.

In addition to the Tulving and Gold (1963) study used in this chapter as an example of how context facilitates word identification, see Morton (1964, 1969), Klein and Klein (1973), and Smith and Spoehr (1974). Morton (1982) outlines his influential "logogen" model, which proposes that words are represented in the brain in a form accessible in a variety of ways, for example through their sound, spelling, meaning, and grammatical function. Warrington and Shallice (1979) argue from neuropsychological premises that "word form" has direct access to the "semantic system," assumed to be the source of meaningfulness. For a summary of the arguments of the present chapter and preceding three chapters, see Smith and Holmes (1971). In related studies demonstrating the effect of meaningfulness, Rothkopf and Coatney (1974) show that reading rate is determined by the reader's expectations of information in the text, and Rothkopf and Billington (1974) that comprehension is improved when answers to specific questions are sought and found. Smith and Kleiman (1979) summarize many experiments showing that a preceding context "somehow activates the meaning of the possible next word," Carpenter and Just (1975, 1977) examine how reading normally involves the integration of new contextual information with what is already known (again demonstrating that learning and comprehension are inseparable).

Cohen (1970) and Neisser and Beller (1965) provide experimental demonstrations that meaning can be sought without the identification of words. In tasks involving a search through word lists, it took no longer to find an example of a category (such as "any flower") than to find a specific word in that category (such as *daisy*). Search tasks of this kind basically require rejecting irrelevant items on the list (much as we quickly dispose of names we are *not* looking for in a telephone directory) and show that it is not necessary to identify a word specifically to decide that it does not fall into a particular category (set of alternatives) in which we are interested. Spragins, Lefton, and Fisher (1976) have demonstrated that meaning is so prepotent that it will interfere with a search in which meaning is actually irrelevant. Neisser (1967) has an extensive discussion of such search tasks and the light they throw on visual decision-making; for a more recent review see Martin (1979). In a study entitled "Meaning in Visual Search" that is *not* about reading, Potter (1975) reports that viewers recognize pictures as accurately and almost as fast when all they know in advance is the "meaning" (given by a name or title, such as "a boat") as when they have already seen the picture itself. McNeill and Lindig (1973) show that context effects exist with spoken language just as with written (see also Miller, Heise, & Lichten, 1951).

Use of contextual information to identify words deleted completely from text is the basis of the *Cloze test* (Taylor, 1957; Neville & Pugh, 1976–1977), frequently employed to estimate the comprehensibility of a passage or the comprehension of a reader (although it is theoretically indefensible to expect any book to be equally readable to more than a few readers or to summarize the ability of any reader in a single score). The text in a Cloze test has words deleted at certain regular or systematic intervals, for example:

A moth's ears are located——the sides of the rear——part of its thorax and——directed outward and backward into——constriction that separates the thorax——the abdomen. Each ear is——externally visible as a small——, and within the cavity is——transparent eardrum.

Suppose six passages of this kind are presented to 10 readers who are asked to fill in as many spaces as they can, scoring as a correct response every guess that coincides with the word that was actually deleted from a space. One way of interpreting a high score for a particular space would be that there are very few alternative words that could be put in that position—the uncertainty is low. And the only reason that uncertainty is low in that position is that most of the alternative words have been eliminated by information acquired from other parts of the passage, from the words that have not been removed. Passages that get a relatively large number of missing words correctly replaced may therefore be regarded as more easily comprehensible than those whose spaces are more dubious; thus this type of score is sometimes interpreted as a measure of the "intelligibility" or "readability" of a passage. On the other hand, a reader who succeeds in completing correctly a relatively large number of missing words might be regarded as one who is able to make greater use of the redundancy in the passage and who therefore comprehends it more. The Cloze test demonstrates that meaning is not something that suddenly appears when we have read to the end of a sequence of words, nor does it accumulate word by word from left to right across the page. Some clues to every deleted word in the example would be lost if all the words coming after the gap were removed. Indeed, a good strategy on any occasion when difficulty is encountered in comprehending print is to read further ahead instead of immediately going back to reread whatever preceded the troublesome passage.

Learners and Context

A variety of studies have demonstrated the readiness of children to make use of context in early reading (if they are so permitted), for example, Klein, Klein, and Bertino (1974), Golinkoff (1975/76), and Doehring (1976); see also McFarland and Rhodes (1978). Rosinski, Golinkoff, and Kukish (1975) conclude that meaning is irresistible to children; it can interfere with performance on a task because they cannot ignore it. Such studies also tend to show that use of context and reading ability increase together. This correlation is often attributed to the fact that better readers can make more use of context; less often the possibility is considered that use of context makes better readers. For the relation between ability and use of context see also Clay and Imlach (1971) and Samuels, Begy, and Chen (1975–1976). For analyses of children's errors, what K. Goodman calls "windows on the reading process," see K. Goodman (1965, 1969), Weber (1968), and Clay (1969). Studies of children's misreadings tend to highlight the important fact that many of the errors, especially those made by better readers, preserve the meaning of the context, and also that errors which make a difference to meaning are often subsequently corrected by children who are reading for meaning (and therefore are not errors that need be a great cause for concern). Children who read more literally, perhaps because of an emphasis on "accuracy" during instruction, may however make nonsensical errors without being aware of them.

The paradigm example of a child learning to read by meaning alone, without any possibility of decoding to sound, must be that of Helen Keller. Henderson (1976) reports the case of a deaf child who learned to recognize 4,400 printed words in nine months at the age of six by relating them to manual signs in a meaningful context, basically in response to the child's own spontaneous inquiries. Ewoldt (1981) demonstrates that deaf children read in the same way as hearing children.

Eye Movements

The particular order and location of fixations is not a reliable guide to how readers comprehend text, especially as reading rate increases. (In the same way, the intermittent manner in which our gaze wanders around a room is not particularly suggestive of the stable perception of the room that the brain constructs.) Nevertheless, Just and Carpenter (1980) claim to present a new theory of reading based on points of fixation. Rayner, Well, and Pollatsek (1980) demonstrate that the eyes pick up more visual information on the right of a fixation than on the left (in English). For other discussions of fixations and comprehension see Kolers (1976), Kieras and Just (1984), Just and Carpenter (1984), Rayner (1983), and Groner, McConkie, and Menz (1985).

Subvocalization

Edfelt (1960) concluded that good readers engage less in "silent speech" than poor readers and that an easy text results in less subvocalization than a difficult one (which to me reflects the same underlying factor—all texts are difficult for poor readers). Kleiman (1975) in a carefully controlled study showed that recoding to speech was not necessary for the understanding of individual words ("lexical access") but might be useful while "semantic integration" takes place, in other words when there might be a heavier demand on short-term memory. Baddeley, Eldridge, and Lewis (1981) argue that while memory is helped by subvocalization, inappropriate articulation requirements in experiments can disrupt short-term memory. Swanson (1984) has also shown that the need for subvocalization (which he calls "phonological recoding") increases as load on memory increases, for example in the face of "comprehension questions." The need is also greater for younger readers or when reading is difficult. In any case, comprehension has to occur prior to phonological recoding; words cannot be subvocalized meaningfully in any other way. Pugh (1978) discusses both speed reading and the elimination of subvocalization and concludes that neither interferes with comprehension.

NOTES TO CHAPTER 10, READING, WRITING AND THINKING, pp. 164-179.

Comprehension and Thinking

Reading and thinking are fundamentally inseparable, especially when reading is discussed or researched under the heading of comprehension. Comprehension might be considered as reading from a thinking point of view. Vygotsky (1978) defined thinking as "internalized action," which could also be regarded as a definition of reading. In a special "literacy" issue of *Harvard Educational Review*, Scribner and Cole (1978) argue that literacy does not change the basic way in which people reason. The contrary view is widely held, for example by Olson (1977).

In any aspect of thinking, what we know already—our "prior knowledge"— is obviously an important factor in what we can accomplish. Tierney and Cunningham (1984) discuss the importance of building up and "activating" background knowledge prior to reading. Basically this is common sense—the more we know about a topic before reading, the more we understand. But there is a decidedly mechanistic tone about theorizing which talks of the provision, utilization, and activation of any aspect of thought, which in practice can lead teachers to spend more time on preparation for reading than on reading itself, although reading is a major source of prior knowledge. Prior knowledge can on occasion be detrimental, if the text asserts something contrary to what the reader predicts (Alvermann, Smith, & Readance, 1985), especially if there are differences between the cultural perspectives of the text and the world-view of the reader (Lipson, 1983, 1984).

Kimmel and MacGinitie (1984) have shown that children may perseverate with inappropriate hypotheses while reading (and presumably in other circumstances). This is not necessarily the fault of the readers, however. Children can often cope well with paragraphs or entire texts where the "main idea" is at the beginning. But many school texts are not written in this way. Simmel and MacGinitie show that school texts often begin with examples, analogies and even refutations, and make their point clear only at the end. Nicholson and Imlach (1981) found that prior knowledge and text could compete when children were required to answer questions about their reading. Eight-year-olds could incorrectly impose their own expectations on narrative, but on the other hand they could also "be assailed by every word in the paragraph"—a phrase first used in an important article by Thorndike (1977). Baddeley, Logie, Nimmo-Smith, and Brereton (1985) analyzed the "components" of fluent reading, and found the two major factors to be vocabulary and working memory span, both of which relate to the sense which a reader can make of a text. Paradoxically, O'Brien and Myers (1985) demonstrated that comprehension difficulty could improve recall, because readers spent more time looking back. Confounding comprehension in this way is not recommended as a strategy for improving memory.

August, Flavell, and Clift (1984) showed that skilled fifth-grade readers noticed inconsistencies in stories (a missing page) more often than less skilled readers, which may simply indicate that better readers have more experience in reading. Noticing the inconsistencies in sense did not necessarily interfere with recall of detail. Beebe (1980) found that errors made by silent readers reduced both comprehension and recall—unless the errors were corrected or "semantically acceptable," in which case both comprehension and recall improved. Beebe's study shows clearly that reading is primarily an effort after sense. Juel and Holmes (1981) noted that poor readers spend less time on difficult words when reading silently than when reading aloud, when presumably the expectations of others control how the reading is done. In comparing oral and silent reading of sentences, the authors noted that the "same cognitive processes" were involved; reading for meaning is important in both.

Comprehension in reading does not necessarily take place immediately, or all at once. Samuels (1979) and O'Shea, Sindelar, and O'Shea (1985) have shown, not surprisingly, that reading the same text more than once improves fluency, comprehension and memory, especially for "poor readers" or for reading difficult texts. The effect is particularly pronounced if readers are cued to read for comprehension rather than for accuracy. This research underlines an important general point: It is usually more effective to read a text *quickly*, more than once, than to plod through it slowly once only. Initial "skimming," and even browsing through an entire book by glancing at occasional pages, adds to prior knowledge and facilitates subsequent efforts to make sense of the entire text.

Baldwin, Peleg-Bruckner, and McClintock (1985) wondered whether "prior knowledge" itself facilitated reading, or whether the facilitation was attributable to the added interest that prior knowledge probably indicates. They found that for seventh- and eighth-grade children, the two factors were separate and additive. Not surprisingly, it is better to have both than to have interest without knowledge or knowledge without interest.

An ingenious eye-movement experiment by Just and Carpenter (1984) demonstrates that readers can make fast and accurate recovery from errors. When presented with sentences where mistakes of interpretation were almost certain to occur—such as with the word "sewer" in the sentence "There is also one sewer near our home who makes terrific suits"—readers made rapid and economical "regressive" eye movements directly to the misleading words. There were other references to eye-movement studies and "misleading texts" in the Notes to Chapter 9. Thompson (1981) defends the proposition that reading is generally a predictive activity, but not "hypothesis-testing." Prediction reduces alternatives (as argued in the present book), while hypothesis-testing focuses too much on a single possibility. For a brief consideration of Neisser's (1977) anticipatory model of cognition from a reading point of view, see Doehring and Aulls (1981).

Reading Speed

Carver (1985) criticizes studies that claim to demonstrate fast rates of reading. He asserts that "comprehension" is rarely adequately defined or measured in such studies and holds that unless readers comprehend the author's thoughts on a sentence-by-sentence basis (a procedure to which he gives the special name of *rauding*), then "skimming" rather than reading is taking place. Demonstration of rauding under laboratory conditions involves tests of recall of detail which constitute great impositions on memory. Not surprisingly, Carver's experimental subjects fail to meet such a criterion at speeds of more than 600 words a minute. But it can be argued that no one reading in normal circumstances would ever try to remember the detail of every sentence of a novel or even of a business letter. Few people could read a novel if they expected to be tested on the detail of every sentence, the kind of "educational" requirement that often makes textbooks and literature unreadable for many students. Inability to remember detail does not mean that a book was not comprehended, or even that every sentence in that book was not comprehended at the appropriate time. Carver's rauding would be inefficient reading in most circumstances. His own studies showed that "speed readers" were able to write an adequate 100-word summary of a 6000-word text after perusing it for four minutes. From a different point of view, British researchers Harding, Beech, and Sneddon (1985) found that the reason more proficient readers aged from five to nine years old appeared to "process larger units of information" was that they read faster and therefore had less of a memory handicap. Potter (1984), using a technique that delivers individual words at a controlled rate to readers (Forster, 1970), found that college students preferred a rate of 360 words a minute. At 720 words a minute, almost all the words could be read but ideas "seem to pass through the mind without being adequately retained"—on a sentence-by-sentence basis at least. At 960 to 1680 words a minute, most viewers felt they could not see most of the words or understand individual sentences, although they could be shown to have acquired some understanding. Potter, Kroll, Yachzel, and Harris (1980) corroborated that it is memory that takes time in reading. Increasing the rate of reading from 180 to 600 words a minute left comprehension unaffected but reduced memory for detail.

Comprehension and Context

There is some research showing that poor readers use context more than fluent readers (Stanovich, 1980, 1981, 1986; Stanovich, Cunningham & Feeman, 1984; Perfetti & Roth, 1981; Perfetti, Goldman, & Hogaboam, 1979). These experimental results might appear contrary to the position argued in this book that poor readers use less nonvisual information. The resolution of this apparent paradox is that when reading is difficult, all readers *need* context more, and as Thompson (1981) points out, "good and poor readers" reading the same text are not doing equivalent reading—one is reading easy material and the other difficult. In the experimental conditions, poor readers are forced to rely on context and every other source of available help. But there is a related factor. Experimenters, especially those with a cognitive science orientation, typically define "context" as a few words on the page on either side of a "target word" in contrived situations that emphasize word identification or memory. There is much more to nonvisual information than adjacent words on a page. Nonvisual information includes all of a reader's relevant prior knowledge, plus understanding of the text *as a whole*. In fact, adjacent words on the page should be considered *visual information*—they are not "context" so much as additional features to be analysed if individual word identification is emphasized and difficult. And the less nonvisual information a reader can bring to bear, the more visual information, in the form of distinctive features from the text, need to be identified. In such circumstances, readers may need supplementary features outside the boundaries of target words in order to identify those words. Conversely, experienced readers (or readers reading "easy" texts) need attend to fewer distinctive features from individual words or from surrounding words as they read, as illustrated in Figure 1.3 in Chapter 1.

Stanovich calls his view of reading *interactive-compensatory*, to indicate that readers "interact" with texts (which is indisputable), and that they compensate for local difficulties they have by attending more to surrounding detail. The point about compensation is correct, but only in situations that focus on accurate word identification rather that purposeful, meaningful reading. It could also be argued that children who cannot identify particular words on sight in contrived experimental or instructional situations are forced to use context as much as they can since phonics won't work for them.

None of the studies of "context effects" demonstrate that reading is necessarily a matter of identifying one specific word after another, although the experimental designs often suggest that this is the assumption of the researchers. Other theorists (including myself) use the term context much more broadly to include the text as a whole, the purpose of the author, and the reader's general intentions and expectations. A few theorists go even further and include the "social context" of reading as well, for example, Harste, Woodward, and Burke (1984); Heap (1980); and Iser (1978). To recapitulate the view presented in this book, features of sequences of letters are analyzed but the letters themselves need not be identified when the reader's objective is the identification of words. And features of sequences of words may be analyzed without the words themselves being identified when the purpose of reading is to find specific kinds of sense in the text. Readers can go straight to meaning in the text by means of prediction. Reading is not a matter of identifying word after word. The eyes may appear to focus on individual words during reading (Just & Carpenter, 1980), but they have to be focused somewhere. The particular focal point does not necessarily indicate that words are being identified one at a time. Freebody and Anderson (1983) dispute Stanovich's compensatory-interactive model, arguing that comprehension and prior knowledge override text factors. But they add that it is not always easy for young readers to switch away from individual word identification (if that has become a habitual practice) especially if there are problems related to vocabulary, text cohesion, or "schema availability" (the relevant prior knowledge).

Becker (1982) argues that skilled readers can employ two alternative "strategies": (1) identifying and trying to put together meaning from successive words (the bottom-up view) or (2) "context driven," emphasizing the sense of the passage. The latter is more of a top-down point of view—but typically still puts the text in charge. The "context" is the surrounding text, not the purposes and understanding of the reader. Aaronson and Ferres (1984a) similarly identify two reading strategies. College students, both slow and fast readers, could employ (1) a "structure oriented strategy" when reading for retention, or (2) a "meaning oriented strategy" when reading for comprehension. In the latter case "lexical and structural information" related primarily to individual words was lost. Fifth graders could also employ the two strategies but more often tended to use them together for both recall and comprehension, indicating less flexibility than more experienced readers.

In many of the kind of experiments that I have discussed, there is often a confusion between *decoding* (in order to identify an unfamiliar word, to say what it is) and what is termed *phonological recoding*, in order to find a meaning for the word. *Phonological recoding* means putting a word into spoken language form (albeit silently) in order to "access the internal lexicon," and obtain a meaning. The phonological recoding view regards written language as parasitical on speech, and says in effect that we cannot recognize the meaning of written words by the look of them, but rather have to convert them into spoken language form in order to make sense of them from their sound. Unfortunately, some theorists talk about decoding as if that automatically means getting the meaning, although phonological recoding would be a necessary additional theoretical step. Words can be identified without being understood. On the other hand, phonological recoding does not entail decoding. It is possible to name a familiar word and to find a meaning for it from the appearance of the word as a whole, without going through decoding of letters or syllables. And phonological recoding itself is by no means an essential part of reading. As argued in Chapter 9, meaning can be brought directly to the visual representation of words, without any spoken language representation, as is obviously the case for homophones like *their* and *there*, which have identical sounds but whose meaning is easily distinguished by their appearance. Once again the decoding and recoding experiments demonstrate the untoward emphasis on words in reading research that Goodman (1982) has pointed out. Reading is not normally a matter of extracting and putting together the meaning of individual words, but of bringing relevant meaning to texts.

Other Aspects of Reading

Margaret Meek Spencer (1987) emphasizes that reading always requires a text that is read for a particular purpose, a consideration which she thinks is overlooked in textbooks which treat reading in the abstract. A similar point is strongly made by Iser (1978), who says reading requires not only a reader, but a context in which the reading is taking place. Obviously the authors of textbooks cannot specify a particular situation every time they refer to "reading," but the point is well taken that the manner in which reading transpires at any particular time depends on the person reading, the text being read, and all the circumstances of the occasion. For an excellent review of reading as a constructive process, still topical after twenty years, see Ryan and Semmell (1969). Langer (1951) and Iser (1978) both assert that a reader's involvement with a story is like involvement in actual events.

Benton (1979) identifies four characteristics of the "reading state." It is active, creative, unique (to the individual who is reading), and cooperative (between the reader and the author). For a deep understanding of how children perceive narrative, see Meek (1982), and other chapters in the same volume. For general discussions of comprehension in reading, see Flood (1984) and J.

Langer (1982a). In reviewing the 1979–1980 report of the U.S. National Assessment of Reading, J. Langer (1982b) noted that the 100,000 students examined (aged 9, 13, and 17) could all comprehend reading passages and form judgments on them, though some had difficulty in elaborating or explaining their own ideas. The problem, Langer thought, was the emphasis on the "right answer," even when students were invited to give their own interpretations.

Torrance and Olson (1985) report that good readers talk in more complex utterances, and use a wider range of abstract words related to thinking and language. Olson (1977) argues that literacy makes people civilized.

Huey (1908) speaks such quiet common and scientific sense about reading (despite some rather dated anxieties about the "hygiene" of certain reading habits) that many theorists, including the present author, have been tempted to claim him as an intellectual predecessor. For histories of research on reading and on reading instruction see Venezky (1977), Mathews (1966), and Davies (1973). For comparative surveys of approaches to reading in different countries see Downing (1973) and Gray (1956). The Russian view, very much outside-in, is provided by Elkonin in Downing (1973), while Sakamoto (1976) discusses reading in Japan. Edited volumes covering various points of view include Singer and Ruddell (1976), Merritt (1976), and three volumes of Resnick and Weaver (1979). There are several chapters on reading in a two-volume international compendium on language edited by Lenneberg and Lenneberg (1975). For a general compendium of reading research, from a variety of points of view, see Downing and Leong (1982). Hochberg and Brooks (1976) discuss intentional aspects of reading, and Searle (1980) is an interesting but technical article on intention and language generally.

A typical alternative approach to both theory and instruction from that of the present volume is that of Venezky (1976), who states explicitly at the outset of his book that "reading is the translation from writing to a form of language from which the reader is already able to derive meaning," an assertion for which I think there is no evidence and which is probably untestable. Kavanagh and Mattingly (1972), LaBerge and Samuels (1977), and Reber and Scarborough (1977) present collections of papers on various aspects of reading and language generally, most of them from an outside-in point of view. Outstanding among such papers is one by Gough (1972), entitled "One Second of Reading" (which is as much of the process that is considered). Gough asserts that reading must progress from letters through sounds to words and finally meaning, and presents an elaborate diagram of these stages. But the arrows on the flowchart come to a theoretical full stop at comprehension, which is relegated to a mystical area of the brain called TPWSGWTAU (the place where sentences go when they are understood) presided over by a magician named Merlin. Groff (1977) pleads for phonics from an educational point of view.

Reading and Writing

Most contemporary researchers into reading pay some attention to writing as well. They look at how readers and authors must collaborate with each other, at what reading and writing have in common, and also at what knowledge of reading and of writing contribute to each other. Good introductions to many of these topics are Nystrand (1986) and J. Langer and Smith-Burke (1982). Jensen (1984) reprints a number of *Language Arts* articles on the "reading/writing connection."

In an issue of *Language Arts* devoted to the same topic, Tierney and Pearson (1983) discuss reading and writing as similarly creative "composing" activities, and conclude that "what drives reading and writing is . . . desire to make sense of what is happening, to make things cohere." The discussion of the implicit contract between readers and writers that enables their expectations and intentions to meet in the conventions of the text is developed more fully, and more from the writer's point of view, in F. Smith (1982). Tierney and LaZansky (1980) also refer to the rights and responsibilities of readers and writers as "a contractual agreement." Eckhoff (1983) shows how children's reading influences what they write. If their primers contained "stories" in which each sentence was on a separate line, children wrote their own stories in the same way. If their reading was richer and more conventional, so was their writing. Calkins (1980) found that children learned more about punctuation from their reading than from instruction and used more punctuation as a consequence. The children also adopted stylistic features of the texts they read, such as beginning sentences with "And" or ending them with "too." For a general argument that children learn to write by reading, see Smith (1983b). Stotsky (1983) documents how better (more experienced) readers tend to be better writers and to produce more "syntactically mature" writing. She also found, however, that studies that used writing as an exercise to improve writing had little effect on reading. She cites several studies showing that additional reading may be as good as, or even better than, grammar study in improving writing. Jaggar, Carrara, and Weiss (1986) also examine the mutual influence of childrens' reading and narrative writing; see also Hansen, Newkirk, and Graves (1985).

NOTES TO CHAPTER 11, LEARNING ABOUT THE WORLD AND ABOUT LANGUAGE, pp. 180–197.

Language Learning

Important discussions of the way in which meaning is the basis of language learning include Bloom (1973), Halliday (1975), and Nelson (1973, 1974). Bloom, Rocissano, and Hood (1976) elaborate on the contribution of adult-child dialogues to language learning, and Harper (1975) considers the manner in which children actually control adult behavior to make learning possible. Bruner (1975, 1978) argues that the origin of language in children lies in their joint activities with adults, for example, from four to six months they begin to follow the direction of their parent's gaze (Scarfe & Bruner, 1975), as well as showing signs of turn-taking. See also Moerk (1977) and Moskowitz (1978). Tough (1974) also stresses that children learn language through use, not through prescription or instruction.

Many researchers have looked at how mothers help babies to learn language, for example by "scaffolding" a meaning around the use of language (Ninio & Bruner, 1978). Shatz (1978) describes how infants understand what adults mean before they understand what they say—and thereby look as if they know more than they do. Clark and Hecht (1983) review research showing how comprehension precedes the production of language. Bridges, Sinha, and Walkerdine (1981) demonstrate how infants figure out the intentions of their mothers, taking into account the circumstances in which their mothers are talking, in order to understand what they are saying. Urwin (1982) describes how convergence of gaze becomes the basis for a shared frame of reference, and Wells and Nicholls (1985) consider shared activities. Nelson (1985) proposes that children learn primarily through being involved in meaningful "events" with adults. For a semiotic perspective, see Bates (1979).

Children do not learn to talk by imitation, unless imitation is defined very specifically as the deliberate use of adult utterances on appropriate occasions to achieve the same ends as adults, when the utterances are in fact already understood. For further discussion of the active and meaningful nature of imitation by children, and of its utility as a research tool, see Bloom, Hood, and Lightbown (1974) and Slobin and Welsh (1973). Certainly adults do not usually babble (in the infantile sense) yet the roots of meaningful language can be detected in infant babbling (Weir, 1962). Krashen (1976) is an important article on the *unconscious* nature of language learning.

On "metacognition"—or knowing whether and how you know something— see especially Flavell (1979) and A. Brown (1980, 1982). Flavell (1979) argues that children cannot monitor their own or other people's mental states very well, and do not have a very good understanding of goals or tasks, actions, or strategies. Flavell, Speer, Green, and August (1981) tape-recorded children working on a building-block task and reported that the children not only did not understand the task but also did not understand that they were not communicating with each other adequately. But in a commentary on this study in the same monograph, Grover J. Whitehurst raises the critical question of whether the children lack independent metacognitive skills or simply experience. Brown (1980) extends her analysis to the use of study time by good and poor readers, and their relative ability in such tasks as selecting "main ideas." Once again the "skills versus experience" question should arise, but Brown believes that older students can in fact benefit from insights into the workings of their own memories. Derry and Murphy (1986) review current efforts to train learning abilities in systematic ways, and conclude "executive learning skills cannot be trained easily or by direct instruction alone, but must be developed gradually and automated over an extended period of time."

An excellent introduction to Piagetian thought on children's language learning, emphasizing that it can only be understood by taking into account what a child knows already, is available in Sinclair (1970) and Sinclair-de-Zwart (1972). Additional general references on language learning are given below. Important studies of infant learning abilities generally, before they even turn their attention to language, are described by T. Bower (1971, 1974), Fantz (1964, 1966), Kagan (1970), and Nelson (1985). At the other extreme, the importance of meaningfulness in second language learning is discussed by McLaughlin (1977), Fillion, Smith, and Swain (1976), and Krashen (1985).

More generally, the notion that the same principles underlie both comprehension and learning has been argued by Greeno (1974), and by Haviland and Clark (1974). Donaldson and Reid (1982) demonstrate that children are natural hypothesis-testers and rule users, with a strong drive and enormous ability to make sense of the world and of what people say—especially with the help of others. See also Donaldson's (1982) excellent book on children's thinking and learning, in which she argues that children can reason perfectly well if "logical" aspects of tasks are embedded in meaningful contexts.

A classic and controversial work on the biological basis of language learning is Lenneberg (1967). There are many texts on the development of language in children, including R. Brown (1973), Slobin (1979), Bloom (1970), Gleason (1985), Chukovsky (1968), Menyuk (1971), and two books with an educational emphasis, Cazden (1972) and Dale (1976). Miller (1977) is a delightful short book on the ease with which children learn language and on the difficulty adults experience in trying to study them doing so. There are also a number of edited volumes containing important original chapters, including Collins (1979), Moore (1973), Olson (1980), and F. Smith and Miller (1966). Wood (1981) examines the development of both verbal and nonverbal communication in infants, and in an edited volume, Golinkoff (1983) brings together prominent psychologists, sociologists, anthropologists and educators for a more theoretical look at the transition from "prelinguistic" to linguistic communication. Bain (1983) is an advanced volume examining many social aspects of the development of language and behavior generally. The more general argument that comprehension and learning are inseparable is in Smith (1975), and a more complete discussion of demonstrations, engagement and sensitivity in Smith (1981a).

Vocabulary

In an intensive study, Carey (1978) estimates that six-year-olds have mastered (to some degree) an average of 14,000 words, noting that "this massive vocabulary growth seems to occur without much help from teachers." According to Carey, there is first a "fast mapping" when a child hypothesizes a probable general meaning for a new word. A gradual process of refining and adding "partial knowledge" of meaning ensues on successive encounters, with from four to ten encounters required for word learning to be "complete." A similar incremental learning assumption was adopted by Nagy and Anderson (1984) and Nagy, Herman, and Anderson (1985) who used a sophisticated technique for estimating the vocabulary growth of high school students. They concluded that the students were learning an average of 3000 new words *every year*—mostly from reading—independently of whether direct vocabulary instruction was provided by the teacher. They estimated that fifth graders could encounter more than a million words a year, between 15,000 and 55,000 of which would be unknown. From empirically derived probabilities that something would be learned of these unfamiliar words on every encounter, they calculated that a "typical middle-grade student" would learn between 1500 and 8250 words a year, an average of 4,875. (See also Herman, Anderson, Pearson, & Nagy, 1987.) All of these researchers see reading as the primary source of vocabulary development, and great limitations to methods of teaching based on word lists and direct instruction.

Children required to learn specific new words in contrived experimental contexts—typically artificial words embedded in half a dozen unrelated sentences—usually find the task difficult. McKeown (1985), for example, required 30 fifth graders to figure out the meaning of artificial words in short sentences like "Eating lunch is a narp thing to do," and found that good readers could accomplish the task, but not poor readers (although these presumably had difficulty in reading the sentences in the first place). She concluded that "the meaning-acquisition process" is complex and difficult, even for high ability readers. But this may be a case of what might be called the Laboratory Fallacy, which asserts that children who have difficulty on an artificially-contrived learning (or comprehension or memory) task, will have similar difficulty in all situations. Schatz and Baldwin (1986) showed that "context cues" are not usually reliable predictors of word meaning—not in experimental situations where texts are brief and assembled in a contrived manner. The more naturalistic approach of Nagy and Anderson and their colleagues that I have just cited suggests a different conclusion, although the technique of embedding unfamiliar words in minimal context is common in laboratories and classrooms. For third-grade children's vocabulary development—estimated at about 5000 words a year—see M. Smith (1941). See also Anglin (1980).

Learning as a Social Event

Vygotsky (1978) succinctly explains the social nature of learning: "Every function in the child's cultural development appears twice, on two levels. First on the social, and later on the psychological level" (p. 57). He sees an interweaving of biological "elementary" processes and sociocultural "higher" functions, imposed neither from within nor from outside but mediated always by a dialectic between individual and society. All "higher" functions like memory, attention and perception, develop from actual relations between people which become internalized. "For the young child, to think means to recall; but for the adolescent, to recall means to think." There is a "practical intelligence" before speech, but language plays an essential role in the development of higher mental functions—it enables children to become objects of their own behavior. Brown and Ferrara (1985) examine Vygostky's theories closely, noting that children perform better and learn better with adult assistance at the *upper* level of their ability.

Walkerdine (1982) makes similar arguments in a semiotic context. She holds that language, thinking and "context" are not separate systems but are jointly related to a basic human need to know how signs of all kinds are interpreted. In a complex and subtle discussion, Walkerdine (who has some differences with Vygotsky) also proposes the centrality of metaphor in children's thought and learning. See also Bridges, Sinha, and Walkerdine (1981) on learning through language. Urwin (1982) similarly argues that learning reflects social interaction, with a semiotic emphasis on the importance of "signs." Clark and Hecht (1983) look at the relation of understanding, speech, and learning.

Motivation

The role of motivation in learning needs perhaps to be clarified, especially because children are frequently blamed for failure to learn because of lack of motivation. However, learning frequently takes place in the absence of conscious motivation, for example the effortless growth of vocabulary. And the presence of motivation does not guarantee learning. We have all failed to learn things we have been highly motivated to learn, on which we may have expended considerable effort and "time on task." Learning normally depends not on effort but on the demonstrations, collaboration, engagement, and sensitivity that I discussed in this chapter. Interest and expectation of learning are better predictors of learning than overt motivation. At best, motivation has the beneficial effect of putting learners into situations where demonstrations and collaboration are likely to be found. And of course, anyone motivated not to learn, or anticipating failure, is likely to find the expectation fulfilled.

An Alternative Perspective

There are basically two alternative psychological theories about learning, the extremes of which are diametrically opposed. The *behaviorist* view is that all learning is *habit formation*, and that the only data of importance are the observable circumstances in which habits are established. The *cognitive* view is that learning involves the *acquisition of knowledge,* and that what is interesting is the unobservable manner in which knowledge is structured and organized by the brain. The present book, obviously, has a cognitive (but not cognitive science) bias.

The most famous contemporary exponent of behaviorism is B. F. Skinner, whose very name has become a conditioned response to the box (actually a cage) that he invented and in which many of the principles of behaviorist theory have been analyzed and elaborated. In the Skinner box the behavior of rats, pigeons, fish, worms, and other living organisms has been studied and extrapolated, with considerable facility, to describe and even explain the behavior of human beings. Behaviorists assert that all behavior can be understood—in Skinnerian terminology "predicted and controlled"—in terms of *habits* established by the *reinforcement* of a *response* in the presence of a particular *stimulus.*

A response, quite simply, is a piece of observable behavior; not an idea, or a prediction, or an emotion, or a memory—all of these are unobservable, and therefore in the behaviorist view "fictions"—but an explicit movement or physical change. A stimulus, also quite simply, is an occasion for a response. A red light is the stimulus for stopping a car; the words, "pass the salt, please" are the stimulus for passing the salt; a baby is a stimulus for protective and nuturant behavior, and the printed word *cat* is a stimulus for the spoken word "cat." Learning is the establishing, or conditioning, of a bond between a particular stimulus and response, the establishing of a habit. The actual nature of the habit is determined by S-R (stimulus-response) contingencies. If a pigeon is conditioned to peck at a disk when a red light shines, then the S-R bond will be formed between the red light and a peck at the disk.

Reinforcement determines whether conditioning actually takes place. A particular S-R bond will be established only if the behaving organism is reinforced in a particular way while responding in the presence of a stimulus. Positive reinforcement is anything that increases the probability that a response will recur in the presence of a particular stimulus; negative reinforcement reduces that probability. In everyday life positive reinforcement is associated with reward, negative reinforcement with punishment. (However, there are differences between punishment and negative reinforcement. Negative reinforcement, such as the withholding of a reward, reduces the probability that a type of behavior will recur in the future. Punished behavior is likely to recur as soon as the punishment is stopped; the removal of punishment is positively reinforcing.)

After that slab of definition, examples are in order. I shall offer two: one animal and one human. Imagine a rat in a box equipped with stimulus, response, and reinforcement apparatus—a Skinner box, in other words. In this particular box there are two stimuli: a red light and a green light, and two available responses in the form of levers that the rat can press, one on the left and one on the right. The reinforcement apparatus is a chute down which a pellet of food may be dropped. Ignoring for a moment the question of how the rat first learns to make the right kinds of responses, we shall watch the acquisition of an S-R habit. The rat is at 85% of its normal body weight, so it is no surprise that a pellet of food is positive reinforcement. The rat pushes one of the levers when no light is on, and nothing happens. A red light comes on, but it pushes the "wrong" lever, and still nothing happens. Eventually, the rat pushes the "correct" lever when the red light comes on, and it receives positive reinforcement, the reward of a pellet of food. But if it pushes the same lever when the green light comes on, there is, of course, no pellet. Very soon the rat is pushing one lever every time the red light comes on, and the other lever for the green. Quite a complex piece of discriminative behavior has been conditioned. Similar behavior can be conditioned in quite a different way, by negative reinforcing the animal if the correct response is not made—for example, with a mild electric shock.

The second example reveals a child in a classroom also equipped with stimulus, response, and reinforcement apparatus, but not called a Skinner box. The stimulus apparatus is called a teacher, who asks questions, and the response apparatus is the child's voice. The child is not at 85% of normal body weight, but then the child will not be reinforced with pellets of food. The stimulus apparatus holds up a card bearing the word *cat,* and the child responds by gazing mutely out of the window. There is no reinforcement. The child responds by uttering the word "dog." There is no reinforcement. Eventually the child utters the word "cat," and is reinforced: The teacher smiles, or says "Correct" or "Very good" or "Go out and play now," or stops referring to the child sarcastically as a genius, or does something else that is a reinforcer by our operational definition. This increases the probability of the child's saying "cat" when confronted with the printed word *cat.*

The process of setting up the exact kind of behavior that it is desired to reinforce is known as *shaping.* The term is appropriate; the behavior is literally molded by a series of *successive approximations.* Consider again the lever-pressing rat, from the moment an untrained animal—"naive" is the felicitous term employed—is first put into the box. The experimenter, to show the rat how it is to be reinforced, drops a pellet of food down the chute into a food tray, and the rat eats and looks for more. The next problems is to get the rat to focus attention on the lever. If the experimenter waited until the rat actually pushed the lever, it might take all day. Instead, the experimenter reinforces the rat for a very rough approximation, namely, entering the end of the box at which the levers are situated. Very quickly the rat "learns"[1] that it is reinforced

---

[1] Even with behaviorist theory there is a temptation to put the descriptions into everyday cognitive words like "learns," "thinks," and "decides," although a behaviorist would simply say that the probability of a particular response is increased.

only at the end of the cage, but by then the experimenter reinforces only if the rat comes to the corner where the levers are. The rat concentrates its attention on that particular corner and inevitably bumps against one of the levers, for which again it is reinforced. As soon as the experimenter has got the rat to push the lever, the serious business begins of reinforcing only when the rat pushes the right lever at the right time. The whole process takes an experienced trainer less time to accomplish than to describe. Training a naive rat to lever-press to a particular light or sound is a five-minute laboratory demonstration. And once the shaping has been accomplished the rest of the training and data collection can be controlled quite automatically, programmed circuits organizing S-R contingencies so that every move by the conditioned animals is inexorably followed by a predetermined consequence.

By an associated process called *chaining*, quite elaborate sequences of behavior can be built up out of small elements. As a rather trivial example, pigeons can be trained to play table tennis. In both shaping and chaining the underlying principle is the same, made quite explicit in the terminology of the behaviorist experimenter: first get one piece of behavior *under control*. Once a system is established by which an organism will respond in order to receive reinforcement, the schedule of reinforcement can be adapted to develop the particular pattern of behavior required. What happens when the rat gets too fat on all those constant pellets of food, or a teacher runs out of rewards for the child? The remarkable fact is that the actual reinforcer comes to play only a minor part in the conditioning process once behavior has been brought under control. In fact the conditioning of really complex behavior is accomplished in the absence of reinforcement. Once reinforcement is expected, the experimenter works on the expectation. Pie in the sky is the most effective reinforcer of all.

In contrast to the behaviorist point of view, cognitive psychologists see human learners as discriminating experience-seekers and creative decision-makers rather than as creatures of habit. In the cognitive view reinforcement influences behavior only because it is informative; it provides feedback about the consequences of behavior. People scale mountains to see what is on the other side, not from force of habit, and they read for pleasure or to find the answers to questions. People do not permit their experiences or their knowledge to be determined for them by chance or inertia. Even children, as the discussion of language learning has tried to show, are selective and self-directed in their interactions with the world.

There can be no answer to the question of which view is "right," behaviorist or cognitive, because the question is inappropriate. Neither side can produce data that will contradict the other; there is no critical experiment that will decide between the two (Dulany, 1974), since basically they are both trying to make the same evidence explicable though in quite different ways. Rather the question should be which theory is the most useful, which sheds the most light in our efforts to understand various aspects of human behavior. No theory can claim to offer a complete account. I have already contrasted behaviorist and cognitive views of language in Chapter 2.

To suggest that reading is learned by reinforcing the conditioned response "cat" in the presence of the visual stimulus *cat* seems to me to leave out all the interesting as well as many of the difficult issues (F. Smith, 1979). In this article I also argue that behaviorism is the favored learning theory of *programmed instruction* because it breaks learning down into small discrete units, gaining control at the expense of sense. As a description of situations in which pigeons and even people are more or less likely to learn, the relevance of behaviorism may be more easily seen. But then it has to be recognized that reinforcement for humans is far more subtle than it might appear to be for animals. As I have argued in this chapter, human learning provides its own motivation and reward. The problem with extrinsic (or irrelevant) reinforcers, such as "token" rewards of money, candy, or grades, is that while they may temporarily make learning more probable, their withdrawal is negatively reinforcing and even punishing. When irrelevant reinforcement is taken away, the desired learning or behavior becomes less probable because it was not acquired for its own sake in the first place (Levine & Fasnacht, 1984; Notz, 1975; Lepper, 1978). For Skinner's own view of learning and teaching, see Skinner (1953, 1968), and for further critiques, McKeachie (1974) and Dember (1974).

NOTES TO CHAPTER 12, LEARNING TO USE WRITTEN LANGUAGE, pp. 198–216.

Learning to Read

Some of the most significant pathfinding research into children's developing understanding of literacy has been done not by educators or psychologists—who tend to look at individuals in isolation, or in a personal relationship to "knowledge"—but by sociologists and anthropologists. The edited volume of Goelman, Oberg, and Smith (1984) contains summaries and reviews of research into the social basis of preschool literacy by workers in a number of disciplines, and also outlines the prevailing methodologies. The primary method of research is not experimental, but observational. *Ethnographic* is the technical term for such research, also called "naturalistic research," and (by Yetta Goodman) "kid-watching." Two of the main findings of this research are that children in all cultures develop insights into the forms and functions of written language before school, and that these insights are based on meaning and use. The research also shows that learning about reading cannot be separated from learning about writing. As the title of this chapter indicates, learning to be literate entails learning how written language is used.

The research has also made clear that children do not need to be economically privileged or the recipients of special kinds of instructional support in order to learn about reading and writing. Ferreiro (1978, 1985), for example, who demonstrated how three- and four-year-olds gain insights about letters, words and sentences, did much of her work in the slums of Mexico City with children whose parents were illiterate. The fact that early readers have not necessarily had advantages is also made by M. Clark (1977) in her classic book on *Young Fluent Readers,* many of whom came from large poor families and were not "good risks" for reading instruction in school. Hall and Guthrie (1982) refer to the danger of the hypothesis that minority groups and the poor use language in ways that systematically put their children at a disadvantage at school. An alternative hypothesis might be that certain approaches to instruction systematically put such children at a disadvantage. Goodman (1970) has also pointed out that children are not taught to read by having their dialect changed or by being regarded as deficient in values, speech or attitudes, just because these are culturally different.

What children learn and think about literacy is largely determined by the practices and attitudes of people around them (Heath, 1982a). In an article that includes a useful list of references up to 1982, Teale (1982) asks how children become able to read and write without formal training, and concludes "Social interaction is the key. Natural literacy development hinges upon the experiences the child has in reading and writing activities which are mediated by literate adults, older siblings, or events in the child's everyday life."

There is an extensive documentation of the remarkable ability of children to make sense of written language without formal instruction, including Goodman (1980), Hiebert (1981), Mason (1980) and Ylisto (1977). Excellent descriptions of children learning to read independently of instruction are provided by Bissex (1980), Clark (1976), Clay (1979), and Torrey (1979). Young children's sensitivity to language generally and their often underrated ability to learn from meaningful adult demonstrations are discussed and illustrated in Gelman (1979). For what teachers can learn from children who learn to read early, see Forester (1977). See also Durkin (1966). In a review giving many examples of children's literacy learning before and during early schooling, Harste, Woodward, and Burke (1984) note that by the age of three, children assume that print is meaningful—an insight acquired from experience rather than from instruction. McCartney and Nelson (1981) show that three-year-old children use "script-based organizations of knowledge" (their own narrative constructions) to understand and recall stories. "Emergent literacy" is a new term, employed in the titles of useful books by Hall (1987) and Teale and Sulzby (1986).

A delightfully perceptive ninety-year-old article entitled "Eleanor Learns to Read" by Harriett Iredell (1898, reprinted in 1982) traces a child's progress through a succession of demands "something like this—Tell me a story. Read me a story. Read me this story. Where is such and such a story? Where does it tell about such and such? What does it say here? What is this word?" Julie Jensen, who as editor of *Language Arts* rediscovered and introduced the Iredell article, notes that Eleanor learned without multi-media, graded, controlled, individualized literacy kits, controlled vocabulary readers, or worksheets.

Reading to Children

Reading to children is frequently recommended, although it is not always made clear what exactly the practice is expected to achieve. Obviously reading to children may interest them in stories (or whatever else is read to them) and also demonstrate the interest and utility that other people find in reading. But every occasion when a child is read to can also be a reading (and writing) lesson, an opportunity to learn more about the conventions and purposes of written language. Teale (1981) reviews what is known—and not known—about parents reading to children. Taylor and Strickland (1986) describe many family story-reading sessions and their benefits to children. Durkin (1984) studied 23 poor black children of "average intelligence" who had frequently transferred schools, who become "successful readers" (reading above "grade level" by grade 5). She found that the children had supportive parents who liked stories and read to them.

Heath and Thomas (1984) provide a fascinating case study of a teenaged, unemployed high school dropout mother of two (co-author Charlene Thomas) herself learning to read in the course of helping her children learn to read. Heath (1985) contributes another poignant biographical study of a parent helping a child learn to read and to think in describing how she helped her own 18-year-old daughter recover from traumatic head injuries after a mountain-climbing accident. In this article Heath emphasizes the importance of opportunities to *talk about* literate matters in order to *remain* literate. Another of her many insightful contributions is an article entitled "What no bedtime story means" (Heath 1982b). Taylor (1983) describes how children learn to read and write in their families.

More generally, Wells (1981, 1985) examines the relationship between "pre-school related activities and success in school," noting also the importance of talking about what is read and written. He also discusses the relationship between parental reading practices and children's ideas of literacy and subsequent success in school. Once again, Vygotsky (1978) becomes relevant with his conception of a "zone of proximal development" where children do things with assistance which they will soon be able to do for themselves.

Literacy and Schooling

The fact that children often learn so much before school, and that cultural influences are so important, does not release schools from responsibility or provide convenient justification for failures of instruction. If children have not received adequate environmental support for embarking upon literacy, then schools must provide it. The ethnographic research shows clearly the collaborative conditions under which learning to read and write takes place. If parents fail to read to children, it is all the more important that teachers do so.

Sulzby (1985) discusses how kindergarten children, some as young as four and a half, begin to make sense of stories, from commenting on pictures to telling a story which gains more and more fidelity to the text. There was always a story behind the children's comments—and the children's versions of the story always made sense. McMahon (1983) showed that even first grade children have little difficulty—and enjoy—coordinating a text they are looking at and a tape-recorded voice reading the text. For a general, research-based review of many aspects of literacy and school, see the edited volume by Raphael (1986).

Intelligence has never been found to be an important factor in learning to read, although reading appears to contribute significantly to intelligence. Stanovich, Cunningham, and Feeman (1984) found only a low relationship between intelligence and reading ability in first-grade children. The correlation was higher by fifth grade, and the researchers attributed the increase to "reciprocal causation." They also found that children who quickly learned to read read well through life, indicating the importance of avoiding obstacles, irrelevancies and confusions in a child's early experiences with literacy.

The influence of instruction on children's behavior has been well documented. Research on how children learn to read rarely remains uncontaminated by the influence that prior instruction has already had on them. Barr (1972, 1974) has written basic papers on the effect of instruction on children's reading. Downing and Oliver (1973–74), Meltzer and Herse (1969), and Jenkins, Bausel and Jenkins (1972) all report on effects of early reading instruction on children. Holdaway (1976) comments on the importance of self-correction for children learning to read and on the risk that some instructional techniques take this responsibility away from them. Eckhoff (1983) was cited in the previous chapter for demonstrating that what children read is revealed in their writing. Juel and Roper/Schneider (1985) report that what children read also shows up in how they read. In particular, texts made up of "decodable" regular words produced children whose main strategy in reading was to sound out unfamiliar words. DeFord (1981) reaches a similar conclusion.

MacGinitie and MacGinitie (1986) argue that an emphasis on "mechanics" in the primary grades teaches students not to read, and they note a de-emphasis on extended writing, literature, and "content-rich reading" in high school. When students have difficulties with a text, teachers respond (or ask other students to respond) rather than bringing students back to the text. In a painstaking book-length analysis of British practices, Hull (1985) shows how the written and spoken language used in reading instruction, and in content areas at all grade levels, is frequently totally incomprehensible to students. He is particularly scathing when textbook or examination questions include words and phrases that students do not understand (because of their ambiguity or vacuous definitions) and complaints are then made that the students cannot read. Hull's book is published in Britain. His occasional use of Anglicisms like "lower school" (junior high) and "sixth form" (twelfth grade) will illustrate for North American teachers his point that one does not have to be ignorant or learning disabled to be confused by unfamiliar uses of common words. MacGinitie (1984), in an article entitled "Readability as a solution adds to the problem" reports that attempting to "simplify" texts by making them conform to formulas restricting word and sentence length can make them more difficult to read. Pearson (1974, 1975) notes that comprehensibility is not improved in early reading books by fragmenting sentences and reducing grammatical complexity, a point made in other ways by Shuy (1981) and by Gourley (1978). Furness and Graves (1980) demonstrate experimentally that emphasis on accuracy (in oral reading) can actually reduce comprehension, just as an emphasis on correct spelling will inhibit children's writing. Paradoxically, both emphases result in less learning of what is supposed to be the object of the correction. Children reluctant to make mistakes will rarely venture beyond what they know already. Hiebert (1983) takes a critical look at ability grouping.

Moore (1983) and Heath (1983) discuss naturalistic methods of assessment in reading instruction. Mayher and Brause (1986) propose that testing may often cripple language education, through pressures on children and control of teachers, while not being closely related to learning to read and write.

Salmon and Claire (1984) made a two-year study of four comprehensive (secondary) schools in Britain and found that classroom collaboration, both socially and in "learning," between teachers and students and among students, resulted in better student understanding of the curriculum.

Mikulecky (1982) compared reading in school that was supposed to prepare students for the workplace, and reading in various occupations. He found that students read less often and less competently than most workers on the job, though the students read easier material to less depth.

Books are often overrated in research and practice. Books have no unique or essential properties for literacy learning, and they are not always the easiest texts to read. Newspapers and magazines often contain material that can attract the attention of the smallest children, depending upon their interests and mood. Krashen (1987) reviews the research on comics, showing that they can be highly productive materials for developing reading interests and ability, and also that comics frequently have rich vocabularies and conceptual content.

Teachers and Programs

Chall (1967) has already been cited for her influential review of instructional methods, leading her to a surprising programmatic decoding conclusion, and Samuels (1976, and LaBerge & Samuels, 1974) has consistently argued for a "subskills" approach to instruction, based on the notion that decoding is a central part of reading, although it becomes so rapid and automatic that it is not in fact detectable in any way. Atkinson (1974) exemplifies the not uncommon view that computers can teach children to read, even though the objectives are typically limited and the theory of reading underlying such programs is rarely evident or adequate. Jonathan Anderson (1984) surveyed commercially available computer software for language and reading in the United States, Britain, and Australia, and concluded that up to 95% is concerned with drills and computer-managed activities. Carroll and Chall (1975) edited a report of the Committee on Reading of the U.S. National Institute of Education, discussing the research that was available or required to take advantage of modern technology and produce universal literacy. In a review of the Carroll and Chall book, D. Olson (1975) notes that not one of the contributing researchers queried the underlying assumption that technology could eradicate illiteracy. Eisner (1982) criticizes the idea that improved techniques and tighter evaluation will increase learning. For a general discussion of how language instruction can be fragmented into absurdity, see Shannon (1983, 1986) and F. Smith (1981b, 1986).

A more reasoned and most readable brief discussion of choices in reading instruction is provided by Williams (1979), although she tends to see the opposite of a phonics approach as "whole word," which is not the perspective of most people opposed to phonics drills, and pays little attention to meaningfulness. Indeed, drilling with flashcards and meaningless word lists can be just as confusing and misleading for children. Another important recent article about instruction is Durkin (1981). K. Goodman has several times made trenchant counterattacks against hard-line "decoding" critics, against Gleitman and Rozin in two issues of *Reading Research Quarterly* in 1973, and against Mosenthal in the same journal in 1976/77. Goodman also clarifies his and my points of view with respect to such "interactive" theories as Rumelhart's (1977) in K. Goodman (1981) and more generally and vigorously in K. Goodman (1979).

"Whole language" is the instructional philosophy that reflects most consistently the view that meaning and "natural language" are the basis of literacy learning. (The approach becomes somewhat distorted when publishers announce that they are producing "whole language materials," a contradiction in terms.) Kenneth and Yetta Goodman are the theorists most closely identified with the origin and development of the whole language approach. Many TAWL (Teachers Applying Whole Language) groups have been established, especially in the United States and Canada. For discussions of whole language teaching and its underlying philosophy, see Goodman (1986a), Newman (1985), Taylor, Blum, and Logsdon (1986), Gunderson and Shapiro (1987), and Morrow and Weinstein (1986). Goodman sums up the whole language view:

> Many school traditions seem to have actually hindered language development. In our zeal to make it easy, we've made it hard . . . primarily by breaking whole (natural) language up into bite-size, but abstract little pieces. We took apart the language and turned it into words, syllables, and isolated sounds. Unfortunately, we also postponed its natural purpose—the communication of meaning—and turned it into a set of abstractions, unrelated to the needs and experiences of the children we sought to help. (1986a, p. 7)

See also Goodman (1986b) for his views on basal readers.

The whole language movement, and the theory and research underlying it, do not always receive their due. *Becoming a Nation of Readers,* the report of the National Academy of Education's Commission on Reading (Anderson, Hiebert, Scott, & Wilkinson, 1985) was castigated in the following manner by the editor of the International Reading Association's Annual Review of Reading Research (Weintraub, 1986):

> There's no guarantee that the big name is synonymous with quality. Even when well-funded and headed by a blue ribbon committee, a supposedly comprehensive review may be narrowly based, considerably less than comprehensive, and biased in its election of what is included and what is excluded. . . . I happen to concur that a very selective body of literature was included and some rather critical research excluded.

For social aspects of literacy and learning, see Ong (1982), Levine (1986), and several chapters in Olson, Torrance, and Hildyard (1985). Margaret Meek Spencer (Meek, 1982; 1984) is insightful on social aspects of literacy instruction, and also on the place of literature in teaching children to read. See also Meek, Armstrong, Austerfield, Graham, and Plackett (1983) regarding a not always encouraging and successful struggle to help adolescents to read. Atwell (1987) also examines teaching reading and writing to adolescents. For articles based on Yetta Goodman's concept of "kid watching" (more formally, teachers as researchers), see Jaggar and Smith-Burke (1985). An excellent compendium of recent research in reading and writing (termed "comprehension and composition") is Squire (1987). Hedley and Baratta (1985) contains important articles on reading, learning and thinking generally, including ethnographic research. Tuman (1987) examines social attitudes towards reading and reading instruction.

Among alternative points of view not so far mentioned, see Ehri and Wilce (1985), also Gough and Hillinger (1980), who go so far as to assert that learning to read is an unnatural act (referring specifically to their own view that beginning readers must learn to rely on letter-sound relations to identify words). On the other hand, Krashen (1985) examines the evidence and arguments that both spoken and written language are learned only by comprehension. He also examines the emotional blocks that can stand in the way of such learning. In "Learning to Read at Forty-Eight", Yatvin (1982) shares insights gained in belated efforts to learn to read Hebrew.

Important journals related to reading research are the International Reading Association's *Reading Research Quarterly* and the National Council of Teachers of English's *Language Arts*. Significant annual volumes are the International Reading Association's *Annual Review of Reading Research* and the National Reading Conference's Yearbooks (e.g. Niles & Lalik, 1985).

Metalinguistic Awareness

The notes to the previous chapter included references related to the general role of metacognition in learning—the awareness of one's own thought processes. Metalinguistic awareness is metacognition specifically related to linguistic matters, particularly (in the case of reading and writing) to the nature of written language. It is not clear that such awareness plays an important role in learning, or indeed, that such awareness can take place until after learning has occurred. It is difficult to see how terms like "letter," "word," and "sentence" can have any meaning to anyone who cannot read. Many people able to converse fluently cannot say what the difference is between nouns and verbs, or active and passive sentences, not to mention verbalizing the complexities of transformational grammars and the conventions of cohesion. Nevertheless, some theorists not only feel that metalinguistic understanding is essential for learning to read, but they define learning to read in terms of such understanding. Mason (1979) for example, in an article entitled "When do children begin to read?", associates reading with realizing that letters are discriminable patterns related to sounds. Downing (1970) found that the words "word" and "sound" were poorly understood by five-year-olds, who thought for example that "fish and chips" could be one word and that the word "sound" could be used for a variety of noises (which is of course true in normal circumstances). One implication of confusion of this kind might be that time is wasted that is spent talking about reading rather than actually helping children to read. Downing, Ollila, and Oliver (1975) discovered not surprisingly that there were cultural differences in children's "concepts" of reading and writing. They found that 72 Indian kindergarten children knew less than 92 non-Indian children about "the technical language of literacy." The difference is obviously attributable to differences (though not necessarily defects) in experience rather than instruction. The authors use typical but unfortunate evaluative language for such differences, remarking of the Indian children that "their concepts of the communicative function of reading and writing were significantly immature" and "their perception of phonemes was significantly less well developed." In their introduction to an edited book on metalinguistics, Downing and Valtin (1985) note:

> During the 1970s there was a rapid increase in metacognition and metalinguistics . . . For educators these developments presented a glittering array of new ideas that promised to throw light on children's thinking processes in learning how to read . . . However, the variety of independent theoretical approaches and their accompanying terminologies has been somewhat confusing.

In the same volume, Downing (1985) argues that reading can be broken down into subskills that require deliberate training and "task awareness," while Ehri (1985) emphasizes spelling instruction as a way to make children aware of the relation between words they hear and words they see. Metacognitive and metalinguistic theorists typically emphasize relationships of sound and spelling in reading rather than meaning. They also stress the role of cognitive *strategies*.

A. Brown (1982), for example, discusses "self-regulatory strategies" that contribute to "learning how to learn from reading," including predicting, planning, checking and monitoring knowledge of one's own abilities. Metacognitive strategies in reading are also discussed extensively in Forrest-Pressley and Waller (1984). Brown cites extensive documentation that better readers are more efficient and effective at such tasks, though there is always the chicken-and-egg problem of whether the competence produces better readers or that experienced readers naturally gain more competence. She relates her notion of "autocritical skills" to aspects of Vygotsky's (1978) socialization theory—that collaboration provides criticism and other cognitive resources which are then internalized. Lack of such collaboration is sometimes attributed to "disadvantaged homes," for example by Feuerstein, Jensen, Hoffman, and Rand (1985), who assert that such children from such backgrounds suffer "mediational deprivation." Brown herself contrasts "disadvantaged" with middle-class children on metacognitive competences. However, she also notes that teachers treat good and poor readers differently. Shannon (1985, 1985) has reviewed a mass of research indicating that schoolchildren who are identified as poor readers, or likely to be poor readers, do less reading, less interesting reading, more difficult reading, more exercises, and receive less assistance than other children. Hiebert (1983) looked at the consequences of ability grouping and also found that more able readers get the most meaningful reading with an emphasis on meaning, while the others received a greater emphasis on accuracy (which of course makes reading more difficult). See also Stanovich (1986) on the "Matthew effect" (that the rich get richer) in reading. Stanovich acknowledges that the main reason good readers get better is the differential treatment they receive in school (but as a believer with Gough and Hillinger (1980) that reading is an "unnatural act," he favors "surgical strikes" of specific skill instruction for children with problems.) Metacognitive instruction tends to become a matter of more questions in preset sequences, or more drills, before reading actually begins, according to Langer (1982a, 1982b).

Further evidence that teachers get back what they teach is provided by Mosenthal (1983), who found that teachers who concentrated on a single text and right answers got student responses showing little sign of prior knowledge or other reading. Teachers who encouraged broader thinking got more extensive and reflective responses. See also Allingston (1980) on the way in which teachers interrupt during primary-grade oral reading. Anderson, Mason, and Shirey (1984) looked closely at "reading groups" in the primary grades and concluded "There is a cornucopia of evidence that could be cited to support a stress on meaning in the reading group," compared with an emphasis on accurate oral reading. The article is a concise, readable outline of the general and educational research supporting the view that people learn and remember more when conditions require them to understand the material. The authors term this "the law of meaningful processing."

Dyslexia and Learning Disabilities

Of the allocation of blame for children's failure to learn to read there is no end. Guthrie (1973) offers one of many surveys of various systems for characterizing the disabilities of children who seem unable to capitalize on the resources available to modern reading pedagogy. Such children are frequently labeled "learning disabled," a diagnosis that is vigorously criticized by Glenn (1975) and Hart (1976). Serafica and Sigel (1970) note that some "reading disabled" children have superior visual discrimination to normal readers.

Staller (1982) reviews research on the relationship between neurological impairment and reading disability, and concludes that it is not yet possible to relate dyslexic behavior to specific neurological correlates. Berninger and Colwell (1985) studied 241 children aged between ages 6 and 12 identified as having no problem, a possible problem, or a definite problem in reading—and could find no support for the use of neurodevelopmental and educational measures in the diagnosis of specific learning disabilities. Dorman (1985) criticizes research that defines or diagnoses dyslexia, because there is no agreement on what would constitute neurological evidence of neurological dysfunction in relation to reading. He concludes that "insistence upon the inclusion of [central nervous system] dysfunction in the definition and diagnosis of dyslexia seems to be putting the cart before the horse, in the sense that the neurological basis of any or all developmental reading disorders remains hypothetical." Lipson and Wixson (1986) also review reading disability research and conclude that it must "move away from the search for causative factors within the reader and toward the specification of the conditions under which different readers can and will learn." Rather than accepting deficit explanations for reading problems, Wong (1982) proposes metacognitive factors, such as inadequate self-monitoring and self-questioning (in other words, attention to the meaning of what is read). Calfee (1983) says that dyslexia ought to be viewed as a problem with the development of the mind (i.e. experience) rather than a disease of the brain. Vellutino (1987) found no evidence that dyslexia is due to a visual deficit, nor to support remediation based on exercises to improve visual perception. He adds "In any case, not enough is yet known about how the brain works to enable anyone to devise activities that would have a direct and positive effect on neurological functions responsible for such basic processes as visual perception, cross-modal transfer and serial memory." Instead he recommends lots of assisted reading.

Johnston (1985) examined three case studies of adult reading disability and found "overwhelming feelings of inadequacy and confusion," anxiety, rational and irrational use of self-defeating strategies, conflicting motives, and inappropriate attributions of cause and blame, all going back to the individual's earliest reading experiences. Clay (1979) suggests that children become reading failures by learning the wrong things. Downing (1977) argues that society creates reading disabilities, for example, by artificially establishing "critical periods" for learning and through inappropriate expectations and stereotypes. Graham (1980) shows that "learning disabled" readers may have the same word recognition skills as children who are succeeding. In a careful examination of thirty years of research into reading failure, Hamill and McNutt (1981) could find no relationship to intelligence, perceptual or motor abilities, reasoning or even affective factors, and only a marginal correlation with spoken-language ability. Patterson (1981) reviews neuropsychological approaches to reading generally.

The consequences of reading failure are rarely adequately stressed. Reichardt (1977) talks of children "playing dead or running away" from reading situations, defensive reactions among "reading handicapped students" whose physiological responses to reading ranged from complete apathy to hypertension. More generally, Seligman (1975) discusses "learned depression" (due to lack of control over failures) and "learned laziness" (due to lack of control over rewards), both consequences of situations where the learner lacks control and understanding.

Despite all the conjectures, it should not be surprising that no one has actually succeeded in finding a specific reading center or system in the architecture of the brain. Literacy has not existed as a cultural phenomenon long enough for the brain to develop specialized reading processes. One might just as meaningfully suggest areas of the brain dedicated to cycling or sewing. It has been known for over 100 years that one side of the brain (nine times out of ten the left) is essential for the production and comprehension of language (except in infants, whose brains are much more labile). But this asymmetry does not mean that only one side of the brain is involved in language. All thinking activities involve the entire brain. Different people obviously have different preferences—some like listening to music and others would rather look at pictures—but this does not mean that they lack parts of their brains. Looking at pictures, listening to music, and reading and writing involve experience, knowledge, and feelings, and cannot be restricted to one area of the brain. It is a naive interpretation of neurological, language, and learning research to imagine that reading can be learned with the left side of the brain or with the right. There could only be specific reading disabilities if there are specific learning abilities—and no one has ever suggested what those might be.

GLOSSARY

This list does not attempt to define words as a dictionary does, but rather indicates the general way that certain terms are employed in this book. Figures in parentheses indicate the chapter in which a term was first used or primarily discussed. Terms in *italics* themselves appear elsewhere in the glossary.

Aesthetic reading: Reading done primarily for experience; contrasted with *efferent reading* (3).

Artificial intelligence: The study of electronic or mechanical systems designed to emulate human language and thought (preface).

Cat and dog problem: The fact that *distinctive features* cannot be explicitly taught but must be learned by the testing of *hypotheses* (11).

Category interrelationships: The various ways in which *cognitive categories* can be combined as a basis for *prediction* or action (1).

Channel capacity: Limit to the amount of *information* that can pass through any part of an information-processing system (3).

Cognition: A particular organization of knowledge in the brain, or the process of organizing such knowledge (1). See *cognitive structure*.

Cognitive categories: Prior decisions to treat some aspects of experience as the same, yet as different from other aspects of experience; the constantly developing framework of *cognitive structure* (1).

Cognitive questions: The specific information sought by the brain to make a decision among alternatives; the range of a *prediction* (1).

Cognitive science: An area of common concern in psychology, linguistics, and the design of computer systems, related to the manner in which knowledge can be acquired, stored, retrieved, and utilized (preface).

Cognitive structure: The totality of the brain's organization of knowledge; everything an individual knows (or believes) about the world. Comprises *cognitive categories, feature lists,* and *category interrelationships.* Also referred to as *long-term memory* and the *theory of the world in the head* (1).

Comprehension: The interpretation of experience; relating new information to what is already known; asking *cognitive questions* and being able to find answers to them; a state, the absence of confusion (1).

Constraint: The exclusion or reduced probability of certain alternatives; the mechanism of *redundancy* (3).

Context: The setting, physical or linguistic, in which words occur and that places constraints on the range of alternatives that these words might be (2).

Context-dependent language: Spoken or written language coherent within itself and not related to the concurrent physical situation in which it occurs (2).

Conventions: Arbitrary or accidental forms of behavior made meaningful by mutual understanding of and respect for their use and implications (2).

Criterial set: A set of *distinctive features* within a *feature list* that permits an *identification* to be made on minimal information from a given set of alternatives (7).

Criterion level: The amount of information an individual requires to make a particular decision, varying with the perceived uncertainty of the situation and the perceived risk and cost of making a mistake (3).

Decoding to sound: The view that reading is accomplished by transforming print into actual or subvocalized (implicit) speech through the exercise of *spelling-to-sound correspondences.* See also *phonological recoding* (8).

Declarative knowledge: See *propositional knowledge* (1).

Deep structure: The meaningful aspect of language; the interpretation of *surface structure* (2).

Demonstrations: Displays, by people or artifacts, of how something is done (11).

Discourse structure: Conventions concerning the organization of language, for example, turn-taking and interruption in speech, and paragraphing and repetition in texts (2).

Distinctive features: *Significant differences* among visual (or acoustic) patterns, that is differences that make a difference. For reading, any aspect of *visual information* that permits distinctions to be made among alternative letters, words, or meanings (1,3,6). See also *feature lists.*

Distributional redundancy: Reduction of *uncertainty* because alternatives are not equally probable (6,7). May exist in letters or words (and, if an individual's mannerisms are sufficiently well-known, expressions). See also *featural redundancy.*

Efferent reading: Reading done primarily for information; contrasted with *aesthetic reading* (3).

Engagement: The interaction of a brain with a *demonstration;* the act of learning (11).

Ethnographic research: Observation of behavior in natural contexts; nonintrusive research; also termed "naturalistic research"; contrasted with controlled experimentation (12).

Event knowledge: Hypothesized mental representations of patterns of behavior in specific events; clusters of related expectations. See *scheme* (1).

Expectations: See *prediction.*

Featural redundancy: In reading, *redundancy* among the *distinctive features* of print as a consequence of constraints upon letter or word occurrence (6,7).

Feature analysis: A theory of pattern recognition proposing that visual configurations such as digits, letters, or words are identified by the analysis of *distinctive features* and their allocation to *feature lists;* in contrast to *template theory* (6).

Feature list: A cognitive specification or "set of rules" for particular combinations of *distinctive features* that will permit *identification* in reading (6).

Feedback: Information that permits a decision whether an *hypothesis* is right or wrong (appropriate or inappropriate) in *learning* (11).

Fixation: The pause for the selection of *visual information* as the gaze rests at one place in the text between *saccades* (4).

Functional equivalence: Specification of the same *cognitive category* by two or more *feature lists* (7).

Grammar: See *syntax.*

Grapheme: A letter of the alphabet, one of 26 alternatives (8).

Hypothesis: A tentative modification of cognitive structure (*cognitive categories, feature lists,* or *category interrelationships*) that is tested as a basis for *learning* (11).

Identification: In reading, a cognitive decision among letter, word, or meaning alternatives based on the analysis of selected *visual information* in print (6–9).

Immediate meaning identification: The *comprehension* of language without the prior identification of words (9).

Immediate word identification: The *identification* of a word on sight, without *information* from another person and without the prior *identification* of letters or letter combinations within the word (7).

Information: Any property of the physical environment that reduces *uncertainty,* eliminating or reducing the probability of alternatives among which a perceiver must decide (3).

Learning: The modification or elaboration of *cognitive structure,* specifically the establishment of new or revised *cognitive categories, category interrelationships,* or *feature lists* (11).

Letter-sound correspondence: See *spelling-to-sound correspondence.*

Lexical access: Computer-derived metaphor for making sense of words in reading or speech through reference to an internal *lexicon* (2).

Lexicon: A hypothesized mental store of knowledge about words, including their sound, spelling, and meaning. See *lexical access, logogen* (2).

Logogen: A theoretical construct for all the knowledge an individual has about a word; an entry in the internal *lexicon* (2).

Long-term memory: The totality of an individual's knowledge and beliefs about the world, including summaries of past experience in the world and ways of interacting with it (5).

Meaning: A relative term; the interpretation that a reader places upon text (the answer to a *cognitive question*). Alternatively, the interpretation an author or third party expects a reader to place upon text. The consequences of *comprehension* (1).

Meaningful(ness): In reading, a text that is relevant to a reader's purpose, *expectations,* and *understanding.*

Mediated meaning identification: An inferior alternative to *immediate meaning identification*, attempting to derive meaning by the prior identification of words (9).

Mediated word identification: A less efficient alternative to *immediate word identification*, requiring information from letters or letter combinations within the word (8).

Memory: See *sensory store, short-term memory*, and *long-term memory*.

Metacognition: Thought about one's own thinking, understanding, or learning (1).

Metalanguage: Language about language (2).

Metalinguistic awareness: Understanding of metalanguage, notably the way aspects of spoken and written language may be discussed in reading instruction (12).

Noise: A signal that conveys no information (3).

Nonvisual information: Prior knowledge "behind the eyes" that reduces *uncertainty* in advance and permits *identification* decisions with less *visual information* (4).

Orthography: Spelling; the arrangement of letters in words (8).

Perception: *Identification* decisions made by the brain; subjective awareness of these decisions (4).

Phoneme: One of about 40 discriminable classes of *significantly different* speech sounds in English. (Other languages have different sets of roughly the same number of phonemes) (8).

Phonetics: The scientific study of the sound structure of speech; has nothing to do with reading (8). See *phonics*.

Phonics: Reading instruction based on the assumption that reading is decoding to sound and requires learning *spelling-to-sound correspondences* (8). Sometimes mistakenly referred to as *phonetics*.

Phonological recoding: Transforming written words to sound in order to understand their meaning (as opposed to understanding written words directly) (8).

Prediction: The prior elimination of unlikely alternatives; the remaining set of alternatives among which an *identification* decision will be made from (in reading) selected *visual information* in print (1).

Procedural knowledge: Knowledge of integrated sequences of behavior; see also *propositional knowledge, event knowledge* (1).

Propositional knowledge: Knowledge in the form of internalized statements, (such as "facts," proverbs, formulae); also referred to as *declarative knowledge* (as opposed to *procedural knowledge* (1).

Psycholinguistics: An area of common concern in psychology and linguistics studying how individuals learn and use language.

Redundancy: *Information* that is available from more than one source. In reading, may be present in the *visual information* of print, in the *orthography*, the *syntax*, the *meaning*, or in combinations of these sources. Redundancy may be *distributional* or *sequential*. Redundancy must always reflect *nonvisual information;* prior knowledge on the part of the reader permits redundancy to be used (3).

Regression: An eye movement *(saccade)* from right to left along a line or from bottom to top of a page (4).

Saccade: Movement of the eyes as the gaze moves from one *fixation* to another in reading (4).

Scenario: A generalized mental representation of conventional patterns of behavior in specific situations. See also *scheme* (1).

Scheme: A generalized mental representation of complex patterns of behavior or events;

also referred to as *schema*, plural *schemata*. See also *scenario, script, event knowledge* (1).

Script: A generalized mental representation of conventional behavior on specific occasions (1).

Semantics: The meaningful aspect of language; the study of this aspect (2).

Sensitivity: The prior learning state of the brain; readiness for *engagement;* absence of expectation that learning will not occur (11).

Sensory store: In vision, the very brief retention of *visual information* while *identification* decisions are made; also called the *visual image* (5).

Sequential redundancy: Reduction of *uncertainty* attributable to *constraints* on the number or relative probability of likely alternatives in *context* (7,9); may exist among letters or words and as a consequence of a reader's or listener's expectations. See also *featural redundancy.*

Short-term memory: The limited and constantly changing content of what is attended to at any particular moment (5).

Significant difference: A difference in the physical properties of an event that forms the basis of an *identification* decision (6).

Situation-dependent language: Spoken or written language referring to and made meaningful by the concurrent physical situation in which it occurs (2).

Specification: A constantly changing outline in a reader's (or writer's) mind about the structure and content of a text; the basis of *prediction* in reading (6).

Spelling-to-sound correspondence: The co-occurrence of a particular letter or group of letters in a written word and the assumed sound of the same part of the word in speech (8).

Surface structure: The physical properties of language; for reading—*visual information* (2).

Syntax: The manner in which words are organized in meaningful language; also referred to as "grammar" (2).

Tachistoscope: A projector or other viewing device with a shutter or timer controlling the presentation of *visual information* for brief periods of time (4).

Template theory: A theory of pattern recognition that visual configurations such as digits, letters, or words can be identified by comparison with prestored representations or templates in the brain; in contrast to *featural analysis* (6).

Text: A meaningful (or potentially meaningful) instance of written language; can range from a word to an entire book.

Theory: In science, a summary of a scientist's past experience, the basis for interpreting new experience and for predicting future events (1).

Theory of the world in the head: The brain's *theory;* also known as *cognitive structure* and *long-term memory* (1).

Transformational grammar: Part of the theory of the world in the head of every language user; the bridge between *deep structure* and *surface structure* (2).

Uncertainty: The amount of *information* required to make an *identification* decision, determined by the number of alternative decisions that could be made, the perceived probability of each alternative, and the individual's *criterion level* for making the decision (3).

Understanding: See *comprehension.*

Visual image: See *sensory store.*

Visual information: In reading, *information* that is available to the brain through the eyes from the *surface structure* of print, for example, from the inkmarks on a page (4).

REFERENCES

Aaronson, Doris, and Steven Ferres, Reading strategies for children and adults: Some empirical evidence, *Journal of Verbal Learning and Verbal Behavior*, 1984a, *23*, 189–220.

Aaronson, Doris, and Steven Ferres, The word-by-word reading paradigm: An experimental and theoretical approach, in D. E. Kieras, and M. A. Just (eds.), *New Methods in Reading Comprehension Research* (Hillsdale, NJ: Erlbaum Associates, 1984b).

Allingston, R., Teacher interruption behavior during primary-grade oral reading. *Journal of Educational Psychology*, 1980, *72*, 3, 371–377.

Alvermann, Donna E., Lynn C. Smith, and John E. Readance, Prior knowledge activation and the comprehension of compatible and incompatible text, *Reading Research Quarterly*, 1985, *20*, 4, 420–436.

Anderson, I. H., and W. F. Dearborn, *The Psychology of Teaching Reading* (New York: Ronald, 1952).

Anderson, John R., *Cognitive Psychology and Its Implications* (San Francisco: Freeman, 1980).

Anderson, John R., and Gordon H. Bower, *Human Associative Memory* (Washington, DC: Winston, 1973).

Anderson, Jonathan, The computer as tutor, tutee, tool in reading and language. *Reading*, 1984, *18*, 2, 67–78.

Anderson, Richard C., Elfrieda H. Hiebert, Judith A. Scott, and Ian A. G. Wilkinson, *Becoming a Nation of Readers: The Report of the Commission on Reading* (Washington, DC: National Academy of Education, 1985).

314

Anderson, Richard C., Jana M. Mason, and Larry Shirey, The reading group: An experimental investigation of a labyrinth. *Reading Research Quarterly*, 1984, *20*, 1, 6–38.

Anderson, Richard C., and Andrew Ortony, On putting apples into bottles: A problem in polysemy, *Cognitive Psychology*, 1975, *7*, 167–180.

Anderson, Richard C., and Pearson, P. David, A schema-theoretic view of basic processes in reading comprehension, in P. David Pearson (ed.), *Handbook of Reading Research* (New York: Longman, 1984).

Anderson, Richard C., and J. W. Pichert, Recall of previously unrecallable information following a shift in perspective, *Journal of Verbal Learning and Verbal Behavior*, 1978, *17*, 1–12.

Anderson, Richard C., R. E. Reynolds, D. L. Schallert, and T. E. Goetz, Frameworks for understanding discourse, *American Educational Research Journal*, 1977, *14*, 367–381.

Anglin, Jeremy, Acquiring linguistic skills: A study of sentence construction in preschool children, in D. R. Olson, (ed.), *The Social Foundations of Language* (New York: Norton, 1980).

Applebee, Arthur N., A sense of story, *Theory Into Practice*, 1977, *16*, 342–347.

Armbruster, Bonnie B., and T. H. Anderson, Content area textbooks, in Richard C. Anderson, Jean Osborn and Robert J. Tierney (eds.), *Learning to Read in American Schools: Basal Readers and Content Texts* (Hillsdale, NJ: Lawrence Erlbaum Associates, 1984).

Atkinson, Richard C., Teaching children to read using a computer, *American Psychologist*, 1974, *29*, 169–178.

Attneave, Fred, *Applications of Information Theory to Psychology* (New York: Holt, Rinehart and Winston, 1959).

Attneave, Fred, How do you know?, *American Psychologist*, 1974, *29*, 493–499.

Atwell, Nancie, *In the Middle: Writing, Reading and Learning With Adolescents* (Upper Montclair, NJ: Boynton/Cook, 1987).

August, Diane L., John H. Flavell, and Renee Clift, Comparison of comprehension monitoring of skilled and less skilled readers. *Reading Research Quarterly*, 1984, *20*, 1, 39–53.

Averbach, E., and A. S. Coriell, Short-term memory in vision, *Bell Systems Technical Journal*, 1961, *40*, 309–328.

Baars, Bernard J., *The Cognitive Revolution in Psychology* (New York: Guilford, 1986).

Baddeley, A. D., M. Eldridge, and V. J. Lewis, The role of subvocalisation in reading, *Quarterly Journal of Experimental Psychology*, 1981, *33A*, 439–454.

Baddeley, A. D., and K. Patterson, The relation between long-term and short-term memory, *British Medical Bulletin*, 1971, *27*, 3, 237–242.

Baddeley, Alan, Robert Logie, Ian Nimmo-Smith, and Neil Brereton, Components of fluent reading, *Journal of Memory and Language*, 1985, *24*, 1, 119–131.

Baer, Donald M., and John C. Wright, Developmental psychology, in Mark A. Rosenzweig and Lyman W. Porter (eds.), *Annual Review of Psychology*, 1975, *25*, 1–82.

Bain, Bruce (ed.), *The Sociogenesis of Language and Human Conduct* (New York: Plenum, 1983).

Baldwin, R. Scott, and James M. Coady, Psycholinguistic approaches to a theory of punctuation, *Journal of Reading Behavior*, 1978, *10*, 363–375.

Baldwin, R. Scott, Ziva Peleg-Bruckner, and Ann H. McClintock, Effects of topic interest and prior knowledge on reading comprehension, *Reading Research Quarterly*, 1985, *20*, 4, 497–504.

Barclay, J. R., The role of comprehension in remembering sentences, *Cognitive Psychology*, 1973, *4*, 229–252.

Barlow, John A., Mass line leadership and thought reform in China, *American Psychologist*, 1981, *36*, 3, 300–309.

Baron, Jonathan, Orthographic and word-specific mechanisms in children's reading of words, *Child Development*, 1979, *50*, 60–72.

Baron, Jonathan, and C. Strawson, Use of orthographic and word-specific knowledge in reading words aloud, *Journal of Experimental Psychology: Human Perception and Performance*, 1976, *2*, 386–393.

Barr, Rebecca C., The influence of instructional conditions on word recognition errors, *Reading Research Quarterly*, 1972, *7*, 509–529.

Barr, Rebecca C., The effect of instruction on pupil reading strategies, *Reading Research Quarterly*, 1974, *10*, 555–582.

Barr, Rebecca, Commentary: Studying classroom reading instruction, *Reading Research Quarterly*, 1986, *21*, 3, 231–236.

Bartlett, Frederick C., *Remembering: A Study in Experimental and Social Psychology* (London: Cambridge University Press, 1932).

Bates, Elizabeth, *Language and Context* (New York: Academic Press, 1976).

Bates, Elizabeth, *The Emergence of Symbols: Cognition and Communication in Infancy* (New York: Academic Press, 1979).

Baumann, James F., and Karen Wilson Schneider, *Apprehension span of adult fluent readers: A clarification of J. M. Cattell's classic research on letter and word perception*, Madison, Wisconsin Research and Development Center for Individualized Schooling Teaching Report #520, 1979.

Beck, Isabel L., Margaret G. McKeown, Richard C. Omanson, and Martha T. Pople, Improving the comprehensibility of stories: The effects of revisions that improve coherence, *Reading Research Quarterly*, 1984, *19*, 3, 263–277.

Becker, Curtis A., The development of semantic context effects: Two processes or two strategies?, *Reading Research Quarterly*, 1982, *17*, 4, 482–502.

Beebe, Mona J., The effect of different types of substitution miscues on reading, *Reading Research Quarterly*, 1980, *15*, 3, 324–336.

Beers, Terry, Commentary: Schema-theoretic models of reading: Humanizing the machine, *Reading Research Quarterly*, 1987, *22*, 3, 369–377.

Benton, Arthur L., The neuropsychology of facial recognition, *American Psychologist*, 1980, *35*, 2, 176–186.

Benton, Michael, Children's responses to stories, *Children's Literature in Education*, 1979, *10*, 2, 68–85.

Berdiansky, Betty, Bruce Cronnell, and John A. Koehler, *Spelling-Sound Relations and Primary Form-Class Descriptions for Speech-Comprehension Vocabularies of 6-9 Year-Olds*, Southwest Regional Laboratory for Educational Research and Development, Technical Report No. 15, 1969.

Berninger, Virginia Wise, and Sarah O. Colwell, Relationships between neurodevelopmental and educational findings in children aged 6 to 12 years, *Pediatrics*, 1985, *75*, 697–702.

Besner, D., E. Davelaar, D. Alcott, and P. Parry, Wholistic reading of alphabetic print: Evidence from the FDM and the FBI, in Henderson, Leslie (ed.), *Orthographies and Reading: Perspectives from Cognitive Psychology, Neuropsychology, and Linguistics* (Hillsdale, NJ: Lawrence Erlbaum Associates, 1984).

Beveridge, Michael (ed.), *Children Thinking Through Language*, (London: Arnold, 1982).

Bissex, Glenda L., *Gnys at Wrk: A Child Learns to Write and Read* (Cambridge, MA: Harvard University Press, 1980).

Black, Alison, Paul Freeman, and Philip N. Johnson-Laird, Plausibility and the comprehension of text, *British Journal of Psychology*, 1986, *77*, 1, 51–62.

Bloom, Lois, *Language Development: Form and Function in Emerging Grammars* (Cambridge, MA: MIT Press, 1970).

Bloom, Lois, *One Word at a Time: The Use of Single Word Utterances Before Syntax* (The Hague: Mouton, 1973).

Bloom, Lois, Lois Hood, and Patsy Lightbown, Imitation in language development: If, when, and why, *Cognitive Psychology*, 1974, *6*, 380–420.

Bloom, Lois, Lorraine Rocissano, and Lois Hood, Adult-child discourse: Developmental interaction between information processing and linguistic knowledge, *Cognitive Psychology*, 1976, *8*, 521–552.

Blough, Donald S., Pigeon perception of letters of the alphabet, *Science*, 1982, *218*, 397–398.

Boulding, Kenneth E., Human knowledge as a special system, *Behavioral Science*, 1981, *26*, 93–102.

Bower, Gordon H., Experiments on story understanding and recall, *Quarterly Journal of Experimental Psychology*, 1976, *28*, 511–534.

Bower, Gordon H., John B. Black, and Terrence J. Turner, Scripts in memory for text, *Cognitive Psychology*, 1979, *11*, 177–220.

Bower, Thomas G. R., The object in the world of the infant, *Scientific American*, 1971, *225*, 30–47.

Bower, Thomas G. R., *Development in Infancy* (San Francisco: Freeman, 1974).

Brand, H., Classification without identification in visual search, *Quarterly Journal of Experimental Psychology*, 1971, *23*, 178–186.

Bransford, John D., J. R. Barclay, and Jeffrey J. Franks, Sentence meaning: A constructivist vs. interpretive approach, *Cognitive Psychology*, 1972, *3*, 193–209.

Bransford, John D., and Jeffrey J. Franks, The abstraction of linguistic ideas, *Cognitive Psychology*, 1971, *2*, 331, 350.

Bransford, John D., and Barry S. Stein, *The Ideal Problem Solver: A Guide for Improving Thinking, Learning and Creativity*, (New York: Freeman, 1984).

Bransford, John D., Barry S. Stein, and Nancy J. Vye, Helping students learn how to learn from written texts, in M. H. Singer (ed.), *Competent Reader, Disabled Reader: Research and Application* (Hillsdale, NJ: Lawrence Erlbaum Associates, 1982).

Bridges, Allayne, Chris Sinha, and Valerie Walkerdine, The development of comprehension, in Gordon Wells, *Learning Through Interaction: The Study of Language Development*, (Cambridge: Cambridge University Press, 1981).

Britton, Bruce K., and John B. Black (eds.), *Understanding Expository Text*, (Hillsdale, NJ: Lawrence Erlbaum Associates, 1985).

Broadbent, Donald E., The word-frequency effect and response bias, *Psychological Review*, 1967, *74*, 1–15.

Broadbent, Donald E., and Margaret H. P. Broadbent, Some further data concerning the word frequency effect, *Journal of Experimental Psychology (General)*, 1975, *104*, 297–308.

Broerse, A. C., and E. J. Zwaan, The information value of initial letters in the identification of words, *Journal of Verbal Learning and Verbal Behavior*, 1966, *5*, 441–446.

Bronowski, Jacob, *The Origins of Knowledge and Imagination* (Princeton, NJ: Yale University Press, 1978).

Brooks, Lee, Spatial and verbal components of the act of recall, *Canadian Journal of Psychology*, 1968, *22*, 349–368.

Brown, Ann L., Metacognitive development and reading, in Rand C. Spiro, Bertram C. Bruce, and William F. Brewer, *Theoretical Issues in Reading Comprehension: Perspectives from Cognitive Psychology, Linguistics, Artificial Intelligence, and Education* (Hillsdale, NJ: Lawrence Erlbaum Associates, 1980).

Brown, Ann L., Learning how to learn from reading, in Langer, Judith A. and M. Trika Smith-Burke (eds.), *Reader Meets Author/Bridging the Gap* (Newark, DE: International Reading Association, 1982).

Brown, Ann L., and Roberta A. Ferrara, Diagnosing zones of proximal development, in J. S. Wertsch (ed.), *Culture, Communication and Development* (New York: Cambridge University Press, 1985).

Brown, H. D., Categories of spelling difficulty in speakers of English as a first and second language, *Journal of Verbal Learning and Verbal Behavior*, 1970, *9*, 232–236.

Brown, Roger, *A First Language: The Early Stages* (Cambridge, MA: Harvard University Press, 1973).

Brown, Roger and David McNeill, The "tip of the tongue" phenomenon, *Journal of Verbal Learning and Verbal Behavior*, 1966, *5*, 4, 325–337.

Bruner, Jerome S., On perceptual readiness, *Psychological Review*, 1957, *64*, 123–152.

Bruner, Jerome S., *Beyond the Information Given* (collected papers) (New York: Norton, 1973).

Bruner, Jerome S., The ontogenesis of speech acts, *Journal of Child Language*, 1975, *2*, 1–19.

Bruner, Jerome S., Acquiring the uses of language, *Canadian Journal of Psychology*, 1978, *32*, 204–218.

Bruner, Jerome S., *Actual Minds, Possible Worlds* (Cambridge, MA: Harvard University Press, 1986).

Bruner, Jerome S., and D. O'Dowd, A note on the informativeness of parts of words, *Language and Speech*, 1958, *1*, 98–101.

Butler, Christopher S., *Systemic Linguistics* (London: Batsford, 1985).

Calfee, Robert C., *Human Experimental Psychology* (New York: Holt, Rinehart and Winston, 1975).

Calfee, Robert, The mind of the dyslexic. In Elinor Linn Hartwig (ed.), *Annals of Dyslexia, Vol. 33* (Baltimore, MD: Orton Dyslexia Society, 1983).

Calfee, Robert C., Memory and cognitive skills in reading acquisition, in Drake D. Duane and Margaret B. Rawson (eds.), *Reading, Perception and Language* (Baltimore: York Press, 1974).

Calfee, Robert C., Richard Arnold, and Priscilla Drum, Review of *The Psychology of Reading* (by Eleanor Gibson and Harry Levin), in *Proceedings of the National Academy of Education*, 1976, *3*, 1–80.

Calkins, Lucy, When children want to punctuate: Basic skills belong in context. *Language Arts*, 1980, *57*, 567–573.

Caplan, David (ed.), *Biological Studies of Mental Processes* (Cambridge, MA: MIT Press, 1980).

Carey, Susan, The child as word learner, in M. Halle, J. Breslin and George A. Miller (eds.), *Linguistic Theory and Psychological Reality* (Cambridge, MA: MIT Press, 1978).

Carpenter, Patricia M., and Meredyth Daneman, Lexical retrieval and error recovery in reading: A model based on eye fixations, *Journal of Verbal Learning and Verbal Behavior*, 1981, *20*, 137–160.

Carpenter, Patricia A., and Marcel A. Just, Sentence comprehension: A psycholinguistic processing model of verification, *Psychological Review*, 1975, *82*, 45–73.

Carpenter, Patricia A., and Marcel A. Just, Integrative processes in comprehension, in David LaBerge and S. Jay Samuels (eds.), *Basic Processes in Reading: Perception and Comprehension* (Hillsdale, NJ: Lawrence Erlbaum Associates, 1977).

Carroll, John B., and Jeanne S. Chall (eds.), *Toward a Literate Society* (New York: McGraw-Hill, 1975).

Carroll, John B., Peter Davies, and Barry Richman, *The American Heritage Word Frequency Book* (Boston: Houghton Mifflin, 1971).

Carroll, John B., and R. O. Freedle (eds.), *Language Comprehension and the Acquisition of Knowledge* (Washington, DC: Winston, 1972).

Carver, Ron, How good are some of the world's best readers? *Reading Research Quarterly*, 1985, *20*, 4, 389–419.

Cattell, James McKeen, Ueber die Zeit der Erkennung und Benennung von Schriftzeichen, Bildern und Farben, *Philosophische Studien*, 1885, *2*, 635–650; translated and reprinted in A. T. Poffenberger, (ed.), *James McKeen Cattell, Man of Science, 1860-1944* (Vol. 1) (Lancaster, PA: Science Press, 1947).

Cazden, Courtney B., *Child Language and Education* (New York: Holt, Rinehart and Winston, 1972).

Cermak, Laird S., and Fergus I. M. Craik, (eds.), *Levels of Processing in Human Memory* (Hillsdale, NJ: Lawrence Erlbaum Associates, 1979).

Chafe, Wallace L., *Meaning and the Structure of Language* (Chicago: University of Chicago Press, 1970).

Chall, Jeanne S., *Learning to Read: The Great Debate* (New York: McGraw-Hill, 1967).

Cherry, Colin, *On Human Communication* (3rd ed.). (Cambridge, MA: MIT Press, 1978).

Chomsky, Carol, Reading, writing and phonology, *Harvard Educational Review*, 1970, *40*, 2, 287–309.

Chomsky, Carol, Write first, read later, *Childhood Education*, 1971, *47*, 6, 296–299.

Chomsky, Carol, Approaching spelling through invented spelling, in Lauren B. Resnick and Phyllis A. Weaver (eds.), *Theory and Practice of Early Reading* (Hillsdale, NJ: Lawrence Erlbaum Associates, 1979).

Chomsky, Noam, *Syntactic Structures* (The Hague: Mouton, 1957).

Chomsky, Noam, Review of *Verbal Learning* (by B. F. Skinner), *Language*, 1959, *35*, 26–58.

Chomsky, Noam, *Aspects of the Theory of Syntax* (Cambridge, MA: MIT Press, 1965).

Chomsky, Noam, *Language and Mind* (New York: Harcourt, 1972).

Chomsky, Noam, *Reflections on Language* (New York: Pantheon, 1975).

Chomsky, Noam, and Morris Halle, *Sound Pattern of English* (New York: Harper & Row, 1968).

Chukovsky, Kornei (tr. Miriam Morton), *From Two to Five* (Berkeley: University of California Press, 1968).

Clark, Eve V., and Barbara Frant Hecht, Comprehension, production, and language acqusition. *Annual Review of Psychology*, 1983, *34*, 325–349.

Clark, Herbert H., and Eve V. Clark, *Psychology and Language* (New York: Harcourt Brace Jovanovich, 1976).

Clark, Margaret M., *Young Fluent Readers* (London: Heinemann Educational Books, 1976).

Clay, Marie M., Reading errors and self-correction behavior, *British Journal of Educational Psychology*, 1969, *39*, 1, 49–56.

Clay, Marie M., Theoretical research and instructional change: A case study, in Lauren B. Resnick, and Phyllis A. Weaver, (eds.), *Theory and Practice of Early Reading* (Hillsdale, NJ: Lawrence Erlbaum Associates, 1979).

Clay, Marie M., and Robert H. Imlach, Juncture, pitch and stress and reading behavior variables, *Journal of Verbal Learning and Verbal Behavior*, 1971, *10*, 133–139.

Cofer, Charles N., Constructive processes in memory, *American Scientist*, 1973, *61*, 5, 537–543.

Cohen, Gillian, Search times for combinations of visual, phonemic and semantic targets in reading prose, *Perception and Psychophysics*, 1970, *8*, 5B, 370–372.

Collins, W. Andrew (ed.), *Children's Language and Communication: The Minnesota Symposia on Child Psychology* (Vol. 12) (Hillsdale, NJ: Lawrence Erlbaum Associates, 1979).

Cosky, Michael J., The role of letter recognition in word recognition, *Memory and Cognition*, 1976, *4*, 2, 207–214.

Craik, Fergus I. M., and Robert S. Lockhart, Levels of processing: A framework for memory research, *Journal of Verbal Learning and Verbal Behavior*, 1972, *11*, 671–684.

Crismore, Avon (ed.), *Landscapes: A State-of-the-Art Assessment of Reading Comprehension Research, 1974-1984* (Bloomington, IN: Indiana University Language Education Dept., 1985).

Crowder, Robert G., *Principles of Learning and Memory* (Hillsdale, NJ: Lawrence Erlbaum Associates, 1976).

Culler, Jonathan, *The Pursuit of Signs: Semiotics, Literature, Deconstruction* (Ithaca, NY: Cornell University Press, 1981).

Dale, Philip S., *Language Development: Structure and Function* (New York: Holt, Rinehart and Winston, 1976).

Davies, W. J. Frank, *Teaching Reading in Early England* (London: Pitman, 1973).

de Beaugrande, Robert, *Text, Discourse, and Process. Toward a Multidisciplinary Science of Texts. Advances in Discourse Processes Vol. 4* (Norwood, NJ: Ablex, 1980).

de Beaugrande, Robert, Design criteria for process models of reading, *Reading Research Quarterly*, 1981, *16*, 2, 261–315.

de Beaugrande, Robert, and P. Dressler, *Introduction to Text Linguistics* (New York: Longman, 1981).

Deely, John, *Introducing Semiotic* (Bloomington: Indiana University Press, 1982).

DeFord, Diane E., Literacy: Reading, writing and other essentials, *Language Arts*, 1981, *58*, 5, 652–658.

Dember, William N., Motivation and the cognitive revolution, *American Psychologist*, 1974, *29*, 3, 161–168.

den Buurman, Rudy, Theo Roersema, and Jack F. Gerrison, Eye movements and the perceptual span in reading, *Reading Research Quarterly*, 1981, *16*, 2, 227–235.

Derry, Sharon J., and Debra A. Murphy, Designing systems that train learning ability: From theory to practice. *Review of Educational Research*, 1986, *56*, 1, 1–39.

Dishner, Ernest K., Thomas W. Bean, and John E. Readence (eds.), *Reading in the Content Areas: Improving Classroom Instruction* (Dubuque, IA: Kendall/Hunt, 1981).

Doehring, Donald G., Acquisition of rapid reading responses, *Monographs of the Society for Research in Child Development*, 1976, *41*, 2, no. 165.

Doehring, Donald, and Mark Aulls, Implications of Neisser's cognitive theory for models of reading acquisition, *Reading/Canada/Lecture*, 1981, *1*, 1, 46–52.

Doggett, David, and Larry G. Richards, A reexamination of the effect of word length on recognition thresholds, *American Journal of Psychology*, 1975, *88*, 583–594.

Donaldson, Margaret, *Children's Minds* (Glasgow: Fontana/Collins, 1978).

Donaldson, Margaret, and Jessie Reid, Language skills and reading: A developmental perspective, in A. Hendry (ed.), *Teaching Reading: The Key Issues* (London: Heinemann Educational Books, 1982).

Dorman, Casey, Defining and diagnosing dyslexia: Are we putting the cart before the horse? *Reading Research Quarterly*, 1985, *20*, 4, 505–508.

Douglas, Mary (ed.), *Rules and Meanings: The Anthropology of Everyday Knowledge* (Harmondsworth: Penguin, 1968).

Downing, John, Children's concepts of language in learning to read, *Educational Research*, 1970, *12*, 106–112.

Downing, John (ed.), *Comparative Reading* (New York: Macmillan, 1973).

Downing, John, How society creates reading disability, *Elementary School Journal*, 1977, *77*, 274–279.

Downing, John, *Reading and Reasoning* (New York: Springer-Verlag, 1979).

Downing, John, Task-awareness in the development of reading skills, in John Downing and Renate Valtin (eds.), *Language Awareness and Learning to Read* (New York: Springer-Verlag, 1985).

Downing, John, and Che Kan Leong, *Psychology of Reading* (New York: Macmillan, 1982).

Downing, John, and Peter Oliver, The child's conception of "a word," *Reading Research Quarterly*, 1973–74, *4*, 9/4, 568–582.

Downing, John, Lloyd Ollila, and Peter Oliver, Cultural differences in children's concepts of reading and writing, *British Journal of Educational Psychology*, 175, *45*, 312–316.

Downing, John, and Renate Valtin (eds.), *Language Awareness and Learning to Read* (New York: Springer-Verlag, 1985).

Dreyfus, Hubert L., and Stuart E. Dreyfus, *Mind Over Machine* (New York: The Free Press, 1986).

Dulany, Don E., On the support of cognitive theory in oppostion to behavior theory: A methodological problem, in Walter B. Weiner and David S. Palermo (eds.), *Cognition and the Symbolic Process* (Hillsdale, NJ: Lawrence Erlbaum Associates, 1974).

Dunn-Rankin, Peter, The similarity of lower case letters of the English alphabet, *Journal of Verbal Learning and Verbal Behavior*, 1968, *7*, 990–995.

Dunn-Rankin, Peter, Perceptual characteristics of words, in R. Groner, G. W. McConkie, and C. Menz (eds.), *Eye Movements and Human Information Processing* (North-Holland: Elsevier Science, 1985).

Durkin, Dolores, *Children Who Read Early* (New York: Teachers College Press, 1966).

Durkin, Dolores, What is the value of the new interest in reading comprehension?, *Language Arts*, 1981, *58*, 1, 23–43.

Durkin, Dolores, Poor black children who are successful readers: An investigation, *Urban Education*, 1984, *19*, 53–76.

Eckhoff, Barbara, How reading affects children's writing, *Language Arts*, 1983, *60*, 5, 607–616.

Eco, Umberto, *Semiotics and the Philosophy of Language* (Bloomington, IN: Indiana University Press, 1984).

Edfeldt, A. W., *Silent Speech and Silent Reading* (Chicago: University of Chicago Press, 1960).

Ehri, Linnea C., How orthography alters spoken language competencies in children learning to read and spell, in J. Downing, and R. Valtin (eds.), *Language Awareness and Learning to Read* (New York: Springer-Verlag, 1985).

Ehri, Linnea C., and Lee S. Wilce, Movement into reading: Is the first stage of printed word learning visual or phonetic?, *Reading Research Quarterly*, 1985, *20*, 2, 163–179.

Eisner, Elliot, *Cognition and Curriculum: A Basis for Deciding What to Teach* (New York: Longman, 1982).

Ellis, Andrew W., *Reading, Writing and Dyslexia: A Cognitive Analysis* (London: Lawrence Erlbaum Associates, 1984).

Erdmann, B., and R. Dodge, *Psychologische Untersuchungen ueber das Lesen auf Experimenteller Grundlage* (Halle: Niemeyer, 1898).

Ericsson, K. Anders, William G. Chase, and Steve Falcon, Acquisition of a memory skill, *Science*, 1980, *208*, 1181–1182.

Ewoldt, Carolyn., A psycholinguistic description of selected deaf children reading in sign language, *Reading Research Quarterly*, 1981, *17*, 1, 58–89.

Eysenck, Michael W. *A Handbook of Cognitive Psychology* (Hillsdale, NJ: Lawrence Erlbaum Associates, 1984).

Fantz, Robert L., Visual experience in infants: Decreased attention to familiar patterns relative to novel ones, *Science*, 1964, *146*, 668–670.

Fantz, Robert L., Pattern discrimination and selective attention, in A. H. Kidd, and Jeanne L. Rivoire (eds.), *Perceptual Development in Children* (New York: International Universities Press, 1966).

Ferreiro, Emilia, What is written in a written sentence?: A developmental answer, *Journal of Education*, 1978, *160*, 4, 25–39.

Ferreiro, Emilia, Literacy development: A psychogenetic perspective, in D. R. Olson, N. Torrance, and A. Hildyard (eds.), *Literacy, Language and Learning: The Nature and Consequences of Reading and Writing* (Cambridge, MA: Cambridge University Press, 1985).

Ferreiro, Emilia, and Ana Teberosky, *Literacy Before Schooling* (Exeter, NH: Heinemann Educational Books, 1982).

Feuerstein, Reuven, Mogens Jensen, Mildred B. Hoffman, and Yaacov Rand, Instrumental enrichment: An intervention program for structural cognitive modifiability, in Judith W. Segal, Susan F. Chipman, and R. Glaser (eds.), *Thinking and Learning Skills, Vol. 1: Relating Instruction to Research* (Hillsdale, NJ: Lawrence Erlbaum Associates, 1985).

Fillion, Bryant, Frank Smith, and Merrill Swain, Language "basics" for language teachers: Towards a set of universal considerations, *Language Arts*, 1976, *53*, 7, 740–745.

Fillmore, Charles J., The case for case, in Emmon Bach and Robert J. Harms (eds.), *Universals in Linguistic Theory* (New York: Holt, Rinehart and Winston, 1968).

Fillmore, Charles J., and D. Terrance Langedoen (eds.), *Studies in Linguistic Semantics* (New York: Holt, Rinehart and Winston, 1971).

Flavell, John H., Metacognition and cognitive monitoring, *American Psychologist*, 1979, *34*, 10, 906–911.

Flavell, John H., James Ramsey Speer, Frances L. Green, and Diane L. August, The development of comprehension monitoring and knowledge about communication, *Monographs of the Society for Research in Child Development*, 1981, *46*, 5, 192.

Flood, James, Introduction to Understanding Reading Comprehension, in J. Flood (ed.), *Understanding Reading Comprehension* (Newark, DE: International Reading Association, 1984).

Fodor, Janet Dean, *Semantics* (New York: Crowell, 1977).

Fodor, Jerry A., Tom Swift and his procedural grandmother, *Cognition*, 1978, *6*, 229–247.

Fodor, Jerry A., *The Language of Thought* (Cambridge, MA: Harvard University Press, 1979).

Fodor, Jerry A., M. F. Garrett, E. Walker, and C. H. Parkes, Against definitions, *Cognition*, 1980, *8*, 263–367.

Forester, Anne D., What teachers can learn from 'natural readers', *Reading Teacher*, 1977, *31*, 160–166.

Forrest-Pressley, Donna-Lynn, and T. Gary Waller, *Cognition, Metacognition and Reading* (New York: Springer-Verlag, 1984).

Forster, Kenneth I., Visual perception of rapidly presented word sequences of varying complexity, *Perception and Psychophysics*, 1970, *8*, 215–221.

Fraisse, Paul, Perceptual processing of words and drawings, in Victor Sarris and Allen Parducci (eds.), *Perspectives in Psychological Experimentation: Toward the Year 2000* (Hillsdale, NJ: Lawrence Erlbaum Associates, 1984).

Fredericksen, C. H., Representing logical and semantic structure of knowledge acquired from discourse, *Cognitive Psychology*, 1975, *7*, 371–458.

Freebody, Peter, and R. C. Anderson, Effects of vocabulary difficulty, text cohesion, and schema availability on reading comprehension, *Reading Research Quarterly*, 1983, *18*, 3, 277–294.

Freire, Paulo, *Pedagogy of the Oppressed* (New York: Herder and Herder, 1972).

Friedman, Sarah L., Kenneth A. Klivington, and Rita W. Peterson (eds.), *The Brain, Cognition and Education* (Orlando, FL: Academic Press, 1986).

Friendly, Michael L., In search of the M-gram: The structure of organization in free recall, *Cognitive Psychology*, 1977, *9*, 188–249.

Fries, Charles C., *Teaching and Learning English as a Foreign Language* (Ann Arbor: University of Michigan Press, 1945).

Fromkin, Victoria, and Robert Rodman, *An Introduction to Language* (New York: Holt, Rinehart and Winston, 1983).

Furness, David W., and Michael F. Graves, Effects of stressing oral reading accuracy on comprehension, *Reading Psychology*, 1980, *2*, 1, 8–14.

Gardner, Howard, *Frames of Mind* (New York: Basic Books, 1983).

Gardner, Howard, *The Mind's New Science* (New York: Basic Books, 1987).

Garner, Wendell R., *Uncertainty and Structure as Psychological Concepts* (New York: Wiley, 1962).

Garner, Wendell R., To perceive is to know, *American Psychologist*, 1966, *21*, 1, 11–19.

Garner, Wendell R., Good patterns have few alternatives, *American Scientist*, 1970, *58*, 34–42.

Garner, Wendell R., *The Processing of Information and Structure* (Hillsdale, NJ: Lawrence Erlbaum Associates, 1974).

Gazzaniga, M. S., *The Bisected Brain* (New York: Appleton, 1970).

Gelb, J., *A Study of Writing* (Chicago: University of Chicago Press, 1963).

Gellatly, Angus (ed.), *The Skillful Mind* (Milton Keynes, England: Open University, 1986).

Gelman, Rochel, Preschool thought, *American Psychologist*, 1979, *34*, 10, 900–905.

Geyer, John J., Perceptual systems in reading: The prediction of a temporal eye-voice span constant, in H. K. Smith (ed.), *Perception and Reading* (Newark, DE: International Reading Association, 1968).

Gibbs, Raymond W. Jr., Literal meaning and psychological theory, *Cognitive Science*, 1984, *8*, 275–304.

Gibson, Eleanor J., Learning to read, *Science*, 1965, *148*, 3673, 1066–1072.

Gibson, Eleanor J., and Harry Levin, *The Psychology of Reading* (Cambridge, MA: MIT Press, 1975).

Gilhooly, K. J., *Thinking: Directed, Undirected and Creative* (London: Academic Press, 1982).

Gillhooly, W. B., The influence of writing system characteristics on learning to read, *Reading Research Quarterly*, 1973, *8*, 2, 167–199.

Glaser, Robert, Education and thinking: The role of knowledge, *American Psychologist*, 1984, *39*, 2, 93–104.

Gleason, Jean Berko (ed.), *The Development of Language* (Colombus, OH: Merrill, 1985).

Gleitman, Lila R., and Paul Rozin, Teaching reading by use of a syllabary, *Reading Research Quarterly*, 1973 (a), *8*, 4, 447–483.

Gleitman, Lila R., and Paul Rozin, Phoenician go home? (A response to Goodman), *Reading Research Quarterly*, 1973 (b), *8*, 4, 494–501.

Glenn, Hugh W., The myth of the label "learning disabled child," *Elementary School Journal*, 1975, *75*, 6, 357–361.

Glucksberg, S., and J. H. Danks, *Experimental Psycholinguistics: An Introduction* (Hillsdale, NJ: Lawrence Erlbaum Associates, 1975).

Glusko, Robert J., The organization and activation of orthographic knowledge in reading aloud, *Journal of Experimental Psychology (Human Perception and Performance)*, 1979, *5*, 674–691.

Glynn, Shawn M., and Frances J. DiVesta, Control of prose processing via instructional and typographical cues, *Journal of Educational Psychology*, 1979, *71*, 5, 595–603.

Goelman, Hillel, Antoinette Oberg, and Frank Smith (eds.), *Awakening to Literacy* (Portsmouth, NH: Heinemann Educational Books, 1984).

Golden, Joanne M. and John T. Guthrie, Convergence and divergence in reader response to literature, *Reading Research Quarterly*, 1986, *21*, 4, 408–421.

Golden, Richard M., A developmental neural model of visual word perception, *Cognitive Science*, 1986, *10*, 3, 241–276.

Goldstein, Ira, and Seymour Papert, Artificial intelligence, language and the study of knowledge, *Cognitive Science*, 1977, *1*, 84–123.

Golinkoff, Roberta Michnick, A comparison of reading comprehension processes in good and poor readers, *Reading Research Quarterly*, 1975–76, *11*, 623–659.

Golinkoff, Roberta Michnick (ed.), *The Transition from Prelinguistic to Linguistic Communication* (Hillsdale, NJ: Lawrence Erlbaum Associates, 1983).

Goodman, Kenneth S., A linguistic study of cues and miscues in reading, *Elementary English*, 1965, *42*, 639–643.

Goodman, Kenneth S., Reading: A psycholinguistic guessing game, *Journal of the Reading Specialist*, 1967, *6*, 126–135.

Goodman, Kenneth S., Analysis of oral reading miscues: Applied psycholinguistics, *Reading Research Quarterly*, 1969, *5*, 1, 9–30.

Goodman, Kenneth S., Dialect rejection and reading: A response, *Reading Research Quarterly*, 1970, *5*, 4, 600–603.

Goodman, Kenneth S., The 13th easy way to make learning to read difficult, *Reading Research Quarterly*, 1973, *8*, 4, 484–493.

Goodman, Kenneth S., The know-more and the know-nothing movements in reading: A personal response, *Language Arts*, 1979, *56*, 6, 657–663.

Goodman, Kenneth S., Letter to the editors, *Reading Research Quarterly*, 1981, *16*, 3, 477–478.

Goodman, Kenneth S., *Language and Literacy: The Selected Writings of Kenneth S. Goodman* (Frederick Gollasch, ed.), *Vol. 1: Process, Theory, Research. Vol. 2: Reading, Language and the Classroom Teacher* (Boston: Routledge and Kegan Paul, 1982).

Goodman, Kenneth S., *What's Whole in Whole Language* (Richmond Hill, ON: Scholastic, 1986a).

Goodman, Kenneth S., (for the National Council of Teachers of English Reading Commision), Basal readers: A call for action, *Language Arts*, 1986b, *63*, 4, 358–363.

Goodman, Yetta M., The roots of literacy, (edited by Malcolm P. Douglass), *Proceedings, Claremont Reading Conference, 44th Annual Yearbook*, Claremont, CA, 1980.

Goody, Jack, and Ian Watt, The consequences of literacy, in P. P. Gigliolo (ed.), *Language and Social Context* (London: Penguin, 1972).

Gough, Philip B., One second of reading, in James F. Kavanagh and Ignatius G. Mattingly (eds.), *Language by Ear and by Eye* (Cambridge, MA: MIT Press, 1972).

Gough, Philip B., and M. L. Hillinger, Learning to read: An unnatural act, *Bulletin of the Orton Society*, 1980, *30*, 180–196.

Gourley, Judith W., This basal is easy to read—or is it?, *The Reading Teacher*, 1978, *32*, 174–182.

Graham, Steven, Word recognition skills of learning disabled children and average students, *Reading Psychology*, 1980, *2*, 1, 23–33.

Gray, William S., *The Teaching of Reading and Writing: An International Survey* (Paris: UNESCO, 1956).

Greene, Judith, *Psycholinguistics: Chomsky and Psychology* (London: Penguin, 1972).

Greeno, James G., Learning and comprehension, in Lee W. Gregg (ed.), *Knowledge and Cognition* (Hillsdale, NJ: Lawrence Erlbaum Associates, 1974).

Gregory, Michael, and Susanne Carroll, *Language and Situation* (London: Routledge, Kegan and Paul, 1978).

Gregory, R. L., *Eye and Brain: The Psychology of Seeing* (New York: McGraw-Hill, 1966).

Gregory, R. L., *The Intelligent Eye* (New York: McGraw Hill, 1970).

Grimes, Joseph E., *The Thread of Discourse* (The Hague: Mouton, 1975).

Groff, Patrick, The new anti-phonics, *Elementary School Journal*, 1977, 77, 323–332.

Groner, R., George W. McConkie, and C. Menz (eds.), *Eye Movements and Human Information Processing* (North-Holland: Elsevier Science, 1985).

Gunderson, Lee, and Jon Shapiro, Some findings on whole language instruction, *Reading-Canada-Lecture*, 1987, *5*, 1, 22–26.

Guthrie, John T., Models of reading and reading disability, *Journal of Educational Psychology*, 1973, *65*, 9–18.

Haber, Lyn R., Ralph N. Haber, and Karen R. Furlin, Word length and word shape as sources of information in reading, *Reading Research Quarterly*, 1983, *18*, 2, 165–189.

Haber, Ralph N., and Lyn R. Haber, The shape of a word can specify its meaning, *Reading Research Quarterly*, 1981, *16*, 3, 334–345.

Hall, Nigel, *The Emergence of Literacy* (Sevenoaks, Kent, UK: Hodder and Stoughton, 1987).

Hall, William S., and Larry F. Guthrie, Situational differences in the use of language, in Langer, Judith A. and M. Trika Smith-Burke (eds.), *Reader Meets Author/Bridging the Gap* (Newark, DE: International Reading Association, 1982).

Halliday, Michael A. K., Language function and language structure, in John Lyons (ed.), *New Horizons in Linguistics* (London: Penguin, 1970).

Halliday, Michael A. K., *Explorations in the Functions of Language* (London: Arnold, 1973).

Halliday, Michael A. K., *Learning How to Mean: Explorations in the Development of Language* (London: Arnold, 1975).

Halliday, Michael A. K., *An Introduction to Functional Grammar* (Baltimore, MD: Arnold, 1985).

Halliday, Michael A. K., and Ruqaya Hasan, *Cohesion in English* (London: Longman, 1976).

Hamill, Donald D., and Gaye McNutt, *The Correlates of Reading* (Austin, TX: Pro-Ed, 1981).

Hansen, Jane, Thomas Newkirk, and Donald Graves, *Breaking Ground: Teachers Relate Reading and Writing in the Elementary School* (Portsmouth, NH: Heinemann Educational Books, 1985).

Harding, Leonora M., John R. Beech, and William Sneddon, The changing pattern of reading errors and reading style from 5 to 11 years of age, *British Journal of Educational Psychology*, 1985, *55*, 45–52.

Hardyck, C. D., and L. F. Petrinovich, Subvocal speech and comprehension level as a function of the difficulty level of reading material, *Journal of Verbal Learning and Verbal Behavior*, 1970, *9*, 647–652.

Harper, Lawrence V., The scope of offspring effects: From caregiver to culture, *Psychological Bulletin*, 1975, *82*, 5, 784–801.

Harste, Jerome C., and Diane Stephens, *Toward Practical Theory: A State of Practice Assessment of Reading Comprehension Instruction* (Bloomington, IN: Language Education Department, Indiana University, 1985).

Harste, Jerome C., Virginia A. Woodward, and Carolyn L. Burke, *Language Stories and Literacy Lessons* (Portsmouth, NH: Heinemann Educational Books, 1984).

Hart, Leslie A., Misconceptions about learning disabilities, *National Elementary Principal*, 1976, *56*, 1, 54–57.

Hausman, Carl R., Can computers create?, *Interchange*, 1985, *16*, 1, 27–37.

Havelock, Eric A., *Origins of Western Literacy* (Toronto: Ontario Institute for Studies in Education, 1976).

Haviland, Susan E., and Herbert H. Clark, What's new? Acquiring new information as a process in comprehension, *Journal of Verbal Learning and Verbal Behavior*, 1974, *13*, 512–521.

Heap, James, What counts as reading: Limits to certainty in assessment, *Curriculum Inquiry*, 1980, *10*, 265–292.

Heath, Shirley Brice, *Ways With Words* (Cambridge, MA: Cambridge University Press, 1982a).

Heath, Shirley Brice, What no bedtime story means: Narrative skills at home and school, *Language in Society*, 1982b, *11*, 49–76.

Heath, Shirley Brice, Research currents: A lot of talk about nothing, *Language Arts*, 1983, *60*, 4, 999–1007.

Heath, Shirley Brice, Being literate in America: A sociohistorical perspective, in Jerome A. Niles and Rosary V. Lalik (eds.), *Issues in Literacy: A Research Perspective* (Rochester, NY: National Reading Conference, 34th Yearbook, 1985).

Heath, Shirley Brice, and Charlene Thomas, The achievement of pre-school literacy for mother and child, in H. Goelman, A. A. Oberg, and F. Smith (eds.), *Awakening to Literacy* (Exeter, NH: Heinemann, 1984).

Heckenmueller, E. G., Stabilization of the retinal image: A review of method, effects and theory, *Psychological Review*, 1965, *63*, 157–169.

Hedley, Carolyn, and Anthony N. Baratta (eds.), *Contexts of Reading* (Norwood, NJ: Ablex, 1985).

Henderson, John M., Learning to read: A case study of a deaf child, *American Annals of the Deaf*, 1976, *121*, 502–506.

Henderson, Leslie, Writing systems and reading processes, in L. Henderson (ed.), *Orthographies and Reading: Perspectives from Cognitive Psychology, Neuropsychology, and Linguistics* (Hillsdale, NJ: Lawrence Erlbaum Associates, 1984a).

Henderson, Leslie (ed.), *Orthographies and Reading: Perspectives from Cognitive Psychology, Neuropsychology, and Linguistics* (Hillsdale, NJ: Lawrence Erlbaum Associates, 1984b).

Herman, Patricia A., Richard C. Anderson, P. David Pearson, and William E. Nagy,

Incidental acquisition of word meaning from expositions with varied text features, *Reading Research Quarterly*, 1987, *22*, 3, 263–284.

Hiebert, Elfrieda H., Developmental patterns and interrelationships of preschool children's print awareness, *Reading Research Quarterly*, 1981, *16*, 2, 236–260.

Hiebert, Elfrieda H., An examination of ability grouping for reading instruction, *Reading Research Quarterly*, 1983, *18*, 231–255.

Hochberg, Julian E., *Perception* (2nd ed.) (Englewood Cliffs, NJ: Prentice-Hall, 1978).

Hochberg, Julian E., and Virginia Brooks, Reading as intentional behavior, in H. Singer, and Robert B. Ruddell, *Theoretical Models and Processes of Reading* (2nd ed.) (Newark, DE: International Reading Association, 1976).

Holdaway, Don, Self-evaluation and reading development, in John E. Merritt (ed.), *New Horizons in Reading* (Newark, DE: International Reading Association, 1976).

Howe, M. J. A., and Linda Singer, Presentation variables and students' activities in meaningful learning, *British Journal of Educational Psychology*, 1975, *45*, 52–61.

Howes, D. H., and R. L. Solomon, Visual duration threshold as a function of word-probability, *Journal of Experimental Psychology*, 1951, *41*, 401–410.

Hudson, Judith A., Memories are made of this, in Katherine Nelson, *Event Knowledge*. (Hillsdale, NJ: Lawrence Erlbaum Associates, 1986).

Huey, Edmund Burke, *The Psychology and Pedagogy of Reading* (New York: Macmillan, 1908; reprinted Cambridge, MA: MIT Press, 1968).

Hull, Robert, *The Language Gap: How Classroom Dialogue Fails* (London: Methuen, 1985).

Huttenlocher, Janellen, and Deborah Burke, Why does memory span increase with age? *Cognitive Psychology*, 1976, *8*, 1, 1–31.

Iredell, Harriett, Eleanor learns to read, *Education*, 1898, *19*, 4, reprinted in *Language Arts*, 1982, *59*, 7, 668–671.

Iser, Wolfgang, *The Art of Reading: A Theory of Aesthetic Response* (London: Routledge and Kegan Paul, 1978).

Jaggar, Angela M., Donna H. Carrara, and Sara E. Weiss, The influence of reading on children's narrative writing (and vice versa), *Language Arts*, 1986, *63*, 3, 292–300.

Jaggar, Angela, and M. Trika Smith-Burke (eds.), *Observing the Language Learner* (Newark, NJ: International Reading Association, 1985).

Jakobson, Roman, and Morris Halle, *Fundamentals of Language* (The Hague: Mouton, 1956).

Jaynes, Julian, *The Origins of Consciousness in the Breakdown of the Bicameral Mind* (Boston: Houghton Mifflin, 1976).

Jaynes, Julian, Consciousness and the voices of the mind. *Canadian Psychology*, 1986, *27*, 2, 128–140.

Jenkins, James J., Remember that old theory of memory? Well, forget it!, *American Psychologist*, 1974, *29*, 11, 785–795.

Jenkins, J. R., R. B. Bausel, and L. M. Jenkins, Comparison of letter name and letter sound training as transfer variables, *American Educational Research Journal*, 1972, *9*, 75–86.

Jensen, Julie M. (ed.), *Composing and Comprehending* (Urbana, IL: National Conference on Research in English, 1984).

Johnson, Neal F., On the function of letters in word identification: Some data and a preliminary model, *Journal of Verbal Learning and Verbal Behavior*, 1975, *14*, 1, 17–29.

Johnson-Laird, Philip, Procedural semantics and mental models, in J. Mehler, Edward C. T. Walker, and M. Garrett (eds.), *Perspectives on Mental Representation* (Hillsdale, NJ: Lawrence Erlbaum Associates, 1982).

Johnston, J. C., and J. L. McClelland, Perception of letters in words: Seek not and ye shall find, *Science*, 1974, *184*, 1192–1193.

Johnston, Peter H., Understanding reading disabillity: A case study approach, *Harvard Educational Review*, 1985, *55*, 2, 153–177.

Jones, Edward E., Interpreting interpersonal behavior: The effects of expectancies, *Science*, 1986, *234*, 41–46.

Juel, Connie, and Betty Holmes, Oral and silent reading of sentences. *Reading Research Quarterly*, 1981, *15*, 545–568.

Juel, Connie, and Diana Roper/Schneider, The influence of basal readers on first grade reading, *Reading Research Quarterly*, 1985, *20*, 2, 134–152.

Just, Marcel Adam, and Patricia A. Carpenter (eds.), *Cognitive Processes in Comprehension* (Hillsdale, NJ: Lawrence Erlbaum Associates, 1977).

Just, Marcel Adam, and Patricia A. Carpenter, A theory of reading: From eye fixations to comprehension, *Psychological Review*, 1980, *87*, 6, 329–354.

Just, Marcel Adam, and Patricia A. Carpenter, Using eye fixations to study reading comprehension, in D. E. Kieras, and M. A. Just (eds.), *New Methods of Reading Comprehension Research* (Hillsdale, NJ: Lawrence Erlbaum Associates, 1984).

Kagan, Jerome, The determinants of attention in the infant, *American Scientist*, 1970, *58*, 298–306.

Kail, Robert, *The Development of Memory in Children* (San Francisco: Freeman, 1979).

Katz, Jerrold J., Chomsky on meaning, *Language*, 1980, *56*, 1, 1–41.

Kavanagh, James F., and Ignatius G. Mattingly (eds.), *Language by Ear and by Eye* (Cambridge, MA: MIT Press, 1972).

Kieras, David E., and Marcel A. Just (eds.), *New Methods in Reading Comprehension Research* (Hillsdale, NJ: Lawrence Erlbaum Associates, 1984).

Kimmel, Susan, and Walter H. MacGinitie, Identifying children who use a persevative text processing strategy, *Reading Research Quarterly*, 1984, *19*, 2, 162–172.

Klahr, D., Chase, W. G., and E. A. Lovelace, Structure and process in alphabetic retrieval, *Journal of Experimental Psychology: Learning, Memory and Cognition*, 1983, *9*, 462–277.

Klatzky, Roberta L., *Human Memory: Structures and Processes* (2nd ed.) (San Francisco: Freeman, 1980).

Kleiman, Gary M., Speech recoding in reading, *Journal of Verbal Learning and Verbal Behavior*, 1975, *14*, 323–339.

Klein, Gary A., and Helen Altman Klein, Word identification as a function of contextual information, *American Journal of Psychology*, 1973, *86*, 2, 399–406.

Klein, Helen Altman, Gary A. Klein, and Mary Bertino, Utilization of context for word identification in children, *Journal of Experimental Psychology*, 1974, *17*, 79–86.

Kintsch, Walter, *The Representation of Meaning in Memory* (Hillsdale, NJ: Lawrence Erlbaum Associates, 1974).

Kintsch, Walter, and T. A. van Dijk, Recalling and summarizing stories, *Language*, 1975, *40*, 98–116.

Kintsch, Walter, and T. A. van Dijk, Towards a model of text comprehension and production, *Psychological Review*, 1978, *85*, 363, 394.

Kolers, Paul A., Reading and talking bilingually. *American Journal of Psychology*, 1966, 79, 357–376.

Kolers, Paul A., Reading is only incidentally visual, in Kenneth S. Goodman, and James T. Fleming (eds.), *Psycholinguistics and the Technology of Reading* (Newark, DE: International Reading Association, 1967).

Kolers, Paul A., Three stages of reading, in Harry Levin and Joanna P. Williams (eds.), *Basic Studies on Reading* (New York: Basic Books, 1970).

Kolers, Paul A., Specificity of operations in sentence recognition, *Cognitive Psychology*, 1975, 7, 289–306.

Kolers, Paul A., Buswell's discoveries, in R. A. Monty and J. W. Senders (eds.), *Eye Movements and Psychological Processes* (Hillsdale, NJ: Lawrence Erlbaum Associates, 1976).

Kolers, Paul A., and M. Eden (eds.), *Recognizing Patterns: Studies in Living and Automatic Systems* (Cambridge, MA: MIT Press, 1968).

Kolers, Paul A., and M. T. Katzman, Naming sequentially presented letters and words, *Language and Speech*, 1966, 9, 2, 84–95.

Kolers, Paul A., and Henry L. Roediger, III, Procedure of Mind, *Journal of Verbal Learning and Verbal Behavior*, 1984, 23, 425–449.

Kosslyn, Stephen M., *Image and Mind* (Cambridge, MA: Harvard University Press, 1980).

Krashen, Stephen D., Formal and informal linguistic environments in language acquisition and language learning, *TESOL Quarterly*, 1976, 10, 2, 157–168.

Krashen, Stephen D., *Inquiries and Insights* (Hayward, CA: Alemany Press, 1985).

Krashen, Stephen D., *Comics Book Reading and Language Development* (Victoria, British Columbia: Abel Press, 1987).

Krueger, Lester E., Familiarity effects in visual information processing, *Psychological Bulletin*, 1975, 82, 6, 949–974.

Krueger, Lester E., Robert H. Keen, and Bella Rublevich, Letter search through words and nonwords by adults and fourth-grade children, *Journal of Experimental Psychology*, 1974, 102, 5, 845–849.

Kuhn, Thomas, *The Structure of Scientific Revolutions* (Chicago: University of Chicago Press, 1970).

Kutas, Marta, and Steven A. Hillyard, Reading senseless sentences: Brain potentials reflect semantic anomaly, *Science*, 1980, 207, 203–204.

LaBerge, David, and S. Jay Samuels, Towards a theory of automatic information processing in reading, *Cognitive Psychology*, 1974, 6, 293–323.

LaBerge, David, and S. Jay Samuels, (eds.), *Basic Processes in Reading: Perception and Comprehension* (Hillsdale, NJ: Lawrence Erlbaum Associates, 1977).

Lakoff, George, *Women, Fire, and Dangerous Things: What Categories Reveal About the Mind* (Chicago: University of Chicago Press, 1987).

Langer, Judith A., From theory to practice: A prereading plan, *Journal of Reading*, 1981, 25, 2, 152–156.

Langer, Judith A., Facilitating text processing: The elaboration of prior knowledge, in J. A. Langer, and M. T. Smith-Burke (eds.), *Reader Meets Author/Bridging the Gap* (Newark, DE: International Reading Association, 1982a).

Langer, Judith A., Reading, thinking, writing . . . and teaching, *Language Arts*, 1982b, 59, 4, 336–341.

Langer, Judith A., and M. Trika Smith-Burke (eds.), *Reader Meets Author/Bridging the Gap* (Newark, DE: International Reading Association, 1982).

Langer, Suzanne K., *Philosphy in a New Key* (Cambridge, MA: Harvard University Press, 1951).

Larsen, Steen F., Procedural thinking, programming, and computer use, in E. Hollnagel, G. Mancini, and D. Woods (eds.), *Intelligent Decision Aids in Process Environments* (Berlin: Springer-Verlag, 1986).

Lawler, R. W., and M. Yazdani (eds.), *Artificial Intelligence and Education (Vol. 1). Learning Environments and Tutoring Systems* (Norwood, NJ: Ablex, 1987).

Lenneberg, Eric H., *Biological Foundations of Language* (New York: Wiley, 1967).

Lenneberg, Eric H., and Elizabeth Lenneberg (eds.), *Foundations of Language Development: A Multidisciplinary Approach*, 2 vols. (New York: Academic Press, 1975).

Lepper, Mark R. (ed.), *The Hidden Cost of Reward* (Hillsdale, NJ: Lawrence Erlbaum Associates, 1978).

Levin, Harry, Successions in psychology (review of Bernard J. Baars, *The Cognitive Revolution in Psychology*), *Science*, 1987, *236*, 1683–1684.

Levine, Frederic M., and Geraldine Fasnacht, Token rewards may lead to token learning, *American Psychologist*, 1974, *29*, 816–820.

Levine, K., *The Social Context of Literacy* (London: Routledge and Kegan Paul, 1986).

Levy, Betty Ann, Speech analysis during sentence processing: Reading and listening, *Visible Language*, 1978, *12*, 81–102.

Lewis, Donald J., Psychobiology of active and inactive memory, *Psychological Bulletin*, 1979, *86*, 1054–1083.

Liben, Lynn S., *Piaget and the Foundations of Knowledge* (Hillsdale, NJ: Lawrence Erlbaum Associates, 1983).

Liberman, Alvin M., F. S. Cooper, D. F. Shankweiler, and M. Studdert-Kennedy, Perception of the speech code, *Psychological Review*, 1957, *54*, 358–368.

Liberman, Isabelle Y., and Donald Shankweiler, Speech, the alphabet and teaching to read, in Lauren B. Resnick and Phyllis A. Weaver (eds.), *Theory and Practice of Early Reading* (Vol. 2) (Hillsdale, NJ: Lawrence Erlbaum Associates, 1979).

Lieberman, Philip, *The Biology and Evolution of Language* (Cambridge, MA: Harvard University Press, 1984).

Lindsay, Peter H., and Donald A. Norman, *Human Information Processing* (2nd ed.) (New York: Academic Press, 1977).

Lipson, Marjorie Y., The influence of religious affiliation on children's memory for text information, *Reading Research Quarterly*, 1983, *18*, 4, 448–457.

Lipson, Marjorie Y., Some unexpected issues in prior knowledge and comprehension, *The Reading Teacher*, 1984, *37*, 760–764.

Lipson, Marjorie Y., and Karen K. Wixson, Reading disability research: An interactionist perspective, *Review of Educational Research*, 1986, *56*, 1, 111–136.

Llewellyn-Thomas, E., Eye movements in speed reading, in *Speed Reading: Practices and Procedures, No. 10* (Newark, DE: University of Delaware Reading Study Center, 1962).

Lott, Deborah, and Frank Smith, Knowledge of intra-word redundancy by beginning readers, *Psychonomic Science*, 1970, *19*, 6, 343–344.

Lyons, John, *Semantics*, 2 vols. (Cambridge, MA: Cambridge University Press, 1977).

MacGinitie, Walter H., Readability as a solution adds to the problem, in Richard C.

Anderson, Jean Osborn, and Robert J. Tierney (eds.), *Learning to Read in American Schools: Basal Readers and Content Texts* (Hillsdale, NJ: Lawrence Erlbaum Associates, 1984).

MacGinitie, Walter H., and Ruth K. MacGinitie, Teaching students not to read, in S. de Castel, A. Luke, and K. Egan (eds.), *Literacy, Society, and Schooling* (Cambridge, MA: Cambridge University Press, 1986).

Mackworth, Norman H., Visual noise causes tunnel vision, *Psychonomic Science*, 1965, *3*, 67–68.

Macnamara, John, Cognitive basis of language learning in infants, *Psychological Review*, 1972, *79*, 1, 1–13.

Magee, Bryan, *Popper* (London: Fontana, 1973).

Makita, Kiyoshi, The rarity of reading disability in Japense children, *American Journal of Orthopsychiatry*, 1968, *38*, 4, 599–614.

Makita, Kiyoshi, Reading disability and the writing system, in J. E. Merritt (ed.), *New Horizons in Reading* (Newark, DE: International Reading Association, 1976).

Mandler, George, Organization and memory, in K. W. Spence, and J. T. Spence (eds.), *The Psychology of Learning and Motivation* (Vol. 1) (New York: Academic Press, 1967).

Mandler, George, Recognizing: The judgment of previous occurrence, *Psychological Review*, 1980, *87*, 3, 252–271.

Mandler, George, *Cognitive Psychology: An Essay in Cognitive Science* (Hillsdale, NJ: Lawrence Erlbaum Associates, 1985).

Mandler, Jean Matter, A code in the node: The use of a story schema in retrieval, *Discourse Processes*, 1978, *1*, 14–35.

Mandler, Jean Matter, *Stories, Scripts, and Scenes: Aspects of Schema Theory* (Hillsdale, NJ: Lawrence Erlbaum Associates, 1984).

Mandler, Jean Matter, and Marsha S. Goodman, On the psychological validity of story structure, *Journal of Verbal Learning and Verbal Behavior*, 1982, *21*, 507–523.

Mandler, Jean Matter, and N. S. Johnson, Remembrance of things parsed: Story structure and recall, *Cognitive Psychology*, 1977, *9*, 111–151.

Marcel, Tony, Unconscious reading: Experiments on people who do not know that they are reading, *Visible Language*, 1978, *12*, 4, 391–404.

Marchbanks, Gabrielle, and Harry Levin, Cues by which children recognize words, *Journal of Educational Psychology*, 1965, *56*, 2, 57–61.

Marr, David, *Vision* (San Francisco: Freeman, 1982).

Marshall, John C., and F. Newcombe, Syntactic and semantic errors in paralexia, *Neuropsychologia*, 1966, *4*, 169–176.

Martin, Maryanne, Top-down processing and target search in reading, *Perceptual and Motor Skills*, 1979, *48*, 467–470.

Mason, Jana M., When do children begin to read?: An exploration of four-year-old children's letter and word reading competencies, *Reading Research Quarterly*, 1980, *15*, 2, 203–227.

Massaro, Dominic W., *Experimental Psychology and Information Processing* (Skokie, IL: Rand McNally, 1975).

Massaro, Dominic W., and David Klitzke, Letters are functional in word identification, *Memory and Cognition*, 1977, *5*, 292–298.

Masson, Michael E. J., and Linda S. Sala, Interactive processes in sentence comprehension and recognition, *Cognitive Psychology*, 1978, *10*, 244–270.

Mathews, M. M., *Teaching to Read: Historically Considered* (Chicago: University of Chicago Press, 1966).

Mattingly, Ignatius G., Reading, linguistic awareness, and language acquisition, in J. Downing and R. Valtin (eds.), *Language Awareness and Learning to Read* (New York: Springer-Verlag, 1985).

Mayher, John S., and Rita S. Brause, Learning through teaching: Is testing crippling integrated language education?, *Language Arts*, 1986, *63*, 4, 390–396.

Mayor, Barbara M., and Anthony K. Pugh (eds.), *Language, Communication and Education* (London: Croom Helm, 1987).

McCartney, K., and Katherine Nelson, Children's use of scripts in story recall, *Discourse Processes*, 1981, *4*, 59–70.

McClelland, James L., Putting knowledge in its place: A scheme for programming parallel processing structures on the fly, *Cognitive Science*, 1985, *9*, 1, 113–146.

McClelland, James L., and David E. Rumelhart, An interactive activation model of context effects in letter perception: Part I. An account of basic findings, *Psychological Review*, 1981, *88*, 375–407.

McConkie, George W., and Keith Rayner, The span of the effective stimulus during a fixation in reading, *Perception and Psychophysics*, 1975, *17*, 578–586.

McCusker, Leo X., Michael L. Hillinger, and Randolph G. Bias, Phonological recoding and reading, *Psychological Bulletin*, 1981, *89*, 2, 217.

McFarland, Carl E., Jr., and Deborah H. Rhodes, Memory for meaning in skilled and unskilled readers, *Journal of Experimental Child Psychology*, 1978, *25*, 199–207.

McGee, Lea M., Awareness of text structure: Effects on children's recall of expository text, *Reading Research Quarterly*, 1982, *17*, 4, 581–590.

McKeachie, W. J., The decline and fall of the laws of learning, *Educational Researcher*, 1974, *3*, 3, 7–11.

McKeown, Margaret G., The acquisition of word meaning from context by children of high and low ability, *Reading Research Quarterly*, 1985, *20*, 4, 482–496.

McLaughlin, Barry, Second-language learning in children, *Psychological Review*, 1977, *84*, 3, 438–459.

McMahon, Margaret L., Development of reading-while-listening skills in the primary grades, *Reading Research Quarterly*, 1983, *19*, 1, 38–52.

McNeill, David, Developmental psycholinguistics, in F. Smith, and G. A. Miller (eds.), *The Genesis of Language* (Cambridge, MA: MIT Press, 1967).

McNeill, David, *The Acquisition of Language: The Study of Developmental Psycholinguistics* (New York: Harper & Row, 1970).

McNeill, David, So you think gestures are nonverbal?, *Psychological Review*, 1985, *92*, 3, 350–371.

McNeill, David, and Karen Lindig, The perceptual reality of phonemes, syllables, words, and sentences, *Journal of Verbal Learning and Verbal Behavior*, 1973, *12*, 4, 419–430.

McPeck, John E., *Critical Thinking and Education* (Oxford: Martin Robertson, 1981).

Meek, Margaret, *Learning to Read* (London: Bodley Head, 1982).

Meek, Margaret, Speaking of shifters, in M. Meek and Jane Miller (eds.), *Changing*

English: Essays for Harold Rosen (London: Heinemann Educational Books, 1984).

Meek, Margaret, Stephen Armstrong, Vicky Austerfield, Judith Graham, and Elizabeth Plackett, *Achieving Literacy: Longitudinal Studies of Adolescents Learning to Read* (London: Routledge and Kegan Paul, 1983).

Meltzer, Nancy S., and Robert Herse, The boundaries of written words as seen by first graders, *Journal of Reading Behavior*, 1969, *1*, 3–14.

Menyuk, Paula, *The Acquisition and Development of Language* (Englewood Cliffs, NJ: Prentice-Hall, 1971).

Merritt, John E. (ed.), *New Horizons in Reading* (Newark, DE: International Reading Association, 1976).

Meyer, Bonnie J. F., Prose analysis: Purposes, procedures, and problems, in B. K. Britton and J. B. Black (eds.), *Understanding Expository Text* (Hillsdale, NJ: Lawrence Erlbaum Associates, 1985).

Meyer, David E., and Roger W. Schvaneveldt, Facilitation in recognizing pairs of words: Evidence of a dependence between retrieval operations, *Journal of Experimental Psychology*, 1971, *90*, 227–234.

Michotte, A., *La Perception de la Causalité* (Louvain: Institut Supérieur de Philosophie, 1946).

Mikulecky, Larry, Job literacy: The relationship between school preparation and workplace actuality, *Reading Research Quarterly*, 1982, *17*, 3, 400–419.

Miller, George A., *Language and Communication* (New York: McGraw-Hill, 1951).

Miller, George A., The magical number seven, plus or minus two: Some limits on our capacity for processing information, *Psychological Review*, 1956, *63*, 81–92.

Miller, George A. (ed.), *Mathematics and Psychology* (New York: Wiley, 1964).

Miller, George A., Some preliminaries to psycholinguistics, *American Psychologist*, 1965, *20*, 15–20.

Miller, George A., *Spontaneous Apprentices: Children and Language* (New York: Seabury, 1977).

Miller, George A., Jerome S. Bruner, and Leo Postman, Familiarity of letter sequences and tachistoscopic identification, *Journal of Genetic Psychology*, 1954, *50*, 129–139.

Miller, George A., Eugene Galanter, and Karl H. Pribram, *Plans and the Structure of Behavior* (New York: Holt, Rinehart and Winston, 1960).

Miller, George A., G. A. Heise, and W. Lichten, The intelligibility of speech as a function of the context of the test materials, *Journal of Experimental Psychology*, 1951, *41*, 329–335.

Miller, George A., and Philip N. Johnson-Laird, *Language and Perception* (Cambridge, MA: The Belknap Press of Harvard University Press, 1975).

Miller, George A., and Patricia E. Nicely, An analysis of perceptual confusions among some English consonants, *Journal of the Acoustical Society of America*, 1955, *27*, 338–353.

Minsky, Marvin, K-lines: A theory of memory, *Cognitive Science*, 1980, *4*, 117–133.

Moerk, Ernest L., *Pragmatic and Semantic Aspects of Early Language Development* (Baltimore, MD: University Park Press, 1977).

Moore, David W., A case for naturalistic assessment of reading comprehension, *Language Arts*, 1983, *60*, 4, 957–969.

Moore, Timothy E. (ed.), *Cognitive Development and the Acquisition of Language* (New York: Academic Press, 1973).

Morris, Charles, *Signs, Language and Behavior* (New York: Prentice-Hall, 1946).

Morris, Joyce M., *Langage in Action* (London: Macmillan Education, 1974).

Morris, Joyce M., New phonics for initial literacy, *Australian Journal of Reading*, 1982, *5*, 2, 52–60.

Morrow, Lesley Mandel, and Carol Simon Weinstein, Encouraging voluntary reading: The impact of a literature program on children's use of library centers, *Reading Research Quarterly*, 1986, *21*, 3, 330–346.

Morton, John, The effects of context on the visual duration threshold for words, *British Journal of Psychology*, 1964, *55*, 2, 165–180.

Morton, John, Interaction of information in word recognition, *Psychological Review*, 1969, *76*, 2, 165–178.

Morton, John, Disintegrating the lexicon: An information-processing approach, in Jacques Mehler, Edward C. T. Walker, and Merrill Garrett, *Perspectives on Mental Representation* (Hillsdale, NJ: Lawrence Erlbaum Associates, 1982).

Mosberg, Ludwig, A response: Comments on 'Language by Eye and by Ear,' in Frank B. Murray, and John J. Pukulski (eds.), *The Acquisition of Reading: Cognitive, Linguistic and Perceptual Prerequisites* (Baltimore, MD: University Park Press, 1978).

Mosenthal, Peter, The influence of social situation on children's classroom comprehension of text, *Elementary School Journal*, 1983, *8*, 5, 537–547.

Moskowitz, Breyne Arlene, The acquisition of language, *Scientific American*, 1978, *12*, 92–108.

Moyer, Sandra B., and Phillis L. Newcomer, Reversals in reading diagnosis and remediation, *Exceptional Children*, 1977, *43*, 424–429.

Nagy, William E., and Richard C. Anderson, The number of words in printed school English, *Reading Research Quarterly*, 1984, *19*, 304–330.

Nagy, William E., Patricia A. Herman, and Richard C. Anderson, Learning words from context, *Reading Research Quarterly*, 1985, *20*, 2, 233–253.

Navon, David, Forest before trees: The precedence of global features in visual perception, *Cognitive Psychology*, 1977, *9*, 353–383.

Naylor, Hilary, Reading disability and lateral asymmetry: an information-processing analysis, *Psychological Bulletin*, 1980, *87*, 3, 531–545.

Neisser, Ulric, *Cognitive Psychology* (New York: Appleton, 1967).

Neisser, Ulric, *Cognition and Reality* (San Francisco: Freeman, 1977).

Neisser, Ulric, Components of intelligence or steps in routine procedures?, *Cognition*, 1983, *15*, 189–197.

Neisser, Ulric, and H. K. Beller, Searching through word lists, *British Journal of Psychology*, 1965, *56*, 349–358.

Nelson, Katherine, Structure and strategy in learning to talk, *Monographs of the Society for Research in Child Development*, 1973, *38*, 149.

Nelson, Katherine, Concept, word and sentence: Interrelations in acquisition and development, *Psychological Review*, 1974, *81*, 4, 267–285.

Nelson, Katherine, *Making Sense: Development of Meaning in Early Childhood* (New York: Academic Press, 1985).

Nelson, Katherine, *Event Knowledge* (Hillsdale, NJ: Lawrence Erlbaum Associates, 1986).

Neville, Mary H., and A. K. Pugh, Context in reading and listening: Variations in approach to Cloze tasks, *Reading Research Quarterly*, 1976–77, *12*, 1, 13–31.

Newman, Edwin B., Speed of reading when the span of letters is restricted, *American Journal of Psychology*, 1966, *79*, 272–278.

Newman, Judith M. (ed.), *Whole Language: Theory and Use* (Portsmouth, NH: Heinemann Educational Books, 1985).

Newman, Judith M., Online: Using a database in the classroom, *Language Arts*, 1986, *63*, 3, 315–319.

Newson, John, and Elizabeth Newson, Intersubjectivity and the transmission of culture: On the social origins of symbolic functioning, *Bulletin of the British Psychological Society*, 1975, *28*, 437–446.

Nicholson, Tom, and Robert Imlach, Where do their answers come from? A study of the inferences which children make when answering questions about narrative stories, *Journal of Reading Behavior*, 1981, *13*, 2, 111–129.

Niles, Jerome A., and Rosary V. Lalik (eds.), *Issues in Literacy: A Research Perspective* (Rochester, NY: National Reading Conference, 34th Yearbook, 1985).

Ninio, A., and Jerome S. Bruner, The achievement and antecedents of labelling, *Journal of Child Language*, 1978, *5*, 5–15.

Nisbett, Richard E., and Timothy DeCamp Wilson, Telling more than we can know: Verbal reports on mental processes, *Psychological Review*, 1977, *84*, 3, 231–259.

Norman, Donald A., *Memory and Attention: An Introduction to Human Information Processing* (New York: Wiley, 1969; 2nd ed. 1976).

Norman, Donald A., and Daniel G. Bobrow, Descriptions: An intermediate stage in memory retrieval, *Cognitive Psychology*, 1979, *11*, 107–123.

Norman, Donald A., and David E. Rumelhart, *Explorations in Cognition* (San Francisco: Freeman, 1975).

Notz, William W., Work motivation and the negative effects of extrinsic rewards, *American Psychologist*, 1975, *30*, 9, 884–891.

Nystrand, Martin, *The Structure of Written Communication* (Orlando, FL: Academic Press, 1986).

Oatley, Keith, *Perceptions and Representations: The Theoretical Bases of Brain Research and Psychology* (New York: The Free Press, 1978).

O'Brien, Edward J., and Jerome L. Myers, When comprehension difficulty improves memory for text, *Journal of Experimental Psychology: Learning, Memory and Cognition*, 1985, *11*, 1, 12–21.

Olson, David R., Language and thought: Aspects of a cognitive theory of semantics, *Psychological Review*, 1970, *77*, 257–273.

Olson, David R., Review of *Towards a Literate Society* (edited by J. B. Carroll and J. Chall), in *Proceedings of the National Academy of Education*, 1975, *2*, 109–178.

Olson, David R., From utterance to text: The bias of language in speech and writing, *Harvard Educational Review*, 1977, *47*, 3, 257–281.

Olson, David R. (ed.), *The Social Foundations of Language and Thought* (New York: Norton, 1980).

Olson, David R., Nancy Torrance, and Angela Hildyard (eds.), *Literacy, Language and Learning: The Nature and Consequences of Reading and Writing* (Cambridge, MA: Cambridge University Press, 1985).

Olson, Gary M., Memory development and language acquisition, in T. E. Moore (ed.), *Cognitive Development and the Acquisition of Language* (New York: Academic Press, 1973).

Olson, Gary M., Susan A. Duffy, and R. L. Mack, Thinking-out-loud as a method for studying real-time comprehension processes, in D. E. Kieras, and M. A. Just (eds.), *New Methods in Reading Comprehension Research* (Hillsdale, NJ: Lawrence Erlbaum Associates, 1984).

Ong, Walter J., *Orality and Literacy: The Technologizing of the Word* (London: Methuen, 1982).

Ortony, Andrew (ed.), *Metaphor and Thought* (Cambridge, MA: Cambridge University Press, 1979).

O'Shea, Lawrence J., Paul T. Sindelar, and Dorothy J. O'Shea, The effects of repeated readings and attentional cues on reading fluency and comprehension, *Journal of Reading Behavior*, 1985, 17, 2, 129–142.

Paivio, Allan, *Imagery and Verbal Processes* (New York: Holt, Rinehart and Winston, 1971).

Palmer, F. R., *Semantics: A New Outline* (Cambridge, MA: Cambridge University Press, 1976).

Paris, S. G., and A. Y. Carter, Semantic and constructive aspects of sentence memory in children, *Developmental Psychology*, 1973, 9, 109–113.

Park, Soji, and Tannis Y. Arbuckle, Ideograms vs. alphabets: Effects of script on memory in 'biscriptal' Korean subjects, *Journal of Experimental Psychology (Human Learning and Memory)*, 1977, 3, 631–642.

Pastore, R. E., and C. J. Scheirer, Signal detection theory: Considerations for general application, *Psychological Bulletin*, 1974, 81, 12, 945–958.

Patterson, Karalyn E., Neuropsychological approaches to the study of reading, *British Journal of Psychology*, 1981, 72, 151–174.

Pearson, P. David, The effects of grammatical complexity on children's comprehension, recall and conception of certain semantic relations, *Reading Research Quarterly*, 1974–75, 10, 155–192.

Pearson, P. David, and Alice Studt, Effects of word frequency and contextual richness on children's word identification abilities, *Journal of Educational Psychology*, 1975, 67, 1, 89–95.

Peirce, Charles S., *Collected Papers* (Cambridge, MA: Harvard University Press, 1931–1958).

Perfetti, Charles A., Psychosemantics: Some cognitive aspects of structural meaning, *Psychological Bulletin*, 1972, 78, 4, 241–259.

Perfetti, Charles A., S. R. Goldman, and T. W. Hogaboam, Reading skill and the identification of words in discourse context, *Memory and Cognition*, 1979, 4, 273–282.

Perfetti, Charles A., and S. Roth, Some of the interactive processes in reading and their role in reading skill, in A. M. Lesgold and C. A. Perfetti (eds.), *Interactive Processes in Reading* (Hillsdale, NJ: Lawrence Erlbaum Associates, 1981).

Phillips, John L. Jr., *Piaget's Theory: A Primer* (San Francisco: Freeman, 1981).

Piaget, Jean, *The Construction of Reality in the Child* (New York: Basic Books, 1954).

Piaget, Jean, and Barbel Inhelder, *The Psychology of the Child* (New York: Basic Books, 1969).

Piattelli-Palmarini, Massimo, *Language and Learning: The Debate Between Jean Piaget and Noam Chomsky* (Cambridge, MA: Harvard University Press, 1980).

Pierce, J. R., *Symbols, Signals and Noise: The Nature and Process of Communication* (New York: Harper & Row, 1961).

Pierce, J. R., and J. E. Karlin, Reading rates and the information rate of a human channel, *Bell Systems Technical Journal*, 1957, *36*, 497–516.

Pillsbury, W. B., A study in apperception, *American Journal of Psychology*, 1897, *8*, 315–393.

Pinker, Steven, Visual cognition: An introduction, *Cognition*, 1984, *18*, 1–63.

Piper, David, Teaching story grammar: Some reasons for caution, *Canadian Journal of English Language Arts*, 1987, *10*, 1, 30–37.

Polanyi, Michael, *The Tacit Dimension* (Garden City, NY: Doubleday, 1966).

Popper, Karl R., *Objective Knowledge: An Evolutionary Approach* (Oxford: Clarendon Press, 1973).

Popper, Karl R., *Unended Quest: An Intellectual Autobiography* (London: Fontana/Collins, 1976).

Potter, Mary C., Meaning in visual search, *Science*, 1975, *187*, 965–966.

Potter, Mary C., Rapid serial visual presentation (RSVP): A method for studying language processing, in D. E. Kieras, and M. A. Just (eds.), *New Methods in Reading Comprehension Research* (Hillsdale, NJ: Lawrence Erlbaum Associates, 1984).

Potter, Mary C., J. F. Kroll, B. Yachzel, and C. Harris, Comprehension and memory in rapid sequential reading, in R. Nickerson (ed.), *Attention and Performance VIII* (Hillsdale, NJ: Lawrence Erlbaum Associates, 1980).

Pribram, Karl H., *Languages of the Brain* (Englewood, NJ: Prentice-Hall, 1971).

Pritchard, R. M., Stabilized images on the retina, *Scientific American*, 1961, *204*, 6, 72–78.

Puff, Richard C. (ed.), *Memory Organization and Structures* (New York: Academic Press, 1977).

Pugh, Anthony K., *Silent Reading* (London: Heinemann Educational Books, 1978).

Pylyshyn, Z. W., What the mind's eye tells the mind's brain: A critique of mental imagery, *Psychological Bulletin*, 1973, *80*, 1–24.

Pylyshyn, Z. W., Imagery theory: Not mysterious, just wrong, *Behavioral and Brain Sciences*, 1979, *2*, 561–563.

Quastler, Henry, Studies of human channel capacity, in Colin Cherry (ed.), *Information Theory* (London: Butterworths, 1956).

Raphael, Taffy E. (ed.), *The Contexts of School-Based Literacy* (New York: Random House, 1986).

Rayner, Keith, Visual attention in reading: Eye movements reflect cognitive processes, *Memory and Cognition*, 1977, *5*, 443–449.

Rayner, Keith, Eye movements in reading and information processing, *Psychological Bulletin*, 1978, *85*, 618–660.

Rayner, Keith (ed.), *Eye Movements in Reading* (New York: Academic Press, 1983).

Rayner, Keith, A. D. Well, and A. Pollatsek, Asymmetry of the effective visual field in reading, *Perception and Psychophysics*, 1980, *27*, 537–544.

Read, Charles, Pre-school children's knowledge of English phonology, *Harvard Educational Review*, 1971, *41*, 1, 1–34.

Reber, A. S., and D. Scarborough (eds.), *Toward A Psychology of Reading* (Hillsdale, NJ: Lawrence Erlbaum Associates, 1977).

Reder, Lynne M., The role of elaboration in the comprehension and retention of prose: A critical review, *Review of Educational Research*, 1980, *50*, 1, 5–53.

Reichardt, Konrad W., Playing dead or running away—defense mechanisms during reading, *Journal of Reading*, 1977, *20*, 706–711.

Reicher, G. M., Perceptual recognition as a function of meaningfulness of stimulus material, *Journal of Experimental Psychology*, 1969, *81*, 275–280.

Reid, L. Starling, Towards a grammar of the image, *Psychological Bulletin*, 1974, *81*, 6, 319–334.

Resnick, Lauren B., and Phyllis A. Weaver (eds.), *Theory and Practice of Early Reading*, 3 vols. (Hillsdale, NJ: Lawrence Erlbaum Associates, 1979).

Restle, F., Theory of serial pattern learning, *Psychological Review*, 1970, 77, 481–495.

Rhode, Mary, and Bruce Cronnell, *Compilation of a communication skills lexicon coded with linguistic information*, Los Alamitos, CA: Southwest Regional Laboratory for Educational Research and Development Technical Report #58, 1977.

Rock, Irvin, *The Logic of Perception* (Cambridge, MA: MIT Press, 1983).

Rosch, Eleanor, and B. B. Lloyd, *Cognition and Categorization* (Hillsdale, NJ: Lawrence Erlbaum Associates, 1978).

Rosen, Harold, The importance of story, *Language Arts*, 1986, *63*, 3, 226–237.

Rosenberg, Steven, and Herbert A. Simon, Modelling semantic memory: Effects of presenting semantic information in different modalities, *Cognitive Psychology*, 1977, *9*, 293–325.

Rosenblatt, Louise, M., *The Reader: The Text: The Poem* (Carbondale, IL: Southern Illinois University Press, 1978).

Rosenblatt, Louise M., "What facts does this poem teach you?" *Language Arts*, 1980, *57*, 4, 386–394.

Rosinski, Richard R., Roberta Michnick Golinkoff, and Karen S. Kukish, Automatic semantic processing in a picture-word interference task, *Child Development*, 1975, *46*, 1, 247–253.

Rothkopf, Ernst Z., and M. J. Billington, Indirect review and priming through questions, *Journal of Educational Psychology*, 1974, *66*, 5, 669–679.

Rothkopf, Ernst Z., and Richard P. Coatney, Effects of readability of context passages on subsequent imspection rates, *Journal of Applied Psychology*, 1974, *59*, 6, 679–682.

Rotman, Brian, *Jean Piaget: Psychologist of the Real* (Ithaca, NY: Cornell University Press, 1977).

Rozin, Paul, Susan Poritsky, and Raina Sotksy, American children with reading problems can easily learn to read English represented by Chinese characters, *Science*, 1971, *171*, 1264–1267.

Rumelhart, David, Schemata: The building blocks of cognition, in R. C. Spiro, B. C. Bruce, and W. F. Brewer (eds.), *Theoretical Issues in Reading Comprehension: Perspectives from Cognitive Psychology, Linguistics, Artificial Intelligence, and Education* (Hillsdale, NJ: Lawrence Erlbaum Associates, 1980).

Rumelhart, David E., and James L. McClelland, An interactive activation model of context effects in letter perception: Part II. The contextual enhancement effect and some tests and extensions of the model, *Psychological Review*, 1981, *89*, 60–94.

Rumelhart, David E., and Andrew Ortony, The representation of knowledge in memory, in Richard C. Anderson, Rand J. Spiro, and William E. Montague (eds.), *Schooling and the Acquisition of Knowledge* (Hillsdale, NJ: Lawrence Erlbaum Associates, 1977).

Rumelhart, David E., and Patricia Siple, Process of recognizing tachistoscopically presented words, *Psychological Review*, 1974, *81*, 99–118.

Ryan, Ellen Bouchard, and Melvyn I. Semmel, Reading as a constructive language process, *Reading Research Quarterly*, 1969, *5*, 1, 59–83.

Sachs, Jacqueline S., Memory in reading and listening to discourse, *Memory and Cognition*, 1974, *2*, 1A, 95–100.

Sadowski, Mark, An exploratory study of the relationships between reported imagery and the comprehension and recall of a story, *Reading Research Quarterly*, 1983, *19*, 1, 110–121.

Sakamoto, Takahiko, Writing systems in Japan, in John E. Merritt (ed.), *New Horizons in Reading* (Newark, DE: International Reading Association, 1976).

Salmon, Phillida and Hilary Claire, *Classsroom Collaboration* (London: Routledge and Kegan Paul, 1984).

Sampson, Geoffrey, *Writing Systems: A Linguistic Introduction* (Stanford, CA: Stanford University Press, 1985).

Samuels, S. Jay, Letter-name versus letter-sound knowledge in learning to read, *Reading Teacher*, 1971, *24*, 604–608.

Samuels, S. Jay, Automatic decoding and reading comprehension, *Language Arts*, 1976, *53*, 323–325.

Samuels, S. Jay, The method of repeated readings, *The Reading Teacher*, 1979, *32*, 403–408.

Samuels, S. Jay, Gerald Begy, and Chau Ching Chen, Comparison of word recognition speed and strategies of less skilled and more highly skilled readers, *Reading Research Quarterly*, 1975–76, *1*, 11(1), 72–86.

Santa, John L., Carol Santa, and Edward E. Smith, Units of word recognition: Evidence for the use of multiple units, *Perception and Psychophysics*, 1977, *22*, 285–591.

Scarfe, M., and Jerome S. Bruner, The capacity for joint visual attention in the infant, *Nature*, 1975, *25*, 265–266.

Schank, Roger B., What's a schema anyway? Review of Roy O. Freedle (ed.), *New Directions in Discourse Processing* (Vol. 2) (Norwood, NJ: Ablex, 1979), *Contemporary Psychology*, 1980, *25*, 10, 814–816.

Schank, Roger B., *Reading and Understanding: Teaching from the Perspective of Artificial Intelligence* (Hillsdale, NJ: Lawrence Erlbaum Associates, 1982).

Schank, Roger B., and R. Abelson, *Scripts, Plans, Goals, and Understanding* (Hillsdale, NJ: Lawrence Erlbaum Associates, 1977).

Schatz, Elinore Kress, and R. Scott Baldwin, Context cues are unreliable predictors of word meanings, *Reading Research Quarterly*, 186, *21*, 4, 439–454.

Schneider, Walter, and Richard M. Shiffrin, Controlled and automatic human information processing: I. Detection, search, and attention, *Psychological Review*, 1977, *84*, 1, 1–66.

Scribner, Sylvia, and Michael Cole, Literacy without schooling: Testing for intellectual effects, *Harvard Educational Review*, 1978, *48*, 4.

Searle, John R., The intentionality of intention and action, *Cognitive Science*, 1980, *4*, 47–70.

Sebasta, Sam, Why Rudolph can't read, *Language Arts*, 1981, *5*, 545–548.

Seidenberg, Mark S., The time course of phonological code activation in two writing systems, *Cognition*, 1985, *19*, 1–30.

Selfridge, Oliver, and Ulric Neisser, Pattern recognition by machine, *Scientific American*, 1960, *203*, 2, 60–68.

Seligman, Martin E. P., *Helplessness: On Depression, Development and Death* (San Francisco: Freeman, 1975).

Serafica, F. C., and I. E. Sigel, Styles of categorization and reading disability, *Journal of Reading Behavior*, 1970, *2*, 105–115.

Shallice, Tim, and Elizabeth K. Warrington, Word recognition in a phonemic dyslexic patient, *Quarterly Journal of Experimental Psychology*, 1975, *27*, 187–199.

Shannon, Claude E., Prediction and entropy of printed English, *Bell Systems Technical Journal*, 1951, *30*, 50–64.

Shannon, Patrick, The use of commercial reading materials in American elementary schools, *Reading Research Quarterly*, 1983, *19*, 1, 68–85.

Shannon, Patrick, Mastery learning in reading and the control of teachers and students, *Language Arts*, 1984, *61*, 5, 484–493.

Shannon, Patrick, Reading instruction and social class, *Language Arts*, 1985, *62*, 6, 604–613.

Shannon, Patrick, Teachers' and administrators' thoughts on changes in reading instruction within a merit pay program based on test scores, *Reading Research Quarterly*, 1986, *21*, 1, 20–35.

Sharkey, Noel E., and D. C. Mitchell, Word recognition in a functional context: The use of scripts in reading, *Journal of Memory and Language*, 1985, *24*, 2, 253–270.

Shatz, Marilyn, On the development of communicative understandings: An early strategy for interpreting and responding to messages, *Cognitive Psychology*, 1978, *10*, 271–301.

Shiffrin, Richard M., Locus and role of attention in memory systems, in P. M. A. Rabbitt and S. Dornic (eds.), *Attention and Performance V* (New York: Academic Press, 1975).

Shuy, Roger W., Four misconceptions about clarity and simplicity, *Language Arts*, 1981, 58, 3, 557–561.

Silverman, Wayne P., Can 'words' be processed as integrated units?, *Perception and Psychophysics*, 1976, *20*, 2, 143–152.

Simon, Herbert A., How big is a chunk?, *Science*, 1974, *183*, 482–488.

Simon, H. A., Cognitive science: The newest science of the artificial, *Cognitive Science*, 1980, *4*, 33-46.

Sinclair, Hermina, The transition from sensory-motor behavior to symbolic activity, *Interchange*, 1970, *1*, 3, 119–126.

Sinclair-de Zwart, Hermina, Language acquisition and cognitive development, in John B. Carroll, and R. O. Freedle (eds.), *Cognitive Development and the Acquisition of Language* (Washington, DC: Winston, 1972).

Singer, Harry, Learning to read and skilled reading: Multiple systems interacting within and between the reader and the text, in J. Downing and R. Valtin (eds.), *Language Awareness and Learning to Read* (New York: Springer-Verlag, 1985).

Singer, Harry, and Robert B. Ruddell (eds.), *Theoretical Models and Processes of Reading* (2nd ed.) (Newark, DE: International Reading Association, 1976).

Skinner, B. F., *Science and Human Behavior* (New York: Macmillan, 1953).

Skinner, B. F., *Verbal Behavior* (New York: Appleton, 1957).

Skinner, B. F., *The Technology of Teaching* (New York: Appleton, 1968).

Skinner, B. F., Cognitive science and behaviorism, *British Journal of Psychology*, 1985, *76*, 3, 291–301.

Slater, Wayne H., Revising inconsiderate elementary school expository text: Effects on comprehension and recall, in J. A. Niles and Rosary V. Lalik (eds.), *Issues of Literacy: A Research Perspective* (Rochester, NY: National Reading Conference, 34th Yearbook, 1985).

Slobin, Dan I., *Psycholinguistics* (2nd ed.) (Glenview, IL: Scott Foresman, 1979).

Slobin, Dan I., and C. A. Welsh, Elicited imitation as a research tool in developmental psycholinguistics, in Charles A. Ferguson and Dan I. Slobin (eds.), *Readings in Child Language Acquisition* (New York: Holt, Rinehart and Winston, 1973).

Smith, Edward E., and Glenn M. Kleiman, Word recognition: Theoretical issues and instructional hints, in Lauren B. Resnick and Phyllis A. Weaver (eds.), *Theory and Practice of Early Reading* (Vol. 2) (Hillsdale, NJ: Lawrence Erlbaum Associates, 1979).

Smith, Edward E., Edward J. Shoben, and Lance J. Rips, Structure and process in semantic memory: A featural model for semantic decisions, *Psychological Review*, 1974, *81*, 3, 214–241.

Smith, Edward E., and Kathryn T. Spoehr, The perception of printed English: A theoretical perspective, in B. H. Kantowitz (ed.), *Human Information Processing: Tutorials in Performance and Cognition* (Hillsdale, NJ: Lawrence Erlbaum Associates, 1974).

Smith, Frank, The use of featural dependencies across letters in the visual identification of words, *Journal of Verbal Learning and Verbal Behavior*, 1969, *8*, 215–218.

Smith, Frank, *Comprehension and Learning* (New York: Holt, Rinehart and Winston, 1975).

Smith, Frank, Learning to read by reading: A brief case study, *Language Arts*, 1976, *53*, 3, 297–299.

Smith, Frank, Making sense of reading—and of reading instruction, *Harvard Educational Review*, 1977 (a), *47*, 3, 386–395.

Smith, Frank, The uses of language, *Language Arts*, 1977 (b), *54*, 6, 638–644.

Smith, Frank, Conflicting approaches to reading reasearch and instruction, in Lauren B. Resnick, and Phyllis A. Weaver (eds.), *Theory and Practice of Early Reading* (Vol. 2) (Hillsdale, NJ: Lawrence Erlbaum Associates, 1979).

Smith, Frank, Demonstrations, engagement and sensitivity: A revised approach to language learning, *Language Arts*, 1981a, *58*, 1, 103–112.

Smith, Frank, Demonstrations, engagement and sensitivity (2): The choice between people and programs, *Language Arts*, 1981b, *58*, 6, 634–642.

Smith, Frank, *Writing and the Writer* (New York: Holt, Rinehart and Winston, 1982); (London, Heinemann Educational Books, 1982).

Smith, Frank, *Essays into Literacy* (Portsmouth, NH: Heinemann Educational Books, 1983a).

Smith, Frank, Reading like a writer, *Language Arts*, 1983b, *60*, 5, 558–567.

Smith, Frank, *Insult to Intelligence* (New York: Arbor House, 1986).

Smith, Frank, *Joining the Literacy Club* (Portsmouth, NH: Heinemann Educational Books, 1987a).

Smith, Frank, *How Education Backed the Wrong Horse* (Victoria, British Columbia: Abel Press, 1987b; reprinted in Smith, 1987a).

Smith, Frank, and Peter Carey, Temporal factors in visual information processing, *Canadian Journal of Psychology*, 1966, *20*, 3, 337–342.

Smith, Frank, and Kenneth S. Goodman, On the psycholinguistic method of teaching reading, *Elementary School Journal*, 1971, 177–181.

Smith, Frank, Deborah Lott, and Bruce Cronnell, The effect of type size and case alternation on word identification, *American Journal of Psychology*, 1969, *82*, 2, 248–253.

Smith, Frank, and Deborah Lott Holmes, The independence of letter, word and meaning identification in reading, *Reading Research Quarterly*, 1971, *6*, 3, 394–415.

Smith, Frank, and George A. Miller (eds.), *The Genesis of Language* (Cambridge, MA: MIT Press, 1966).

Smith, Mary K., Measurement of the size of general English vocabulary through the elementary grades and high school, *Genetic Psychology Monographs*, 1941, *24*, 311–345.

Sperling, George, The information available in brief visual presentations, *Psychological Monographs*, 1960, *74*, 11, Whole No. 498.

Spencer, Margaret Meek, *How Texts Teach What Readers Learn* (Victoria, British Columbia, Abel Press, 1987).

Sperry, R. W., Hemisphere disconnection and unity in conscious awareness, *American Psychologist*, 1968, *23*, 723–733.

Spiro, Rand J., Bertram C. Bruce, and William F. Brewer (eds.), *Theoretical Issues in Reading Comprehension. Perspectives from Cognitive Psychology, Linguistics, Artificial Intelligence, and Education* (Hillsdale, NJ: Lawrence Erlbaum Associates, 1980).

Spoehr, K. T., and S. W. Lehmkuhle, *Visual Information Processing* (San Francisco: Freeman, 1982).

Spragins, Anne B., Lester A. Lefton, and Dennis F. Fisher, Eye movements while reading and searching spatially transformed text: A developmental examination, *Memory and Cognition*, 1976, *4*, 1, 36–42.

Squire, James R. (ed.), *The Dynamics of Language Learning* (Urbana, IL: National Conference on Research in English, 1987).

Squire, Larry S., Mechanisms of memory, *Science*, 1986, *232*, 1612–1619.

Staller, Joshua, Neurological correlates of reading failure, in Martin H. Singer (ed.), *Competent Reader, Disabled Reader: Research and Application* (Hillsdale, NJ: Lawrence Erlbaum Associates, 1982).

Stanovich, Keith E., Toward an interactive-compensatory model of individual differences in the development of reading fluency, *Reading Research Quarterly*, 1980, *15*, 32–71.

Stanovich, Keith E., Attentional and automatic context effects in reading, in A. M. Lesgold and C. A. Perfetti (eds.), *Interactive Processes in Reading* (Hillsdale, NJ: Lawrence Erlbaum Associates, 1981).

Stanovich, Keith E., Matthew effects in reading: Some consequences of individual differences in the acquisition of literacy, *Reading Research Quarterly*, 1986, *21*, 4, 360–407.

Stanovich, Keith E., Anne E. Cunningham, and Dorothy J. Feeman, Intelligence, cognitive skills and early reading progress, *Reading Research Quarterly*, 1984, *19*, 3, 278–303.

Stein, Nancy L., and C. G. Glenn, An analysis of story comprehension in elementary school children, in R. R. Freedle (ed.), *New Directions in Discourse Processing* (Vol. 2) (Norwood, NJ: Ablex, 1979).

Steinberg, Danny, *Language, Mind and the World* (New York: Longman, 1982).

Steinberg, Danny D., M. Harada, M. Tashiro, and H. Harper, Acquiring written language as a first language by deaf children, *Working Papers in Linguistics*, 1980, *12*, 3, University of Hawaii.

Steinberg, Danny, and Jun Yamada, Are whole word *kanji* easier to learn than syllable *kana? Reading Research Quarterly*, 1978–79, *14*, 4, 88–89.

Sternberg, Robert J., Components of human intelligence, *Cognition*, 1983, 15, 1–48.

Sternberg, Robert J., Human intelligence: The model is the message, *Science*, 1985, *230*, 4730, 1111–1118.

Stevenson, V. (ed.), *Words: The Evolution of Written Languages* (London: Methuen, 1983).

Stotsky, Sandra, Research on reading/writing relationships: A synthesis and suggested directions, *Language Arts*, 1983, *60*, 627–642.

Stubbs, Michael, *Discourse Analysis: The Sociolinguistic Analysis of Natural Language* (Oxford: Blackwell, 1982).

Sulzby, Elizabeth, Children's emergent reading of favorite story books: A development study, *Reading Research Quarterly*, 1985, *20*, 4, 458–481.

Swanson, H. Lee, Phonological recoding and suppression effects in children's sentence comprehension, *Reading Research Quarterly*, 1984, *19*, 4, 393–403.

Swets, John A., The receiver operating characteristic in psychology, *Science*, 1973, *182*, 990–1000.

Swets, John A., W. P. Tanner, Jr., and T. G. Birdsall, Decision processes in perception, *Psychological Review*, 1961, *68*, 301–320.

Tannen, Deborah, Oral and literate strategies in spoken and written narrative, *Language*, 1982a, *58*, 1–21.

Tannen, Deborah, *Spoken and Written Language: Exploring Orality and Literacy* (Norwood, NJ: Ablex, 1982b).

Taylor, Denny, *Family Literacy. Young Children Learning to Read and Write* (Exeter, NH: Heinemann Educational Books, 1983).

Taylor, Denny, and Dorothy S. Strickland, *Family Storybook Reading* (Exeter, NH: Heinemann Educational Books, 1986).

Taylor, Insup, *Introduction to Psycholinguistics* (New York: Holt, Rinehart and Winston, 1976).

Taylor, Insup, and M. Martin Taylor, *The Psychology of Reading* (New York: Academic Press, 1983).

Taylor, Nancy E., Irene H. Blum, and David M. Logsdon, The development of written language awareness: Environmental aspects and program characteristics, *Reading Research Quarterly*, 1986, *21*, 2, 132–149.

Taylor, Stanford E., *The Dynamic Activity of Reading: A Model of the Process* (Huntington, NY: Educational Developmental Laboratories, Inc., Bulletin No. 9, 1971).

Taylor, Stanford E., Helen Frackenpohl, and James L. Pettee, *Grade Level Norms for the Components of the Fundamental Reading Skill* (Huntington, NY: Educational Developmental Laboratories, Inc., Bulletin No. 3, 1960).

Taylor, W. L., "Cloze" readability scores as indices of individual differences in comprehension and aptitude, *Journal of Applied Psychology*, 1957, *41*, 19–26.

Teale, William H., Parents reading to their children: What we know and need to know, *Language Arts*, 1981, *58*, 8, 902–912.

Teale, William H., Toward a theory of how children learn to read and write naturally, *Language Arts*, 1982, *59*, 6, 555–570.

Teale, William H., and Elizabeth Sulzby, *Emergent Literacy* (Norwood, NJ: Ablex, 1986).

Thompson, G. Brian, Toward a theoretical account of individual differences in the acquisition of reading skill, *Reading Research Quarterly*, 1981, *15*, 4, 596–599.

Thorndike, E., Reading as reasoning: A study of mistakes in paragraph reading, *Journal of Educational Psychology*, 1977, *9*, 77–110.

Thorndike, E. L., and I. Lorge, *The Teacher's Word Book of 30,000 Words* (New York: Teachers College, 1944).

Tierney, Robert J., and J. W. Cunningham, Research on teaching reading comprehension, in P. D. Pearson (ed.), *The Handbook of Reading Research* (New York: Longman, 1984).

Tierney, Robert J., and Jill LaZansky, The rights and responsibilities of readers and writers: A contractual agreement, *Language Arts*, 1980, *57*, 6, 606–613.

Tierney, Robert J., and James Mosenthal, Discourse comprehension and production: Analyzing text structure and cohesion, in J. A. Langer and M. Trika Smith-Burke (eds.), *Reader Meets Author/Bridging the Gap* (Newark, DE: International Reading Association, 1982).

Tierney, Robert J., and P. David Pearson, Toward a composing model of reading, *Language Arts*, 1983, *60*, 5, 568–580.

Tinker, Miles A., Fixation pause duration in reading, *Journal of Educational Research*, 1951, *44*, 471–479.

Tinker, Miles A., Recent studies of eye movements in reading, *Psychological Bulletin*, 1958, *54*, 215–231.

Tinker, Miles A., *Bases for Effective Reading* (Minneapolis: University of Minnesota Press, 1965).

Torrance, Nancy, and David R. Olson, Oral and literate competencies in early school years, in David R. Olson, Nancy Torrance, and Angela Hildyard (eds.), *Literacy, Language and Learning: The Nature and Consequences of Reading and Writing* (Cambridge, MA: Cambridge University Press, 1985).

Torrey, Jane W., Learning to read without a teacher: A case study, *Elementary English*, 1969, *46*, 550–556.

Torrey, Jane W., Reading that comes naturally: The early reader, in T. G. Walker, and G. E. Mackinnon (eds.), *Reading Research: Advances in Theory and Practice* (Vol. 1) (New York: Academic Press, 1979).

Tough, Joan, Children's use of language, *Educational Review* (Birmingham University, 1974) *26*, 3, 166–179.

Treisman, Anne M., Strategies and models of selective attention, *Psychological Review*, 1969, *76*, 3, 282–299.

Tulving, Endel, How many memory systems are there?, *American Psychologist*, 1985a, *40*, 385–398.

Tulving, Endel, Memory and consciousness, *Canadian Journal of Psychology*, 1985b, *25*, 1–12.

Tulving, Endel, and Cecille Gold, Stimulus information and contextual information as determinants of tachistoscopic recognition of words, *Journal of Experimental Psychology*, 1963, *66*, 319–327.

Tulving, Endel, and Donald M. Thomson, Encoding specificity and retrieval processes in episodic memory, *Psychological Review*, 1973, *80*, 5, 352–373.

Tulving, Endel, and Michael J. Watkins, Structure of memory traces, *Psychological Review*, 1975, *82*, 4, 261–275.

Tuman, Myron C., *A Preface to Literacy: An Inquiry into Pedagogy, Practice, and Progress* (Tuscaloosa: University of Alabama Press, 1987).

Underwood, Geoffrey (ed.), *Strategies of Information Processing* (London: Academic Press, 1978).

Urwin, Cathy, The contribution of nonvisual information systems and language to knowing oneself, in Michael Beveridge (ed.), *Children Thinking Through Language* (London: Arnold, 1982).

Vachek, J., *Written Language* (The Hague: Mouton, 1973).

van Dijk, Teun A., *Macrostructures: An Interdisciplinary Study of Global Structures in Discourse, Interaction and Cognition* (Hillsdale, NJ: Lawrence Erlbaum Associates, 1980).

van Dongen, Richard, Children's narrative thought, at home and at school, *Language Arts*, 1987, *64*, 1, 79–87.

Vellutino, Frank R., Dyslexia, *Scientific American*, 1987, *256*, 3, 34–41.

Venezky, Richard L., English orthography: Its graphical structure and its relation to sound, *Reading Research Quarterly*, 1967, *2*, 75–106.

Venezky, Richard L., *The Structure of English Orthography* (The Hague: Mouton, 1970).

Venezky, Richard L., *Theoretical and Experimental Base for Teaching Reading* (The Hague: Mouton, 1976).

Venezky, Richard L., Research on reading processes: A historical perspective, *American Psychologist*, 1977, *32*, 339–345.

Vygotsky, Lev S., *Language and Thought* (Cambridge, MA: MIT Press, 1962).

Vygostky, Lev S., *Mind in Society: The Development of Higher Psychological Processes* (Cambridge, MA: Harvard University Press, 1978).

Walker, Carol H., and Bonnie J. F. Meyer, Integrating information from text: an evaluation of current theories, *Review of Educational Research*, 1980, *50*, 421–437.

Walkerdine, Valerie, From context to text: A psychosemiotic approach to abstract thought, in M. Beveridge (ed.), *Children Thinking Through Language* (London: Arnold, 1982).

Walters, Gloria S., Melvin K. Komoda, and Tannis Y. Arbuckle, The effects of concurrent tasks on reading: Implications for phonological recoding, *Journal of Memory and Language*, 1985, *24*, 1, 27–45.

Wanner, Eric, and Lila Gleitman (eds.), *Language Acquisition: The State of the Art* (Cambridge, MA: Cambridge University Press, 1982).

Warrington, Elizabeth K., and Tim Shallice, Semantic access dyslexia, *Brain*, 1979, *102*, 43–63.

Weaver, Phyllis, and Fredi Shonkoff, *Research Within Reach* (Washington, DC: National Institute of Education, 1978).

Weber, Rose-Marie, The study of oral reading errors: A survey of the literature, *Reading Research Quarterly*, 1968, *4*, 96–119.

Weintraub, Sam, The fuzzy area of literature reviews, in Sam Weintraub, Helen K. Smith, Nancy L. Roser, Walter J. Moore, Michael W. Kibby, Kathleen S. Jongsma, and Peter L. Fisher (eds.), *Summary of Investigations Relating to Reading, July 1, 1984 to June 30, 1985* (Newark, DE: International Reading Association, 1986).

Weir, Ruth H., *Language in the Crib* (The Hague: Mouton, 1962).

Wells, Gordon, *Learning Through Interaction: The Study of Language Development* (Cambridge, MA: Cambridge University Press, 1981).

Wells, Gordon, Preschool literacy-related activities and success in school, in D. R. Olson, N. Torrance, and A. Hildyard (eds.), *Literacy, Language and Learning: The Nature and Consequences of Reading and Writing* (Cambridge, MA: Cambridge University Press, 1985).

Wells, Gordon and J. Nicholls, *Language and Learning: An Interactional Perspective* (Lewes, UK: Falmer, 1985).

Wheeler, D. D., Processes in word recognition, *Cognitive Psychology*, 1970, *1*, 59–85.

Whorf, B. L., *Language, Thought and Reality* (Cambridge, MA: MIT Press, 1956).

Wildman, Daniel, and Martin Kling, Semantic, syntactic and spatial anticipation in reading, *Reading Research Quarterly*, 1978–79, *14*, 2, 128–164.

Wilkinson, Andrew M. (ed.), The context of language, *Educational Reviews*, 1971, *23*, 3.

Williams, Joanna, Reading instruction today, *American Psychologist*, 1979, *34*, 10, 917–922.

Winograd, Terry, What does it mean to understand language?, in Donald A, Norman (ed.), *Perspectives on Cognitive Science* (Norwood, NJ: Ablex, 1981).

Wong, Bernice Y. L., Understanding learning disabled students' reading problems: Contributions from cognitive psychology, *Topics in Learning and Learning Disabilities*, 1982, 43–50.

Wood, Barbara S., *Children and Communication* (Englewood Cliffs, NJ: Prentice-Hall, 1981).

Woodworth, Robert S., *Experimental Psychology* (New York: Holt, 1938).

Woodworth, Robert S., and H. Schlosberg, *Experimental Psychology* (New York: Holt, Rinehart and Winston, 1954).

Yates, Jack, The content of awareness is a model of the world, *Psychological Review*, 1985, *92*, 2, 249–284.

Yatvin, Joanne, Learning to read at forty-eight, *Language Arts*, 1982, *59*, 8, 822–828.

Ylisto, Ingrid P., Early reading responses of young Finnish children, *The Reading Teacher*, 1977, *31*, 167–172.

Young, Andrew W., and Andrew W. Ellis, Asymmetry of cerebral hemispheric function in normal and poor readers, *Psychological Bulletin*, 1981, *89*, 1, 183–190.

Zipf, Paul, *Semantic Analysis* (Ithaca, NY: Cornell University Press, 1960).

AUTHOR INDEX

I

Imlach, R. H., 280, 282
Inhelder, B., 223
Iredell, H., 297
Iser, W., 285, 286

J

Jaggar, A. M., 288, 302
Jakobson, R., 265
Jaynes, J., 257
Jenkins, J. J., 260
Jenkins, J. R., 299
Jenkins, L. M., 299
Jensen, J. M., 288
Jensen, M., 304
Johnson, N. F., 269
Johnson, N. S., 226, 238, 260
Johnson-Laird, P. N., 224, 227, 235
Johnston, J. C., 269
Johnston, P. H., 306
Jones, E. E., 251
Juel, C., 282, 299
Just, M. A., 176, 220, 224, 249, 256,
    257, 267, 278, 280, 283, 285

K

Kagan, J., 290
Kail, R., 261
Karlin, J. E., 253, 256
Katz, J. J., 232
Katzman, M. T., 255
Kavanagh, J. F., 287
Keen, R. H., 270
Kieras, D. E., 220, 249, 267, 280
Kimmel, S., 281
Kintsch, W., 223, 237
Klahr, D., 227
Klatzky, R. L., 260
Kleiman, G. M., 223, 278, 280
Klein, G. A., 279
Klein, H. A., 279
Kling, M., 224
Klitzke, D., 269
Klivington, K. A., 249
Koehler, J. A., 137, 271

Kolers, P. A., 152, 229, 250, 255, 259,
    264, 269, 280
Komoda, M. K., 274
Kosslyn, S. M., 260
Krashen, S. D., 259, 289, 290, 300, 303
Kroll, J. F., 284
Krueger, L. E., 252, 270
Kuhn, T., 221
Kukish, K. S., 279
Kutas, M., 225

L

LaBerge, D., 287, 301
Lakoff, G., 225, 235
Lalik, R. V., 303
Langendoen, D. T., 234
Langer, J. A., 287, 288, 305
Langer, S. K., 286
Larsen, S. F., 248
Lawler, R. W., 249
LaZanski, J., 288
Lefton, L. A., 256, 278
Lehmkuhle, S. W., 264
Lenneberg, Elizabeth, 287
Lenneberg, Eric H., 287, 290
Leong, C. K., 209, 287
Lepper, M. R., 296
Levin, H., 241, 249, 274
Levine, F. M., 296
Levine, K., 203
Levy, B. A., 277
Lewis, D. J., 258
Lewis, V. J., 281
Liben, L. S., 223
Liberman, A. M., 239
Liberman, I. Y., 273, 274
Lichten, W., 278
Lieberman, P., 235
Lightbown, P., 289
Lindig, K., 254, 278
Lindsay, P. H., 246, 251, 258, 264
Lipson, M. Y., 281, 305
Llewellyn-Thomas, E., 256
Lloyd, B. B., 225
Lockhart, R. S., 258
Logie, R., 282

SUBJECT INDEX

Page numbers in *italic* indicate entries in Notes; page numbers in **bold face** indicate glossary entries.

A

Aesthetic reading, *248*, **308**
Alphabet, 134–137, 210, *275-276*
  recognition, 104
  utility, 141
Ambiguity of words, *see* Words
Ambiguous figures, 11, 126
Apprehension, 153
  see also Comprehension
Artificial intelligence, *248*, **308**
Auditory system, 51

B

Babies, *see* infants
Behavioristic view, *292-296*
Bits, defined, *242-243*
Boredom, 188
Brain
  hemispheric dominance, 83–86, *257*

C

Case grammar, *see* Generative semantics
Cat and dog problem, 127, 181, 199, **308**
Categories, 110, *275*
  in cognitive structure, 9, **308**
  interrelationships, 12, 187, **308**
  learning, 187
  rules, 11, 110
Children
  and comprehension, 184–186
  and learning, 181–187
  and learning to read, 208–209
  and meaning, 159–160
  and memory, 90
  and reading, 151, *296-301*
Chinese writing, 141–142, 152–153, *273*, *275*
Chomsky, N., *230-234*
  see also Transformational grammar

359